For the past hundred years, the social survey has been a major tool of social investigation, and its use has also been linked to social reform. Starting with the landmark surveys of Charles Booth in London and Jane Addams in Chicago, social surveys in both Britain and the United States investigated poverty, unemployment and other difficult social conditions. While in Britain there was marked continuity between the early studies of Booth and others, and the type of social research being done as late as the 1950s and 1960s, in the United States the social survey movement exercised curiously little impact upon later developments within empirical social science. By the 1930s, this method of investigation had virtually disappeared from the US scene.

This book traces the history of the social survey in Britain and the United States (with two chapters on Germany and France). It discusses the aims and interests of those who carried out early surveys, and the links between the social survey and the growth of empirical social science. The use of maps to portray social conditions was one of the survey method's major contributions to social scientific research, and examples of the early maps are included in the volume. The contributors are drawn from a range of disciplines, including history, sociology, political science, demography and geography.

The social survey in historical perspective, 1880–1940

The social survey
in historical perspective
1880–1940

EDITED BY

Martin Bulmer
Kevin Bales and
Kathryn Kish Sklar

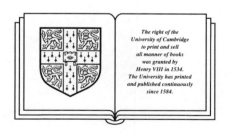

The right of the
University of Cambridge
to print and sell
all manner of books
was granted by
Henry VIII in 1534.
The University has printed
and published continuously
since 1584.

CAMBRIDGE UNIVERSITY PRESS
Cambridge
New York   Port Chester
Melbourne   Sydney

Published by the Press Syndicate of the University of Cambridge
The Pitt Building, Trumpington Street, Cambridge CB2 1RP
40 West 20th Street, New York, NY 10011, USA
10 Stamford Road, Oakleigh, Melbourne 3166, Australia

© Cambridge University Press 1991

First published 1991

Printed in Great Britain at the
University Press, Cambridge

British Library cataloguing in publication data
The Social Survey in Historical Perspective, 1880–1940.
1. Social sciences. Research, history
I. Bulmer, Martin II, Bales, Kevin III. Sklar, Kathryn
Kish
300.72

Library of Congress cataloguing in publication data
The Social Survey in Historical Perspective, 1880–1940 / edited by
Martin Bulmer, Kevin Bales, and Kathryn Kish Sklar.
p. 000 cm.
Includes index.
ISBN 0 521 36334 9
1. Social surveys – United States – History. 2. Social surveys –
Great Britain – History. I. Bulmer, Martin. II. Bales, Kevin.
III. Sklar, Kathryn Kish.
HN29.S645 1991
300'.723 – dc20   90-38520   CIP

ISBN 0 521 36334 9 hardback

UP

Contents

⧉ *Figures* ⧉

⧉ *Tables* ⧉

◙ *Maps* ◙

Colour plates   *between pages* 12 *and* 13

1. Map of *Jewish East London* showing the ethnic composition of Whitechapel and Stepney from map prepared by George E. Arkell in 1901. From *The Jew in London: A Study of Racial Character and Present-Day Conditions, being two essays prepared for the Toynbee Trustees*, by C. Russell and H. S. Lewis (London: T. Fisher Unwin, 1901).

2. Charles Booth's poverty map of Whitechapel and Stepney in East London in 1893. From Charles Booth, *Life and Labour of the People in London* (London: Macmillan Co., 1893), extract from Supplemental map.

3. Nationalities map showing social composition of the population in the neighbourhood of Hull House in Chicago, 1895, (extract). From Residents of Hull-House, *Hull-House Maps and Papers: A Presentation of Nationalities & Wages in a Congested District of Chicago, together with Comments & Essays on Problems growing out of the Social Conditions* (Boston: Thomas Crowell and Co, 1985).

4. The Seventh Ward of Philadelphia. The distribution of negro inhabitants throughout the ward and their social condition in 1897. From W. E. B. Du Bois, *The Philadelphia Negro* (Philadelphia: University of Pennsylvania, 1899), extract from frontispiece.

5. Map showing the predominant racial groups among the population in the West End, Boston in 1903. From Robert Woods, *Americans in Process: A Settlement Study by Residents and Associates of the South End House* (Boston: Houghton Mifflin, 1903), following page 46.

6. Poverty map of Whitechapel and Stepney in East London in 1930. From Hubert Llewellyn-Smith (ed.), *The New Survey of Life and Labour in London* (London: P. S. King, 1930–36), vol. 4, Poverty maps.

Black and white

⑤ *Contributors* ⑤

KEVIN BALES (editor) is a sociologist who is Senior Lecturer in Social Research at the Polytechnic of Central London. He was previously Chief Research Officer at the Economic and Social Research Council Data Archive at the University of Essex. His present research interests are in the fields of the history of social research, modern social research methods, and in developing social theory. His publications include many articles on criminology and applications of social research, and *Man in the Middle: The Life and Work of Charles Booth* (forthcoming).

MARTIN BULMER (editor) is a sociologist who teaches in the Department of Social Science and Administration at the London School of Economics and Political Science, University of London. His research interests include the history of the social sciences in the twentieth century, the application of research to policy, the sociology of informal social care, the sociology of privacy, and the study of research training in higher education. His recent publications include (as editor, with J. Lewis and D. Piachaud) *The Goals of Social Policy* (1989), *The Social Basis of Community Care* (1987), and (as editor) *Social Science Research and Government* (1987). He is also an editor of the journal *Ethnic and Racial Studies*.

KATHRYN KISH SKLAR (editor) is an historian who specialises in the study of American women and social movements. She is Distinguished Professor of History at the State University of New York, Binghampton, having previously taught at the University of California, Los Angeles and at the University of Michigan. Her current research studies women reformers and the creation of the American welfare state between 1880 and 1930, with a focus on Florence Kelley (1859–1932). Her publications include *Catherine Beecher: A Study in American Domesticity* (1973), (as editor) *Notes of Sixty Years: the Autobiography of Florence Kelley, 1859–1926* (1986), '"The Greater part of the Petitioners are Female": The Reduction by Statute of Women's Working Hours in the Paid Labor Force, 1840–1917', in Gary Cross (ed.), *The International History of the Shortening of the Workday* (1988).

STEVEN R. COHEN has taught at Columbia University and currently teaches at the Trinity School in New York.

ROGER DAVIDSON is Senior Lecturer in Economic and Social History and Associate Director of the International Office at Edinburgh University. His previous research focused on the formulation of welfare and industrial relations policy in late-nineteenth- and twentieth-century Britain, and on the role of information in British policy-making processes. He is currently working on a study of the social politics of venereal diseases in twentieth-century Scotland. His publications include *Whitehall and the Labour Problem in Late-Victorian and Edwardian Britain* (1985) and (as editor, with P. White) *Information and Government: Studies in the Dynamics of Policy-Making* (1988).

ALAIN DESROSIÈRES is a statistician who is a member of the Research Department at the Institut National de la Statistique et des Études Économiques in Paris, the statistical office of the French government. He is also a member of the Groupe de Sociologie Politique et Morale of the Ecole des Hautes Etudes en Sciences Sociales in Paris. His present research interests centre on the ways by which the social sciences achieve 'hard things', i.e. quantifiable and precise knowledge, on the model of the natural sciences, by establishing a connection between political, social and cognitive tools. The history of mathematical statistics, of social classification, or of sample surveys provide examples of such constructions. His publications include (with L. Thévenot), *Les catégories socioprofessionelles*, (1988), a study of the history and construction of social classifications.

IRMELA GORGES is a sociologist who is a Privatdozentin at the Institut für Soziologie of the Freie Universität of Berlin. She had conducted various empirical projects on adult education, participation (*Mitbestimmung*) and legal aid for the underprivileged. Currently, she is taking part in an interdisciplinary research group on the non-technical constituencies of the development of CAD/CAM-systems at the Technische Universität of Berlin. Her current teaching and research interests are the history of sociology as well as the history of methods of empirical social research and the social history of new technologies. Her publications include *Sozialforschung in Deutschland 1872–1914* (2nd edn 1986) and *Sozialforschung in der Weimarer Republik 1918–1933* (1986).

E. P. HENNOCK is Andrew Geddes and John Rankin Professor of Modern History at the University of Liverpool. He is founder and Director of its Centre for the History of Social Policies, whose members, drawn from several departments, have an interest in the historical dimension of policy-making in a variety of spheres and teach an M.A. programme in social policy history. His own work on the history of social policy has combined the study of the political and the social with a particular interest in the history of ideas. Originally a student of urban history and the author of *Fit and Proper Persons. Ideal and Reality in Nineteenth Century Urban Government* (1973), he has subsequently published articles on social theory and the study of poverty, as well as *British Social Reform and German Precedents. The Case of Social Insurance 1880–1914* (1987). His main research interests at present are in the comparative history of social policy in Britain and Germany.

SETH KOVEN is an Assistant Professor of History at Villanova University, Pennsylvania, where he teaches European social and economic history, and British and women's history. His current research interests focus on women's voluntary associations and state welfare policies and programmes in Great Britain. He is author of *Culture and Poverty: The London Settlement House Movement, 1870–1914* (Routledge, forthcoming) and is co-editing with Sonya Michel, *Gender and the origins of Welfare States in Europe and North America.*

JANE LEWIS is an historian and a Reader in the Department of Social Administration at the London School of Economics & Political Science. Her teaching and research interests are in the twentieth-century history of social policy and of gender. Her main publications are: *The Politics of Motherhood* (1980), *Women in England 1870–1950* (1984), *What Price Community Medicine?* (1986), *Daughters Who Care* (1988). She is currently working on a study of marriage and marriage counselling in the post-war period and a book on later Victorian and Edwardian women social reformers.

JENNIFER PLATT is Professor of Sociology at the University of Sussex. Her main teaching interests are in research methods and the social structure of industrial societies. She has a longstanding research interest in the sociology of empirical social research, and in recent years has been working on a variety of topics in the history of sociological research methods, especially in the USA in c. 1920–1960. Some relevant publications are *Realities of Social Research* (1976), 'The Development of the "Participant Observation" Method in Sociology: Origin Myth and History', *Journal of the History of the Behavioral Sciences* (1983), 'Stouffer and Lazarsfeld: Patterns of Influence' in H. Kuklick and E. Long (eds.), *Knowledge and Society*, vol. 6, (1986), 'Functionalism and the Survey: the Relation of Theory and Method', *Sociological Review*, (August 1986).

STEPHEN P. TURNER is Graduate Research Professor in the Department of Philosophy at the University of South Florida. His most recent book was *The Impossible Science* (with J. Turner), a history of American Sociology. He has previously published books on Max Weber and Durkheim and on the philosophy of the social sciences, and articles on many topics, including the history of American geology. He is presently working on a history of 'mainstream' American Sociology.

EILEEN JANES YEO is a social historian in the School of Cultural and Community Studies at the University of Sussex. Her teaching focuses mainly on class and gender themes in modern British history and in comparative perspective, and on the social history of language and concepts. She has had a longstanding research interest in the history of social science and has also written extensively on British working-class and radical culture. Her publications include *The Unknown Mayhew* (1971) with E. P. Thompson, and *Popular Culture and Class Conflict, 1590–1914* (1981) with Stephen Yeo. She has also been active in community groups engaged in analysis and action, writing and publishing a book on *Social Science, Class and Gender in Britain, 1789 to 1914* for Virago Books and working on another about *Meanings of Motherhood from 1750 to the Present.*

Social investigation is an important part of the social history of industrial societies since the nineteenth century, and throws light on the development of both social policy and the social sciences. This collection of papers deals with one particular period and one type of social investigation, concerning the two generations between 1880 and the beginning of the Second World War. In 1880 social investigation was a burgeoning phenomenon but the social survey in the sense in which that term is used in this book did not exist. By 1940 such inquires were much more common, and the beginnings of the modern sample survey, which was to become integral to the post-war world, were by then already apparent.

This collection seeks to identify what were some of the most important innovations in the social survey in this period, what those who conducted surveys thought they were doing, what impact their research had upon opinion and debates at the time, and what was the longer-term significance of particular investigations. A variety of different types of research activity are embraced, which share sufficient common features to justify the appellation 'survey'. The main focus is upon developments in both Britain and the United States, including exchanges between them, with a glance at developments in France and Germany. There are important differences in national traditions of social investigation which are only touched on here, but it is hoped that the collection has enough of an international focus to avoid parochialism.

A significant theme of the papers here is the relationship between research and social action. Most of the early social surveyors were not detached and dispassionate academics but people with practical and political ideals and interests. Many of them undertook inquiries as much out of a desire to understand the world the better to change it as out of dispassionate interest. Thus, as well as illuminating the role of knowledge-production in the history of social policy, the collection provides a case study in the tensions between involvement and detachment in social inquiry.

Other important themes concern the place of white women and racial minorities in the history of the social survey. It is no accident that several of the pioneer surveyors were women, or that the leading American sociological surveyor was African–American. Evaluating the contributions made by such researchers and understanding the implications of their minority status are among the aims of the collection presented here. Enjoying unprecedented access to higher education in the 1870s and 1880s, but lacking professional employment commensurate with their training, middle-class white women created their own channels of influence. They addressed their energies to a multitude of social issues raised by industrial capitalism, recognising the necessity of documenting social problems as a first step toward solving them.

In an era of fierce racial prejudice and the accommodationist philosophy advanced by Booker T. Washington, the educational opportunities for middle-class African–American men were more restricted than those of white women. An exception to this rule was W. E. B. Du Bois who applied his learning to social investigation and sought to illuminate the social conditions in which members of his race lived. Neither women nor African–Americans gained admission to the nascent academic disciplines that dominated social inquiry in the following generation, but they illuminate the centrality of social conscience and empirical curiosity to the early development of social science.

The idea of this book began in the summer of 1983 when Kevin Bales and Kitty Sklar were both working in the Archives of the British Library of Political and Economic Science at the LSE in London. Kevin proposed that the early history of the social survey as a method of social investigation should be made known to a wider audience, and together they started planning a collection which was the ancestor of the present one. As the project developed, they were joined by Martin Bulmer, who independently had an interest in the history of the social survey and in the origins of social investigation in Britain and the United States more generally.

Plans took a further step forward when Kitty Sklar and Martin Bulmer met at the University of California, Los Angeles in July 1987, and Kitty suggested the value of a conference which would bring the contributors to the book together, since most of them did not know each other and some were historians and some social scientists. Support was obtained from the Nuffield Foundation for some travel and subsistence costs of overseas participants, and a successful conference was held at the Polytechnic of Central London in March 1989, with twenty-one participants from Britain, the United States, France and West Germany. Apart from the contributors to this book, we would like to thank Mark Abrams, Anna Davin, Vivien Hart, Greta Jones, Dirk Käsler, Michael Rose, Simon Szreter, Pat Thane and Richard Wiggins for joining us in that conference and making valuable suggestions which have helped in revising the papers for publication.

Work analysing the bibliographical data on the history of the social survey in Britain and the United States shown in maps 8 to 11 and in figures 1.1 and 1.2 was done by Cynthia Brown, our research assistant, in the spring of 1989. Four other sources of funding remain to be acknowledged. Kevin Bales' original work on Charles Booth's poverty surveys, in 1982–3, was supported by the Joseph Rowntree Memorial Trust and its director, Robin Guthrie. Cynthia Brown's work was supported by a grant to Martin Bulmer from the Social Research Division of the London School of Economics and Political Science. The inclusion of colour maps in this book has been made possible by a grant to Martin Bulmer from the British Academy under its Small Personal Research Grants Scheme, and by a grant to Kevin Bales for research dissemination by the Joseph Rowntree Memorial Trust. We are glad to have this opportunity to acknowledge their support. Alain Desrosières and Irmela Gorges participated in the March conference as a result of their membership of the Franco–German–British Working Group on the History of Empirical Social Research and Statistics, of which Martin Bulmer and Jennifer Platt are also members. Financial support from the Centre Nationale de la Recherche Scientifique and of the Deutsche Forschungsgemeinschaft made possible meetings of this group.

One of the particularly worthwhile consequences of the March 1989 conference was the juxtaposition of historical and social science perspectives upon the social survey. Traces of the tension between them remain in this collection, but we believe that the combination of the two perspectives has been very fruitful. The historian is more prone to concentrate upon the particular, and on the effects of a particular time and place, whereas the social scientist seeks to frame general statements about a class of investigations. Nevertheless, the two can usefully be set side by side. The historian may be more likely to emphasise the importance of historical processes of change, the social scientist the universal features of a class of activities termed 'social survey'. Yet evident in these chapters is a common desire to understand the origins of modern empirical social investigation, itself an important part of the history of both social policy and of the social sciences.

CHAPTER ONE

The social survey in historical perspective

MARTIN BULMER, KEVIN BALES AND KATHRYN KISH SKLAR

Since antiquity, governments have collected information about the people whom they governed as a by-product of administration. As a consequence, they have also found it useful and necessary to design methods to gather such data. The population census – counting the numbers of people living within a given territory – was one of the first such inquiries. At the time of the birth of Jesus, for example, Joseph and Mary were travelling to Bethlehem to be registered in a census. For the most part, however, such inquiries were confined to basic headcounts.

The social survey is a direct descendant of this type of inquiry, although much broader in scope. The origins of the investigation of the condition of the working or labouring classes in modern times may be traced to the late eighteenth century. Interest intensified with the creation of the Statistical Societies in the 1830s, with their roots in Benthamism and political economy,[1] and as a result of the early public health inquiries. A variety of developments in early- and mid-Victorian England, discussed by Eileen Yeo in chapter 2, preceded the emergence of the scientific social survey in the 1880s. Social investigation is a broader category than the social survey, and the Victorian period in particular saw the flowering of a variety of forms of social investigation which are part of the immediate pre-history of the social survey. The social survey as a tool of scientific inquiry is not much more than 100 years old.

The appearance of the social survey in the latter part of the nineteenth century followed the development of social investigation. Both may be attributed in broad terms to the confluence of upper- and middle-class concern about the negative effects of large-scale urbanisation and industrialisation in Western Europe and North America with the growth of a desire to investigate society scientifically and on a more systematic basis than before.[2] The sources from which the social survey grew were various,

1

government censuses being only a minor contributor. Throughout the nineteenth century there were investigations into public health, housing, family life and employment, particularly as these affected the working classes.. The investigations were carried out by private individuals (many of them, in the later nineteenth century, women of some social position), certain professions (associated with, in particular, medicine), members of voluntary associations concerned with social welfare, a few journalists and (by the end of the century) one or two academic scholars.

Although the methods of inquiry varied, there was some common ground. From the time of Charles Booth onwards, the term 'social survey' came increasingly to be applied to the inquiries. Indeed, for a period in the United States what became known as the Social Survey Movement flourished, engaging significant numbers of private, government and academic researchers. These inquiries signified increasing upper- and middle-class interest in the condition of the working classes as well as a desire to intervene – a desire both to remedy want and disease through voluntary or state action and to achieve a greater degree of social control through the use of scientific expertise.

The social survey defined

The types of social survey treated in this book are richly varied and not easily defined in a wholly consistent manner. The *Encyclopaedia of the Social Sciences* (*ESS*) published in the 1930s, edited by Alvin Johnson, provides one of the most adequate definitions.

In its broadest sense a social survey is a first hand investigation, analysis and coordination of economic, sociological and other related aspects of a selected community or group. Such a survey may be undertaken primarily in order to provide material scientifically gathered upon which social theorists may base their conclusions; or its chief purpose may be to formulate a programme of amelioration of the conditions of life and work of a particular group or community. Although either type of survey may yield results of value to the other, scope and method are governed chiefly by the initial purpose of the study. The first type was introduced into sociological thought by Frédéric Le Play in the middle of the nineteenth century and has resulted in a rich and varied literature as well as in a less definite but nevertheless powerful influence, particularly in French and German sociology. The latter, while gaining much from the impetus of Le Play's studies of working men's family budgets, had its actual inception in England in the last quarter of the century with the work of Charles Booth and his associates, and has attained its fullest development in the United States. Thus the social survey as a method for the study and analysis of social phenomena as well as for the application of a programme of social planning is of comparatively recent origin, although it had been envisaged by thinkers belonging to an earlier period.[3]

This definition brings out well the dual involvement of social scientists and social reformers in the history of the social survey, and the interplay between them. It is important to stress that before 1940 the social survey was not associated particularly closely with academic social science, which was in any case itself quite small in scale. The modern scientific sample survey, established by academics such as Rensis Likert and Paul Lazarsfeld, government statisticians such as P. C. Mahalanobis and Louis Moss, and market researchers such as Henry Durant and Mark Abrams, has developed since that time.[4] Before that period, a variety of individuals and groups, only a minority of them academics, contributed to the establishment of the social survey and it is with them that we are concerned here.

Several specific characteristics distinguish the social survey from the modes of social investigation that preceded it. A social survey involved field work, the collection of data at first hand by a social investigator rather than reliance upon reports by others or on pre-existing data. Surveys attempted to achieve comprehensive rather than haphazard coverage, albeit (in most of the studies discussed in this book) within a local rather than a national area. The data in surveys related to individuals, families and households rather than aggregates, and were analysed accordingly. Survey research involved the attempt, however primitive, at counting and quantifying the phenomena with which it was concerned. And the social survey developed in close relationship with public policy and social reform.

From its inception, the social survey was intimately associated with social action. Whether or not studies were done with a reform purpose, they were thought of as illuminating current public debates about the condition of the working classes. This concern was well captured in David Glass' definition in Chamber's Encyclopaedia: 'a scientific study of social conditions and social problems, within a limited geographical setting, the objectives of that study being implicitly or explicitly related to social policy'.[5] Social surveyors varied in their degree of detachment from the issues of the day, but almost all were concerned not simply to anatomise and classify in the manner of early anthropologists, but to throw light on matters of current social and political controversy and to promote social amelioration if not social intervention. As Mark Abrams, one of its chief British practitioners, wrote:

Occasionally surveys originate in an abstract desire for more knowledge about the structure and workings of a society; more frequently, however, they are carried out as an indispensable first step in measuring the dimensions of a social problem, ascertaining its causes, and then deciding upon remedial action ... Most surveys have been concerned with curing obviously pathological social conditions.[6]

What actual methods were involved in the conduct of a social survey in the period before 1940? The *ESS* definition quoted earlier does not adequately answer this question. In the late twentieth century we tend to be over-influenced by the contemporary sample survey, and run the danger of reading into social surveys of the past elements drawn from today's practices. It is hard to escape an implicitly Whiggish history.[7]

A fundamental change in the concepts guiding the acquisition of social knowledge accompanied the rise of the social survey. This change is visible in the difference between Henry Mayhew's examination of the London poor in the middle of the nineteenth century and Charles Booth's surveys three decades later. Booth conceptualised the problem differently, conducted a larger-scale inquiry, attempted to measure the phenomena with which he was concerned, and collected data from multiple observers rather than relying upon a single observer. Some historians will protest at the periodisation implicit in such a distinction, and maintain that social survey-type inquiries were taking place earlier in the nineteenth century. But even though some features of the survey method predated the emergence of the modern local social survey, inquiries using those features were not yet mature social surveys.[8]

This slow and uneven development is apparent in the contributions which follow. At the end of our period, there was a degree of discontinuity between the social survey in the United States before 1940 and the rise of the modern sample survey after 1940. Alain Desrosières follows the emergence of the idea of representative sampling and shows the lack of lineal development in its course. E. P. Hennock traces the evolution of the study of poverty, showing the twists and turns in its emergence as a measurable concept in British social science.

Slow and uneven development also characterised other features such as the role of the investigator, how the data were actually collected, and the analysis of the results. Charles Booth, for example, did not rely upon interviewers but upon School Board Visitors; however, Seebohm Rowntree *did* use interviewers, and reliance upon first-hand methods of data collection rather than reports from middle-class observers acquainted with the working class gradually became standard procedure. The emergence of the interview, however, was not an inevitable process. (We still await a full history of its development.) Thus, the term 'social survey' embraced a wide variety of research practices, sharing some common elements in terms of conceptualisation, extent, measurement and first-hand data collection, and also building concretely upon what had gone before.

THE PRE-HISTORY OF THE SOCIAL SURVEY

In Britain, the most important early landmark in systematic inquiries was Domesday Book of 1086. Some authors, such as Caradog Jones in 1948,[9] have treated William the Conqueror's Domesday Book as the beginning of social surveys in Britain. Domesday Book's listings, of course, were more about property than about people, but it did initiate a tradition of inquiry which carried forward to the end of the nineteenth century. In the seventeenth and eighteenth centuries, enumeration with a purpose steadily increased and became less likely to be carried out by government than by interested private individuals. At the same time the focus of the investigations broadened, from administrative and economic information about people to demographic and social topics.

This process of inquiry prior to the mature social survey may be thought of as having four phases or aspects. The first, starting in the seventeenth century, was the tradition of 'political arithmetic'. The second, in the first half of the nineteenth century, shifted the emphasis from population characteristics to the investigation of social problems by both government and private individuals in the 'statistical movement'. A third trend, mixed up with the second but to some extent distinct from it and gaining impetus throughout the nineteenth century, studied social conditions as a weapon in the arsenal of 'ameliorism' and social reform. The fourth, part of ameliorism in Britain but distinct from it in France, was the collection of data by direct observation. All four phases were preliminary to the social surveys considered in this book, and the methods of inquiry used did not constitute surveys in the sense defined earlier.

Political arithmetic

'Political arithmetic' has the longest pedigree. It is usually thought to begin with John Graunt and William Petty in the Restoration.[10] Their publication in 1662 of the *Natural and Political Observations on the Bills of Mortality* linked social and economic measures and included a crude life-expectancy table. Petty was the more active of the two and had earlier accomplished the *Down Survey* in 1652, a careful assessment of life and property in Ireland under Henry Cromwell. A general register of demographic information was urged by Petty during period of the Commonwealth and after the Restoration, but this was never realised. It was Petty who coined the term 'political arithmetic'.

The contributory causes of this seventeenth-century flowering included the advances in natural sciences which a few sought to emulate in the study of society, population growth amidst the absence of reliable demographic data, the development of insurance which required a firmer numerical foundation, and mercantilist beliefs that population size played an important part in the wealth and power of the nation. Yet the flowering was comparatively short-lived. Petty died in 1687, and for the following century there was little of note that qualifies for the history of social inquiry being pursued here.

This is not to say that social statistics were entirely quiescent in the eighteenth century. Demographic record-keeping expanded slowly and rudimentary analyses were carried out by Sir Peter Pett, Charles Davenant and Gregory King. Halley's life-expectancy tables were used for the first time in the calculation of life insurance. Cullen sees in the work of King and Halley the 'almost instantaneous' reduction of political arithmetic into demography.[11] In the process, political arithmetic lost William Petty's reformist zeal but served to inform contemporary debate about the population question.

Throughout the eighteenth century there were fears that the population had fallen since the Glorious Revolution of 1688. Methods used to estimate population were inadequate, being based on the window tax, but calls for a census were resisted in part due to fear of new taxes.[12] The complexion of the population debate changed radically after the publication of Malthus's *Essay on Population* in 1798, when concern about under-population was replaced with concern about over-population. Malthus' work, although the best known, was only one of several striking developments at the end of the eighteenth century. Another was the application of demographic methods to medical problems in the work of Gilbert Blane. A third was the entry into English of the word 'statistics'.

In 1791 'statistics' was firmly ensconced in the language with the publication of Sir John Sinclair's *Statistical Account of Scotland*, which surveyed that country demographically, economically and socially through descriptive accounts of each locality obtained from local parsons and schoolmasters.[13] By 1797 the *Encyclopaedia Britannica* described 'statistics' as 'a word lately introduced to express a view or a survey of any kingdom, county or parish'. The synthesis of this form of statistics with the population question contributed to the introduction of the national population census.

The intellectual spur to the successful establishment of the census, where previous efforts had failed, owed more to the efforts of John Rickman than to the publication of Malthus' book. Rickman pressed Parliament, which responded not to the long-term demographic case but to the need to assess demand for food in the wake of the disastrous harvest of 1800. A retrospective census was collected from parish records going back to 1700 along with the first census in 1801. Thereafter, a regular census was performed every ten years. Significant improvements in the method of enumeration were introduced in 1841, when details about all individuals were first recorded by enumerators.

THE STATISTICAL MOVEMENT

Around the beginning of the nineteenth century a qualitative change occurred in how society was viewed. Morality, religion and authority had been challenged earlier, in the scientific revolution of the seventeenth century, for example, but this scepticism and resort to empirical inquiry had not extended, demography apart, to the study of society. The eighteenth-century *philosophes* used evidence about primitive peoples, but they were at heart philosophers who did not have a sense of puzzlement about the state of contemporary society. That inquisitiveness began to arise among people who were in touch with fellow citizens outside their own strata of society, and sought to establish more precisely the facts of the conditions under which those people lived.[14] This interest was sharpened by the gathering pace of urbanisation and industrialisation as people were brought together in ever-more-concentrated settlements which aggravated problems of health, overcrowding, and the lack of recreation space, especially compared with with rural society.

The period after 1800 saw a significant extension of the scope of social inquiry in Britain. In particular, the establishment of a number of Statistical Societies in many cities provided a focus for discussing the inquiries to which the growing curiosity about social conditions were leading. The first to be founded was the Manchester Statistical Society in 1833. Its work was motivated by the peculiarly Victorian blend of an urge to attack moral evils and to 'elevate the physical condition' of workers.[15] One of its innovations was the employment of agents, such as the 'intelligent Irishman ... himself a handloom weaver', to survey 4,102 weaver families in 1834. Most notable among the new societies was the London Statistical Society, formed in 1834 by Richard Jones, T. R. Malthus, Charles Babbage, Adolphe Quetelet and Adam Sedgwick. Its original aims were defined as 'procuring, arranging and publishing Facts calculated to illustrate the Conditions and Prospects of Society'.[16] Quetelet's importance is discussed shortly, but it was not the academic founders but some of its early members − such as

Edwin Chadwick and William Farr – who addressed questions of relief policy or public health, who were the most active investigators and who moved the Society's work more into the field of social investigation.

In preparing the Poor Law Report of 1834, Chadwick had brought social inquiry closer to the process of government policy-making. Subsequently, as Secretary of the Poor Law Commissioners, he prepared the *Report on the Sanitary Condition of the Labouring Population*, which graphically described the social and health conditions of urban areas in which epidemic diseases such as cholera were rife. Concerns with urban poverty, welfare and sanitary improvement were growing. In its first ten years, Statistical Society discussions centred on health and social conditions including education, generating that 'peculiar pattern of British empirical sociology' in which demography and the study of poverty predominate.[17]

William Farr, on the other hand, was influential in the development of vital statistics. He made important contributions in his work on the causes of cholera and in his studies of the connection between cholera and density of population. He was working in a time receptive to the statistical approach. As G. M. Young observed, 'it was the business of the [eighteen] thirties to transfer the treatment of affairs from a polemical to a statistical basis, from Humbug to Humdrum. In 1830 there were hardly any figures to work on. Even the census was far from perfect .... But statistical inquiry was a passion of the time.'[18] Farr had benefited from studying medicine in Paris, where he was also taught medical statistics and his interest was aroused in the quantitative study of the incidence of disease. International contacts emerge at several points in this book, and are explicitly discussed by Jennifer Platt in chapter 13. He was one early example of the extent to which investigators in one country learnt from those working in another.

In some ways Farr was a typical member of the Statistical Society of the 1830s and 1840s, but, having a sophisticated understanding of statistics for the time, he never assumed that facts alone constituted a science. He was a distinguished member of that group of medical members of the early statistical societies who made notable contributions to the measurement of social phenomena, ancestors of the epidemiologists and community health specialists of today. Public health was a major social issue directly related to the life chances of the industrial working class. In the British medical profession, 'a tradition of local investigation connected with efforts to improve the condition of the poor. Physicians, especially those affiliated with dispensaries, were frequently the first professional people to gain extensive and direct experience with the lives of the poorest classes of cities.'[19]

The incidence of disease, compared with some other phenomena, was relatively easy to enumerate in terms of deaths and cases of sickness. Statistical inquiries were seen by some medical people as a way of improving medicine, through finding order and regularity in complex events. Quetelet's influence was strong here. The development of life tables, for example, exemplified the search for regularities in socio-medical phenomena. Farr was an important figure in the development of medical and demographic statistics not least because from his position in the General Register Office he continually emphasised their relevance to policy and administration. Like Victorian administrative reformers such as Chadwick and Simon, social investigation was seen by Farr as a necessary part of state activity.

By 1850, six distinct types of agency carrying out social investigations may be distinguished. Royal Commissions investigated social conditions, as did parliamentary committees. Government officials such as Chadwick and Sir John Simon conducted inquiries, while in some fields government inspectors were a source of information. After 1837 the work of the General Register Office, in which Farr was the prime mover, gradually grew in importance.[20] And private individuals carried out studies which were reported at the meetings of the Statistical Societies. None of these six types included what would fifty years later have been recognised as a social survey, with the possible exception of studies accomplished by the London and the Manchester Statistical Societies. Social conditions were itemised by means of information collected from correspondents around the country, informants giving first-hand testimony under interrogation before commissions and committees, augmented by other first-hand observation, particularly by medical investigators. Only in the demographic field was systematic effort made to gather individual data, and here the census and vital registration rather than a purpose-designed inquiry[21] was the main vehicle.

Controversy arose about the place of values in such investigations. Though driven to greater or lesser extents by the desire to improve social conditions – particularly to check the scourge of epidemic diseases – investigators sought to rest their case on facts rather than values. The aspirations of the Statistical Society were clear enough. Its prospectus stated: 'The Statistical Society will consider it to be the first and most essential rule of its conduct to exclude carefully all Opinions from its transactions and publications – to confine its attention rigorously to facts – and, as far as it may be possible, to facts which can be stated numerically and arranged in tables'.[22] In reality, it was hard to keep a clear distinction between facts and values and between facts and theories. All observers framed their observations in terms of theories, and these coloured their interpretations.[23] Moreover, some though not all investigators, whether government servants or private individuals, were interested in pursuing social reform, so that a purely detached and disinterested conception of social inquiry, though it was part of the rhetoric of the statistical societies, was an inadequate foundation for their work.

Adolphe Quetelet

On the continent the development of social inquiry was somewhat different though one of its key figures, Adolphe Quetelet, sparked off the creation of the Statistical Society of London during his visit to the British Association for the Advancement of Science in 1833. Quetelet was born in Ghent in 1796; in his youth he had literary and artistic interests before being trained as a mathematician. He then became interested in astronomy, and on a visit to Paris in 1823 to pursue this interest became acquainted with the French mathematicians Fourier and La Place and with their work on probability. This gave him the idea of applying statistical ideas to the measurement of the human body. On his return to Belgium he became involved in designing a Belgian census, and followed this up with studies of human stature and of criminal tendencies in the Belgian population. A third study of the distribution of populations by weight followed. From the various studies, Quetelet published *On the Development of Man and his Faculties* in 1835, a book bearing the subtitle 'physique sociale'.[24]

The 'laws' from which Quetelet sought to construct his social physics were initially based on his observation of relationship between physical characteristics and rates of crime and marriage over time and between countries. He then studied the distribution of these characteristics and found that they tended to conform to a normal or binomial form. Though his best-known statement of his ideas was published in 1869, in fact he had formed them thirty years earlier. The ideas which had the strongest appeal to analysts of society were those concerning what he called 'moral statistics' about crime, marriage, suicide, public disorder and intellectual capacities.

Quetelet was important in introducing some major statistical ideas into social inquiry, although with hindsight the way in which he worked them out failed to realise their full potential — for example, he did not apply ideas about probability to the occurrence of events. His view of social causation was a deterministic one, influenced by his training in science. He was a statistician, relying on data derived from administrative sources and not collecting his own. For this reason he does not belong to the survey tradition, though his methods of analysis provided pointers to the survey, in his studies of the distribution of physical and social characteristics. His 'moral statistics' had parallels with the Durkheimian conception of social inquiry at the end of the century, although the Durkheimians were critical of his use of averages and in 1912 Halbwachs wrote a monograph attacking Quetelet's approach.[25]

Quetelet was an important figure in the history of social science research. Not for nothing was Paul Lazarsfeld's chair at Columbia named for him. He was tutor to Prince Albert before his marriage to Queen Victoria, and it was undoubtedly due to his influence that the Prince Consort became in 1840 the patron of the London Statistical Society. Many British social investigators and reformers of the nineteenth century, as various as Florence Nightingale and Francis Galton, paid homage to his work as a moral statistician, but as Stephen Cole observes, this was more of a gesture than a sign of intellectual consolidation and development.[26]

Indeed, one of the characteristics of many of these developments in the statistical investigation of social conditions was their non-cumulative quality. One may speculate about why this was so. Cole puts the main emphasis upon the lack of institutionalisation of British empirical social research during the nineteenth century. Lacking scientific occupational positions, agreement on common problems and tools, mechanisms for socialisation into the research role, and (apart from the *Journal of the Statistical Society*) avenues of communication, effort remained fragmented. Philip Abrams' more subtle account stresses changes in the political culture to which the statisticians failed to adapt, and the fact that social science developed largely outside their orbit due to their resistance to its more theoretical concerns and their espousal of a version of pure empiricism.

AMELIORISM AND SOCIAL REFORM

Alongside the empiricist inquiries of the statisticians, a moral concern with social conditions fuelled an urge to investigate and change them.

If Victorian England produced Mr Gradgrind and the Commissioners of Fact, it also produced Charles Dickens. If it produced many men like Sir Robert Giffen, it also produced some like Seebohm Rowntree. This is not a question of sharp antithesis. Again and again we find the concern for facts and for rationalisation mixed up with a counteracting moral sensibility ... For many Victorians the moral perspective carried imperatives of its own at least as powerful as those of empirical science.[27]

Beginning in the 1830s, quantitative social research acquired a more distinctly moral tone.[28] Utilitarian Christianity, which had informed the work of many of the members of the Statistical Societies, gained a wider acceptance and led to putative social investigations. To accomplish these studies there was 'an extraordinary growth of voluntary bodies concerned with policies of moral improvement'[29] which saw social science as applied Christianity. Such ameliorists promulgated a belief that the way to social reform lay via the improvements of individuals rather than of society. This belief in the efficacy of improving individuals fostered a shift in the focus of social investigation from social organisations to individuals and families, as well as from research to legislation – in Philip Abrams' words, from promoting the measuring of society to promoting social measures. 'Moral statistics' about crime and prisons, alcohol consumption, sexual behaviour, health and education became a prime focus for attention, a trend paralleled in Belgium and France in the work of Quetelet and his followers, a tradition that Durkheim and his school were later to take up.

The ameliorist approach was embodied in the National Association for the Promotion of Social Science (NAPSS). This association was founded in 1857 and soon came to dominate what was then considered social investigation in the period between its founding date and the 1880's, including the concerns of the London Statistical Society. It organised annual conferences, sought to influence Parliament to legislate on social issues, and relied heavily on the influence of its prestigious membership to achieve reform.[30] Its intellectual base, however, was more uncertain. As Abrams observes, ameliorist analyses

settled the issue of causes too quickly, too uncritically and too atomistically. Social problems were rooted in individual moral weakness and in the conjunction of personal weakness and temptations offered to weakness by certain kinds of social situation. A two-pronged policy science was called for: to show how individual character could be fortified against temptation; and to show how to eliminate vicious situations.[31]

Moral perceptions were so strong and so clear that although there was often awareness of structural conditions leading to social problems, there was seldom any sustained effort to analyse or generalise these structural linkages. Ultimately, appeals were always made to moral and political principles, not to empirically grounded generalisations or to a theoretical system of explanation. In keeping with this orientation, the investigations did not emphasise the gathering of new information, still less innovative approaches to research methods. The NAPSS worked through the framing of opinion among its members and their influence in government, a process

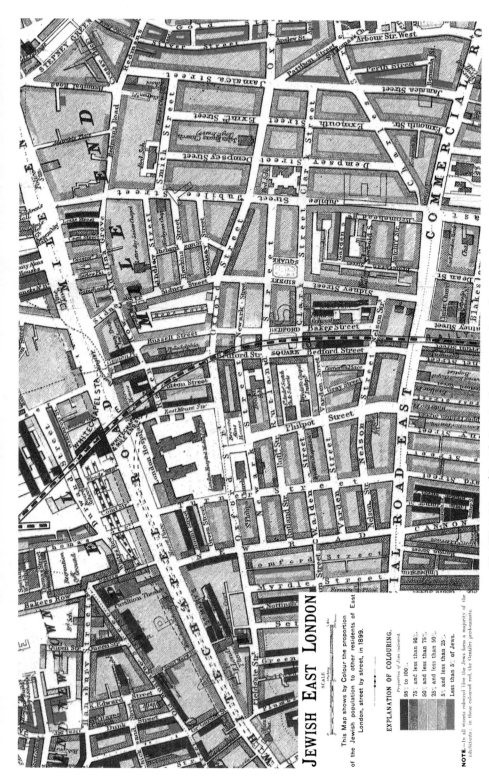

JEWISH EAST LONDON

SCALE

This Map shows by Colour the proportion
of the Jewish population to other residents of East
London, street by street, in 1899.

EXPLANATION OF COLOURING.

Proportion of Jews indicated.

95% to 100%.
75% and less than 95%.
50% and less than 75%.
25% and less than 50%.
5% and less than 25%.
Less than 5% of Jews.

NOTE.—In all streets coloured blue the Jews form a majority of the inhabitants: in those coloured red, the Gentiles predominate.

PLATE 1 Map of *Jewish East London* showing the ethnic composition of Whitechapel and Stepney from map prepared by George E. Arkell in 1901.

THE STREETS ARE COLOURED ACCORDING TO TH▮

Lowest class. Vicious, semi-criminal.   Very poor, casual. Chronic want.   Poor. 18s. to 21s. a week for a moderate famil▮

A combination of colours—as dark blue and black, or pink and red—indicates that ▮

PLATE 2 Charles Booth's poverty map of Whitechapel and Stepney
in East London in 1893.

PLATE 3 Nationalities map showing social composition of the population in the neighbourhood of Hull House in Chicago, 1895 (extract).

NATIONALITIES MAP No.I.—POLK STREET TO TWELFTH,
HALSTED STREET TO JEFFERSON, CHICAGO.

FRENCH FRENCH CANADIAN BOHEMIAN SCANDANAVIAN CHINESE COLORED

STORES ETC., NOT BY DWELLINGS.

The Seventh Ward of Philadelphia

The Distribution of Negro Inhabitants Throughout the Ward, and their social condition

(For a more detailed explanation of the meaning of the different grades, see § 46, chap. xv.)

Grade 4: Vicious and Criminal Classes.

Grade 3: The Poor.

Grade 2: The Working People—Fair to Comfortable.

Grade 1: The "Middle Classes" and those above.

Residences of Whites, Stores, Public Buildings, etc.

PLATE 4 The Seventh Ward of Philadelphia. The distribution of negro inhabitants throughout the ward and their social condition in 1897.

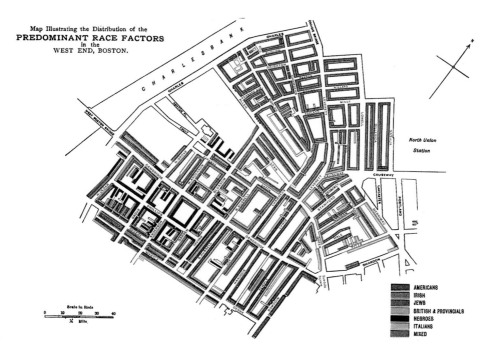

PLATE 5 Map showing the predominant racial groups among the population in the West End, Boston in 1903.

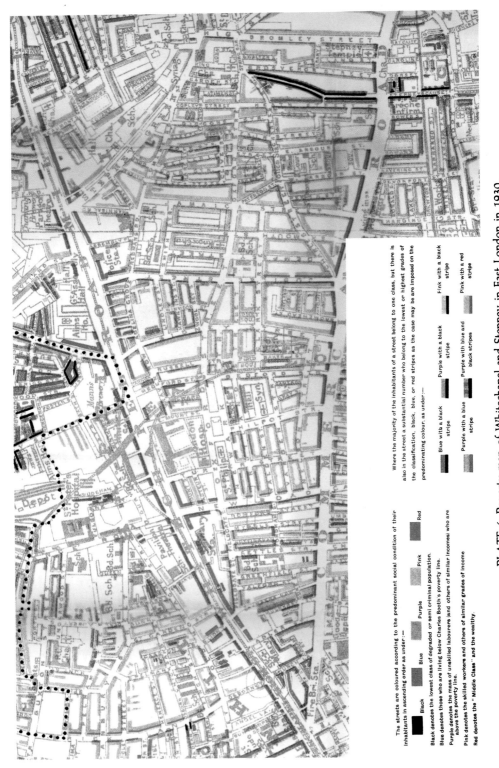

The streets are coloured according to the predominant social condition of their inhabitants in ascending order as under:—

Black   Blue   Purple   Pink   Red

Black denotes the lowest class of degraded or semi criminal population.

Blue denotes those who are living below Charles Booth's poverty line.

Purple denotes the mass of unskilled labourers (and others of similar incomes) who are above the poverty line.

Pink denotes the skilled workers and others of similar grades of income

Red denotes the "Middle Class" and the wealthy.

Where the majority of the inhabitants of a street belong to one class, but there is also in the street a substantial number who belong to the lowest or highest grades of the classification, black, blue, or red stripes as the case may be are imposed on the predominating colour, as under:—

Blue with a black stripe   Purple with a black stripe   Pink with a black stripe

Purple with a blue stripe   Purple with blue and black stripes   Pink with a red stripe

PLATE 6 Poverty map of Whitechapel and Stepney in East London in 1930.

which relegated empirical inquiry into second place. After the demise of the NAPSS, the approach persisted in the Charity Organisation Society, whose members took a moral view of the social behaviour of the lower orders, derived guidance for the relief of want from first principles, and otherwise were not very curious about empirical reality.

By the 1880s the NAPSS had become gravely handicapped by this ameliorist approach and its narrowness of interpretation. It was also hindered by its craving for consensus, and the fact that its channels of influence were into government and to politicians, rather than to officials as in the case of the statisticians. The economic crises of the 1870s called into question the adequacy of the interpretations offered by the NAPSS and by political economists. Thereafter, a more searching and contentious debate about social policy issues eroded the intellectual high ground occupied by the upper-class ameliorists in the NAPSS.

Four overlapping groups challenged their dominance. As social policy became politically a more contentious issue, differences between political parties became sharper and they began to give social issues more prominence in their agendas. Parties, moreover, were becoming more rigidly organised both in Parliament and in the country, and the appeal of a body which sought consensual solutions to problems where different interests were in conflict – whether those of employer and worker or temperance reformer and brewer or whatever – was much reduced. Secondly, the growing trade unions were producing a new group of articulate working-class activists who were not spoken for in any way by the NAPSS. Thirdly, the political left began to offer an ideological explanation of poverty distinctly different from that of the ameliorists. And there was a desire on the part of a few people for a more rigorous and empirical investigation of the matters of political disagreement, less tinged with moral principles and more innovative in its research methods.

OBSERVING LIFE AMONG THE WORKING CLASSES

Mayhew and Le Play

The NAPSS membership belonged to a stratum of society far removed from the working classes whose living and working conditions were exercising British opinion in the 1880s. Though the condition of the lower orders much concerned members of NAPSS, this concern was not based upon the close acquaintance of a detached observer, but rather upon social intercourse in well-defined and unalterable social roles with servants, tenants, workpeople, offenders against the law and 'moral unfortunates' who were the object of philanthropy.[32] Their picture of working-class life was consequently conditioned by their own social position and heavily overlaid with moral judgement.

This makes the work of the journalist Henry Mayhew in mid-century all the more remarkable. Though not a practitioner of the social survey he used an approach that became integral to the survey method half a century later – he went out and talked to ordinary people about their lives and experiences as a disinterested observer. Mayhew was not the first to adopt this approach. Radicals such as William Cobbett and Frederich Engels had used it to good effect before Mayhew, but Mayhew gave new meaning to the practice of detached observation. Acting as the metropolitan correspondent of the *Morning Chronicle*, Mayhew talked to members of the working classes in their own environment at work, in public places and at home. His accounts of various working class occupations, with detailed descriptions of the conditions of life and the economic circumstances of the persons described, were published first in 1849 to 1851 in the paper, and later collected into *London Labour and the London Poor* (1861). Mayhew's qualitative and sympathetic treatment of the working class stands in marked contrast to the moralism characteristic of the ameliorists,[33] though he himself in some of his later writing was not above a strong dose of moralism.[34] One reason for the lack of imitators of Mayhew was the lack of an institutional base for social research.

Different characteristics prevailed in France, but one very important social observer, Le Play, demands attention. Quetelet's attempts to frame laws of 'social physics' had led him into conflict with Auguste Comte in the 1830s. Comte's vision of the contribution made by the social sciences was very different from that in the empirical tradition. Theory had a more salient place in French proto-sociology from an earlier date, though ideas from political economy held powerful sway in Britain, and Spencerian evolutionism later became important for sociology. Just as important as Comte was his fellow graduate of the Ecole Polytechnique, Frédéric Le Play, an engineer by profession, who made notable contributions to the advancement of empirical inquiry in mid-century by his studies of workers in various parts of Europe.[35]

Frédéric Le Play advanced the application of scientific method to the study of society without doing surveys as such. Influenced by his training as an engineer and a statistician, Le Play developed pragmatic methods for the study of working-class family life. Though aiming to construct a science of society, he eschewed Comteian organicism and Quetelet's search for laws in favour of the systematic collection of information about the state of a people. Influenced in his youth by the British political arithmeticians and the German tradition of descriptive statistics, he saw the compilation of economic and social data as the basis of sound administration. In his 1840 monograph *Vues générales sur la statistique*, he argued that government could be made more effective by employing classificatory devices, and presented a model consisting of hundreds of categories and sub-categories derived from the German statistical tradition. He suggested that information on sex, age, level of education, profession and place of residence of each member of the population should be collected, as well as information on intellectual and moral characteristics.[36]

Le Play stands in a French tradition of national population inquiries dating back to Colbert and Vauban in the seventeenth century that were carried out by government, usually via the prefects. In his youth Le Play thought that state statistics were reliable sources, but he came to view such data as not wholly satisfactory, and subject to manipulation. He was also critical of the 'moral statistics' of Quetelet, for he viewed his data as lacking reliability, and he did not share the belief that it was possible to frame laws independent of the individual. Le Play was attracted by the British statistical societies, with whose approach he was in sympathy. They were private, not state bodies, they had moral commitment to social betterment, and their members were politically active to achieve those ends. He saw social research as combining scientific investigation with inquiries which would 'furnish statesmen with a solid basis for resolving social questions'.[37]

By the 1850s, Le Play was convinced that social research should concern itself, not with population characteristics but with the private lives of citizens, particularly their family life. To gain knowledge of this, investigators must use direct observation:

In scientific matters, only direct observation of facts can lead to rigorous conclusions and their acceptance. This principle is acknowledged today in the physical sciences, but it is still unrecognised in social science. The practitioners of social science are generally inspired by preconceived ideas which perpetuate antagonisms and which cannot serve as a basis for systematic action. People imbued with such biases tend to disdain the facts and the conclusions which can be drawn from them. Social science thus remains in a situation comparable to the physical sciences when they were based on the conceptions of astrology and alchemy; social science will not be established until it is founded on observation.[38]

To aid in this task he used the 'monographic method'. Detailed studies were made of particular families in different parts of Europe, the families selected so as to be 'typical' of the stratum to which they belonged. Desrosières discusses this aspect of his work in chapter 8 in this volume.

Noteworthy from the point of view of the survey is Le Play's use of quantitative budget data, which was meticulously collected in line with his belief that every act in a family's life could be traced in its income or outgoings. His studies, published in *Les ouvriers européens* in 1855, combined this quantitative budget analysis with qualitative data about the social circumstances of individual families. In a sense Le Play was conducting surveys, although rather limited in their subject matter, and containing data mixed up with his moral and philosophical beliefs. His lasting influence was upon the town planning survey, mediated through Patrick Geddes and Victor Branford, founders of the Le Play School in Britain, who in turn influenced not the social sciences but modern town planning.[39]

Developments in Germany

In Germany, the situation was rather different. The tradition of collecting statistics about German states, a legacy of the Napoleonic period, influenced Le Play, and was distinctive from developments in Britain. A mixture of geography, administrative law and political theory, the characteristic product combined descriptive accounts of states, their population and system of government, customs and industry, presented as complex classificatory systems. Statistics at an early date became a subject of scholarly inquiry and was used in the education of state officials. This was quite a different tradition from that embodied in the London Statistical Society, being conducted by government rather than private individuals, professionals or aristocrats, and seeking to portray national and demographic characteristics without particular attention to social conditions.

The main developments in Germany took place later in the nineteenth century and early in the twentieth, when a range of social scientists and government officials combined to study the condition of the working class as a result of industrialisation. The setting in which they did so was the *Verein für Sozialpolitik*, in which historical economists such as Schmoller and Brentano as well as the young Max Weber undertook inquiries into the condition of peasants and land labourers.[40] These developments are of note, and are further considered by Irmela Gorges in chapter 12 below.

Their significance should not, however, be exaggerated. In the first place, these German inquiries took place later in the century and drew on British, Belgian and German models already available. They were less innovative than their counterparts already discussed. They relied heavily upon third-party informants such as officials, teachers, ministers, landowners, and others thought to be knowledgeable about the conditions of peasants in their area. These informants sent back their responses in the form of an essay, so that unlike Le Play or Booth, little individual information was collected and often responses were published verbatim rather than being analysed. The main interest of the members lay in analysing and debating the policy issues to which the research materials bore only a tenuous connection. 'The *Verein* surveys did not result in the improvement of social research methods'.[41]

THE RISE OF SOCIAL SURVEY RESEARCH

The history of the social survey is usually dated in Britain to the 1880s when, as economic depression heightened social tensions, social and political groups that had competed in prosperity descended into conflict. The demise of the NAPSS was but one symptom of this crisis, the causes of which lay elsewhere. By the 1880s, the liberal economics and utilitarian Christianity that had served the ruling classes well since the beginning of the nineteenth century were now increasingly called into question. The assumption that increasing production would lead to a sufficiency of goods being distributed was being proved wrong by the extent of poverty. The Victorian concentration on individual philanthropy as a means of alleviating social problems was increasingly shown to be inadequate, and many turned to the possibility of action by the state – beyond the minimal provision through the Poor Law – for more effective relief. Economic liberalism was challenged by the new extensions taking place in political citizenship. The extension of the electoral franchise and the growth of trades unions led to vocal and public criticism of assumptions which had previously been accepted without much questioning by large sections of the upper and middle classes.

One manifestation of these changing circumstances was sporadic social unrest. The Trafalgar Square riots of 1886 caused great anxiety in comfortable circles. 'A new fear came to England, a new self-questioning ... At the same time poverty, unemployment and the demands of the enfranchised people for better things were becoming insistent threats to confidence in self-adjusting social processes and to established English ways of life.'[42] This pressure from below sparked off in sections of the middle and upper classes desire to gather more information with which to frame a practical course in social policy. The systematic accumulation of social facts was seen to be useful as an aid to appropriate social intervention.

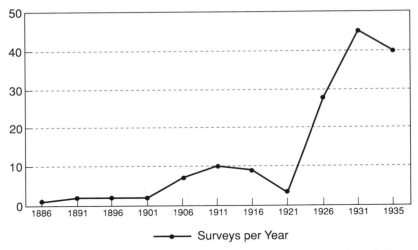

Figure 1.1   UK social surveys by year, 1886 to 1934. Adapted from Wells, 1936.

One particular question which exercised opinion in the middle and upper classes was the extent of poverty. Through the nineteenth century pauperism, as measured by the proportion of the population in receipt of poor relief, fell from 8·8 per cent of the population in 1834 to 4·6 per cent of the population in 1870 and then to just over 3 per cent in 1880. Judged in these terms, poverty was not a significant problem. But careful observers believed otherwise. Mayhew had observed that while 1·87 million people in 1848 were in receipt of poor relief there were, he estimated, 2·25 million people without a gainful occupation, some 14 per cent of the population.[34] In the 1880s, with more trying economic conditions, the problem of poverty became more insistent and the discrepancy between the numbers in receipt of poor relief and the proportion of the population having inadequate incomes due to underemployment, unemployment, family breakdown, ill-health, old age and other misfortunes was more apparent. But how great was the difference and who would provide an answer to the question?

The absence of an adequate institutional base from which to undertake such inquiries was a major obstacle.[44] This base was not provided by the political parties. Government departments did little at this period to gather information on social conditions or else produced figures, as on the Poor Law, which were misleading. Social inquiry was not part of the Poor Law machinery. Voluntary bodies such as the Charity Organisation Society (COS), though they undertook careful casework, could throw little objective light upon the larger picture. With the exception of one or two positions in economics, social science was not institutionalised in universities. And although the parliamentary committee and the Royal Commission were devices for investigating problems, their methods of taking individual evidence were unlikely to lead to a satisfactory overall picture of social conditions.

Existing methods of collecting social data about poverty were patchy and often lacking in reliability. Mayhew's observational approach emphasised vivid insight and detailed description over extensive enumeration. Statistics compiled by central and local government, such as they were, related to administrative function and were neither designed nor collected by people with professional training. The interrogatory methods of committees of inquiry produced impressionistic results which varied between individuals. While some local and national government officials sincerely sought to uncover and use social facts, there was a marked lack of clarity in defining, let alone measuring, poverty.

Charles Booth

The pivotal figure of Charles Booth is treated in two chapters in this book by Kevin Bales and E. P. Hennock. The conventional view which credits Booth with the innovation of the social survey has a good deal of truth in it, though it needs some qualification. The publication of the first volume of Booth's study of poverty in London in 1889 created a sensation. Charles Booth was a wealthy Liverpool shipowner who was annoyed by the lack of a factual basis for the accounts of urban poverty in pamphlets such as *The Bitter Cry of Outcast London* and in articles in the *Pall Mall Gazette* which suggested that one quarter of the population of London were living in poverty. The ongoing public debate about the 'poverty question' was clouded by three questions which had been posed but never sufficiently answered: how many were poor, why were they poor, and what should be done to alleviate poverty? Through careful empirical study Booth sought answers for the East End of London to the first two questions. The *Life and Labour of the People in London*, published in seventeen volumes between 1889 and 1903, is the first great empirical study in the social survey tradition.[45]

Booth's originality, as Kevin Bales shows in chapter 3, lay in his methods of inquiry, not just in how he collected and analysed his data, but in the way he conceptualised the problem of poverty. Booth attempted to introduce precision to the concept of the 'poverty line' where hitherto there had been vagueness, a characteristic which justifies including him as one of the founding fathers of social science.[46] E. P. Hennock discusses this aspect of Booth's work in more detail in chapter 7. Moreover, Booth sought to measure the numbers of the population above and below the poverty line with some precision, even though the classification categories that he used lacked adequate justification. This too differentiated his work from previous studies, and foreshadowed the later use of the social survey for estimating population values with some exactitude. Thirdly, although Booth's study like most of the studies considered in this volume was a local study, its coverage was comprehensive – he aimed to gather information on as large a proportion of the population as was possible and especially on all families with children in the parts of London covered by the survey. Booth was also unusual in using a team of investigators. He and his fifteen assistants (ten men and five women), including Beatrice Potter (later Webb), Hubert Llewellyn Smith, Clara Collett, Ernest Aves and Graham Balfour, constituted a larger group of social investigators than hitherto had worked on a single study.

To obtain the necessary data Booth relied not upon official statistical sources – although the 1881 Census provided essential background information about the districts studied – but on first-hand data about the household circumstances of poor families. These data were not collected directly by his research team but by what Beatrice Webb called the method of the 'wholesale interview'.[47] School Board Visitors, who entered the homes of children attending London schools, were interviewed by Booth to gather information about the circumstances of each family.

The School Board Visitors themselves carried out house-to-house surveys in the districts for which they were responsible in order to locate and enrol children. They were also empowered to collect information on occupations, rents and wages. After a 'pilot test' interviewing the Visitors with two members of his staff, Booth had printed data collection notebooks that categorised the information gained in the interviews. Great care was taken to achieve uniformity in the data collection between the different interviewers, and the information obtained was checked against other sources in an attempt to increase its reliability. The quantitative and qualitative data from the notebooks were analysed by Booth and his staff. The published results were aggregations of the measurable and distillations of the unquantifiable. The findings had direct policy implications and contributed to movements toward social reform and old age pensions in particular.

In recent years there has been some scholarly interest in Booth's work and a degree of controversy over the precise nature of his contribution. This is reflected in the chapters by Kevin Bales and E. P. Hennock. Hennock has already set out the basis for a reinterpretation of Booth's significance in two major articles.[48] One issue where revision is required concerns the precise origins of Booth's interest in the subject of poverty and the influences upon him in the period before 1886, when he began the research. There is no doubt, as Hennock argues, that Booth was much influenced by the intellectual climate of the time, though to describe him as a 'systematiser' perhaps goes too far in playing down his contribution.[49] His originality lay in the conception and design of the inquiry he undertook, as well as in the impact of his finding that 30 per cent of the population of London were living in poverty. There is further disagreement between Bales and Hennock over the reliability of Booth's data, whether or not his survey was based on a non-random sample, the precision of Booth's categorisation of poverty and over Booth's analysis of the causes of poverty.[50]

Other recent work on Booth includes a study by Cullen of Booth's measures of poverty using correlation analysis to demonstrate Booth's application of a 'consistent standard of poverty',[51] an article by Bales on the Booth Archive,[52] an edition of his maps by the London Topographical Society,[53] the computerisation of a sample of some 30,000 households from the Poverty Study,[54] a microfilm edition of his research materials from the British Library of Political and Economic Science[55] and work by historians at the Open University to organise and index his papers.[56]

Booth's research had two important effects on the development of the social survey, independent of any influence his findings may have had. The first of these is that Booth's work popularised survey research. The wide publicity which *Life and Labour* received in America as well as in Europe sparked the interest of widely dispersed individuals who then took up the social survey as a tool to meet their own needs. The surveys discussed in chapters 4 and 6, at Hull House in Chicago and in *The Philadelphia Negro*, both sought to use the community survey as a means of addressing social problems, and both are derivations, albeit with greater policy emphasis, from *Life and Labour*. Secondly, Booth's work served as a template for a large number of early social researchers – Seebohm Rowntree, Jane Addams, W. E. B. Du Bois, among others, who drew heavily upon Booth's methods. A clear example of this transfer of research methods can be been in the shared technique of mapping poverty and ethnicity in sections of London, Chicago and Philadelphia (see plates 2, 3, 4 and the discussion below, pp. 31–35). In the process, important improvements were made, but

Booth's work may be seen as a distinct stimulus from which other surveys developed.

After Booth

The next major survey in Britain, Seebohm Rowntree's study of York, was conducted in 1899 and published in 1901. This further refined both the conceptualisation and measurement of the phenomenon of poverty. Most important, perhaps, it used 'retail' rather than 'wholesale' interviewing, that is to say, people were interviewed directly in their own homes by members of the research team, not indirectly through reports by middle-class professionals with knowledge of individual families. This transition from reliance upon informants who could report on the circumstances of working-class people to reliance upon the response of the people themselves was a most important one. It was not unknown earlier – Mayhew had relied on direct questioning – but prior to Rowntree had not been used in large-scale inquiries. His reliance upon direct questioning seems to have been due partly to the absence of voluntary workers to act as informants, but also his pragmatic discovery that the answers given to direct questions were generally reliable when checked against other sources such as information from neighbours, from employers, and so on.[57] With hindsight the use of interviews appears to be a definite innovation, yet contemporaries questioned their use. Helen Bosanquet argued at the time that since it took 'long years of apprenticeship to be able to judge accurately the real signs of poverty', Rowntree's inexperienced researchers, their visits 'limited to a few minutes', could only lead to inaccurate and untrustworthy statistics.[58]

Hennock in chapter 7 makes clear Rowntree's contribution to poverty studies, which in many respects was more refined than Booth's. Like Booth, Rowntree carried out a complete enumeration of the town. The first social surveyor to use sampling methods was Arthur Lyon Bowley in his studies of poverty in five towns, published as *Livelihood and Poverty* in 1915. Bowley's contribution is considered by Hennock in chapter 7 and Alain Desrosières in chapter 8, and needs little further comment here except to note that this innovation undercut the local social survey, eventually to replace it with the modern sample survey. Once Bowley had shown that it could be done, however, the diffusion of sampling was not inevitable. Like the idea of sampling itself, which Desrosires explores, the use of sampling in practice only emerged slowly and was first seriously taken up by American market researchers between the wars. It was used in social survey research for government and academic research only during and after World War II.

Studies by Booth, Rowntree and Bowley were not the only social surveys being done in Britain. Prior to 1914, a number of community studies carried out in Britain focused upon poverty, housing and employment. Some, though not all, of these studies may be termed social surveys. They ranged from studies of agricultural villages such as Corsley in Wiltshire[59] through neighbourhoods such as East Ham and Lambeth[60] to towns and cities such as Middlesbrough, Norwich, Liverpool and Oxford.[61] These studies reflected earlier developments during the period in which Booth was planning his London survey.

THE CHANGING CLIMATE

Charles Booth is usually hailed as the first social surveyor, but attention is not always drawn to the intellectual ferment of the 1880s and to other developments taking place in the same period. Jane Lewis' chapter on the debates between the Bosanquets and the Webbs reminds us that the social survey formed part of a larger movement for the application of social analysis to the problems of urban industrial society. Throughout the period, the Charity Organisation Society represented one approach to social intervention, centred around individual case work. But other approaches that pointed to more collectivist solutions were also developing, and these had somewhat closer affinities to the use of surveys in social investigation. For example, the Fabian Women's Group under the influence of Mrs Pember Reeves itself carried out surveys.

Two intellectual currents are especially worthy of attention. The 'New Liberalism', which was grounded in Oxford Idealism, and the establishment of the Fabian Society in 1884, grounded in socialism, pointed to trends in middle-class opinion in the left-centre of the political spectrum that inclined towards more collectivist solutions to social problems. The Fabians ultimately became an important element in the establishment of the Labour Party. The new liberals, including figures such as J. A. Hobson, J. L. Hammond and L. T. Hobhouse, were an intellectual group on the left of the Liberal party who made important contributions to political ideas and also, in some cases, to social science. Hobhouse, for example, became the first professor of sociology in England, at the London School of Economics and Political Science. For the most part the members of these groups did not themselves conduct surveys, but they were consumers of them. Groups such as the Fabian Society were developing wider structures of social and political thought within which the results of surveys could be interpreted.

Sidney and Beatrice Webb illustrate this tangential relationship. Though in her youth Beatrice had assisted Booth, in their maturity the Webbs did not undertake studies using the survey method as that term is employed here, though they did use interviews extensively in some of their institutional studies. They were, however, fervent advocates of social research and researchers of substance themselves, and co-founded the London School of Economics and Political Science as an academic centre for the pursuit of social inquiry. Though the problem of institutionalisation was real, and one of the problems of the paucity of researchers was that so few carried on social research that it was difficult to recruit successors to those who did, gradually the activities of persons like the Webbs did create an intellectual context, and eventually an institutional context, within which survey research could flourish.

Another important institutional context, itself a social movement, was the Settlement. The original settlement, Toynbee Hall in the east end of London, was set up in 1884 by the Reverend (later Canon) Samuel Barnett, an Anglican clergyman influenced by John Ruskin, William Morris and the Christian socialism of the period. Its objectives were to 'bridge the gulf that industrialism has created between rich and poor, to reduce the mutual suspicion and ignorance of one class for the other, and to do something more than give charity'. This was to be achieved by the establishment of a voluntary association with residential premises located in an urban working-class area, an institution intermediary between different geographical and social worlds. Its practical aims were threefold: to spread education and culture, enable middle-class people to form personal relationships with members of the working class, and to discover facts about social problems.[62] By 1911, forty-six such settlements had been founded in Britain.

The significance of the Settlement House as a training-ground for socially concerned young people was considerable. Although Canon Barnett at first espoused a person-centred explanation of social pathology, between 1880 and 1900 he moved sharply away from such a COS view of the world toward economic explanations for the causes of social distress and a growing belief in state intervention to provide for the destitute, pensions for the elderly and training schemes for the unemployed.[63]

It is easy in retrospect to poke fun at Settlements, for their high-flown aspirations compared with the reality of 'slumming', for the social distance between their residents and their working-class neighbours, and for their relatively ineffectual impact upon social conditions in their localities. Toynbee Hall, indeed, was built as a 'manorial residence', in nineteenth-century Elizabethan style more characteristic of Oxford than the East End.[64] Yet this urban echo of collegiate life – and its later Britain and American followers – helped to form the world views of a number of influential figures in public life. Canon Barnett's protégés included Alfred Milner, Robert Morant, Arthur Salter and, in social investigation, Hubert Llewellyn Smith (who was in residence while he assisted Booth) and William Beveridge, who indeed was brought in as Sub-Warden in 1903 specifically to sharpen Toynbee Hall's attack on social problems.[65] R. H. Tawney, challenged by the Master of Balliol, Edward Caird, to find out why England had poverty alongside riches, and do something about it, lived there for over four years beginning in 1903, at the same time as Beveridge.[66]

The influence of their ideas and the publicity they gave to the existence of social conditions created a more thoughtful climate for the reception of social surveys. Toynbee Hall was also the training ground for such influential figures as Llewellyn Smith who subsequently played an important part in building up the Statistical Department of the Board of Trade,[67] a parallel development to the social survey in improving quantitative knowledge about the working of the British labour market.

THE AMERICAN CONTEXT AND ITS CONTRASTS WITH BRITAIN

Developments in the United States shared many features of this British experience. In both societies the social survey was shaped by the salience of voluntary effort, of liberal political traditions that restricted government initiatives, and of values promoting 'responsible individualism'. Thus we can speak of an Anglo-American tradition of social survey movements that shared many fundamental features.

Yet as Sklar points out in chapter 4, political, social and economic differences in the two societies produced significant dissimilarities in the development of the social survey. In England, the urge to investigate social conditions bridged academic and political circles more effectively than was the case in the United States. The British civil service facilitated the movement of elite young men from undergraduate study at Oxford and Cambridge to settlements where they worked on social surveys and thence to political offices that gave them the opportunity to bring the knowledge gained to bear on debate within government and to influence policy formation. This easy movement increased the survey's effectiveness as a policy tool in England before 1914, and prolonged its life thereafter. The upper- and middle-class monopoly of voting rights before 1867 meant that civil service control of public policy was firmly established before the working classes gained effective political representation. At the same time, earlier traditions among landed elites who were critical of the effects of industrialisation lent legitimacy, while the increasing political activism of organised labour lent urgency, to state intervention by Victorian and Edwardian officials.

Different political, social and economic conditions in the United States produced different results. State structure was markedly different. The federal system of government, with power divided between the federal, state and county levels, contrasted with the growth towards a unitary British state during the nineteenth and early twentieth centuries.[68] This reflected the much greater geographical, regional and ethnic diversity of the United States.

Party patronage gave wage-earning men unprecedented access to elected and appointed public office, and civil service reform failed dismally as a vehicle for elites to retain control of public life. Patronage also created through the 'spoils system' an alternative welfare system markedly different from the British system of local government.[69] The nation's chief landed gentry — slave-holding southerners — had just been defeated in one of the bloodiest wars in human history, and while that aristocracy produced scathing criticisms of industrial capitalism, their opinions were useless to late-nineteenth century reformers. Meanwhile, the power of the courts in the American political process and the written constitution on which that power was based effectively crippled labour's power in state legislatures by judging such pro-labour statutes unconstitutional. By 1886 the American Federation of Labor had turned its back on government as a means of advancing working-class interests and, limiting itself to skilled craft workers, sought gains through direct negotiations with employers, reinforced with the threat of strikes. The scale of immigration fractured the labour market, hindered trade unionism, and inhibited the development of a social-democratic political movement.[70]

Thus, the American context contained challenges not found in the British milieu. More isolated from political power, unable to draw on traditional criticisms of industrialisation, and less likely to work closely with organised labour, reformers had to make the most of their middle-class resources. They also stood in a different relationship to emerging social science. By the end of the century, there was a different relationship between professional expertise and the developing skills of social investigation than in Britain, one which also had repercussions for conceptions of objectivity and of what constituted social science.[71]

In these circumstances, the social survey became even more important to middle-class reformers. For the objective data provided by the surveys were uniquely effective in mobilising 'public opinion' – that amorphous combination of middle-class and working-class attitudes that activated politicians and labour leaders alike within the American political environment. Surveys could get action (especially when linked with sensationalist press reports) even when 'monster' meetings and petitions could not.

As in England, public health concerns motivated the first social surveys in the United States. One of the earliest was conducted in New York City in 1864 by a municipal reform group that sponsored a building-by-building investigation of city sanitary conditions by physicians, engineers and chemists. Their effort resulted in state legislation that created the Metropolitan Sanitary District, granting sweeping powers to its Board of Health.[72]

These close links between surveys and public policy continued in the 1860s and 1870s with state boards of labour statistics. Beginning with Massachusetts in 1869, such boards were appointed 'to collect, assort, systematize and present in annual reports to the legislature, statistical details relating to all departments of labor'.[73] Their data were often derived from census material, but boards of labor statistics also conducted a wide variety of 'surveys', some of which (measuring housing conditions, for example) were door-to-door, some of which (an inquiry into manufacturers' use of prison labour, for example) were conducted by mail.[74] Though schedules were used, they were surveys only in a loose sense, for workers' and employers' responses were treated as if they were giving evidence based on experience to a legislature or investigatory commission.[75] These investigations became the basis for legislation ranging from mine inspection to the eight-hour day, paralleling some of the British inquiries discussed by Roger Davidson in chapter 14.

Yet the success of the labour boards of statistics was seriously compromised by political patronage which appointed to the boards people loyal to other interests. In this context, voluntary agencies in the 1890s moved once more into the vanguard of social surveys. The most important vehicle for this type of social research was the Settlement House movement.

THE SOCIAL SURVEY IN THE UNITED STATES

The social survey in the United States in the period between 1880 and 1940, while resembling and differing from its British counterpart, directly imitated Booth's work in certain respects.[76]

The first American Settlement House was Neighborhood Guild in New York City, set up in 1886 and becoming the University Settlement in 1891. Hull House in Chicago was founded by Jane Addams in 1889 after returning from a visit to Toynbee Hall. Other settlements followed in Boston, New York and Chicago; by 1910 there were more than 400 American settlements. Of these, the most striking American example of the influence of settlements upon developing social ideas was Hull House. Among its leading residents in the 1890s in addition to Jane Addams were Florence Kelley, pioneer social investigator and later head of the National Consumer's League; Julia Lathrop, later first head of the US Children's Bureau; and Edith Abbott, pioneer in social service education. John Dewey and George Herbert Mead of the University of Chicago were friends of Addams.[77] The residents were young (in their 30s), thoughtful and socially committed. Unlike Toynbee Hall, Hull House was non-sectarian and more explicitly committed to tackling social problems. One historian has called such settlements 'ad hoc graduate schools', and it is indeed realistic to see Hull House (and Toynbee Hall for some of its residents) as a kind of graduate school in social policy and social research before such opportunities existed in universities.

Florence Kelley's work on the *Hull-House Maps and Papers*, discussed by Kathryn Kish Sklar in chapter 4, was one of the earliest American surveys and very much in the Booth tradition. Other studies followed. *The City Wilderness* appeared in 1898, edited by Robert Woods and written by settlement workers attached to Boston's South End House. The settlements tried to reintegrate the city wilderness of isolation and congestion, responding to both the dynamism of city life and the social distance between classes, the corruption and the poverty which they saw around them.

A more specific focus upon poverty was provided in Robert Hunter's 1904 study, *Poverty*. A resident of Hull House after graduating from the University of Indiana in 1896, he was influenced by Booth and Rowntree as well as by Riis' *How the Other Half Lives* in 1890. Hunter attempted to place the study of the phenomenon on an objective basis by adopting a Rowntree-style absolute definition of poverty, which he set as US $460 a year for an average sized family in the North and US $300 a year in the rural South. On this basis he estimated that 12 per cent of the American population (10 million out of 82 million) were poor. This was concentrated in northern industrial areas where 6·6 million, or 20 per cent of the population, were poor. Only about 4 million out of America's 10 million

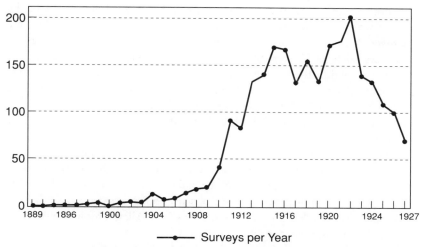

Figure 1.2   US social surveys by year, 1889 to 1927. Adapted from Eaton and Harrison, 1930.

poor received any public relief. Like Booth, Hunter focused upon the structural conditions producing poverty, particularly low wages and unemployment.

The role of the Settlement House movement in publicising social conditions was not confined to poverty. Indeed issues such as child labour, the treatment of juveniles in the court system, sweated labour and poor housing conditions loomed as large if not larger in their concerns. At the state level some notable innovations were effected, for example the establishment of the Illinois Juvenile Court in 1899.[78] Such instances of legislative influence were typically a result of the efforts of reformers to add new responsibilities to government.

Another notable early social survey, somewhat apart from this tradition, was W. E. B. Du Bois' study of *The Philadelphia Negro*, published in 1899. A neglected classic of American sociology, this study of social conditions in the inner city by a young black sociologist was notable for its thoroughness and detachment. Unlike the Settlement House surveys, Du Bois was not intent upon social reform but sought in a detached manner to describe social conditions in a study closely modelled upon the approach of Booth. This study is discussed further in chapter 6, while the relationship between the social survey and academic sociology is examined in chapters 10 and 11.

These studies of urban conditions were distinctive, often providing the only information available on various aspects of urban living in the late nineteenth and early twentieth centuries, apart from the writings of journalists such as Lincoln Steffens or novelists like Upton Sinclair. Yet what developed in the first decade of the twentieth century was arguably more distinctive, for these early settlement studies bore quite a close resemblance to their British counterparts. The Social Survey Movement, which was best expressed in the Pittsburgh Survey of 1906–9, was different.

It was different because it emerged from the charity movement, and the belief among significant numbers of social workers that the roots of social problems were to be found in society rather than in the individual. The origins of the Pittsburgh study were obscure, but it appeared to originate in a request from the chief probation officer of the Allegheny Juvenile Court to Paul U. Kellogg, managing editor of *Charities and the Commons*, the leading social work journal, asking that a study be made of social conditions in Pittsburgh. Initial work was funded by the New York COS and then the newly-established Russell Sage Foundation made a grant of US $47,000 for the main study. Kellogg himself took charge. He had had some social science training at Columbia, including courses from Franklin Giddings, but he was primarily a journalist. Most of his staff were drawn from the world of philanthropy and social service.

Steven Cohen discusses the Survey in detail in chapter 9 and examines some of the academic links of the investigators. Though bearing some resemblance to Booth in approach, the Pittsburgh Survey was more in the nature of investigative journalism, with much less emphasis upon quantification, and where numbers were used, they were used descriptively rather than analytically.[79] If the Pittsburgh Survey differed in its methods, it also differed in outcome. When published, a great effort was made to feed back the results of the research to the locality in which it had been carried out, by means of publicity and exhibits. This gave surveys of this type a completely different character, for they became exercises in community self-study more than scientific examinations of social questions.

Indeed, the success of the Pittsburgh Survey was followed by the establishment of the Department of Survey and Exhibits at the Russell Sage Foundation, which between 1912 and 1931 supported a very large number of local surveys.[80] Shelby M. Harrison was the director, and a bibliography which he compiled in 1930 shows 2,775 surveys carried out by 1927.[81] These included the Springfield Survey, which he himself directed.

The American Social Survey Movement had run out of steam by 1930 and disappeared shortly thereafter. Before that, however, the United States had seen a vogue for 'surveys' in various fields of social activity in the 1920s, some of which produced work of distinct social scientific value. This brings us back to the ambiguity of the term 'survey', for the term was used to refer to factual inquiries in a number of fields such as education, crime and religious belief, where it meant little more than 'factual investigation'. City crime surveys, for example, the first of which was conducted by Columbia political scientist Raymond Moley in Cleveland, Ohio, were studies of the extent of lawlessness in particular cities and of the operation of the legal system. Some surveys, such as the Illinois Crime Survey, produced work of lasting importance when social scientists were commissioned to produce studies of particular topics. John Landesco's study of organised crime in Chicago is a case in point.[82]

A different development, the Country Life movement and the Church survey movement gave rise to a number of inquiries which have some claim to be regarded as surveys. The Institute of Social and Religious Research, which emerged out of the latter, carried out numbers of surveys of religious belief, and it was under their auspices that the Lynds carried out their sociological study of *Middletown* in the mid-1920s.[83] This in turn gives rise to the question of where the boundary lies between the social survey and the community study, including academic studies such as those discussed by Stephen Turner. Though there are some common elements, the two modes of investigation are distinct in terms of extensiveness, precision and attempts at measurement.

SOCIAL MAPPING

Charles Booth's descriptive maps of urban poverty are often referred to as a landmark in social topography, and their appearance in 1891 did receive very wide attention. But the craft of making maps of the social environment and of human activities had made significant advances throughout the nineteenth century, and what happened in the 1890s can be traced back to developments earlier. By the 1860s maps of economic activities were common, particularly about consumption and transport. There were motivations other than the economic which led to maps of the social environment.[84] Two themes predominated. One was the Victorian concern for the moral welfare of the population (especially the working classes), the second the requirement for maps for the campaigns fought against disease in the 1840s. The maps made by Charles Dupin in both France and Britain in the 1820s were examples of the first.

His map of the educational attainment of the population was the first choropleth map, one in which 'enumerated data are assumed to be averages applying equally to all sections of the appropriate districts'.[85] Within a decade many social researchers, including Quetelet, were making maps of 'moral statistics'. In 1829 the first maps of crime were made by Balbi and Guerry, but it was Quetelet's maps of crime published three years later which were particularly innovative. In his maps of crime against the person and against property, he attempted to show a smoothed distribution with gradations in tone according to the principle of the darker the greater. One result of the translation of his study into English and German by 1842 was a general acceptance and adoption of his style of gradation shading.

The 1841 Census of Ireland used shaded maps to illustrate population density as well as a number of social characteristics. In 1849, Joseph Fletcher published the 'Moral Statistics of England and Wales',[86] which included maps of crimes, imprisonments, ignorance (as measured by illiteracy), bastardy and, significantly, pauperism.

Henry Mayhew's studies in the 1860s included maps of criminal statistics, within which he included a number of non-criminal measures such as the sex ratio. In these maps, counties were shaded black or white to indicate whether the incidence of a measured variable fell above or below the national mean. One of Mayhew's maps, showing 'the intensity of criminality in each county in England and Wales', is reproduced as Map 1. At the same time Guerry was brought to a meeting of the British Association by William Farr to discuss his latest edition of maps, which used paired maps to contrast the relative incidence of a number of crimes in the various parts of England and Wales and France. As with Mayhew's maps, the emphasis in social mapping was moving in a sociological direction.

Mapping the incidence of disease was one of the earliest forms of social topography, particularly since disease was often associated with environmental features such as swamps. For nineteenth-century Europe, the central concern was cholera, and fifty-three maps of its incidence and spread had been published by 1832. The most famous of the medical maps of this period was Dr John Snow's plotting of the incidence of cholera around a single polluted pump in Soho in central London, showing the association between proximity to the pump and mortality. Snow later used similar techniques to demonstrate significantly varying death rates by area served by different water companies. It was a short step from such maps of human density or disease to maps of social conditions.

One of the maps of the Census of Ireland of 1841 classed housing into four classes, and shaded areas according to the percentage of the population

MAP

SHOWING THE NUMBER OF THE CRIMINAL OFFENDERS TO EVERY
10,000 OF THE POPULATION;

OR

THE INTENSITY OF THE CRIMINALITY

IN EACH COUNTY OF

ENGLAND AND WALES.

*** The counties printed *black* are those in which the number of Criminals is *above* the average.

The counties left *white* are those in which the number of Criminals is *below* the average.

The average has been calculated from the returns for the last ten years.

Northumberland 8·2

Cumberland 7·1

Durham 7·8

Westmorland 8·1

Yorkshire 11·4

Lancaster 18·5

Chester 22·6

Derby 10·5

Nottingham 11·8

Lincoln 12·8

North Wales 7·2

Salop 14·9

Stafford 17·9

Leicester 17·2

Rutland 13·9

Norfolk 17·4

Worcester 25·0

Warwick 21·6

Northampton 14·2

Huntingdon 14·1

Cambridge 14·7

Suffolk 15·7

Hereford 15·8

Bedford 15·2

Hertford 17·5

Essex 19·4

South Wales 8·4

Monmouth 18·0

Gloucester 26·1

Oxford 17·8

Buckingham

Middlesex

Wilts 18·9

Berks 12·9

Surrey 16·3

Kent 16·4

Somerset 19·9

Hants 17·7

Sussex 15·3

Devon 14·7

Dorset 14·5

Cornwall 8·0

Map 1   The intensity of criminality in each county of England and
Wales.
From Henry Mayhew, *London Labour and the London Poor.*

occupying fourth (poorer) class housing. The colouring of the map bears resemblances to the approach later used by Booth. A very similar map was prepared by Edwin Chadwick, in shades of brown, showing classes of housing and especially the 'less cleansed districts', to accompany his 1842 report on sanitary conditions.

There is apparently a gap between these developments in the early part of the century and Charles Booth's use of maps half a century later. Booth seems to have been impressed by some of these early models, though firm evidence is lacking. His 'Descriptive Map of London Poverty' was an important means of presenting the large amount of information which he had collected. Booth used the social classification which he had developed as a basis for colouring his poverty map. He used Black for Class A, the poor, through to Yellow for Class H, the wealthy; areas in transition were shown by mixing the colours in stripes (see plate 2). The original maps were very detailed, being plotted on twenty-five inch Ordnance Survey plans. It was a sociological use of maps, for the colour codes represented more than specific attributes such as housing conditions. They were meant to represent social classes, encapsulating a range of characteristics in a single measure. Other black and white maps used by Booth are shown in maps 2 to 4. The impact of Booth's colour maps was considerable, following the wide publicity which followed the publication of *The Life and Labour of the People in London*. The maps, for example, were exhibited at the Paris Exhibition.[87] They also served as an example to other social investigators.

One of the first of these were the residents of Hull-House who published *Hull-House Maps and Papers* in 1895. In the section describing the maps written by Agnes Sinclair Holbrook she wrote:

The great interest and significance attached to Mr Charles Booth's maps of London have served as warm encouragement; and although the eyes of the world do not centre upon this third of a square mile in the heart of Chicago as upon East London when looking for the very essence of misery, and although the ground examined here is very circumscribed compared with the vast areas covered by Mr Booth's studies, the two works have much in common ... the greater minuteness of this study will entitle it to a rank of its own ... and as an illustration of a method of research.[88]

The Hull House maps used the same colour scheme on their Wage Map which coloured each household according to income; they also included a map of nationalities (part of which is reproduced as plate 3) which used different colours for the eighteen nationalities represented in their 'third of a square mile'.

Unlike Booth, who classified whole streets into particular categories of poverty and coloured them accordingly, the Hull-House maps classified individual dwellings plotted on maps into groups (see plate 3). This approach was also followed by W. E. B. Du Bois in *The Philadelphia Negro* (see plate 4) almost certainly in imitation. A few later studies also used maps. A map of Jewish London was produced in 1901 closely modelled on Booth (plate 1). Robert Woods's settlement study in Boston of 1903 included two colour maps of the industrial character of the population and its racial composition. The latter is shown in plate 5. Booth, *Hull-House Maps and Papers* and *The Philadelphia Negro* stand out as unusual in their use of colour mapping to show social conditions.

Black-and-white maps were more common, though still not very widely used. The Pittsburgh Survey used maps to show relationships between social problems and the urban environment (see map 5) but did not explore the relationships involved in detail. The survey also included a dramatic 'death calendar' shown as map 6. A few of the later Social Survey Movement surveys, such as the Springfield survey, used maps with an analytic rather than purely descriptive purpose (map 7). During the 1920s, the use of maps in sociological research was taken further by the work of Ernest Burgess and his students at the University of Chicago, which used maps extensively as an aid to ecological analysis to plot, analyse and theorise the characteristics of different natural areas and zones of the city.[89] An example from Zorbaugh's *The Gold Coast and the Slum* is shown in map 12. Thereafter thematic mapping became the preserve of geographers.[90] At least as far as survey research was concerned, this excursion into social mapping around 1900 demonstrated discontinuity rather than continuity. Maps did not generally become part of the survey method, though in Britain in the 1930s colour maps were extensively used in the *New Survey of Life and Labour in London*. An extract is shown in plate 6. This, however, was very much a throw-back to Booth, replicating his work almost slavishly rather than looking more innovatively toward the future.

WOMEN REFORMERS AND SOCIAL ACTION

In both England and the United States the birth of social science occurred under circumstances that invited the participation of women. Closely linked as it was with reform agendas, and not yet ensconced in universities, early social science was oriented toward the solution of many practical problems that also engaged the energies of women reformers: poor law or charity administration for example, and women's rights. Frances Power Cobb in

England and Caroline Dall in the United States exemplified women whose reform activities carried them into the mainstream of social science undertakings in their respective societies.[91]

The social settlement movement deepened this trend between 1890 and 1920. Settlements gave middle-class women (along with men) the opportunity to experience the conditions of working-class life, to engage in collective study of these conditions, and to take collective action to change them. Among English settlements, Toynbee Hall and its imitators were predominantly male institutions, though women's settlements existed, starting with the Women's University Settlement in Southwark in 1887.[92] The effort to enhance settlements as a practical training ground for male graduates of elite universities prompted such leaders as Samuel Barnett, founder of Toynbee Hall, deliberately to discriminate against women. As Meacham described the situation:

A resident's sense that he had not left Oxford or Cambridge far behind was reinforced by the general absence of women. Although Barnett was a convinced feminist and supporter of women's suffrage, he believed, according to his wife, that the introduction of female residents would encourage the impression that the settlement had been 'captured' by women and thereby frighten the ablest university men away.[93]

In the United States, however, women were founders and leaders of the best-known settlements.

Due partly to the differing positions of the settlement movements in the two societies, partly to the greater access American women had to higher education, American settlements attracted life-long commitments from the nation's foremost women reformers. Jane Addams, Florence Kelley, Julia Lathrop, and Grace Abbott each played a major role in reshaping the responsibility of American governments – state and federal – for human welfare. Each was a political force as well as a social reformer. For example, when Jane Addams seconded Theodore Roosevelt's nomination as the Progressive party candidate for the presidency in 1912, she received as great an ovation as TR himself.[94] In England, women were important in the settlement movement, but the most politically-powerful women reformers – Beatrice Webb, Margaret McDonald, and Lady Emilia Dilke – were not affiliated with it.

Perhaps because the American settlement movement did not function as it did in England as a civil-service training ground, women were not crowded out of its leadership ranks. Perhaps because, proportionate to the population, many more women had access to higher education in the United States, a larger population of talented women with university training chose the settlement movement as a life-long alternative to family life. Women leaders in the English movement, like English men, typically remained only a few years and then moved on to other work. In the United States they stayed, using the settlement as a staging ground for other work, much of which was devoted to pioneering labour and social legislation. This life-long collective living and working context facilitated innovative work of all sorts, including the early social survey discussed by Sklar in chapter 4.

Settlements also performed an important educational function, as a kind of proto-graduate school of social policy. The rapid development of the social sciences in the United States preceded the establishment of settlements by a small margin. The American Social Science Association developed around the platform of civil service reform, and was followed by the establishment of the separate social sciences at several leading universities before the end of the century.[95] Some social scientists in these universities, as is clear from the chapters by Kathryn Sklar, Steven Cohen and Stephen Turner, then became sources of advice and inspiration for early American social survey researchers. Close relations were maintained between settlements and some academic social scientists.[96]

This is not to say that women were not important for social investigation in Britain, for they were. Beatrice Potter and Clara Collett worked with Booth as his assistants and Beatrice later became one of the most formidable minds involved in early-twentieth-century social policy, as McBriar's account of her role on the Royal Commission on the Poor Law of 1905–1909, discussed by Jane Lewis, makes amply clear. Of studies carried out before 1914 mentioned earlier (page 23), those by Davies, Pember-Reeves, Bell and Butler were by women. Lady Bell's study of Middlesbrough, for example, was carried out by the wife of the ironmaster who made unusually careful and precise observations of social conditions in the working-class areas of the town for someone in her social position. The role of social investigator was one which upper middle-class women could play without social ostracism, though they could not, Mrs Webb excepted, aspire to the same political prominence as their counterparts in the United States, and they could not frequently occupy the vanguard of social inquiry.

For racial minorities in the United States, the situation was different, and much less advantageous. For all the barriers of social discrimination erected against them at this period, upper-middle-class women were able to construct their own institutions capable of sustaining their lives as reformers, and from these positions of strength they worked successfully with white men. These institutions could even, in Florence Kelley's case, sustain her when she was separated from her husband with three young children – a considerable departure from the normal social conventions of her class. For the black sociologist W. E. B. Du Bois, access to the vanguard of social inquiry was more sporadic and elusive. It is true that, unlike Kelley, he was able to gain a PhD (in history) at a leading university, Harvard, but thereafter his institutional resources remained problematic. Initially he prospered, conducting the research for his stunning social survey *The Philadelphia Negro*, with support from a Quaker philanthropist in the city, and not apparently suffering from the absence of institutional affiliations or from the racist attitudes of the University of Pennsylvania towards a black scholar.

On completing the study, the only openings available to Du Bois were in black colleges. He accepted an appointment at Atlanta University, an all-black institution, and taught there for the next eleven years, attempting to mount a research programme on the condition of black Americans with negligible research resources, additions to which he was unable to obtain from external sources because he was black. If women suffered from discriminatory obstacles placed in their way by men, black scholars and social investigators suffered these but in addition from *social* ostracism of a more pernicious kind. Because they taught and researched in a segregated system, their work and their very existence was ignored in the white world. Du Bois, whose case is discussed further in chapter 6, was a distinguished black sociologist whose work was far in advance of its time, yet he gained virtually no recognition in American sociology before 1910, when he apparently abandoned an academic career in frustration and despair.

FORWARD FROM 1914

Developments in the United States after 1914 are discussed more fully in chapters 11 and 13, but as a generalisation, and with the significant exception of statistical inference, it may be said that after 1914 the social survey developed more rapidly and achieved more outstanding results in the United States than in Britain, and at the same time underwent a change in form. This book stops in 1940, in part because this is a natural break before the rise to eminence of the modern sample survey, in part because the post-1940 period for the United States is covered in detail in Jean Converse's history and for Britain in chapters by Frank Whitehead and Gerald Hoinville in an earlier collection on the history of British sociological research.[97] The same generalisation may be offered for the post-1940 period. Although there are major survey research organisations and centres in Western Europe, governmental, commercial and academic, the intellectual leadership in modern sample survey research has lain in the United States, which has tended to remain in the forefront of intellectual fertility, analytic inventiveness and methodological innovation.

The connections between the two countries are traced in more detail by Jennifer Platt in chapter 13, but the gap seems to have opened up after 1914. On a purely quantitative basis, whereas Eaton and Harrison's bibliography for the United States lists 2,775 surveys up to 1927, A. F. Wells' essay on the local social survey in England and Wales of 1935 listed only 156.[98] One reason for this was clearly the Great War. Britain not only suffered a million dead, a vast increase in national debt and outmoded industrial structure, but in the four years after the war no surveys at all were published, a hiatus of nine years in all, at a time when the Social Survey Movement was at its height in the United States and the social sciences were becoming strongly established for the first time in American universities. The comparison is somewhat misleading since different kinds of surveys were involved, but nevertheless the difference of scale is very striking.

A. F. Wells explained the difference from the United States in terms that Britain had a more centralised system of government and therefore had less need of large numbers of separate surveys. He also observed that most surveys in 1935 were still being conducted by people who were not professional social researchers, and there was no body concerned with the funding of surveys, as there was in the Russell Sage Foundation in the United States. This was not the whole story, however. The large discrepancy owed something to the type of survey carried out, the American surveys being aimed at local audiences conceived in a more populist tradition, and the receptivity to such social knowledge within the political system in the United States as a whole being considerably greater at this period.

One tendency apparent in Britain after 1914 was toward more specialised surveys. Whereas from the time of Booth to 1914, twenty-two major surveys of cities or towns were carried out, from 1918 to 1935 only fourteen such community surveys were conducted. On the other hand, forty-two out of fifty surveys of 'special topics' (such as living conditions, delinquency or unemployment) in the whole period between 1889 and 1935 were carried out after the First World War, and eight of the ten surveys on industrial topics. There were sixty-three post-war surveys of housing and planning, reflecting the priority which improving housing conditions had at this period.

Surveys were of two types, the community surveys and those concerned with the social consequences of the Great Depression of the early 1930s, particularly in the fields of unemployment and health. The community surveys followed quite closely on the model of Booth, seeking to establish the facts and leaving the policy implications to others. In the 1920s Bowley re-studied his four towns. The largest of the community surveys of this period, funded by the Laura Spelman Rockefeller Memorial and then by the Rockefeller Foundation, the *New Survey of Life and Labour in London*, was designed not only as a replication of Booth's original study forty years later, but was directed by one of his original assistants, Sir Hubert Llewellyn Smith, GCB, recently retired as permanent secretary of the Ministry of Labour.[99] The consultative committee included another of Booth's original team, Sir George Duckworth, as well as Sidney Webb (now Lord Passfield) and Arthur Bowley. Intellectually the *New Survey* was most unexciting, since it contained few innovations, conceptual or methodological, apart from the use of random sampling under the influence of Bowley, now Professor of Statistics at the London School of Economics, where the *New Survey* was conducted between 1929 and 1936.

Other major urban studies were carried out in the early 1930s by Ford in Southampton and Caradog Jones on Merseyside, the latter also supported by the Rockefeller Foundation.[100] Rowntree began a second survey of York in 1935, modifying somewhat his definition of poverty but still aiming at complete coverage. In analysing the results, Rowntree drew probability samples of varying sizes from his data to compare with the results of the total enumeration, showing that in most respects the accuracy of sampling was born out by the test.[101] There was a range of smaller studies, such as Henry Mess' study of Tyneside and H. Jennings' of Brynmawr in South Wales.[102] There was a certain vogue for the community self-study, but this produced relatively few results.

The studies of the human consequences of the depression were more vivid and immediate, and included studies done both outside and within the academic community. A few of the studies demonstrated the exchange with the United States, one, E. W. Bakke's *The Unemployed Man*, being a study carried out in Greenwich, England, by an American social psychologist from Yale, which incorporated techniques from American sociological research.[103] Other studies done by British authors included Fenner Brockway's *Hungry England*,[104] the Pilgrim Trust study *Men Without Work*,[105], Hutt, and Simon and Inman on housing, and Boyd-Orr and Titmuss on nutrition and health.[106] There was a number of more local and narrowly focused studies such as Allaway's study of milk supply in Sheffield (1931) and Evans and Boyd's of the use of leisure in Hull (1933).[107]

In general, although these studies and the community surveys produced much new social information, they did not represent much progress beyond that achieved by Booth, Rowntree and Bowley in the earlier period either conceptually or methodologically. Neither in their sampling nor in methods of data collection were there significant innovations, while the absence of social science theory or even concepts in most of them rendered severely limited their use for scientific purposes. Almost all were geographically confined to one or several particular areas – they were still essentially *local* studies. The idea that social surveys could be conducted on a *national* basis only emerged gradually, and in Britain only feebly before 1940. When it did become established, using probability sampling, the nature of the social survey was considerably altered, though not out of all recognition. Particularly in Britain, less so in the United States, there was a considerable measure of continuity between the geographically local surveys which are the subject of this book and the modern sample survey.

After Bowley's pioneering work, the application of sampling in national studies in Britain may be traced to market research and opinion polling in the 1930s. From 1928, George Gallup had been successfully using probability sampling for marketing and political research in the United States. In 1936 Henry Durant established the British counterpart of Gallup's organisation, the British Institute of Public Opinion (BIPO). The BIPO drew random samples of between 2,000 and 15,000 people in political polling and market research. In April 1938, Henry Durant predicted Shirley Summerskill's victory in the West Fulham by-election to within one per cent, a result he attributed to beginner's luck. Later in the same year, Saul Rae achieved the same accuracy in predicting the outcome of the Oxford by-election. Rae weighted his data 'because the maidservants answering the door could not supply the information for the members of the household'.[108] In 1937, the BBC randomly selected 2,000 radio license holders as a 'panel' for listener research.

Other interwar developments, such as the last days of the Le Play school of Geddes and Branford, Mass-Observation[109] and the work of Lancelot Hogben and his group on *Political Arithmetic* had only a marginal bearing on survey research. The establishment of the Government Social Survey during the war[110] and the beginnings of academic social survey research after 1945, lay in the future. Only in statistics did Britain have a clear lead over the United States. The traffic to sit at the feet of Karl Pearson, R. A. Fisher, G. Udny Yule and A. L. Bowley in the University of London continued until well into the 1930s. Leading American survey researchers such as Samuel Stouffer learnt advanced inferential statistics from them and returned to apply those methods to good effect in the United States. Until after 1940, however, the English statisticians had little impact upon British survey practice.

CONCLUSION: FROM LOCAL TO NATIONAL SOCIAL SURVEY

To stop as this book does in 1940 is in one sense artificial, for about that time the modern national sample survey emerged. Its great early achievements had either just happened, as in the case of Gallup's triumph over the *Literary Digest* in 1936, or lay in the future, as in the case of the work of Rensis Likert and Samuel Stouffer in the US government and the armed forces during the war, Paul Lazarsfeld and Robert Merton at the Columbia Bureau or the young recruits to the UK Government Social Survey during and after the war.

This collection of papers is a study of the geographically local social survey between 1880 and 1940 in Britain and the United States. Prior to 1880 there had been a wide variety of nineteenth century social investigations, but none in the mode of the survey as defined at the beginning of this chapter. There was thus a distinctive transition in terms of social scientific method between the world of Mayhew and the Massachusetts Bureau of Labor Statistics on the one hand and the world of Booth, W. E. B. Du Bois and the Pittsburgh Survey on the other.

What distinguished Booth from Mayhew, W. E. B. Du Bois from Ray Stannard Baker, Bowley from R. H. Tawney, was the urge to present systematic and defensible numerical statements about the problem studied based on a large-scale data collection exercise derived from questioning individuals. Such an appeal to 'objectivity' and 'science' is one which a number of contributors to the book view with considerable scepticism. The historians in particular are more inclined to emphasise the historically-specific features of particular inquiries. A longer term view, however, is also of value.

The local survey of social conditions and the modern sample survey were of a kind, with differences. The local survey was closer to social reform and amelioration, to political action and to non-academic institutions; the modern sample survey aspired to be part of social science, to inform rather than prescribe, and became in time established in the academic world as well as in bureaucratic social survey organisations outside it. It rested on probability sampling, permitting a national picture to be developed from a comparatively small number of cases. In terms of the criteria identified above, the two types of survey bore a considerable resemblance to each other, and this is perhaps strongest in their aspirations in the direction of systematic knowledge. It would be misleading to claim that all the surveys discussed in this book were primarily intended to contribute to building the scientific study of society. Nevertheless, they did so, and it is due in part to this heritage that the social survey, which began as a tool of criticism of the condition of industrial societies, is a century later, for better or worse, such an integral part of their functioning.

NOTES

1 Cf. M. J. Cullen, *The Statistical Movement in Early Victorian Britain: The Foundations of Empirical Social Research* (Hassocks, Sussex: Harvester, 1976).

2 '[S]ocial research and social policy derived essentially from professional middle-class anxieties to main the stability of institutions by correcting the measured costs and inefficiencies of social wastage.' O. R. McGregor, 'Social Research and Social Policy in the Nineteenth Century', *British Journal of Sociology*, 8 (1957), 146–57.

3 Social Survey' in *The Encyclopaedia of the Social Sciences* (New York: Macmillan, 1933).

4 J. Converse, *Survey Research in the United States: Roots and Emergence 1890–1960* (Berkeley: University of California Press, 1987).

5 D. V. Glass, 'The Social Survey', entry in *Chambers Encyclopaedia*.

6 M. Abrams, *Social Surveys and Social Action* (London: Heinemann, 1951).

7 Cf Douglas E. Ashford, 'The Whig Interpretation of the Welfare State', *Journal of Policy History*, 1, 1 (1989), 24–43.

8 Pauline Young termed them 'scientific' social surveys in her book *Scientific Social Surveys and Research* (New York: Prentice Hall, 1939), ch. 1. This term is not used here, although it is implied, because its overtones may distort the historical discussion.

9 D. Caradog Jones, *Social Surveys* (London: Hutchinson, 1948).

10 Cullen, *Statistical Movement*.

11 Cullen, *Statistical Movement*, p. 7.

12 Jones, *Social Surveys*; D. V. Glass, *Numbering the People* (Farnborough, Hants.: Saxon House, 1973)

13 Cf. Raymond Kent, *A History of British Empirical Sociology* (Aldershot: Gower, 1981), pp. 13–14.

14 Nathan Glazer, 'The Rise of Social Research in Europe', in Daniel Lerner (ed.), *The Human Meaning of the Social Sciences* (New York, 1959); Cullen, *Statistical Movement*; McGregor, 'Social Research and Social Policy'.

15 Cullen, *Statistical Movement*; T. S. Ashton, *Economic and Social Investigation in Manchester 1833–1933* (Manchester: Manchester University Press, 1934); M. Rose, 'Culture, Philanthropy and the Manchester Middle Classes', in A. J. Kidd and K. W. Roberts (eds.), *City, Class and Culture* (Manchester University Press, 1985), pp. 103–17.

16 I. D. Hill, 'Statistical Society of London – Royal Statistical Society. The First Hundred Years: 1834–1934', *Journal of the Royal Statistical Society A*, 147, 2 (1984), 130–9; L. Goldman, 'The Origins of British "Social Science": Political Economy, Natural Science

and Statistics, 1830–1835', *The Historical Journal*, 26, 3 (1983), 587–616; see also David Elesh, 'The Manchester Statistical Society', in A. Oberschall (ed.), *The Establishment of Empirical Sociology: Studies in Continuity, Discontinuity and Institutionalisation* (New York: Harper and Row, 1972), pp. 31–72.

17 P. Abrams, *The Origins of British Sociology: 1834–1914* (Chicago: University of Chicago Press, 1968), p. 17. See also S. and O. Checkland (eds.), *The Poor Law Report of 1834* (Harmondsworth: Penguin, 1974).

18 G. M. Young, *Victorian England: Portrait of an Age* (second edition, Oxford: Oxford University Press, 1963), p. 32.

19 John M. Eyler, *Victorian Social Medicine: The Ideas and Methods of William Farr* (Baltimore, Md.: Johns Hopkins University Press, 1979), p. 30.

20 Cf. M. Nissel, *People Count: A History of the General Register Office* (London: HMSO, 1987).

21 I.e. an inquiry which was designed to investigate a particular topic in depth, rather than an all-purpose general investigation such as the census.

22 Hill, 'Statistical Society', p. 133.

23 Political economy was particularly influential. Cf. P. Abrams, pp. 8–12.

24 Cf. P. Lazarsfeld, 'Quantification in Sociology', in H. Woolf (ed.), *Quantification: A History of the Meaning of Measurement in the Natural and Social Sciences* (Indianapolis: Bobbs-Merrill, 1961), pp. 147–203.

25 Lazarsfeld, 'Quantification', 172–3.

26 Stephen Cole, 'Continuity and Discontinuity in Science: A Case Study in Failure', in Oberschall (ed.), *Establishment*, pp. 73–129, an essay about empirical social research in Victorian England.

27 P. Abrams, p. 31.

28 For one example, see J. P. Kay, *The Moral and Physical Condition of the Working Classes Employed in the Cotton Manufacture of Manchester* (1832).

29 Kay, *Moral and Physical Condition*, p. 38.

30 E. Yeo, 'Social Science and Social Change: A Social History of Some Aspects of Social Science and Social Investigation in Britain 1830–1890', DPhil thesis, University of Sussex, 1973; L. Goldman, 'The Social Science Association, 1857–86: A Context for Mid-Victorian Liberalism', *English Historical Review*, 100 (1986), 95–134.

31 P. Abrams, p. 40.

32 An illuminating insight into the rigidity and distance in relations between social strata is provided by the diary of a London barrister who secretly married his servant: see Derek Hudson, *Munby: Man of Two Worlds – The Life and Diaries of Arthur J Munby, 1828–1910* (London: John Murray, 1972).

33 Cf. E. Yeo, 'Mayhew as a Social Investigator', in E. P. Thompson and E. Yeo (eds.), *The Unknown Mayhew* (Harmondsworth: Penguin, 1973), pp. 56–109.

34 Cf. *London Labour and the London Poor*, Book IV.

35 Cf. I. Hacking, *The Taming of Chance* (Cambridge: Cambridge University Press, 1990), pp. 133–41.

36 C. B. Silver, 'Introduction' in C. B. Silver (ed.) *Frédéric Le Play on Family, Work and Social Change* (Chicago: University of Chicago Press, 1982), pp. 1–134.

37 Silver, *Le Play*, p. 48.

38 Silver, *Le Play*, p. 52.

39 For a brief discussion, see M. Bulmer, 'The Development of Sociology and of Empirical Social Research in Britain', in Bulmer (ed.), *Essays on the History of British Sociological Research* (Cambridge: Cambridge University Press, 1985), pp. 10–11.

40 Cf. A. Oberschall, *Empirical Social Research in Germany, 1848–1914* (The Hague: Mouton, 1965). For a comparison between the Verein and the British NAPSS and the American Social Science Association, see L. Goldman, 'The Social Science Association and the Absence of Sociology in Nineteenth Century Britain', *Past and Present*, 114 (February 1987), 133–71.

41 Goldman, 'Social Science Association', pp. 161–71.

42 H. M. Lynd, *England in the Eighteen-Eighties* (London: Cass and Co., 1945), p. 414.

43 M. Rose, *The Relief of Poverty 1834–1914* (London: Macmillan, 1972), pp. 14–17.

44 The theme of the lack of institutionalisation of empirical social research in the nineteenth century has been pursued by several scholars, notably Anthony Oberschall, Stephen Cole and Philip Abrams. At the end of the century, Reba Soffer has argued, sociology was held back by espousal of a limiting evolutionary theory and by internal conflicts between the groups around Hobhouse, Geddes and Pearson, which hindered its establishment as an effective academic subject which might have underpinned empirical social research; 'Why do Disciplines Fail? The Strange Case of British Sociology', *English Historical Review*, 97, 385 (1982), 767–802.

45 M. C. Booth, *Charles Booth: A Memoir* (London: Macmillan, 1918); T. S. and M. B. Simey, *Charles Booth: Social Scientist* (London: Oxford University Press, 1960); H. W. Pfautz, *Charles Booth on the City: Physical Pattern and Social Structure* (Chicago: University of Chicago Press, 1967); K. B. Bales, *Man in the Middle: The Life and Work of Charles Booth* (London: Routledge, forthcoming).

46 T. S. Simey, 'Charles Booth, in T. Raison (ed.), *The Founding Fathers of Social Science* (rev. edn; London: Scolar Press, 1979), pp. 108–15.

47 B. Webb, *My Apprenticeship* (Harmondsworth: Penguin, 1938), p. 275.

48 E. P. Hennock, 'Poverty and Social Theory in England: The Experience of the Eighteen-Eighties', *Social History* 1 (January 1976), pp. 67–91, and 'The Measurement of Poverty: From the Metropolis to the Nation, 1880–1920', *Economic History Review*, 2nd series 40, 2 (1987), 208–27.

49 Hennock, 'Poverty and Social Theory', p. 79.

50 Cf. Hennock, 'Poverty and Social Theory', pp. 80–4.

51 M. J. Cullen, 'Charles Booth's Poverty Survey: Some New Approaches', in T. C. Smout (ed.), *The Search for Wealth and Stability: Essays in Economic and Social History presented to M. W. Flinn* (London: Macmillan, 1979), p. 172.

52 K. B. Bales, 'Reclamation of Antique Data: Charles Booth's Poverty Study One Hundred Years On', *Urban History Yearbook*, 1986.

53 David Reeder and the London Topographical Society, *Charles Booth's Descriptive Map of London Poverty 1889*, Maps with Introduction (London: London Topographical Society, Publication no. 130, 1987).

54 K. B. Bales and Michael D. Hughes, *Sample of 35,000 Households from Charles Booth's Poverty Study Notebooks*, data set lodged with the Inter-University Consortium of Political and Social Research, Ann Arbor, Mich.: University of Michigan, 1986.

55 K. B. Bales and Research Publications (eds.), *Life and Labour of the People of London: the Charles Booth Collection 1885–1905 from the British Library of Political and Economic Science, London* (Reading: Research Publications–Harvester Microform with listing and guide, 1988).

56 Rosemary O'Day, 'Retrieval riches – Charles Booth's *Life and Labour of the People in London*', *History Today*, 39 (1989), 29–35.

57 Cf. C. Marsh, 'Informants, respondants and Citizens', in Bulmer (ed.), *Essay on the History of British Sociological Research*, pp. 206–27.

58 Helen Bosanquet, *The Poverty Line* (pamphlet), Occasional paper no 11, Third Series, Charity Organisation Society, undated [c. 1900].

59 M. F. Davies, *Life in an English Village: An Economic and Historical Survey of the Parish of Corsley in Wiltshire* (London: T. Fisher Unwin, 1909).

60 E. G. Hurworth and M. Wilson, *West Ham: A Study of Social and Industrial Problems* (London: J. M. Dent, 1907); M. Pember Reeves, *Round About a Pound a Week* (London: Bell, 1913).

61 Florence (Lady) Bell, *At the Works: A Study of a Manufacturing Town* (London: Arnold, 1907); C. B. Hawkins, *Norwich: A Social Study* (London; P L. Warner, 1910); Liverpool Economic and Statistical Society, *How the Casual Labourer Lives* (Liverpool: Liverpool Economic and Statistical Society, 1909); C. V. Butler, *Social Conditions in Oxford* (London: Sidgwick and Jackson, 1912).

62 A. Briggs and A. Macartney, *Toynbee Hall: The First Hundred Years* (London: Routledge, 1984).

63 A. McBriar, *An Edwardian Mixed Doubles* (Oxford: Clarendon, 1987), pp. 61–5.

64 S. Meacham, *Toynbee Hall and Social Reform 1880–1914: The Search for Community* (New Haven, Conn.: Yale University Press, 1987).

65 J. Harris, *William Beveridge: A Biography* (Oxford: Clarendon, 1977), pp. 48–9.

66 Cf. R. Terrill, *R. H. Tawney and his Times: Socialism as Fellowship* (London: André Deutsch, 1973), pp. 31–5.

67 Cf. R. Davidson, *Whitehall and the Labour Problem in Late-Victorian and Edwardian England* (London: Croom Helm, 1985).

68 Cf. A. V. Dicey, *Lectures on the Relation between Law and Public Opinion in England during the Nineteenth Century* (London: Macmillan, 1905).

69 Cf. Robert K. Merton, *Social Theory and Social Structure* (New York: Free Press, 1957), pp. 71–82; Alexander B. Callow Jr. (ed.), *The City Boss in America* (New York: Oxford University Press, 1976); Michael B. Katz, *In the Shadow of the Poorhouse; A Social History of Welfare in America* (New York: Basic Books, 1986), pp. 150–7.

70 Cf. W. Sombart, *Why is there No Socialism in the United States?* (edited with an introduction by C. T. Husbands) (London: Macmillan, 1976).

71 Cf. Thomas L. Haskell (ed.), *The Authority of Experts: Studies in History and Theory* (Bloomington: Indiana University Press, 1984); M. Bulmer, 'The Rise of the Academic as Expert', *Minerva*, 25, 3 (Autumn, 1987), 362–74.

72 Jon A. Peterson, 'The Impact of Sanitary Reform upon American Urban Planning, 1840–1890', in Donald A. Krueckeberg (ed.), *Introduction to Planning History in the United States* New Brunswick, NJ: Rutgers University Press, 1983), p. 24; Charles E.

Rosenberg, *The Cholera Years: The United States in 1832, 1849 and 1866* (Chicago: University of Chicago Press, 1962), pp. 186–91.

73 William R. Brock, *Investigation and Responsibility: Public Responsibility in the United States, 1865–1900* (Cambridge: Cambridge University Press, 1984), p. 151.

74 Brock, *Investigation and Responsibility*, pp. 170–4.

75 For a fuller discussion, see Caesar Mavratsas, 'An Episode in the Early History of Social Research: The Massachusetts Bureau of Statistics of Labor and its Methods', unpublished paper, Department of Sociology, Boston University, 1988. The standard work is James Lieby, *Carroll D. Wright and Labor Reform,: The Origin of Labor Statistics* (Cambridge, MA: Harvard University Press, 1960).

76 J. T. Patterson, *America's Struggle Against Poverty 1900–1980* (Cambridge, MA: Harvard University Press, 1981), pp. 6–9.

77 See Mary Jo Deegan, *Jane Addams and the Men of the Chicago School 1892–1918* (New Brunswick, NJ: Transaction, 1988).

78 Cf. R. M. Mennel, *Thorns and Thistles: Juvenile Delinquents in the United States, 1825–1940* (Hanover, NH: University Press of New England, 1973), chs 5 and 6.

79 C. A. Chambers, *Paul U. Kellogg and the Survey: Voices for Social Welfare and Social Justice* (Minneapolis: University of Minnesota Press, 1971), pp. 33–45; S. Cohen, ch. 9 below.

80 J. M. Glenn, S. M. Brandt and F. E. Andrews, *Russell Sage Foundation 1907–1946* (New York: Russell Sage Foundation, 1947).

81 A. Eaton and S. M. Harrison, *A Bibliography of Social Surveys: Reports of Fact-Finding Studies made as a Basis for Social Action: Arranged by Subjects and Localities; Reports to January 1st 1928* (New York: Russell Sage Foundation, 1930)

82 J. Landesco, *Organised Crime in Chicago: Part III of the Illinois Crime Survey, 1929* (Chicago: University of Chicago Press, 1968; first published 1929 by the Illinois Association for Criminal Justice).

83 Converse, *Survey Research in the United States*, pp. 30–1, 36–7.

84 Arthur H. Robinson, *Early Thematic Mapping in the History of Cartography* (Chicago: University of Chicago Press, 1982), esp. ch. 7.

85 Robinson, *Early Thematic Mapping*, p. 157.

86 *Journal of the Statistical Society of London*, 12 (May 1849) 151–76.

87 Today they are deposited at the British Library of Political and Economic Science at the London School of Economics, and may be viewed there.

88 *Hull-House Maps and Papers: A Presentation of Nationalities and Wages in a Congested District of Chicago, Together with Comments and Essays on Problems Growing out of the Social Conditions* (Boston: Thomas Crowell and Co., 1895), p. 11.

89 Cf. M. Bulmer, *The Chicago School of Sociology: Institutionalisation, Diversity and the Rise of Sociological Research* (Chicago: University of Chicago Press, 1984), esp. pp. 154–6. Harold Pfautz, *Charles Booth on the City* (Chicago: University of Chicago Press, 1967) shows that Booth's use of maps anticipated a number of the descriptive forms developed in the Chicago School. How far there was direct influence is uncertain, but Ernest Burgess was familiar with Booth's work, and taught a course on the causes and prevention of poverty in 1921.

90 Cf. D. J. Cuff and M. J. Matson, *Thematic Maps* (London: Routledge, 1982).

91 Eileen Yeo's forthcoming work on women and social science in England analyses Cobb's place in the National Association for the Promotion of Social Science; 'Caroline Wells Healey Dall', in Edward James, Janet James and Paul Boyer (eds.), *Notable American Women*, 3 vols. (Cambridge, MA: Harvard University Press, 1971).

92 Michael Rose in a private communication cautions against the belief that all British settlements were male-dominated, and points out that the women's settlements were more concerned with 'social work' activity – case visiting, mothers clubs, child welfare, etc. – and were the most responsive to the development of social work training. The Womens' University Settlement was much involved in the foundation of Urwick's School of Sociology. These womens' settlements drew more on the Chalmers–Octavia Hill–C. S. Loch school of social thought than the Arnoldian–Greenian philosophy of the men's settlements.

93 Meacham, *Toynbee Hall and Social Reform*, p. 47.

94 Cf. E. Lagemann, 'Jane Addams: An Educational Biography', in *Jane Addams on Education* (New York: Teachers College Press, 1985), pp. 1–42.

95 Cf. Thomas L. Haskell, *The Emergence of Professional Social Science: The American Social Science Association and the Nineteenth Century Crisis of Authority* (Urbana, Il.: University of Illinois Press, 1977).

96 Cf. M. J. Deegan, *Jane Addams and the Men of the Chicago School*.

97 Converse, *Survey Research in the United States*; essays in M. Bulmer (ed.), *Essays on the History of British Sociological Research* (Cambridge: Cambridge University Press, 1985).

98 A. F. Wells, *The Local Social Survey in Great Britain* (London: Allen and Unwin, 1935).

99 Sir H. L. Smith (ed.), *The New Survey of London Life and Labour*, 9 vols. (London: P. S. King, 1930–35).

100 P. Ford, *Work and Wealth in a Modern Port* (London: Allen and Unwin, 1934), and D. C. Jones (ed.), *The Social Survey of Merseyside*, 3 vols. (Liverpool: Liverpool University Press, 1934).

101 B. S. Rowntree, *Poverty and Progress: A Second Social Survey of York* (London: Longman, 1941).

102 H. A. Mess, *Industrial Tyneside: A Social Survey* (London: Ernest Benn, 1928), and H. Jennings, *Brynmawr: A Study of a Distressed Area* (London: Allenson and Co., 1934).

103 E. W. Bakke, *The Unemployed Man* (London: Nisbet, 1933).

104 F. Brockway, *Hungry England* (London: Collanz, 1932).

105 Pilgrim Trust, *Men Without Work* (Cambridge: Cambridge University Press, 1938).

106 J. Boyd Orr, *Food, Health and Income: Report on a Survey of the Adequacy of Diet in Relation to Income* (London: Macmillan, 1936), and R. M. Titmuss, *Poverty and Population* (London: Macmillan, 1938).

107 For further discussion, see Wells, *The Local Social Survey*.

108 M. Harrop, 'Opinion Polls in By-Elections', *Newsletter of the Market Research Society*, 264 (March 1988), 22–3.

109 Cf. A. Calder, 'Mass-Observation 1937–1949', in Bulmer (ed.), *Essays on the History of Sociological Research*, pp. 121–36.

110 Cf. L. Moss, *The Government Social Survey: a history* (London: H.M.S.O., 1991), pp. 1–13

CHAPTER TWO

The social survey in social perspective, 1830–1930

EILEEN JANES YEO

INTRODUCTION

It is conventional to award Charles Booth the prize for carrying out the first social survey. But instead of seeking the real pioneer, it might be more interesting to explore the emergence of the survey habit of mind. Bulmer, Bales and Sklar remind us (in the previous chapter) that surveys have been connected from antiquity with the State. Indeed, Mary and Joseph were going to Bethlehem to be counted in a census. According to the Oxford English Dictionary, from the sixteenth century, the word 'survey' was used mainly to signify the State making inventories of property, provisions or people. In Europe, during the nineteenth century, the connection with the state was double-sided in the sense that State bureaucracies, for example, in Napoleonic France (Desrosières in chapter 8) and later in the Kaiser Reich (Gorges in chapter 12), collected facts about the state of the nation. In Britain, voluntary enthusiasts at first and the State only later developed 'statistics as science' to survey 'the present state of the country, with a view to its future improvement'.[1] Whether voluntary or government effort, the observers were positioned at a height and distance where, separated from the object of scrutiny, they would get an overview of 'the population of a political community'.

The early uses of 'survey' involved a definite and unequal power relationship. This is not to say that social survey is like original sin, incapable of redemption. Nearly every social form is contestable and some of the contradictory potential of the social survey will be noted later. But since the social survey and social research are often treated, by sociologists and historians, as somehow positive or benevolent activities, it is as well to expose a darker dimension revealed in the historical development of language. Survey has usually meant extensive overview: indeed a synonym is 'surview', or a commanding view of the whole. As Stephen Yeo has observed, a survey is not a *sous*vey or a view from below.[2] A more intensive invigilation of an individual by authority was signified by a related word, surveillance, which came into use in English around the time of the French Revolution. Whether the view was close-up or panoramic, the gaze was usually that of people in command or aiming to be in command and the investigation was often being made for purposes of governance (raising taxes for example) or for improving what they saw as social order.

I am interested in the development of science in a context of power relations. My significant historical story would explore how different practices of social science empowered or disabled different groups of people at particular cultural moments.[3] My focus would be on science as a contested activity with the contests being fought out not only between social groups but within individuals whose motivation, never mind their impact, was always complex and often contradictory. But given the space constraints here, I will have to underplay the elements of contest and complexity. I will argue that the social survey and social science have been important to the middle class, at different phases of its historical development, in relation to the working class. In a connected way, I will also argue that the social survey has been linked to the development of a certain kind of interventionist, sometimes punitive, welfare state. As a British historian, I can make these arguments most confidently about Britain but other chapters in this book suggest important comparisons with America and Germany that it might be helpful, if risky, to begin to make.

I want to divide the discussion into five chronological phases which will mainly be set in Britain: firstly, Bourgeois Social Investigation in the Age of Revolutions (1789–1850), secondly The Mayhew Moment (1849–1850), thirdly Social Science and the Professional Middle Class (1850–1890), fourthly, Middle-Class Progressives and the Crisis of Liberalism (1890–1920) and fifthly, and very briefly, Academic Professionals and the Exclusivity of Objectivity (1920–). For the last two phases I will draw heavily on other essays in this book to provide a comparative dimension beyond the British Isles.

Between 1789 and the mid nineteenth century in Britain, social order was in crisis. It was precisely around the time of the French Revolution when the survey habit of mind became much more widespread. Lady Shelley observed how 'the awakening of the labouring classes after the first shock of the French revolution made the upper classes tremble. Every man felt the necessity of putting his house in order'.[4] She could have added, that the rich also tried to order the houses of the poor. Cultural revolutionaries from above, like Evangelical philanthropists, set out to engineer the scientific management of the poor and used door-to-door inquiry not only for initial fact-finding but for ongoing surveillance. Science and religion, far from being opposed, were inextricably intertwined. The two new rapidly spreading faiths, Evangelical Anglicanism and Wesleyan Methodism, fostered habits of methodical examination and disciplined ordering of the self and of the social world as the only possible bulwarks against the ever-surging sea of sin. Another early meaning of survey was the examination of the inner spiritual state. William Wilberforce, the crusader against slavery, even tabulated his weekly expenditure of time, thus making statistical representation of the state of his soul.[5]

Social investigation became more closely tied to the middle class during the 1830s in a changed revolutionary situation. This was the period when the middle class was forging its identity in relation to the classes above and below. The political triumph of 1832 gave the middle class the parliamentary vote and a place in the national constitution alongside the landed interest, although they still had to battle for local political ascendancy. The middle class also worked out their identity in relation to the working classes, which had been turbulent in the 1831 Reform riots and seemed to remain in a state of nearly continuous disorder for the next twenty years. To other eyes the 'disorder' might look impressively orderly, manifested not only in organisation ranging from the Grand National Consolidated Trade Union to the Chartist and socialist movements, but in versions of 'really useful' scientific knowledge, like moral economy as against political economy and social science as against statistical science.[6] The middle class based their claim to public authority on their probity, their industry, the comprehensiveness of their knowledge and on their religious service towards the local working class.

Social surveys were vital in this class connection. While the country gentry had found it easy to know the state of their poor, in the new urban conditions Christian service required new modes of inquiry and techniques of discipline. As Unitarian minister and vice-president of the Bristol Society, Reverend Lant Carpenter insisted, 'in large cities and towns statistical enquiries were of the greatest moment'.[7] From 1833, local business and professional men, Nonconformist as well as Anglican, formed statistical societies in Manchester, London, Birmingham. Belfast, Glasgow, Liverpool, Leeds, Aberdeen and Dublin. There were also American cousins in New York and Boston.

In Britain they spent part of their time acting as embryonic town councils collecting civic statistics. But they spent most of their time and money conducting door-to-door surveys into the condition of the local working classes. Even the London Statistical Society, which, atypically, was dominated by professional men including state servants and academics, and which aimed to carry out statistical inquiry into the state of the country, actually ended up doing surveys of the poor. Carried out by paid agents, this was first-hand inquiry on a large scale. Apologies were given for not visiting *all* working-class families in Manchester and Salford although the 4,102 families 'below the rank of shopkeepers' included every such household in Dukenfield, Staleybridge and Ashton-under-Lyne. In Bristol, 6,000 families were interviewed; in the London parish of St George's in the East the number of families totalled 1,954.[8] There was no question of sampling. Although cripplingly expensive, completeness seemed to be mandatory, perhaps because it was a measure of social service and evidence that an overview (necessary for governance) had been achieved.

The investigations were social discipline rather than poverty surveys. Questions were asked about occupation and place of birth but the emphasis was on what were called moral and intellectual statistics. These spotlighted housing facts which often had implications for sexual order, i.e., number of rooms, number of people in them, number of beds, level of rents, condition of furnishings. Bristol and London also went out of doors to record the sanitary condition of the streets. Overcrowding and confusion, particularly in sleeping arrangements, which 'indiscriminately' mixed up sex, age and family groups was a potent index of disorder. Questions were also asked about literacy, school attendance, religious denomination and church-going. The statisticians had already decided that churches and schools were the key agencies of social discipline to replace the once-resident upper class. The issue was to find out the extent of the need for them.

In this same period, State investigations and inspectors 'spread like contagion'. Between 1832 and 1846, over 100 Royal Commissions were set up. Every bit as much cultural revolutionaries as the evangelical Christians, Benthamites and especially Edwin Chadwick were very active in this work. Benthamite strategy stressed the need for statistics, in the sense of state-tistics, authoritative facts which would lead to legislation which in turn could provide the state inspectors who would insure the ongoing collection of yet more legitimate facts.[9] New State departments were created which spent a good part of their time collecting facts, notably the Statistical Section at the Board of Trade (1833) under the direction of Poulett Thompson and the Registrar General's office (1837) headed by another Benthamite, Dr William Farr. The State investigators were quite happy to select facts to create the knowledge they wanted. Chadwick's crucial *Report on the Sanitary Condition of the Labouring Population of Great Britain* (1842) was a patchwork of quotations from his national network of Poor Law Medical Officers, all making the same kinds of judgements on the same issues, like overcrowding and sexual disorder, which gave the impression of overwhelming unanimity from disparate places and thus unassailable national truth.

THE MAYHEW MOMENT 1849–1850

The local door-to-door surveys and State Commissions of inquiry into working-class life largely fell out of use after 1850. Henry Mayhew's much more radical departure was also firmly blocked off. Indeed, a closer look at Mayhew partly reveals that there were obstacles from within as well as from without. A renegade, he still revealed the power of meanings produced by the middle class. While able to listen seriously and to incorporate the analysis of working people into his investigative practice, he was also magnetically stuck to certain constructions of the poor which were to dominate mid-century middle-class social science.

I would nevertheless insist that in his London investigations for the *Morning Chronicle* newspaper he set out to conduct a poverty survey.[10] However embryonic, he worked with an idea of a poverty line:

Under the term 'poor' I shall include all those persons whose incomings are insufficient for the satisfaction of their wants – a want being, according to my idea, contra-distinguished from a mere desire by a positive physical pain, instead of mental uneasiness accompanying it. I shall consider the whole of the metropolitan poor under three separate phases, according as they *will* work, they *can't* work, and they *won't* work'.

He set up alternative hypotheses about the causes of the poverty of those who will work – like low wages, high prices, improvident habits – and set out to test them. He devised an effective method of industrial survey which involved interviewing a representative cross-section of the workers and 'masters' in a trade and which enabled him to locate poverty and to explore its economic causes at the same time. His brilliant method of calculating wages led him to appreciate that there were incompatible facts from the worker's and from the employer's point of view.

However, when it came to those who 'won't work' Mayhew revealed another side of himself. Here his capacity to listen with understanding broke down and stereotypes began to appear in place of full people. During his visits to lodging houses, he became fixated upon young criminals, an obsession which reached a climax in a letter (31 January 1850) devoted entirely to the role of the lodging house as a school for scandal. In words which were uncharacteristically uncontrolled, he found 'a system of depravity, atrocity and enormity which certainly cannot be parallelled in any nation, however barbarous, not in any age, however "dark"'. The letter ended with a powerful depiction of disorder in a scene of promiscuous sleeping arrangements with teenagers taking part in satanic rituals of dancing half-naked round a flame at midnight! When he left the *Morning Chronicle* newspaper, continued publication on his own and had to sell weekly numbers in order to survive, Mayhew increasingly focused on the obsessive object of the middle-class gaze, 'the perishing and dangerous classes'.

SOCIAL SCIENCE AND THE PROFESSIONAL MIDDLE CLASS 1850–1890

From the 1840's onward, professional men and feminist women were very active in constructing the fraction of the poor called 'the perishing and dangerous classes'. These sections of the middle class were annexing social science to their needs and shaping it accordingly. The 'older' professions, medicine, law and even the clergy were growing numerically and assuming their modern form at this time. They created courses of training and methods of policing to separate the qualified from the unqualified practitioner. As important, the professions began to rest their authority on a mixture of science and service which involved a special relationship with some segment of the working class. Doctors were active in creating a new field of 'sanitary science' just as lawyers were conspicuous in 'reformatory science' where their professional expertise was indispensable for treating the perishing and dangerous classes. Middle-class women trying to move into public work and yet remain respectable tried to transpose their service role in the family to the public sphere and to act as social mothers in relation to the poor. Professional men ratified the scientific credentials of women social workers. Women endorsed the service claims of professional men. In the fields of sanitary and reformatory science which became the concern of two Departments in the National Association for the Promotion of Social Science, this 'communion of labour' was clear.[11]

The Association, which existed between 1857 and 1886, and had a sister body in America, provides a good mirror for fashions in mid-century social investigation. To the extent that facts were to be systematically collected and arranged, the call was for the State to do the job, a call uttered, not least, by State servants prominent in the Association. The shape of the census in 1861 and 1871 was a subject for considerable Association pressure. But more often social facts were simply the experience of professional experts in a position of command in some social institution or 'experiment'. Thus Mary Carpenter, the high priestess of the juvenile delinquency rescue movement, would only trust statistics when collected or interpreted by a person like the Reverend John Clay whose expertise was authenticated in multiple ways as a professional clergyman of the state church working for twenty years as chaplain in Preston Goal, a state institution.[12]

In the Social Science Association the working class were represented as being divided into two basic groups. The perishing and dangerous classes were different from 'the true working class' whose most distinctive feature was their capacity for self-organisation into large working-class movements. For the thirty years of the Association's life, all forms of working-class combination were focused upon the Social Economy Department, with working-class activists taking a prominent part in the discussion. Even trade unions were treated with surprising sympathy although, as on the American social science scene explored by Turner in chapter 10, the co-operative movement, in all of its aspects, was favoured most of all. This concern with the labour movement should warn us against getting stuck in stale representations of the Social Science Association as the bastion of individualistic moral ameliorism soon to be abandoned for amoral detachment and state action. State servants were one of the categories of professional men already strongly represented in the Association, especially those involved in 'state medicine' or public health. Even the Charity Organisation Society, founded under NAPSS auspices, worked in its early years with a clear model of a national economic system in which country people were being pushed into cities where they became casualties by being casualised. COS activists supported employment agencies and trade unions at both terminals to regulate the migratory flow.

To shrug off moral concern as anti-scientific is also to misunderstand deeply the determining features of middle class sensibility. The most dignified self-image of the middle-class or sections within always stressed its own moral commitment, compared with aristocratic profligacy and working-class vice. Middle-class masculinity, as Davidoff and Hall have brilliantly shown, was religious, moral, responsible and protective: professional men could add 'expert' and 'scientific' to the list of virtues.[13] For middle-class women the moral dimension of social science was almost more important. Middle-class statistical science and social science were precisely political economy and the utilitarian science of government with the morality added. These sciences allowed for the study of the moral and intellectual dimensions of human life as well as the activities of the supremely egotistical male seeking wealth and power in the public sphere. As such, they both included the feminine aspects of human nature in the subject matter (especially the moral to which women were supposed to be more attuned) and made possible the entry of women as practitioners into the field.[14] It is naive to think that this structurally important sensibility would simply crumble in the later nineteenth century. Some people moved in ways I will explore in the next section. But it is significant that Helen Bosanquet, in her social economics textbook, *The Strength of the People* (1902), spent most of the chapter entitled 'The Remedy' quoting from Reverend Dr Thomas Chalmers about his work in the 1820s of inspecting and re-forming the character of the Glasgow parish poor.

MIDDLE-CLASS PROGRESSIVES AND THE CRISIS OF LIBERALISM 1880–1920

There was a sharp sense of national crisis in this period which spurred the growth of professional jobs for both men and women and provided a focus for their science and service. In several countries, laissez-faire liberalism appeared inadequate to contain new class challenges. From the 'Great Depression' of the 1870s, the British economic system was seen as failing abroad, in international competition, and at home. Beatrice Webb detected 'a new sense of sin amongst men of intellect and property', a conviction that the economy which had provided stupendous riches for the few had 'failed to provide a decent livelihood or tolerable conditions for a majority of the inhabitants of Great Britain'.[15] As part of this concern, Booth and Rowntree revived the idea of household surveys and measured the incidence of poverty using criteria convincing to the middle class. But it was the physical deterioration of army recruits to the Boer War which dramatised the implications for national vitality and survival in a more alarming way.

Britain's economic rivals also had their internal problems. Inequality was thrown into bold relief in America, where a rapidly growing industrial system, drawing heavily upon immigrant labour, was exploding with unprecedented episodes of class war which the dominant laissez-faire social Darwinism was doing little to check (see below, chapter 4). In Germany, the collapse of an economic boom in 1873 along with the investigations of the Historical School into real economic life, called into question classical economic theory imported from England, and revealed a decline in the living conditions of the workers which could threaten the whole of bourgeois society (see below, Chapter 12).

Everywhere, working-class associations and socialist movements were growing. In Britain, the socialists made a devastating attack on the immorality of the selfish social system, taking over the moral high ground the middle class had always claimed as its own. Many middle-class persons flirted with working-class socialism in Britain between 1883 and 1896. But the accent on self-governance which eliminated the need for any other social group was deeply subversive and deterred a larger-scale, longer-term influx of class renegades. Instead, in several countries, the response of the advanced middle class was to create more acceptable strands of socialism (like collectivism or state socialism) or to create progressive strategies which were seen as alternatives to socialism.[16] In both cases, not only were professional experts given a key role, but emphasis was put on social research as a necessary part of social reform and on the training and therefore professionalising of social scientists who would be leaders of this activity. Here was a way both of jumping on the bandwagon of progress steaming in the direction of social justice for all, and yet of retaining a position in the driver's seat for the progressive middle class. Perhaps it would not be too simple to say that in several countries, social science was partly the way advanced liberals tried to contain socialism and other working-class energy bubbling up from below.

Particularly in Britain, the middle-class moved towards more national definitions of issues – for example, the preoccupation with 'national efficiency'. This led to an expansion of jobs in the State and voluntary sectors to cope with these concerns, which in turn created a cadre of professionals with a vested interest in a more nationalised way of seeing.[17] A national perspective made it possible, as Desrosières suggests in chapter 8 to introduce sampling into survey work in order to produce a nationwide picture of working-class conditions and even, in the climate of intense international rivalry, a comparison between different nations. But it would be oversimple to assume there was a wholesale shift in middle-class sensibility from individualism to collectivism, from philanthropy to State action, from less to more adequate analyses of poverty. As Stefan Collini has argued, individualists and collectivists all accepted some form of the State, just as all were concerned with developing individual moral character, committed to an ideal of service[18] and, in social science circles, in favour of training experts. All could look suspicious from a working-class point of view. Jane Lewis' comparison (below, chapter 5) of the Webbs and the Bosanquets indicates some of the shared assumptions of these supposed polar opposites. Both couples can be taken as epitomes of two tendencies within the progressive middle class in Britain which had their analogues in America as well.

The Bosanquets were synonymous in the period with the Charity Organisation Society which, as Turner shows in chapter 10 below, was also a key feature in the American social science landscape. The COS was not the cave of the dinosaurs or the last bastion of individualistic moral reform. In Britain, as in America, there was no question of dismantling the Poor Law, Public Health or Compulsory Schooling legislation. If anything, the COS sought ways to coordinate voluntary and state action particularly in a small administrative area, like the parish or the ward. The COS was very keen on training for social workers and administrators. Together with the Women's University Settlement and the National Council of Women Workers (both middle-class groupings), they pressed for Schools of Sociology and Social Economics which would give theoretical underpinning to practical work and teach about 'the whole system of social organisation which is moulding the lives of the people'.[19] In the United States, Columbia University's first professors of sociology, of social economy and of social legislation were all intimately tied to the COS world. The COS also supplied key personnel to the Russell Sage Foundation which was vital in funding and servicing ventures for social work training in all parts of the country.[20]

The COS social vision recognised collectivities of all kinds and stressed service within them. Once trained, the Bosanquets envisioned an army of State-salaried social workers who would monitor the very poor family 'with a view to its restoration to independent citizenship'. The Bosanquets applauded the labour movement as a clear index of human development. By contrast to the dependent poor, parasitically attached to the State or to charity, members of labour organisations were independent and capable of service to an entity beyond their own biological families.[21] To the Bosanquets and to New Liberals like L. T. Hobhouse, the LSE's first professor of sociology, the active citizen capable of rational purpose was the highest form of human being. Giddings of Columbia was deeply concerned with using social research to elucidate the conditions, like the cooperative movement and particular forms of community, for maximising 'concerted volition'. Even in detached and scientific Chicago, Robert E. Park and his colleagues were convinced that sociological work had demonstrated that human development involved a necessary transition from living only in the family, the immigrant experience, to the participation in the community, 'the name we give to this larger and more inclusive milieu, outside of ourselves, our family and our immediate neighborhood where the individual maintains not merely his experience as an individual, but his life as a person'.[22]

There were other sections of the middle class both in Britain and America who were much more ambitious about State intervention to rectify the inequalities of power generated by unrestrained capitalism. The Webbs' version of socialism, which was out of step with working-class socialist movements at the time, gave enormous power to the State. In their vision of Industrial Democracy, the State would dominate in a new constitutional ecology which also included trade unions and the cooperative movement. Trained experts would administer this State. 'Above all', said Beatrice, 'we want the ordinary citizen to feel that reforming society is no light matter and must be undertaken by experts especially trained for the purpose'.[23] A key task for the Webbs was creating institutions to train the experts who would run this all-important State; the London School of Economics and Political Science was brought into being to do the job.

Although the American advocates of the welfare state were not so committed to State ownership and the expropriation of the capitalist as the British Fabians, strands of social survey in the USA also looked to the State to referee more actively in encounters between unequal contestants. In chapter 9, Cohen uncovers the theoretical underpinning of the Pittsburgh Survey as an attempt to test the socialist claim that competitive capitalism could not deliver benefits to the workers in an industry. John Commons, the survey director, presided over the Wisconsin school of political economy which rejected socialised ownership and insisted that the State could create conditions which equalised the power of workers, by for example setting minimum wage legislation, requiring workers to sit on company Boards and giving them access to the company books. Sklar's chapter shows how the Hull House investigators were convinced that only legislative protection could create the space in which women workers and their children could have a decent life.

What is interesting and needs to be stressed both about the British Fabians and the American advocates of a welfare state is that both created a version of the nation which was still under the command of the middle class, but this time a middle class scientifically trained, professionally expert and committed to public service. On this basis there was room for cooperation with the COS faction as illustrated by the fact that the COS's School of Sociology and Social Economics moved into the LSE in 1912. This was the period when the explosion of salaried jobs in government, industry and the voluntary sector was being seen as the emergence of a 'nouvelle couche social', or a 'professional proletariat' (now called 'the Professional and Managerial Class'). This grouping was adopted by different tendencies within middle-class social science, by the Fabians as

well as the COS, as the vanguard of a new social order based on service
rather than selfishness.[24] But to the working-class movement, in Britain at
least, service from above was still a poor substitute for a real democracy of
working-class power underpinned by an ethic of mutuality. The democratic
and convivial Friendly Societies had a different vision of a welfare state
where they, not state bureaucrats, would distribute insurance benefits. The
Social Democratic Federation's newspaper, *Justice*, reminded readers that
'Fabianesque "State Socialism" was far removed from genuine Democratic
Socialism' while Reynolds and Woolley, in *Seems So! A Working-Class
View of Politics*, warned that 'the worst tyranny to beware of is that of
intellectuals ordering other people's lives. They are so well intentioned, so
merely logical, so cruel.'[25]

Some of the most interesting survey work of this period seemed both to
challenge expertism and yet expose the middle-class inability to surrender
control, to open other directions for development and yet refuse to follow
them. A case in point is the American Social Survey Movement, the first
to make regular use of the words 'social survey', and analogous to Patrick
Geddes' civics movement in Britain with its headquarters in his Edinburgh
'Outlook tower'[26] (note the positioning: a watchtower high above with
commanding views). Both stimulated local people to undertake investigations of their community and then mount local exhibitions to display the
results, often with visual aids like pictures and maps. The idea was to study
social problems and energise the locality into social action. Both aimed to
catalyse community self-study. But who were the community? In America
the pattern was for local leaders to invite the Russell Sage Foundation to
send in experts to organise a social survey (the Pittsburgh Survey was the
first) which would be carried out with local, volunteer, middle-class help. In
Britain, Geddes adopted as his special audience teachers, architects and local
authorities. It would seem that professional people were being equated with
'the community' and their views actually made to prevail. Perhaps Ernest
Burgess exposed something of the power relations implicit in this work
which could undercut some of its democratic ambition when he asserted
that 'community self-study under expert direction is democracy being at
school to the social scientist. The social survey is to the community what
the demonstration station is to the farmer' (quoted by Bulmer in chapter
11). Here was a moment when social survey was used to legitimate the
claims of certain professionals to special expertise, for example, academics
and social workers in the US and town planners in Britain, while confirming
the service credentials of other emergent professions, whose volunteer
labour in study and action constituted a clear work of social service.

ACADEMIC PROFESSIONALS AND THE EXCLUSIVITY OF OBJECTIVITY AFTER 1920

After World War I, as a number of chapters in this book argue, the center of gravity began to shift from an ideal of professionalism for reform to one of professional detachment. I want briefly to address this argument and chart some of its less obvious directions. The Russian Revolution was a decisive event for this process, particularly and paradoxically in America. In the postwar red scare and witchhunt, university people no longer found it safe to be hopeful about the labour movement or even to harness research to reform. Instead the academic watchword became objectivity for work funded by large foundations like Carnegie and Rockefeller, who had also had their knuckles rapped in 1915 for sponsoring science against labour and were now to operate through more anodyne organisations like the American Council of Learned Societies (founded 1919) and the Social Science Research Council (founded 1924).[27] American intellectuals were reaching the position of prewar German academics whose detached stance was partly a form of protection against the Kaiser Reich and who remained aloof during the postwar socialist period particularly as the economic crisis of the 'twenties deepened (see below, chapter 12). By contrast, in Britain many middle-class progressives, and particularly the Webbs, welcomed the Russian Revolutionary State as the paradigm of the professional proletariet in charge.[28] In British academic sociology the connection between survey and reform was harder to break. None the less, as in America, the academic incorporation of social science was accelerated after the war and this perhaps, in the long run, had a deeper undermining effect.

Increasingly, the various ventures for training social science professionals were absorbed by the universities. By 1930 this process had been completed in America, thereby annexing a space which had included the Schools of Sociology and Social Work and the Settlement Houses, all important women's territory. Yet when Florence Kelley was directing research on her neighbours in the Nineteenth Ward, it was men who actually did the doorstep interviews (Sklar below, chapter 4). Once inside the mixed university, a more old fashioned 'communion of labour' took over, with men controlling the production of knowledge and the administrative hierarchy and with women cast as auxiliaries and assistants. Social work became the practical side of sociology and had less academic status: Home Economics, the less-esteemed women's realm in Economics.[29] Of course, the enclosure and subordination were never complete. A network of women's colleges ensured some places where women had a more controlling role while a number of Government departments and pressure groups, not least the National Consumers' League headed by Kelley, preserved spaces where women continued to carry out social research with reformist intent.

Whether social research or social survey was contained within the University or pursued in its characteristic locations outside, its accessibility was being curtailed. Paradoxically objective science, like some reformist science before, served the purposes of middle-class growth and ascendancy. Whatever its intellectual value, objectivity was to function as exclusive middle-class professional activity. At the same time, another potential was stultified. However partially realised, there had been a recurrent idea of community self-study which, if developed democratically, could open to men and women of all classes and conditions the possibility of producing their own knowledge. In the academic ivory tower, with its rarified élite atmosphere, this potential could but wither and die. Nor did the outside climate seem more favourable. Some characteristic areas for the development of social survey techniques were commercial market research and political opinion polls. In both, large numbers of people were contacted but placed in a passive pose and asked to respond to the agenda of the few survey directors. Yet even as I write this sentence, contradictory examples come to mind which still indicate the possibility of other directions of growth – the instances of participatory survey work in the 1970s and early 80s which produced impressive social analysis both in Brighton, where I live, and in London.[30] Hopefully, the social survey will always remain a contested form.

In a way, the history of the social survey is also a contested form. I was invited to the conference about this book to comment on the 'pre-history' of the social survey. During the lively discussions, I realised that the contributors tended to take two different approaches to the history of social investigation. Although historians and sociologists seemed to move in different directions the two approaches could equally be used by either, so there is no simple issue here of sociology versus history. One group, predominantly sociologists such as Bulmer and Bales, were interested in when and how the various characteristics of an ideal-type social survey came to be. They tended to see the significant historical story as a movement, although not in any simple, continuous, one-way direction, from 'amateur, episodic, reformist' work to social research that was 'professionalised, scientific in orientation and aspired to be cumulative by the 1930s'. They were particularly concerned with projects which embodied the new attitudes and practices, for example Booth's survey as depicted by Bales. Or else they highlighted institutional settings, like the University of

Chicago compared with the Russell Sage Foundation, which made possible professionalism, detachment and science, all seen as considerable and relatively unproblematic achievements.

The other group, including Cohen and Turner, were more historicist in outlook. They regarded science not as an absolute but as an historically evolving category and were concerned with real practices of social investigation in relation to historical contexts. They were concerned with exploring how political as well as institutional settings shaped and constrained these practices of survey work. Thus Cohen stressed how the Pittsburgh survey and a reformist version of science could survive given the right paymasters, like the Russell Sage Foundation and Progressive state government in Wisconsin, while Gorges indicates how a passion for objectivity was partly a way of avoiding distasteful alignment with the Kaiser Reich. This group of contributors took seriously the understanding of science as reformist and open to the community and wanted to know how another meaning of science as detached and professional came to prevail. My own approach was closer to this group but still askew from it because of my emphasis on the power relations of gender and class. The significant story was not the emergence of scientific practice *per se* but how distinct historical practices of science came and went, why some roads were taken and other closed, who won recognition and who lost out.

NOTES

1 The definition by Scots enthusiast, John Sinclair, which was taken over by the next generation of statisticians, e.g., John Cleland in *Glasgow and Clydesdale Statistical Society Transactions* (Glasgow, 1836), p. 52. See Sinclair, *A Code of Political Economy, founded on the Basis of Statistical Inquiries* (Edinburgh, 1821), p. xii.

2 These idea is developed in his forthcoming book, *Whose Story*, to be published by Basil Blackwell.

3 This is the story I am telling in my forthcoming book on *Social Science, Class and Gender in Britain, 1789 to 1914* to be published by Virago Books. I wish to thank Vivien Hart for her helpful reading of an earlier draft of this chapter.

4 *The Diary of Frances, Lady Shelley, 1787–1817*, ed. R. Edgcumbe (London, 1912), pp. 8–9. For an extensive view of Evangelical philanthropy, see The Society for Bettering the Conditions ... of the Poor, *Reports*, 5 vols. (London, 1798–1808); and for a close-up of work in the Evangelical heartland: The Society for Bettering the Condition of the Poor at Clapham, Surrey, *Rules and Regulations* (London, 1817).

5 R. I. and S. Wilberforce, *The Life of William Wilberforce* (London: John Murray, 1838), pp. 194–5.

6 See my forthcoming book and also my 'Social Science and Social Change', PhD thesis, University of Sussex, 1973, chs. 2 and 3, for an analysis of this contest and for local

statistical societies. For more on working-class political economy, see N. Thompson, *The People's Science. The Popular Political Economy of Exploitation and Crisis 1816–1834* (Cambridge: Cambridge University Press, 1984).

7 *Journal of the Statistical Society of London*, 1 (1839), 551.

8 Manchester Statistical Society, *Report ... on the Condition of the Working Classes in an Extensive Manufacturing District in 1834, 1835 and 1836* (London, 1838), p. 5; C. B. Fripp, 'Report of an Inquiry into the Condition of the Working Classes of the City of Bristol', in Bristol Statistical Society, *Proceedings* (Bristol, 1839), p. 10; 'Report ... into the State of the Poorer Classes in St. George's in the East', *Journal of the Statistical Society of London*, 11 (1848).

9 The most searching analysis of this development is in P. Corrigan and D. Sayer, *The Great Arch. English State Formation as Cultural Revolution* (Oxford: Basil Blackwell, 1985), ch. 6. For Benthamite finagling of the facts, see S. E. Finer, 'The Transmission of Benthamite Ideas 1820–1850', in *Studies in the Growth of Nineteenth Century Government*, ed. G. Sutherland (London: Routledge and Kegan Paul, 1972).

10 For my earlier views, see 'Mayhew as a Social Investigator', in *The Unknown Mayhew*, ed. E. P. Thompson and E. Yeo (London: Merlin Press, 1971); p. 54 for his poverty line.

11 This phrase was coined by Anna Jameson in *Sisters of Charity and Communion of Labour: Lectures on the Social Employment of Women* (London: Longman etc., 1859). See my forthcoming book and also my 'Social Science and Social Change', chs 4 and 6–8 for a development of the themes in this section. L. Goldman argues that the NAPSS embodied the science of a successful bourgeoisie compared with America and Germany where relative powerlessness led to an earlier entry into the university and more concern with theory: 'A Peculiarity of the English? The Social Science Association and the Absence of Sociology in Nineteenth-century Britain', *Past & Present*, 114 (1987). For the American Social Science Association, T. Haskell, *The Emergence of Professional Social Science: The American Social Science Association and the Nineteenth-Century Crisis of Authority* (Urbana: University of Illinois Press, 1977); W. Leach, *True Love and Perfect Union. The Feminist Reform of Sex and Society* (New York: Basic Books, 1980).

12 M. Carpenter, *Reformatory Schools for the Children of the Perishing and Dangerous Classes* (London, 1851), p. 20; NAPSS, *Transactions* (1859), pp. 628ff; (1860), p. xxix.

13 L. Davidoff and C. Hall, *Family Fortunes. Men and Women of the English Middle Class, 1780–1850* (London: Hutchison, 1988), pp. 108–14; for professional masculinity, F. Mort, *Dangerous Sexualities. Medico-Moral Politics in England since 1830* (London: Routledge and Kegan Paul, 1987), p. 51.

14 Frances Power Cobbe, 'Social Science Congresses, and Women's Part in Them', *Macmillan's Magazine* (Dec. 1861).

15 B. Webb, *My Apprenticeship* (London: Longmans, Green, 1926), pp. 179, 180. The effect of the Boer War revelations on the growth of the welfare state and expansion of careers for middle-class women are best pointed up in B. Gilbert, *The Evolution of National Insurance in Great Britain. The Origins of the Welfare State* (London: Michael Joseph, 1966), A. Davin, 'Imperialism and Motherhood', *History Workshop*, 5 (Spring, 1978).

16 The best study of the quality of working-class socialism in this period is S. Yeo, 'A

New Life. The Religion of Socialism in Britain, 1883–1896', *History Workshop*, 4 (Autumn, 1977). For the multi-class 'scramble for socialism', S. Yeo, 'Notes on Three Socialisms – Collectivism, Statism and Associationism – Mainly in Late-Nineteenth and Early-Twentieth-Century Britain', in *Socialism and the Intelligentsia, 1880–1914*, ed. C. Levy (London: Routledge and Kegan Paul, 1987). For Fabianism as the socialism of the progressive middle class, see E. Hobsbawm, 'The Fabians Reconsidered', in *Labouring Men. Studies in the History of labour* (London: Weidenfeld and Nicolson, 1964).

17 H. Perkin, *The Rise of Professional Society. England Since 1880* (London: Routledge, 1989), pp. 158–60. E. and S. Yeo, 'On the Uses of "Community": From Owenism to the Present', in S. Yeo (ed.), *New Views of Co-operation* (London: Routledge, 1988), pp. 245–7.

18 S. Collini, *Liberalism and Sociology* (Cambridge: Cambridge University Press, 1979), ch. 1.

19 H. Bosanquet, *Rich and Poor* (London: Macmillan and Co., 1902), p. 8; *Social Work in London 1869–1912* (London: John Murray, 1914), pp. 402ff.

20 S. Slaughter and E. Silva, 'Looking Backwards: How Foundations Formulated Ideology in the Progressive Period', in R. Arnove (ed.), *Philanthropy and Cultural Imperialism. The Foundations at Home and Abroad* (Bloomington: Indiana University Press, 1982), pp. 60–1.

21 Bosanquet, *Strength*, pp. 30–1; Lewis, chapter 10 below, n. 89; Collini, *Liberalism and Sociology*, p. 216.

22 R. E. Park, E. W. Burgess and R. D. Mackenzie, *The City* (Chicago: University Press, 1925), p. 106.

23 B. Webb, *Our Partnership*, ed. B. Drake and M. Cole (London, Longmans, Green, 1948), p. 86; S. and B. Webb, *Industrial Democracy* (London, 1897). Significantly, Hobhouse created a similar blueprint in his early book, *The Labour Movement* (London, 1893).

24 For the affinity of the PMC with collectivist socialism and its incompatibility with working-class associationism, see S. Yeo, 'Notes on Three Socialisms'.

25 For working-class movement views of an alternative welfare state, see S. Yeo, 'Working-class Association, Private Capital, Welfare and the State in the Late-Nineteenth and Early-Twentieth-Centuries', in N. Parry *et al.* (eds.), *Social Work, Welfare and the State*, (London: Edward Arnold, 1979). *Justice*, 9 May 1903; S. Reynolds and B. Woolley, *Seems So!* (London: Macmillan, 1911) p. xxv.

26 P. Mairet, *Pioneer of Sociology. The Life & Letters of Patrick Geddes* (London: Lund Humphries, 1957), p. 70.

27 Slaughter and Silva, 'Looking Backwards', pp. 59–60.

28 E.g., see S. and B. Webb, *Soviet Communism: A New Civilisation* (London: Longmans, Green, 1936). The close continuing link between survey and policy is shown in the work of Richard Titmuss and Peter Townsend, and of the Institute for Community Studies.

29 E.g., QueenSpark Rates Book Group, *Brighton on the Rocks. Montetarism and the Local State* (Brighton: QueenSpark, 1983).

CHAPTER THREE

Charles Booth's survey of Life and Labour of the People in London 1889–1903

KEVIN BALES

Charles Booth was a social researcher but not an academic. A careful examination of his work is required to gain an understanding of how a Victorian merchant, ship-owner, and manufacturer came to make a crucial contribution to social science. Abrams[1] has called Booth a bridge that unites the positivist and reformist traditions of nineteenth century political economy with the empirical social sciences of the twentieth. It was his confrontation with human problems which moved Booth to become that bridge. The ineluctable problem of poverty led Booth to pose certain pivotal questions, and to synthesise and improve research methods in attempting to answer those questions. Booth termed poverty 'the problem of all problems' and he felt a personal responsibility to seek its solution. Where he differed from most of his contemporaries was his inherent pragmatism – problems could be solved, he believed, on the basis of sound information. He employed vigorous analytical techniques in investigation, with the hope that social policy might be redirected on the basis of his research.

His personal philosophy included a compelling sense of social obligation which led him to devote years of his life and a fortune to searching for answers to the social problems he felt most serious. Beatrice Webb described him as 'perhaps the most perfect embodiment of ... the mid-Victorian time-spirit – the union of faith in the scientific method with the transference of the emotion of self-sacrificing service from God to man'.[2] It would be incorrect, however, to think of him as interested only in amelioration, for Booth saw his 'service to man' in the introduction of the exactitude of the natural sciences to social research, and to ending confusion in social policy and opinion. By continuing the improvement of statistical methods in social research and popularising its uses he effected a break with the social philosophers of his time and opened a new direction in the development of the social sciences. Early in his research on poverty he wrote that policy could 'be built out of a big theory, and facts and statistics run in to fit it', but this was not the way he wished to work. Instead he sought to construct through research 'a large statistical framework built to receive an accumulation of facts'. When this framework was filled with all the available data and evidence, then from it might be 'evolved the theory and the law and the basis of more intelligent action'. Carried into practice, the construction of this framework and the collection of information to fill it would consume the efforts of Booth and his research staff for seventeen years. To achieve this 'accumulation of facts', aggregate statistical analysis was combined with observation and participation to present a balanced and human portrait of the life of, what was then, the largest city in the world.

If Booth had underlying theoretical assumptions concerning the social system of nineteenth century London they are implicit in the structure of his research project. The sheer breadth of his work, relating deprivation to the structure of the city's economy and the social and religious influences which affect both, sketches the outline of society as he conceived it. The seventeen volumes of *The Life and Labour of the People in London* reflect English urban society, concentrating, but not reducing, the field of vision. But Booth has been criticised for the absence of explicit theory in his work. As the Simeys put it:

As things were, his unwillingness to discuss the theoretical implications of his work had the unfortunate consequence of leaving his philosophical position suspended as it were in mid-air, between the 'science' of Comtism and the revelation of the Christian religion in one dimension, and in another, between the individualism of the classical economists and the socialism of his supporters in the campaign for old age pensions.[3]

Between Christianity and Comtism, individualism and socialism, deductive theory and inductive analysis, Booth took the middle path, using what he recognised as the best of each. Equally important, he placed man in the middle of his analysis. His work was built up by the collection of information from individuals, sometimes as informants sometimes as respondents, whether the object of study was poverty, industry, or religion. If there was a unifying theoretical concept it was that the life of a complex urban society might be understood by examining the lives of its component individuals and then aggregating their experiences into a representative portrait of that society. In this way Booth addressed the larger social issues of his day, by observing the individuals who were most affected by those issues. In his best-known work this meant searching among the individuals who lived at the heart of poverty.

By the 1880s the question of poverty had beleagured English society for well over 100 years. The industrial revolution had been responsible for a distinct change in social organisation and a fundamental shift in the economy. For some parts of society these changes led to, or added to, their impoverishment. From before the Napoleonic wars a debate had continued concerning the nature of poverty, and society's responsibility to the poor. Contributions to this debate included the work of Adam Smith, Malthus, Bentham, Godwin, Comte, Martineau, Engels, Marx, and Spencer, as well as other religious, political (especially a long tradition of governmental investigations), or social commentators of many orientations. Booth's role in this debate was to address two simple questions which were at the base of the ongoing controversy – how many people were poor, and why were they poor? His goal was to show that the incidence and causes of poverty could be accurately measured. By his own estimation and that of his contemporaries he achieved this goal and in doing so began a chapter in the social sciences which had two important themes. Firstly, he demonstrated the effectiveness of social research and the 'survey method'. The concept of the social survey is now so universally accepted that it is difficult, but important, to remember that many of Booth's contemporaries regarded him as its inventor, and acclaimed this invention as a milestone in scientific progress. Booth's popularising of the survey method had greater impact on the development of sociology in America than in Britain. Within twenty years of the publication of the first volume of *Life and Labour of the People in London* hundreds of community surveys had been accomplished in the cities of the United States, including DuBois' study of Philadelphia, Kellog's study of Pittsburg, and the Hull House study of Chicago. These three studies, in particular, closely approximated Booth's techniques. In Britain social investigation also followed Booth's lead, both Rowntree's study of York, and Bowley's broader research adopted and improved Booth's methodology.

Secondly, Booth's research had an important affect on the way in which social policy was formulated. By demonstrating to the satisfaction of most observers the actual number of people in poverty, and by attempting to determine the frequency of various causes of poverty, he indicated a way in which policy might be designed to meet actual and measured needs. This was especially true of Booth's work on the elderly poor. He found that old age and its problems made up the greatest single cause of pauperism and institutionalisation. Strongly affected by this finding, Booth added his voice to the ongoing campaign for universal old age pensions – a radical proposal in the 1880s. Old age pensions did not become law until 1908, but by then the practice of building policy upon data gathered in social research was much more commonplace.

The research which supported the published works which made up the Poverty Series and the other volumes of *Life and Labour of the People in London* (as well as his work on the aged poor) lasted over seventeen years and required a large research staff. It has often been assumed that Booth must have used virtually all of the information he collected to fill seventeen volumes, but this was not the case. He was, in many respects, more successful at collecting data than at analysing it. In an attempt to build up a complete picture of London his team amassed thousands and thousands of pages of notes, records, and evidence. In the first volume he wrote that 'Of the wealth of my material I have no doubt. I am indeed embarrassed by its mass'.[4] Booth was also methodical in filing and storing the information he collected, for each sub-set of research notes, for example, there is usually a hand-written index or directory. Standardised notebooks were printed for his staff so that information would be collected in a uniform manner. Through his own foresight and that of his family the bulk of these research materials were preserved after the closure of his research office in 1903. In the 1920s a large section of these were deposited in the British Library of Political and Economic Science at the London School of Economics and Political Science. In time more materials were added to this collection, and his personal papers were given to the nearby Library of the University of London.

Over the years some researchers have used these materials. For the most part, however, they have been ignored as researchers preferred to explore the printed volumes of *Life and Labour*. With the advent of new techniques for data collection and analysis it became clear that this wealth of information, and its originator, could still play a vital role in the mainstream of the social sciences. With this in mind it is important to carefully examine Booth's research methods, and to assess their place in the evolution of the social survey.

BOOTH'S RESEARCH METHODS

Booth's idea to systematically confront the 'Poverty Question' was not translated directly into his Poverty Study. To do so would have been out of character and precipitous. In Booth's estimation the Poverty Study was like a large-scale business venture, and required the same amount of preparatory data collection, analysis, and planning to shape its ultimate form. In the same way that Booth had laboriously catalogued all shipping in the Portuguese ports before instituting a service there, he now turned to

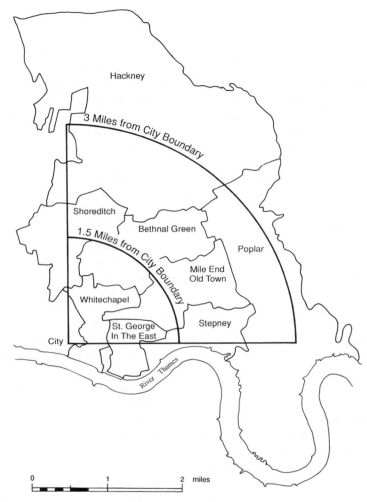

Map 2   Area included in house-to-house poverty survey of Tower
Hamlets, 1886–7. Adapted from Booth 1889.

what available statistics there were to get a broad picture of London's
employment and poverty, his proposed area of study. But he was,
according to Mary Booth, 'still more uncertain as to whether the facts on
which all must depend had been accurately ascertained'.[5] In 1885 Booth
began to concentrate on the need to discover 'these all-important but
elusive facts'.[6] He went first to the Census.

From the 1881 Census returns he hoped to determine the relative distribution of the population amongst various occupational categories. This was not an especially novel exercise, for the Census already collected and categorised employment figures. What was original was Booth's aim of constructing an exact baseline from which discussion of, and policy for, poverty could begin. Through such information he hoped to account for the impact of economic and social change on the 'Condition of the People'. It was an important pilot study, and served to establish working procedures, bringing one of his clerks, Jesse Argyll, into full-time social research, and making contacts in government and the Royal Statistical Society.

The practical value of the Census study was, however, meagre. Booth succeeded more in revealing errors in the way the Census collected employment data than he did in establishing a baseline for the analysis of poverty. In particular he showed that the Census failed 'to distinguish nominal from actual employment, and consequently the great majority of paupers...are returned with the employed'.[7] In other words, the Census might record a man or woman as a Dockworker or a Nurse even though they had not worked for years. He also suggested that issues of immediate importance be investigated through the addition of specific topic-centred questions to an 'omnibus' census. Using this technique, topics which Booth termed 'special subjects', such as urban poverty, could be explored without mounting costly independent research projects. Later in the twentieth century this was to become standard procedure, but at the time his idea was controversial. His work on the census was not well received when he presented his results to a meeting of the Statistical Society in 1886. Several critics implied that Booth, an outsider, a merchant, was playing at the work scholars take seriously. Dr W. Ogle stated that if Booth's ideas on 'special subjects' were incorporated into the census then 'Everyone who had a hobby, or question he was unable to solve. [would think] he could make use of the machinery of the census in order to get the data he wanted'.[8] In the remarks which brought the session to a close the president of the Society, Sir Ranson W. Ranson, congratulated Booth for the 'immense industry he had displayed', but Ranson did not wish to 'undervalue the importance of the objections raised', adding that he could only 'hope that the paper [Booth had presented to the Society] would not be a fruitless one'.[9]

While unsuccessful at the time in altering the procedures for census taking, Booth's work did prepare the ground for his research into poverty in three ways. The first was to convert Booth from an 'ethnographer' and commentator into a social statistical researcher. His previous informal explorations of the East End and discussions with politicians and social reformers had been worthwhile but not directed to any specific result. Now

Table 3.1. *Census notebook: sample page entries – Zion Square 4 April, 1881**

Road or Street	Name and Surname	Relation to Head	Marital Status	Age Males	Age Females	Occupation
19 Zion Sq.	Levi Olstermann	Head	Mar.	29		Cigar Maker
	Hannah Olstermann	Wife	Mar.		24	None
	Joel Olstermann	Son	Unmar.	4		Scholar
	Abraham Olstermann	Son	Unmar.	3		Scholar
	Jacob Olstermann	Son	Unmar.	2 mo.		
18 Zion Sq.	Phillip Cohen	Head	Mar.	38		Tailor
	Martha Cohen	Wife	Mar.		36	None
	Alice Cohen	Daughter	Unmar.		14	Scholar
	Morris Cohen	Son	Unmar.	9		Scholar
	Abram Cohen	Son	Unmar.	7		Scholar
	Fanny Cohen	Daughter	Unmar.		5	Scholar
	Harry Cohen	Son	Unmar.	3		Scholar
18 Zion Sq.	Davis Jacobs	Head	Mar.	55		Commercial Traveller
	Rebecca Jacobs	Wife	Mar.		55	None
	Henry Jacobs	Son	Unmar.	19		Baker
	Isaac Jacobs	Son	Unmar.	17		do.
	Rose Jacobs	Daughter	Unmar.		13	None
17 Zion Sq.	John Harris	Head	Mar.	48		Tailor
	Eliza Harris	Wife	Mar.		42	None
	John Harris	Son	Unmar.	24		Leather Cutter
	Wm Harris	Son	Unmar.	22		Packer
	Elizb. Harris	Daughter	Unmar.		20	Feather curler
	George Harris	Son	Unmar.	14		Scholar
	Julia Harris	Daughter	Unmar.		13	Scholar

* Columns for 'Where born' and 'Deaf and Dumb, etc' are omitted. Zion Sq. is in Civil Parish of Poplar, Borough of Tower Hamlets, Ecclesiastical Parish of St Mathias. PRO reference RG11/508.

a distinct body of information had been analysed in order to address specific questions, it was his first research *project*. Secondly, the Census project shaped his career as a researcher by bringing him into professional contact with other social researchers and especially the members of the Royal Statistical Society. Booth joined the Society in 1885 and presented

Table 3.2. *Booth Notebook : sample page entries – Zion Square 29 December, 1886**

No. in Zion Square	Room	Rent	Occupation	Wife +	Children 3–13	−3	Over 13	Wages	Position
17	3	15/- or 16/-	Tailor	√	−	−	2 girls help	−	poor
18	3	−	Tailor	√	2	−	Daughter	−	poor
18	3	−	Tailor	√	−	−	−	−	poor
19	3	−	Cigar Maker	√	4	−	−	−	poor

Jews and Germans, very poor as a rule, a struggle to live. Trade both in Tailoring and Cigar Making, very bad.**

* LSE Booth collection, Notebook B8. The interviewed School Board Visitor being Mr Bowsher.

+ Meaning 'present'.

** Descriptive notes often follow a block or street's returns.

his paper based on the Census in May 1886. While his paper was not well received, the criticism offered Booth the opportunity to polish and tighten his work. Finally, the work on the Census, as well as that on the Mansion House Enquiry (discussed below), demonstrated to Booth the need to rely on his own resources and skills if he was to successfully address the Poverty Question. For the Census proved as useless as a data source as would the Mansion House Enquiry for the formulation of responsive social policy.

Booth was dissatisfied with the results of this project and with the reception of his work on the Census. Unable to find what he considered trustworthy information on poverty in the public domain, he began to plot his own data collection. The form of the Poverty Study was now taking shape in conversations with Beatrice Potter, Alfred Cripps, Jesse Argyll, and Mary Booth[10] among others. About this time it began to take on its own name, being referred to in correspondence as 'the Inquiry'. By March 1886 Booth had developed an outline plan and had constituted a steering committee, a 'Board of Statistical Research'. It is not clear who was to make up the Board. Alfred Cripps, Beatrice Potter, Maurice Paul, Benjamin Jones (Secretary of the Working Men's Co-operative Society), a person named Radley who was secretary to a trade society (unspecified in Beatrice Webbs' diary) – are the known members. Canon Barnett of Toynbee Hall may also have been invited, but it appears that while many were called few chose to attend. In any event the Board soon dissolved leaving those who were to be research workers on the Inquiry (Maurice Paul, Jesse Argyll, Beatrice Potter) to soldier on under Booth's direction.

Some of those listed above attended a meeting of the 'Board' on 17 April 1886. The next day Beatrice Potter lunched with Canon Barnett, who had not attended. In her diary she records that Barnett 'threw cold water on CB's scheme ... said it was impossible to get the information required and was evidently sceptical of the value of the fact when there'.[11] Undeterred, Booth continued to plan the Inquiry. A sheet of foolscap survives on which Booth has written in pencil:

General aim. To connect poverty and wellbeing with conditions of employment. Incidentally, to describe the industrial peculiarities of London (and of modern towns generally) both as to character of work, character of workers, and of the influences which act upon both.[12]

An extensive research outline followed this opening statement of the intent of the Inquiry (see appendix for complete text). The Simeys believe that this is 'the actual note prepared for consideration by the 'Board'.[13] Clearly, Booth's notes and outline reveal an attempt to link his attempt to measure poverty and employment in the Census with the collection of reliable data to achieve the same end. The way in which Booth framed his research plan is remarkable for its ambition. The outline which follows this research statement is notable for the detail it includes and, also, for what it omits. For an inquiry that, in the first instance, concentrated on poverty and employment, the outline is surprisingly that of a broad economic analysis. The major headings include government regulation, labour organisation, production cost, specialisation, firm size, market elasticity, and distribution. From this outline there is little indication that the subsequent study will look so closely into the lives of the people of the East End. On the other hand this is not a working hypothesis, but the analytical framework which was to receive the data collected.

The method that would complete this plan was being formed through the Spring of 1886. Booth had received a suggestion from Joseph Chamberlain, via Beatrice Potter, recommending the School Board Visitors and their records as a resource for the Inquiry. This was a welcome suggestion, for Booth had, by February 1886, examined then rejected the Census, the Poor Law Unions, charitable societies, and the clergy. Unfortunately, no notes made by Booth at this time survive, but glimpses of the growing Inquiry appear in the letters and diary of Beatrice Webb (née Potter). In March 1886, she wrote to Mary Booth, returning 'the papers sent to me by Charlie'. These papers presumably included outline plans for the 'Board' for she continues:

I should almost divide instructions for the Board, describing in detail the methods and aims of the Inquiry, from a general description of the work which would serve as a credential for inquirers, to give employers and other authorities as an outline of the undertaking.

She, as others, felt somewhat overwhelmed by what Booth proposed to do:

Of course it is a huge business, but if one or two districts or trades could be *thoroughly* worked out, I think the results would be sufficiently valuable ... In any case even if the end be not arrived at, the work will be interesting and *educating*, and give the workers some idea of the scope and direction of an inquiry which might be undertaken by a more powerful body or even by the government.[14]

A few days later she wrote again to Mary Booth. Now it is clear that the School Board Visitors have been chosen:

I think I shall have some time in London and should be glad to undertake my own school board district and the London and St Kath. docks with the Royal Albert further down ... It would certainly be an advantage to have a short resume of the objects of the work without specifying details of clarification? ...

My love to Charlie. I suppose when the scheme is sanctioned by the Board we shall have it in typewriting.[15]

The 'Board' was ineffectual and Booth pushed on with no scheme in 'typewriting'. And while Potter continued to discuss the nature and plan of the research, Booth was anxious to begin and was contacting those who could be helpful. On 6 May Beatrice Potter records in her diary: 'Met at Charles Booth's office Mr. Loch, secretary of the C.O.S. [Charity Organisation Society] Enthusiast for accurate knowledge of the conditions of the poor. Evidently, from his account, there are many who would like to devote themselves to investigation'.[16] In this period other events were pressing Booth to begin his research in earnest. A further stimulus toward initiating his own data collection was Booth's involvement, through the winter of 1885–6, in the Mansion House inquiry 'into the causes of permanent distress in London'. The Mansion House Enquiry was to be an impetus to Booth primarily by what it *did not* achieve.

Following the riots by the poor and unemployed in Trafalgar Square and along Pall Mall in early February 1886 two immediate responses grew up under the aegis of the city of London. The first was the Mansion House Fund for the relief of the distressed. The second, also based at Mansion House, the seat of government for the City of London, involved a request from the Lord Mayor to the Statistical Society to provide assistance in determining the causes of, and solutions for, poverty and 'distress'. Booth probably came to see the Mansion House Enquiry as a significant opportunity lost. With the resources of the Lord Mayor, and the notables selected for the committee, a great deal of 'evidence' was brought to the Enquiry. Unfortunately, the committee conducted itself in the manner of a

Royal Commission. Evidence was collected from public officials and commentators throughout 1886. Questionnaires were issued to those in positions of authority in the East End, such as clergy, relieving officers, and rent collectors asking whether there had been perceptible changes in the condition of the poor and whether the respondent might ascribe those changes to any particular cause. Booth tried to guide the committee into a more statistically sound approach, and directed Jesse Argyll to prepare statistical briefs. His recommendations were noted but not carried out. In the Mansion House Report on Distress we find:

With reference to it [the class of casual labour] the Committee have been much struck with the suggestion of an experienced witness, that great advantage might arise from a careful and exhaustive inquiry into the nature of employments of those who belong to it, the number of persons engaged in each, the probable vitality or cessation of such employments, their trade customs and the like. If such an investigation were carefully made, and a well-drawn report published, it might, it seems to the committee, be practicable for benevolent persons to assist this class more intelligently and more for their ultimate benefit than is at present possible.[17]

This may have been most sage advice offered up by the Committee, the 'remedies' for distress proposed just before and after this recommendation were to remove children from poor homes 'to take them away from evil example and influence, and so to save them'; and to stop charitable donations to poor relief altogether since it only encouraged pauperism. Compared to this reactionary diagnosis and the draconian 'remedies' proposed, Booth's moderate empiricism seems almost radical. As a basis for policy, or as a provider of any real facts, the *Report* was useless. Having seen that one of the few political institutions likely to support the sort of research into poverty that he was planning fail to do so, Booth was forced to rely upon his own resources.

This he did in April 1886 after assembling a meeting of his own Board of Statistical Research. He formed an office and brought in staff, but, in June, 1886, he was called away to New York by the death of one of his business managers. Upon his return to London at the end of July he found 'my secretary and his assistant sore distraught for lack of work from which trouble I pray Heaven they may soon be relieved'.[18] A further delay occurred, however, for Booth 'lost no time in calling on Mr Mather of the School Board, but found that worthy just about to start on a holiday ... till the end of August'.[19] It was agreed with the School Board to begin interviewing the School Board Visitors on the first of September.

During the enforced holiday from late July through August Booth and Potter continued to correspond regularly, discussing especially the essay she was writing on recent advances in Economics (see appendix for transcripts). Her essay was struggling with questions of induction and deduction, and with the nature and relationship of theory and fact. Booth offered the empirical alternative:

Both single facts and strings of Statistics may be true, and clearly demonstrably true, and yet entirely misleading in the way they are used. A framework can be built out of a big theory and facts and statistics run in to fit it — but what I want to see instead is a large statistical framework which is built to receive accumulations of facts out of which at last is evolved the theory and the law and the basis of more intelligent action ... By the way I do not think I should make the possibility of reduction to numerical expression the point as to quantity and quality, though it is true. I fancy that the idea can be taken further in the conception of simple as compared to complex relations.

He went on to warn Potter away from the circular question of induction-deduction (see appendix for complete text). Rather than becoming mired in abstraction, Booth explained, 'I think Political economy needs badly to step back just now. We have had too many hasty deductions and too much cutting out of complicating considerations which never are cut out in nature'.[20]

Booth's assertion that it was necessary to return to basic facts was in accordance with his now developed plan of research. The long conceptualising period of the Poverty Study was nearing an end. At half past seven on the evenings of 1 and 2 September, 1886, Booth and Jesse Argyll interviewed Mr Mather of the School Board and made a first attempt at categorising data from the East End, household by household. The Inquiry had begun.

COLLECTING THE POVERTY DATA

Booth's methods of data collection and its reliability have been the subject of some debate and criticism. Fortunately Booth's own description of those first interviews survives:

We had two successive evenings with Mr Mather on the School Board figures. At the first we got a rough idea of what sort of information was to be had: at the second we made a definite effort at the statement of the facts concerning certain streets. The first evening dealt with very much more picturesque facts than the second, but the second served well enough, and the sorts of streets dealt with are probably more frequently to be met with than the hell-holes and sinks of vice and iniquity first described to us by old Mr Orme, the first visitor we met.[21]

Based on information gathered from these interviews Booth began constructing tables to organise the information. He saw the error in attempting to impose a categorical scheme at the beginning of data collection. About the information on occupations he wrote: 'our idea is that having made our classification we should note down *every* occupation we

Table 3.3. *Distribution of comparable households*

Type of match between households	No.	%
1. Household has same occupations, marital status, and number of children (with ages adjusted and new children less than five years) 1881–1886	21	18·6
2. Household has same marital status, and number of children (with adjustments), but different head's occupation	3	2·8
3. Household has same head's occupation, and marital status, but does not match on number of children	1	0·9
4. Household now headed by widow with the correct number and ages of children	2	1·9
5. Household empty, torn down since 1881, or not recorded in one of the notebooks	43	38·0
6. Household does not match, but is similar on occupation, etc.	43	38·0
Total	113	100·0

hear of, and so make this list in the end a dictionary of Employments'.[22] From a complete inventory of 'Employments' it was hoped forty to fifty 'heads' or categories could be developed. The classification by employment was becoming central to the Inquiry, for it became evident that any data on income would be meagre and perhaps unreliable. After the first interview with a School Board Visitor he wrote in a letter (see appendix for complete text) to Beatrice Potter:

'You will see that I have abandoned to some extent the division by earnings and have fallen back on that by trades. We can get from the Visitors an *opinion* upon the earnings of each man and I should like to find some way of noting this down from averages; but I feel that at the end it is only an opinion and I hesitate to make it the basis of a classification.'[23]

The loss of earnings as a reliable measure did not trouble Booth overmuch, for he felt that occupation as a variable could serve as a method of deducing mean wages, since the variation in earnings within occupations was not great. In any event he determined that other data sources should be used to support wage estimates: 'What is needed is that the Employments should be so arranged as to be capable of research by other means into the facts of income of each class'.[24] The direction of the Inquiry was rapidly falling on his shoulders, for Booth then stated in this letter to Beatrice Potter that he had called a meeting of the 'Board' but expected no one but Maurice Paul to attend.

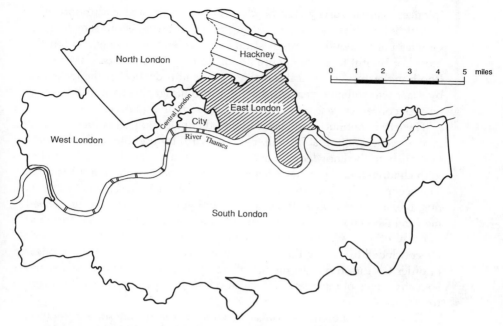

North London

Hackney

0 1 2 3 4 5 miles

East London

Central London

City

West London

River Thames

South London

Map 3   Area included in house-to-house poverty survey of East
London, 1886–9.

At this point in his letter Booth raises a topic which may be
misunderstood. On the seventh hand-written page Booth appears to raise
the question of sampling: 'The plan [of the research] suggested is applicable
either to a complete statement of the whole information touching every
street and every house in London *or to the sampling plan'* (emphasis added).
He continues, 'The "unknown" element will be very considerable in better
districts where it will cover families with children as well as those
without'.[25] By a 'sampling plan' Booth almost certainly did not have in
mind the representative or random sample that would be introduced by
Kiaer in 1895 and pioneered by Bowley as a social science technique in
1906. Karl Pearson was at work on questions of probability sampling
during the period of Booth's Inquiry, but as Kruskal and Mosteller have
pointed out, 'Karl Pearson might have formed the bridge between the two
statistical worlds [natural sciences and social sciences], but he did not'.[26]
Bowley's 1912–14 sample survey of five towns is usually referred to as the

'pioneer' sample survey, and Bowley is often contrasted with Booth who is depicted as either not understanding or not knowing about sampling. As Goyder put it 'Bowley ... used samples in preference to attempts (on the model of Booth) to survey entire populations'.[27] It cannot be claimed that Booth understood statistical sampling, as the introduction of the technique by Kiaer was still nine years away, but it is to his credit as a statistician that he was concerned lest his research fail to be representative.

The letter continues and makes two further methological points. The first is the recognition that it will be necessary to use the collected data cautiously in the knowledge that the information is biased towards families with children (due to the data being collected from School Board Visitors). The second is that the nature of this sample bias will necessitate, as far as possible, its correction – 'to separate ... the young persons and unmarried men and women is an important step; and we can get from the Visitors (and in many other ways) information as to the employments of these classes'. He concluded by saying that each Visitor would need a personal interview in order to 'thrash out his district filling up so many sheets of figures and so many pages of remarks ... If we can *get* the information we shall manage to classify it.'

This letter represents a critical juncture in the history of the Inquiry. Much more than the 'foolscap sheet', this letter lays out a proposed plan of research. Consequently it is important to briefly review the five methodological points Booth makes in this letter:

1. After pilot data collection the information held by the School Board Visitors is determined to be lacking in some respects but generally acceptable. It is recognised that the Visitors may place personal interpretations on the data thus requiring the Inquiry to restrict its collection, as much as possible, to the quantifiable 'facts'.
2. Booth determines that classificatory schemes should grow out of the data rather than be imposed by preconception.
3. Measures of income proven unreliable in the pilot collection are replaced by an occupational classification.
4. The need for secondary sources to support the occupation scheme of wage estimates is noted.
5. The use of some sort of 'sampling plan' is, apparently, considered and rejected. Booth states that the analysis will have to be conducted on the assumption of uniformity, with extra effort focused on collecting data to correct the overemphasis on families with children.

Setting out the problems and plans of the research in this way Booth anticipated a number of his later critics. Problems, such as the bias towards families with children, were evident to him, and were accepted with caution when he believed them to be unavoidable. Booth understood from the beginning that the data which he obtained through the Visitors were far from perfect, he also believed that if he was to answer the research questions he had set himself then these were the best data available.

The interviewing of Visitors continued through the winter of 1886 and into the spring of 1887. A total of sixty-six were interviewed, some by Beatrice Potter. The Visitor who provided the most complete and extensive information may not have been a Visitor at all. She was Ella Pycroft who worked with Potter in the Katherine Buildings as a rent collector cum social worker. Table 3.4 reproduces a page recording information from the Katherine Buildings near St Katherine's Docks. The quality of data varied from Visitor to Visitor, but the preprinted notebooks used by Booth and his staff helped to organise and order what was collected. After the meetings with Mr Mather and Mr Orme which served as a pilot test, three notebooks were prepared by hand with the following column headings: street number; rent per week; no. of rooms; occupation; no. of children 3–13: social status or position; and 'employment of wives or young persons and general remarks'. These first three notebooks were for the use of Booth, Maurice Paul and Jesse Argyll. They began with Mr Bowsher's district in Whitechapel, and continued interviewing through October and November 1886. After they had filled thirty to sixty pages in each of these three notebooks a change occurred in the way the collected information was categorised. The previous system of column headings was altered to read: street number; rent per room; no. of rooms; occupation; wife (meaning wife present and sometimes her occupation); children 3–13; children less than 13; children over 13; wages; and position. The amount of information available on wives and children, and the notes often necessary to describe the family's 'condition' were too lengthy to fit the small column allotted to it in the earlier scheme. To aid in the collection of this additional information, the new order of headings was introduced. Shortly afterward Booth had these headings and columns printed into notebooks. Interviewing the School Board Visitors was the mechanism of the data collection in Booth's survey — the Visitors were themselves the primary data source. Exactly how they came by their information, their veracity, their role in the community, all these must be understood if the Poverty Inquiry is to be understood.

Table 3.4. Examples of cases from household data. Data from the Katherine Buildings – Mile End. School Board Visitor – Miss E. Pyecroft 30 Jan. 1887

House no. (apt. no.)	Rooms	Rent	Occupation	Wife	Children School under 3	Over 13	Wages	Position	Class code
2	1	3/6	Street Sweeper, Dept. of works	1 (means present)	1		20/	regular comfortable	D
3	3	8/6	Carpenter	1, runs a mangle, pays well		1 boy-carpenter 1 girl-service 1 boy-runs errands	35/ to 40/	reg. work at brewery good income	E
4	1	3/6	Carpenter	1, cleans offices earns 10/p.w.	4	1 boy-works on Van.	20/	comfortable now, work some times slack.	D
5	1	3.6	Old man	1, occasion nurse	2	1 boy-carpenter earns 16/p.w.	Army pension 6/ per annum, awfully poor		C
6	1	3/6	Telegraph boy (lives alone – Mother is housekeeper in service)				8/		C
7	1	2/	Aldgate Pension, no work	Widow (alone, receives relief)				Pension 6 per annum	B
8	1	3/6	Bricklayer	1 (very poor now) wife drinks			6d per hr	Irregular work out of work now due to frost	B

End of block – new building, most clean and neat.

THE SCHOOL BOARD VISITORS

While Booth's work is often called the first social survey, in one crucial sense it is not a survey at all. It is actually a detailed and personalised collection of data from middle-class informants, the School Board Visitors (the SBVs). Booth, or one of his assistants, interviewed each Visitor for twenty to thirty hours. The SBV would bring his or her notes and record books (the SBV performed an annual 'survey' in their assigned district), and the researchers would enter the information gained from the Visitor's records or memory into the prepared notebooks. In this way the recorded data follow the street plan of the Visitor's district, proceeding household by household up and down the streets. Aware of possible omissions, the information was scrutinized for accuracy. Booth would inspect a neighbourhood after interviewing a Visitor; compiled data were checked against other aggregate statistics such as those census; and those living and working in the area were asked to give their opinion as to validity of the information.

For the first interviews of the 'pilot' test Booth, Argyll, and Paul would interview each Visitor together. This was done to standardise the questions asked and to agree on the interpretation of the information gained. In the beginning Booth and his staff would not visit any of the streets described in the interview – as Booth explained, 'fearing lest any prejudice of our own should colour the information we received'.[28] Later this decision was rescinded and the neighbourhoods were visited after each interview as a means of checking on the data collected. These checks and the ones mentioned above were sufficient to convince Booth that the data held by the Visitors were capable of bearing the research questions he wished to ask. As he explained to the Royal Statistical Society in 1887:

The School Board Visitors perform amongst themselves a house-to-house visitation. Every house in every street is in their books, and details are given of every family with children of school age. They also begin their scheduling two or three years before the children attain school age, and a record remains in their books of the children who have left school. Most of the visitors have been working in the same district for several years, and thus have an extensive knowledge of the people ... Thus their work keeps them in continual and natural relations with all classes of people.[29]

Booth saw the visitors as a unique source of detailed information, and for his needs they were exceptionally well suited. But the School Board Visitor, whose work was commonplace and well understood in Booth's time, is relatively unknown today. What follows should shed light on the Visitor's role in the East End of London in the 1880s.

A School Board Visitor's position was much sought after. In 1901, several years after Booth's study, over 100 applicants vied for just three SBV vacancies. To fill the three posts the District Board would select from the many applicants around fifteen who would then be examined on Arithmetic, Composition, Dictation, and Tabulation. On the basis of test results and interviews the vacancies would be filled. Once hired, a SBV was paid about £100 per annum. The wage records that remain show a relatively low turnover in these posts, several of those Visitors known to Booth may be traced for many years in the records. (The School Board for London records are, unfortunately, incomplete. Most were destroyed and only 'representative' records were retained, leaving several temporal gaps. It is clear, however, that the SBVs held their jobs for long periods.)

Considering the actual work of the School Board Visitor, it is surprising that the job turnover was not higher, for two reasons. Firstly, the SBVs were sometimes unwelcome among the people they visited, and secondly, they had a tremendous workload. The lack of popularity may be traced to the consequences of compulsory education. In 1871 the London School Board, under powers bestowed by the 1870 Education Act, passed by-laws which would enforce compulsory attendance in school and a fee-paying system. The by-law applied only to those schools charging less than 9d. per week, in other words, it was aimed at working class children who were expected to pay 1d or 2d per week. But, as Lewis notes, 'poverty was not accepted as a legitimate excuse for absence'.[30] It was within the power of the School board to waive the fees of poor pupils, but the Board neglected to take the next step (though it could have legally done so) of opening free schools. Paupers were provided for under an earlier law which required school attendance as a condition of outdoor relief to parents, and the retention of a fee-paying system for the remainder of the population had much to do with the policy of separating the deserving from the undeserving poor.[31] School fees were to be paid to the teacher at the beginning of each week. In London the fees averaged 2d per week and if two children attended from the same family, the second would pay one half the fee unless the school only charged 1d.[32] Many Visitors and commentators of the time pointed out that weekly fees paid for three of four children amounted to 6d or 8d, a large sum when total family income would often be less than a pound, or 6s to 10s for a widow. It was this combination of compulsory attendance with the requirement of fees that made the School Board Visitor more than just an attendance officer.

If the fee was not paid, the Board could exclude the child and then prosecute the parents for the child's absence. This procedure actually added to the number of absences, yet free schools were not established for two main reasons. Firstly, free schools, in the opinion of some officials, would be accessible to an undesirable element of 'gutter children'. Secondly, free schooling was seen by the Board as setting a dangerous precedent which would lead to a call for 'free breakfasts and dinners; free houses and free clothes'.[33]

This chary approach extended to the remittance of fees as well. A number of board members could not believe that the poor were unable to pay the 'school pence'. If they could not, then they were paupers, and should appeal to the Guardians for relief under the Poor Law. The Board saw its work as the problem of ignorance, poverty would be left to the charities and the Poor Law Guardians. On the other side, the parents were not necessarily convinced that compulsory education was a good thing, for it prevented their children from working and bringing home much-needed income, it required a regular weekly outlay (whether the breadwinner was working or not), and many of the subjects taught at the Board school had little practical value.[34]

The School Board Visitor operated between the Board and the parents, charged with gathering exactly that information concerning family poverty which the Board had said was not its concern. Beginning in 1873, whenever a family was being 'visited' for whatever reason:

a common application form was used for the first time to ascertain the family's means, sources of income and rent, whether the breadwinner was unemployed, his prospects of getting work and whether the family had previously requested remission or payment of fees. Visitors were urged to pursue their inquiries with neighbours and employers in order to verify their evidence.[35]

If visited because of a child's absence from school, the parent might then be required to attend a 'B' meeting of the Divisional Committee. The same procedure was followed if the parents were in violation of the bye-laws, in arrears with school fees, or simply applying for a remission of fees. These meetings could be harsh on the parents, who were often required to attend during working hours and were then cross-examined by a board of officers as to the family budget and the personal details of family relationships.

To reduce their liability, parents would sometimes refuse the legal obligation to supply information. Children found in the streets during school hours could not be legally detained, and might also refuse to inform or choose to misinform the SBV.[36] In most areas, and especially in the Southwark and Tower Hamlets districts, parents and children were often so transient as to escape registration altogether.

At their annual conferences the SBVs would discuss the difficult aspects of their work. One speech, reported from the 1885 conference, described West Lambeth:

In one row of houses which he visited with a colleague, out of 108 children, only seven were on the rolls of any school, and the police told him it was unsafe on a Saturday or a Sunday for any constable to go single-handed into that quarter. The attendance officers had to go into places like that; and it was much the same in other large towns. (Hear, hear.)[37]

In addition to the physical threat was the ever present risk of disease and of carrying infection home. In an address to the 1886 conference entitled 'Compulsory Education and its Difficulties', a SBV from South Hackney described some of the homes he visited:

I had to stoop to enter the doorways, and go down two or three steps to enter the room, the number of steps depending very much on the accumulation of filth outside ... When the doors of these shanties were opened, one always noticed that both parent and children were all more or less bleareyed, and pale as death, indeed death is rarely absent from these hovels. In other parts of this district I had many families living in the basement under the pavement, or packed together in small rooms like herrings in a barrel. One was almost stifled in attempting to enter such places ... Think of the reeking stench that fills these staircases, and then you will but faintly realise what it is to enter such places as these.[38]

While difficult for the Visitor, it is obvious from these accounts that Booth had selected excellent informants to learn about the poorest families. As the SBV Pritchard mentioned above 'out of 108 children, only seven were on the rolls' – it is important that it was the SBV who was aware, if no one else was, of the existence of the 'extra' 101 children and their families. The School Board Visitors' brief included an order to register all children who were coming up to school age, and to locate these children they performed the 'house-to-house' visitation Booth described, in doing so they were much more cognisant of all types of households (including these without children) in their areas than were, for example, the Charity Organisation Society visitors who only looked in on those who applied for relief.

Despite the efforts of the SBVs children were often kept home from school depending on the financial and labour needs of the family. Another popular reason given for keeping children from school was the brain-taxing effect of education:

'When you go to a parent to make enquiries why the child is absent from school, you are told the child is suffering from over-pressure. "And what do you mean by that, Mrs Smith?" you ask. "Well, do you see, sir, there's Bill – he keeps a-waking up at nights, a-talking about his sums, and he gets up in bed and looks so wild-eyed, and don't seem to know what he's a-doing of; and as for little Bessie, why she is alus a-dreaming and a-saying her bits of poe'ry she learns at the Board school, and she don't seem right at all, sir. So I says to my old man as the schooling was too much for them.[39]

Clearly the position of the SBV was difficult, caught between a strict and, at times, paradoxical Board and suspicious parents. The School Board Visitors were also very pressed for time. The weekly workload for this, albeit 'white collar' job, was a heavy one.[40] Examining their workload reveals eight major duties:

1. Each SBV was responsible for 3,000 to 6,000 school children in their district.
2. The names of these children were kept in school registers which required inspection each week to isolate the names of 300 or so 'irregular' children.
3. The names of these 'irregular' children would be indexed and a visit scheduled, at the same time an absence report was completed for each child.
4. Additional visits would be made each week to inquire into the backgrounds of parents seeking remission of fees.
5. 'A' notices to parents, the first order to report to the District Board concerning their children's absence, would need to be delivered at a rate of about ten per week.
6. Once a week the SBV might accompany a constable to serve a summons on parents to report to the magistrate's court. Also about once per week the SBV would be needed to testify in the court.
7. While they were about the streets making their 'visits', the SBVs were expected to apprehend any child they found out of school, and fill in form 11A on the spot, after which the child was to be released.
8. Finally, the SBV was to keep 'under surveillance' all children about to reach age five; to keep a list of these children and their birthdays, and to transfer them to the school rolls when appropriate.

These were the tasks Visitors were supposed to accomplish each week. What they were actually able to accomplish was another matter, and certainly informal and more flexible ways of accomplishing these ends were found.

Despite a dedication to the task, the Visitors admitted the strain of their workload. In a paper, calling for a superannuation programme, delivered to their 1885 conference, a Visitor from South Hornsey stated:

The School Board Visitor's work is never done, for apart from his seven or eight hours of peregrination he has an amount of clerical work imposed on him that would frighten many clerks, for this duty not only employs him during the long hours of the night, but occasionally to the small hours of the morning.[41]

For this amount of work they earned salaries which did not provide an especially comfortable life-style. Beatrice Potter described her visits, in May 1887, to one of the SBVs named Kerrigan, a 'most amusing Irishman', who lived in:

the back room of a small working class dwelling – serving for dining, sitting, sleeping, working room of this humble individual, with the most ingenious arrangements for all his functions.[42]

Despite their workload, it must be recognised that the SBVs were not paid for the twenty or so hours they spent being interviewed by Booth's team. Rather, as Booth put it, they 'lent themselves to my purpose'.[43] Booth described the process of working with the Visitors and the notebooks they filled in this way:

Our books are mines of information. They have been referred to again and again at each stage of our work. So valuable have they proved in unforeseen ways, that I only regret they were not more slowly and deliberately prepared; more stuffed with facts than even they are. As it was, we continually improved as we went on, and may be said to have learnt our trade by the time the work was done. At first, nothing seemed so essential as speed. The task was so tremendous; the prospect of its completion so remote; and every detail cost time. In the Tower Hamlets division, which was completed first, we gave on the average $19\frac{3}{4}$ hours work to each School Board visitor; in the Hackney division this was increased to $23\frac{1}{2}$ hours. St. Georges-in-the-East when first done in 1886 cost 60 hours' work with the visitors; when revised it occupied 83 hours.[44]

A salary of £100 per annum placed the SBV's on the lowest rung of the middle-class ladder, but some may not have considered it sufficient for the required workload. Some Visitors were known to 'moonlight', doubling as relieving officers or rent collectors, according to the Royal Commission on Education, 1888. And while most Visitors were conscientious, others were undoubtedly unfit for the job, as in the cases of two SBVs, charged and disciplined by the Board, for sexually harassing housewives.[45]

In spite of the house-to-house visits it is possible that large numbers of children were escaping the notice of the Visitors. In 1887–8, the year after Booth had used the SBVs to survey the East End, the Board appointed one new Visitor to each district with special orders – to find and register those children not on school records, or unknown to the regular SBVs. These 'Street Visitors', as they were called, discovered over 8,000 'vagrant' children in three districts: a number equal to approximately half the listed schoolchildren.[46] When their names were traced through the records, it was found that over half of these 'vagrant' children were actually on school rolls in other districts, but all were playing in the streets, 'loitering, running errands, selling something or scavenging'.[47]

Taken together this description of the work of the School Board Visitors portrays them as a group who should have known the facts on most households with children, but who were often overwhelmed by their workload. A further test of the reliability of the information collected from the School Board Visitors was accomplished by comparing a randomly selected sample of Booth's households with households at the same street addresses in the 1881 Census. Booth's data notebooks and the Census Enumerator books both record marital status, number of children, occupation, certain disabilities, and street address, making comparison possible. (See Tables 3.1 and 3.2; and for distribution of comparable households, table 3.3; table 3.4 is an example from Booth's notebooks). Around 180,000 households are mentioned in Booth's notebooks (with usable information on about 128,000 households) equalling approximately 58 per cent of the estimated 909,000 population of the East End in 1885. Given the gap in time between the Census and Booth's data collected, and the high rate of residential mobility of the time, it was calculated that an exact correspondence of at least 10 per cent must occur between the two data sets if Booth's data were to be assumed reliable. This minimum requirement of ten per cent was exceeded, 18.6 per cent of households in the two sets matched exactly. That result as well as the close similarity in description of non-matching households confirm that Booth's efforts to assemble reliable information was successful. Given the reliability of the information, it is also important to consider the context of its collection.

CONTEXT AND RESULT

Charles Booth collected from the School Board Visitors house-to-house data in the East End at a time of real economic distress. The harsh winter of 1886–87 followed on the preceding year's harsh weather and the resulting economic downturn and social unrest would have accentuated the signs of poverty in London. But it is important to remember that Booth did not set his task as solely to study poverty. He wished to find the numbers in poverty and the causes of poverty as a preliminary to the exploration of the conditions inherent in the employment structure which led to poverty or well-being. Mary Booth writes in her *Memoir* that Booth followed closely the political arguments and proposed policies of the day, but that he had reservations as to:

... whether any of the proposed remedies would be of much avail, doubting not only the soundness of the reasoning on which they were based, but still more uncertain as to whether the facts on which all must depend had been accurately ascertained.[48]

The housing crisis of the period, the failure of the government's response to it and to the question of 'exceptional distress', as well as the changing character of industry and trade in London, would all have been apparent to Booth if not fully understood. Looking back to his personal history and his struggles with larger moral questions, it is apparent that the drive to understand the world which motivated Booth at times also confounded him. For Booth the proper approach to these moral dilemmas was to be formed not through adherence to any dogma, but through decisions based on sound understanding. Booth may have left Comte's positivist 'church', but he persevered in the belief that once Science brought together the full facts, the way would be clear for beneficial social change. By June 1887, when Booth was ready to present the first of his findings to the Statistical Society, his motivations were clearly stated:

It is the sense of helplessness that ties everyone ... To relieve this sense of helplessness, the problems of human life must be better stated. The *a priori* reasoning of political economy ... fails from want of reality. At its base are a series of assumptions very imperfectly connected with the observed facts of modern life. We need to begin with a true picture of the modern industrial organism.[49]

The data Booth collected with which to assemble this true picture were readily accepted in his day. Few questioned the validity or reliability of his data. That this occurred later is an indication of both the increased sophistication of statistical technique and the enhanced sensitivity to the subjectivity of researchers and their respondents. Nevertheless, Booth's data, which have been preserved for modern analysis, are remarkable for the sheer numbers 'surveyed' and the types of information available for each household.

When Booth and his staff had assembled the many notebooks of quantitative and qualitative information for the Poverty Study, they processed it 'by hand'. The published results were primarily aggregations of the measurable and distillations of the unquantifiable. And while the organisation of the research effort was cogent and efficient, the reliability of the research findings must be seen as a function of two interlocking elements: the credibility of the School Board Visitors as discussed above; and the explanatory power of Booth's analytic categories.

These analytic categories have been subjected to a number of modern statistical tests, as has been reported elsewhere. To summarise these tests, in the allocation of households to his class codes and to the groupings which made up the classes on each side of the 'poverty line', Booth was successful for 68 per cent of households as measured by a discriminant analysis. The Simeys believed that, though Booth's estimates were imprecise, 'It must not be assumed ... that the definition itself, or the way in which he applied it to individual families, was unreliable'. They felt that the 'number of dependent children' or the presence of other wage earners was of 'equally great importance' in the classification decision.[50] The analysis, however, showed that it was generally the number of rooms a household occupied and any subjective assessment of the family's condition that was of the greatest importance in Booth's decision to classify a family to a particular group or class. The greatest number of 'misclassified' households (those which the discriminant analysis would have placed in a higher or lower class) occurred within the grey area nearest the 'poverty line'. The analysis also refuted a number of commentators who have asserted that Booth's classifications were unduly influenced by negative subjective judgements passed on the poor by Booth or the School Board Visitors.[51] Subjective judgements were not the most important criteria used to classify households, and when they were part of the classification 'equation' they were more likely to be *positive* assessments of the family's 'situation'. The classification may have been imprecise, but it was not hopelessly subjective, nor could its value judgements be thought to carry any bias *against* the poor.

There have been a number of commentators who have questioned whether the results of the Poverty Survey are reliable and have criticised Booth for his use of classificatory schemes. Interestingly, it seems that the same criticisms of Booth's work are rediscovered in each generation. These criticisms spring from different ideological bases. At the turn of the century Helen Bosanquet was making many of the same points that would later be made by Brown and others, but from the opposite end of the political continuum. Bosanquet was seeking to demolish the concept of the poverty line. As an influential member of the Charity Organisation Society, and one of the writers and supporters of the Majority Report of the Royal Commission on the Poor Law, she felt that Booth's work threatened the basis of moral philanthropy and she saw it as dangerously socialistic. She published a pamphlet (undated, but sometime just after 1900) which attacked both Booth's and Rowntree's work, summarising in this way:

the 'Poverty Line' represents no statistical evidence at all, but is merely a summary of impressions made upon visitors in the course of a visit which must have been frequently, if not always, limited to a few minutes.

This last, concerning the length of visits, was aimed at Rowntree's data collectors whom Bosanquet implies were even less reliable than the School Board Visitors. Then as now the criticism hinged around the idea that Booth (and Rowntree) were counting 'impressions' or 'opinions'. Beatrice Webb later spoke to this point in an article for the Sociological Society:

> The School Board Visitors were going in and out of these houses every day. That was information obtained from personal knowledge, and roughly speaking it would not be far wrong — Jones lives in one room with a certain sized family, earns 20s. and pays 5s. rent. He got such facts as these and then verified them by means of district visitors. I remember that he also utilised the agents for Singer's sewing machines in the same way. He was getting not at the men's opinions, but at their personal knowledge.[52]

Webb was putting the case rather more strongly than Booth did himself, and also more strongly than another of Booth's co-workers on the Poverty Study, Herbert Llewellyn-Smith. In 1895 Llewellyn-Smith explained in a memo to the Board of Trade that the Poverty Study was 'not a house-to-house inquiry', that it was 'not a compilation of statements of the people themselves', that the Visitors were 'not asked to obtain information specially for the inquiry', and that the poverty classification was 'determined by the nett impression left on the mind of Mr. Booth and his secretaries by cross-examination of the School Board Visitors'.[53] These were all points which Booth had made separately in *Life and Labour*, and Llewellyn-Smith did not offer them as criticism but concluded that if the government were to make some sort of 'fresh inquiry' they should proceed 'as nearly as possible on the same lines'. The point of this short review is to demonstrate that many of the same comments and criticisms have been made of the Poverty Study since its publication, centring on whether the Visitors 'impressions' were reliable. Certainly information from any informant or respondent can be questioned as to its veracity. The question which must be asked of the Poverty Study, as with any research attempting to uncover or illuminate social facts, is not just what was in the mind of the investigator, but whether or not the research stands up to empirical testing. When compared to the 1881 Census Booth's data shows a remarkable consistency and reliability. When his classificatory schemes are subjected to statistical tests, they are shown to be internally consistent and clearly differentiating the groups Booth sought to understand. For those reasons there is little point in detailed discussion of the moral suasions and ideological proofs which may be used to question the reliability of the Poverty Survey data. Booth's Poverty Survey may not have been the first true social survey, but in terms of its own aims, and subsequent tests, *it worked*.

Booth's story must also be seen as a key transition in the history of the social survey. His work is the turning point between the social diagnoses of political economy and the embryonic social sciences. The rational and scientific approach which Booth derived, in part, from Comte, stood in contrast to the more subjective and moral measurements of the National Association for the Promotion of the Social Sciences which had held the high ground in social research through the 1870s. The application of this more scientific approach to social science research added new dimensions to survey methodology, initiating what would become the Social Survey Movement. Booth achieved this, not as an originator but as a catalyst. In the 1880s statistics were rapidly improving; agencies which collected social information were increasing in number and spreading their nets; there was a core of educated and motivated workers; and to drive this process along, there was an over-arching sense of social crisis. Into this historical moment Booth launched a prototype for the modern social survey.

What follows is a description of the information Booth collected in the process of researching and writing the *Life and Labour of the People in London*. The survival of these materials is an event rather rare in the history of the social sciences, but one which is very helpful in gaining an understanding of the early social survey.

BOOTH'S DATA

Booth's feat of producing seventeen volumes in as many years has been remarked on many times. He did not work alone, but personally and closely supervised a research staff of three to eight people. Seventeen volumes on a single city, even one as multi-faceted as London, is a daunting task for the reader. And it is the sheer size of Booth's output which has led most researchers to treat the published volumes of *Life and Labour* as the primary source rather than looking behind it to the research materials collected for its production. It would be easy to imagine that to fill seventeen volumes Booth needed to use all of the information he collected. In fact, Booth was so diligent and successful at collecting data of all descriptions that he amassed much more than he actually used in the published work. This fact adds a certain weight to his work – when short descriptions or generalisations found in *Life and Labour* are traced back to Booth's notebooks they are seen to be distillations of many pages of notes and figures. Booth was a categoriser, and enormous amounts of raw data filtered through his hands in order to be systematised and refined. The realisation that there existed large amounts of relatively unused information in the Booth Archive led to the decision to reclaim as much as possible for further

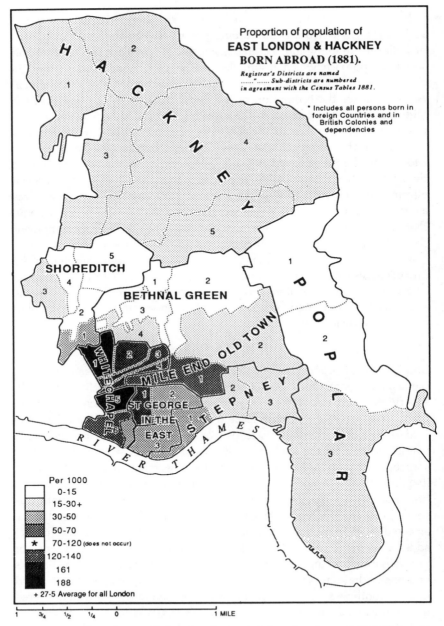

Map 4   Proportion of the population of East London and Hackney
born abroad, 1881.

research. What follows is a very brief description of the collection of information now held in the British Library of Political and Economic Science which was used by Booth to write *The Life and Labour of the People in London*.

The portion of the Booth archive used for *Life and Labour* may be thought of as having three basic forms of information: (1) notebooks in which are recorded interviews and notes; (2) the collected miscellania of any project – collected articles, press clippings, letters, sketches, maps, and synopses; and (3) preprinted notebooks which received distinctly categorised or quantitative information. The notebooks are small, ruled, and bound, and served as the central repository for collected information. Booth listed contents or geographical area or both on the inside cover, often with short notes and the date, which made his (and the modern researchers) task the easier. Taking them by type:

1 INTERVIEW NOTEBOOKS There are approximately (some few fall into more than one category) 314 notebooks recording interviews and notes. Not all, or even most, of these are filled. Booth tended to use one notebook for each topic or area, if ten or twenty or one hundred pages of notes were made on that topic, that would be the number of pages used in the notebook reserved to that topic. The number of notebooks by topic are: religion, 146 notebooks; notes on housing and rents, 29 notebooks; notes on the Police system (collected by George Duckworth), 30 notebooks; on local government, 15 notebooks. In addition are the 81 notebooks on industry or job categories collected for the 'Industry Series'. These 81 notebooks concern 68 industries or types of work. As mentioned not all notebooks are completely filled, but it may be noted as an example that these 81 notebooks contain 5,195 pages of notes; an average of 64 pages of notes per notebook. These interviews conducted for the 'Industry Series' record contracts, hours, rates of pay, production figures, examples of job hazards and health, union bye-laws, work processes, and personal work histories among other things. They cover the full spectrum of occupations from civil servants to charwomen. The interview notebooks also have a system of interior notation, Booth would usually write on the right side of each two-page opening, the left would be used for annotations, a running topic index, and occasionally sketches.

2 MISCELLANY The miscellany of Booth's work are sprinkled, to some extent, throughout the other notebooks, in any notebook an occasional page might note an informant's name, an appointment, or a quick figuring of expenses. In 28 notebooks, Booth has written out a synopsis of the

'Industry Series'. In an album the press notices on his various publications have been saved. One notebook is but a list of community organisations, another, a list of what appears to be every pub in London. These were the pieced together guides to the voluminous amounts of data assembled by Booth and his staff.

3 DATA NOTEBOOKS There are two types of data notebooks. The first, though not preprinted, follow a strict order in the information recorded and concern the cases of 1,457 inmates of institutions. These case histories are divided by institution – Bromley Work House, for example – but the 7 notebooks are, curiously, paginated as one. Each case records: name; home address; condition ('widow since April 4, 1883' or 'imbecile' for example); total number of children; surviving children; children under age 13; occupation; changes of address; relief given; causes of pauperism; relatives (sometimes with short descriptions); general notes – these are the bulk of the case history, and take one-half page to three pages; a statement by the person concerned (not in every case); and visitor's reports.

The second group of preprinted data notebooks is in many ways the heart of the Booth Archive. In these notebooks are recorded all of the information which would be combined to form the Poverty Study. There are forty-six of these notebooks and they contain data collected for an area reaching from Cambridge Circus, the Strand, and Oxford Circus on the West to Bow Creek and the River Lea on the East, but excluding the City of London. The exact area sampled by these data is often misunderstood. In the first volume of *Life and Labour* Booth maps the area 'surveyed' as a quadrant whose radius point is the boundary of the City and Whitechapel at the Thames (see map 2, p. 70). By this reckoning, Hackney, Shoreditch, Bethnal Green, Whitechapel, Mile End Old Town, St George's in the East, Stepney, and Poplar are all included. The districts allotted to all the School Board Visitors who were ultimately interviewed, however, exceeded these boundaries and stretched to the Western points mentioned earlier. At the time the various official administrative boundaries were not rationalised in any way, Booth explained about the London School Board districts that 'These areas unfortunately bear no relation to either the registration sub-districts or to the ecclesiastical parishes, which again differ from each other'.[54] In the second volume of *Life and Labour* Booth explains that the individual family is the unit of analysis used for the study of only East London, Central London, and Battersea (that is, the basis for the analysis in volume 1 in the second edition, and a portion of volume 2). In the first 1889 edition, only Towers Hamlets and Hackney were 'surveyed', subsequent editions enlarged the geographical scope. After that the School Board

Visitors were asked to provide information for the rest of London street by street rather than house-by-house. Booth regretted the loss of employment measures due to this change in the unit of analysis, but noted that 'in order to cover the whole ground in a reasonable time it was necessary to lighten the work'.[55] The forty-six notebooks discussed here are those which record information household by household.

The way information was recorded in the notebooks by Booth and his staff changed slightly as the research got underway. In the autumn of 1886 Booth, Jesse Argyll, and Maurice Paul developed and polished their research technique and the necessary format for data collection. When they first met with the School Board Visitors in the early September 1886, Booth had them begin by 'doing one visitor together, and then dividing our forces so as to each take one'.[56] His intent was to standardise their interview technique as much as possible. Booth was very conscious of the necessity of clear research methods unsullied by preconceptions. He wrote to Beatrice Potter: 'I can and do believe that for some time the *method* of the Inquiry must be formulated and worked before the truths sought are considered, and that meanwhile the truths imagined must be laid aside.'[57]

To collect and categorise the information gained from the School Board Visitors, and to ensure its standardisation, the notebooks were initially given seven categories (as columns) to be completed for each household on a single ruled line. In this way the information for each household could be placed on one line across the page. In the first three notebooks, the ones which Booth, Maurice Paul, and Jesse Argyll used to standardise the interviewing, the categories are handwritten across the top of each page and the columns are pencilled down the page. The column headings in these three notebooks are: 'street number', 'Rent per week', 'no. of rooms', 'Occupation', 'no. children 3–13', 'status or position', 'employment of wives or young persons', and 'general remarks'. This scheme of categories was used as a pilot test of the research method. For the pilot study, 143 pages of notes were collected (33, 50, and 62 respectively in the three notebooks) from nine different Visitors, a pilot sample of just over 2,000 households. Collection of these cases took from mid-September to the end of November 1886. The data collected for this pilot study were not included in the ultimate calculations, a careful check of subsequent notebooks shows the relevant streets of Whitechapel and Mile End Old Town were surveyed again with the improved category scheme. In early December the pilot was wound up, and the system of categories was changed. Exactly how this came about – through a meeting of the staff, or by Booth's own reformulation – is unknown, no record survives. The result was the category-column headings used for most of the research. There were ten categories in the new scheme and notebooks were ordered with these headings printed above the columns (see Table 3.4). The new categories were:

House number
Rooms
Rent
Occupation
Wife
Children 3–13
Children – 3
Over 13
Wages
Position

Into these columns was entered the data which would be analysed for the Poverty Survey.

CONCLUSION

The work of Charles Booth was pivotal in the history of the social survey. Some writers would place him as the last in the long amorphous history of social amelioration and inquiry, others see him as the beginning of a more empirical and quantitative tradition – as the spark which ignited the rapid spread of the social survey movement. For my own part, because of the clarity and rigour of his work, I believe him to be the latter. But whether Booth is placed on one or the other side of that divide, it is clear that an important transition took place. Of course social research took place before Booth, in government, in statistical societies, and by individuals; but after *Life and Labour* there was an explosion of social research. And these new research projects were more like each other than what went before. They synthesised descriptive and statistical techniques, they explored spatial relationships of social measures, and they explicitly or implicitly addressed social problems and social policies. They established a norm of large-scale quantitative social research which formed the basis for the social sciences in the second half of the twentieth century. Booth did not invent the social survey any more than Henry Ford invented the motor car, but Booth's work was important in that it popularised the idea of social research and served as a template for others. He offered up by example social research techniques at a time when the liberal and progressive movements of Britain and the United States were in great need of such tools. After *Life and Labour* progressives on both sides of the Atlantic embraced the social survey as their own special tool for social change. For that reason alone Booth's work and influence deserve attention.

Further attention to, and analysis of, Booth's work is also warranted because of what it holds for modern social scientists. Booth was not a great social theorist, but he was a social scientist of remarkable breadth. The concentration by historians and others on the Poverty Survey has obscured his other, often more mature and thoughtful, work. The aggregated statistics and background materials of his Industry Series are relatively unexplored. The great bulk of directed interviews and participant observation accounts in the Religious Influences Series remain relatively untouched. His tantalising attempts to achieve multivariate explanations for differential birth and death rates by social class have rarely been noticed in the bulk of *Life and Labour*. All these and more wait to be explored by modern researchers.

APPENDIX

We are very fortunate that a good deal of Booth's correspondence survives from the time of the beginnings of his poverty research. In many ways he explains much more clearly than subsequent writers his aims and plans for the poverty study, and his orientation to the nature of social research.

1. To Beatrice Potter, 27 July, 1886

> 6 Grenville Place
> London, SW
> 27 July 1886

Dear Beatrice,

    I humbly beg to report as follows:

I returned to this country on Monday the 21st & after visiting my wife & children & my partner in Liverpool, I came hither, reaching London yesterday afternoon. I found my secretary & his assistant sore distraught for lack of work from which trouble I pray Heaven they may soon be relieved − but I am in truth still in some difficulty as to this as will appear:

    I lost no time in calling upon Mr. Mather of the School Board, but found that worthy just about to start on a holiday or some such diversion, which will last he tells me till the end of August. Under these circumstances I conceive that it is best that I should also take a holiday myself which I am most willing to do & so I count to return to Gradedieu at the end of this week & have agreed with Mr. Mather to begin work with him on the 1st of September. I have also seen Maurice Paul & find him overhead in Examinations & also about to make a holiday being invited he says for some part of the time to the Argoed.

    So all seems to point to a further interval before we get to close quarters with our work, & you see it remains to find something for Mr. Argyle to do. For the younger boy I can provide work in the office below but for Argyle there is very little, & it has occurred to me that he might perhaps be of some use to you in looking up this or that – you being rather far from the British Museum. Can you make any use of him? I could readily explain to him the sort of line you are following, or you could write yourself to him. Please let me know about this by return of post (to 6 Grenville Place).

I have read with great interest your letters to Mary. I could not myself do a long course of reading of the authorities on any subject to save my life, but I must not undervalue the result to those who can – I think such work should be done by deputy as much as possible, or at least strictly divided.

I like your general scheme of an essay on social diagnosis very much – Could Argyle help to work up your sketch of the legislation of the last 50 years – or did you get enough done when yourself at the B.M. to prove your point that 'we are not governed by general principles' beyond controversy. It seems evident to my hasty mind, but people go on as though it were not so – & voluntary action is even more impulsive than political action.

As to the methods of Enquiry. I think I should say that the Statistical Method was needed to give bearings to the results of personal observation or personal observation to give life to statistics. It is to me not so much verification – the figures or the facts may be correct enough in themselves – but they mislead from want of due proportion or from lack of colour, but it is very difficult as you say to state this – to make it near enough & complete enough. I don't think reading will help us, but talking may, & trying to do it over & over is the best plan. The theory & practise must always go hand in hand & there is no key better than a little ignorant self confidence – a humble quality compared to proud reserve, & much more useful.

I think you put the points of Political Economical & Socialist fallacies very well. Self interest a constant quantity & the desire to save the only variable one omitting constructive ability – sound judgement – & even sustained hard work. I fancy this is written in Walker's books (an American Economist) but I have only read a few pages & must look further to be sure; which I will try to do and let you know.

I found Mary very well & the children also – we begin to be fond of Gracedieu & if we go on there shall no doubt take root. I am very glad to hear that Rosie is better.

                                        Yours affectionately,
                                        Charles Booth

2. To Beatrice Potter, 31 July, 1886

                                        Gracedieu
                                        Whitlick,
                                        Leicester.
                                        31 July 1886

Dear Beatrice,

I received your letter just as I was leaving London yesterday. Argyle will be very glad to have some work found for him & took very kindly to the proposal, which I had already made to him in advance, of doing some work for you. I will write to him & set him going in the desired directions & we shall see what he makes of it. If he gets on slowly at first, however, it will be partly because he has still some work at my Census paper – the appendices to which I am printing separate from the paper in order to give the tables to the lending libraries. Mr. Mather promises to give me two evenings running 1st & 2 Sept from

7.30 to make a start on the School board information – which is good. I have also had a talk with Mr. Hey of the Iron-founders, who seems interested, & promises to fill in the figures for his society in London from the end of July returns & let me have them by the 15th August. I shall try to get the printers societies done for the same time & so have something in shape for a September start. Paul [Maurice Paul] has got the figures for one large printing house from the employers side. I think much of the information as to Trades Unions which you need – & which I should like to have also – can be got direct from such a man as Hey.

Your letter interests me very much & I shall be eager to read & criticise whatever you write, in whatever shape you please to send it. Complete or incomplete, rough or polished. I have not got clear in my head the lines of thought or teaching of the leading masters of P. Economy. I get it, or some of it, & then it slips again because of my vile memory. I like your division of your essay into (1) 'Public Opinion' & (2) 'method of investigating and describing facts'. Only for 'demonstrable true' and 'approximately true' I should say 'relatively true' – that is true in the relations in which the facts are used in the picture or description given. That is very badly expressed & I must trust to your sympathetic mind to understand it. It is this relative character or *proportion* of facts to each other, to us, to others, to society at large, & to possible remedies that much be introduced if they are to be of any value at all in social diagnosis. Both single facts, and strings of statistics *may* be true, & demonstrably true, & yet entirely misleading in the way they are used. A framework can be built out of a big theory & facts & statistics run in to fit it, but what I want to see instead is a large statistical framework which is built to receive accumulations of facts out of which at last is evolved the theory and the law & the basis of more intelligent action.

Amongst all the complicated relations of the facts dealt with they must have *one* in common, which is their place in the framework – without this they are of no use for the purpose in hand.

By the way I do not think I should, make the possibility of reduction to numerical expression the point as between quantity & quality, though it is true. I fancy that the idea can be taken further in the conception of simple as compared to complex relations. I suppose that what Jevons means by his 'thing with dimensions' is a thing doubly relative. A desire is only relative to the person who desires – utility is relative to the person desiring something, & also to the means at his disposal. Quality is simply relative to the person who recognises it – a child can appreciate it, as you say.

Quantity is an idea of complex relativity – relative to something else of similar character, while all the while relative also to the person who recognises it.

I agree with you that Jevons' language is jargon & not helpful by any means – but on the other hand I don't know how very clearly to express my own ideas & that is probably a proof that they are not very clear to me.

As to deductive & inductive methods I seem to need both eternally & never could separate them in my mind nor decide which moved first. No induction is possible (I should say) without preceding deduction – nor any deduction without preceeding induction. If induction does not promptly lead to fresh deduction it is barren, & if deduction be not very humble & modest leaning on induction past & demanding increasingly inductive proof for every step it makes forward, it will assuredly go wrong. I think Political Economy needs badly to step back just now – we have had too many hasty deductions & too much cutting out of complicating considerations which are never cut out in nature. Perhaps I need to say that by deduction, or the deductive method I here mean having or finding a theory & looking for the facts; & by induction, or the inductive method, getting the facts & looking for a theory or law.

I am doubtless out of my depth here & I will swim no further lest a cramp o'er take me.

I shall be a fixture here at Gradedieu for 2 or 3 weeks, & then I may have to go to Liverpool rather than London. We cannot look forward now much beyond the coming even I do not think however that we shall have any chance of coming to the Argoed, delightful though it would be. I suppose Mary's first visit will be to her father who is becoming every month weaker & has evidently little more life to live – to be counted that is by months perhaps rather than years, though meanwhile he is very well – only short of strength of heart and lungs.

Mary is exceedingly well & much relieved in mind having got her nurse in the house – & the children & all are well. She sends her love.

Yours affectionately,
Charles Booth

3. Letter to Beatrice Potter, 5 September, 1886

Gracedieu
Whitlick,
Leicester.
5 Sept 1886

Dear Beatrice,

We had two successive evenings with Mr. Mather on the School board figures. At the first we got a rough idea of what was to be had; at the second we made a definite effort at the statement of the facts concerning certain streets. The first even dealt with very much more picturesque facts than the second, but the second served well enough & the sort of streets dealt with are probably more frequently to be met with than the sinks of iniquity and hells upon earth which were described to us by old Mr. Orme, the first visitor we met.

The facts as to 4 streets in Mr. Foote's district (which I think is called St. Pauls, this above Wapping & close to the North London Railway) are given on the enclosed table – we made a rough table to work on & improved it as we went along – the *actual* occupations named are given on the other sheet 'Classified list of Employments'. Every one mentioned (I think) being actually found in these 4 streets – or perhaps some were a remains from the previous night's work.

Our idea is that having made our classification we should note down *every* occupation we hear of, & so make this list in the end a dictionary of employments, classified for our purposes into 40 or 50 heads. So far as we can foresee them we might complete the lists under each head in pencil – but I hope the principle of classification may be made sufficiently clear so that there will be little doubt into which category each subsequent employment will fall.

As to the system of classification you will see that I have abandoned to some extent the division by earnings & have fallen back on that by trades. We can get from the Visitors an *opinion* upon the earnings of each man & I should like to find some way of noting this down for averages; but I feel that the end it is only an opinion & I hesitate to make it the basis of our classification. The character of employment is at any rate a fact & I think that we may so arrange & deal with the information as to this as to make it yield the facts as earnings, in a way that can be proved if disputed. I should like to have the School board Visitors view as one item of evidence.

What is needed is that the employments should be so arranged as to be capable of research by other means into the facts of income of each class – & this will need a good deal of thought. We ought not to make a false start & I have told Mr Mather that I shall delay one or two weeks before beginning the work – & have also called a committee meeting for next Thursday to consider the points. I only fear that nobody will come except Paul & if so we must go on as we best can. I wish you were in London. Could you come for a day? Anyhow you will write your views. Alfred Cripps is no doubt away now & of the others I know nothing.

The plan suggested is applicable to a *complete* statements of the whole information touching every street & every house in London or to the sampling plan. The 'unknown' element will be very considerable in better districts where it will cover families with children as well as those without. In the poorest districts the visitors know pretty well what the people are, children or not, & in any case I think the character of the families with children will be similar in each street to that of those have none.

We only deal with the head of families, but to separate them from the young persons, & the unmarried men & women, is an important step; & we can get from the visitors (& in many other ways) information as to the employments of these classes in each district.

The information will have to be got by personal interview with each visitor & a good many hours of it for each. More than can be had without paying for it, but I think the work may be divided & we shall relegate any female visitors to your care. Once get the system arranged & any one of us may tackle his visitor & thrash out his district filling up so many sheets of figures & so many pages of remarks.

I enclose a letter from Mr. Paul. If we can *get* the information we shall manage to classify it. The pamphlet which Paul is translating seems to be very much to the point & I should be glad to read it (in English).

Will you please return these papers to me at Talbot Court – posting them so that I get them there on *Thursday*. I go to London on Wednesday, going meanwhile to Liverpool. Many thanks for your letter. I am glad Argyle has won a better place in your eyes. He has his good points.

> Ever yours,
> Charles Booth

4. Letter to Beatrice Potter, 10 September, 1886

> 2 Talbot Court E.C.
> 10 Sept 1886

Dear Beatrice,

Many thanks for your letter which is pregnant with ideas. I think we begin to need to meet now to talk things level, & I hope we may meet before I go to New York next month (which will be about the 20th). Our meeting last night consisted, as I have expected, of Paul & myself & we have decided to go ahead.

We have slightly enlarged & improved the tabulation of employments & brought into such shape that each heading can easily be made the subject of a special series of trade Enquiries. The two plans will thus absolutely converge & will fit in as well as can be contrived with the census returns. The scheme thus becomes complete & every bit done will be so much towards the whole statement for London. I don't think the whole work is beyond our reach & I think it *might* be completed in three years. The district figures will be classified according to occupations & the trade figures, starting naturally with occupations, will be classified according to earnings, but I shall try to get at the school board visitors opinions as to earnings also.

We shall start in earnest next week. Paul, Argyle & I doing one visitor together & then dividing our forces so as each to take one, & by then others can come in to the work if they will.

I am very curious to read your paper. Paul says you have found the key but won't tell me what it is. I have been reading Walkers book which seems to contain almost all of my ideas as well as many more & I therefore think it the ablest book I have read. It touches closely on many points which affect us & as I do not think you have had it I sent it to you by parcel post today. I have not done with it & it is not mine so please let me have it back again. I thought you might like to see it before quite finishing your paper.

As to the reviews, there is a good 'discount book seller' near me, 'A Wilson 8 Gracechurch Street', to whom I think you might apply & who would take your instructions as to the forwarding of the magazines as soon as published. They get one from the 25th to the 30th as it may happen. I could arrange it for you if you like. I have spoken to him but did not mention your name.

I go back to Gracedieu tonight but shall be in London all next week.

Yours affectionately

Charles Booth

5. Letter to Beatrice Potter, 21 September, 1886

6 Grenville Place, S.W.

21 Sept 1886

Dear Beatrice,

I am very much interested in your paper. It reached Mary yesterday morning & we had time to read it once through together. I then took it away with me & have read it again. I have made a lot of small notes, mostly unimportant, but which I can send you if you decide to try & place the paper for publication at once. I, however, strongly advise you to let it stand awhile. It is good wine but new, & needs to mature in bottle. You need not touch it, in fact like the wine, it is better left to lie untouched; & meanwhile we should talk the whole subject well over.

I think much of the paper excellent, as it stands, & all of it may readily become so — and moreover I am conscious that I need to ripen as well as, & probably more than, it. So my advice may only amount to the piteous appeal 'Wait for me'.

On your inner thesis my difficulty is that, Professor Marshall notwithstanding, I cannot see how a *science* can be an *organon*, though I can & do believe that for some time the *method* of the Enquiry must be formulated & worked before the truths sought are considered, & that meanwhile the truths imagined must be laid aside. I however am not quite sure that I know what 'an organon of research' means. I cannot translate it, but am supposing that 'method' or 'instrument' of research comes nearly enough to the meaning. Is that so?

I will give the paper to Maurice Paul, but I shall ask him to return it to *me* &, if you do not object, shall take it back to Gracedieu on Friday & give it a Sabbath days thought, &

then if you hold to immediate publication I could sent you some minor suggestions and criticisms. I know also that Mary wants to read the paper again.

Yours ever,
Charles Booth

6. Letter to Professor Alfred Marshall, 18 October, 1886

2 Talbot Court
London E.C.
18 October 1886

Dear Sir,

I have received your very kind note of the 15th & am encouraged by it to venture on asking a favour from you.

I am now engaged (with some others) on an attempt to describe analytically the industrial & social status of the population of London: that is, to state the proportions in which different classes exist, with the actual present condition of each.

It is a very difficult undertaking, & any results obtained will be much open to criticism of all kinds.

What I wish to ask from you is criticism, *in advance*, on the method adopted.

It is proposed to piece together information from as many different sources as possible, so as to make the evidence check & complete itself so far as possible. The framework of the Enquiry will be found in the facts obtainable from the School Board Visitors, who among them, provide something very like a house to house visitation in the poorer districts, & who usually know the occupation & something of the condition of life of every family, where there are school children, in the lower middle class & all below it.

As a trial I have completed a preliminary analysis, from school board information, of a sub-registration district in the East End of London with 20,000 in hab & it is this analysis which I desire to submit to you before going further with the work as much depends on the soundness of the system adopted.

I hope you will excuse the liberty I am taking in asking this favour from you. I had intended to make the request through my friend Mr. Arthur D. Acland with whom I believe you are acquainted, & who is associated in the present attempt; but Mr. Acland is out of town & on receiving your note I decided to write direct.

I am
Yours very truly
Charles Booth

7. Letter to Professor Alfred Marshall, 20 October, 1886

2 Talbot Court E.C.
London
20 October 1886

Dear Sir,

I am much obliged for your kind consent, & now enclose: (by book post)

(1) Notes on the method adopted
(2) Schedules for St Pauls sub. reg. dist.
(3) Summary
(4) Classified list of occupations

The first three explain themselves; the fourth contains all the occupations we have yet come across. The list under each heading will become much longer as we proceed but enough is done to indicate how all sorts of occupations will be dealt with.

I feel I am pressing too much on your good nature in sending you such a mass of materials, but I do not see how to make it any less if our plan is to be fairly laid before you Pray take your own time & do not hesitate to send the most unfavourable criticisms that occur to you.

The clergy of the neighbourhood, as far as I have yet obtained their views, consider the picture given far too favourable & I think myself that class 3 in labour is exaggerated at the expense of class 2.

I obtained yesterday the scheduled results of the Mansion House relief given in this neighbourhood & it would seem from a hasty comparison that, if my figures are correct, not less than half of classes 1, 2, & 3 were relieved. The comparison can be made more exactly when our figures are extended to cover the same area as that dealt with by the Mansion House Committee for St Georges in the East, & may also be made elsewhere in London.

Yours very truly

Charles Booth

8. Letter to Professor Alfred Marshall, 22 May, 1887

Gracedieu Manor

Leicester

22 May 1887

Dear Professor Marshall,

I am very much obliged to you for sending me Mr Herbert Mill's letter & the report of his Liverpool address. May I keep the former? The letter I return herewith.

I have not reached the constructive stage myself, & would rather keep out of it except so far as is needed to forecast the information which is required. I should suppose that suitable members for a self supporting Agricultural community would not be very easily found & that only under the influence of an enthusiasm or religious fervour of some kind could such a community be worked successfully. Its success would be a tour de force – the same capital with the same energy & capacity of management (without the enthusiasm) could in any other field of industry provide a good living for 100 families, if the Capital & Management were given gratis. And at best, with capital & management given & religious enthusiasm to boot, I doubt if more than a bare subsistence would be got out of an agricultural community growing their own food & spinning their own clothes.

Your analysis of London industry (in 'The Housing of the London Poor') seems to me admirable & the constructive portion of your paper is of very great interest to me. I trust we may meet again sometime, as there are many points which I should like further developed, & I should be glad to learn in what ways I could work for you while continuing my East End Enquiry.

My plan is to let the secretaries go on with the Hackney Division, which contains another 400,000 people & completes the East End, doing it on much the same plan as I have used for Tower Hamlets, but with some improvements & to apply to the whole East End an investigation into the leading industries & into the habits of life as well as industry of the different classes.

I shall not open up any new problem but simply enlarge the total field to which the special work will apply.

Yours sincerely

Charles Booth

Transcription of the 'Foolscap Sheet' upon which Booth set out the aims of the Poverty Survey, April 1886.

GENERAL AIM To connect poverty & well-being with Conditions of Employment.

INCIDENTALLY To describe the industrial peculiarities of London (& of modern times generally) both as to character of work & character of workers & the influences which act upon both.

(Subjects)   Points)

I Industrial peculiarities
  Generally

  (a) Organic character & interdependence
    (1) classification
    (2)
    (3)
    (4)
  (b) Official interferences & abnormal condition
    (1) Factory Legislation
    (2) 'Fair Wages for public contracts
    (3) charitable work e.g. for the blind or in homes
    (4)
  (c) Organization of workers
    (1) employers associations
    (2) trades unions
    (3) arbitration
    (4) Cooperation & profit sharing
  (d) Cost of production
    (1) Apportionment
    (2) Increase or decrease
    (3) Race for cheapness
    (4) utilisation of by-products
  (e) Specialisation of effort
    (1) Division of labour
    (2) Interchangeability of labour
    (3)
    (4)
  (f) Captainship
    (1) status of manual labour
    (2) Efficiency of Labour

(3) making and finding a market
(4) Profit
(g) Small vs. large employers
  (1) Elasticity v. rigidity (adaptability)
  (2) Personal v. impersonal relations
    a. with customers
    b. with men employed
  (3) Adequate & inadequate capital
(h) machinery of distribution
  (1) middlemen
  (2) making for stock
  (3) Speculative trading
  (4) Bankruptcy
(i) Character of demand
  (1) Effect of fashion
  (2) Seasons
  (3) Displacement of one article by another
  (4) Expansion & contraction of trade
(j) Trade abuses
  (1) as concern the consumer
  (2) as concern the worker
  (3)
(k) Comparative mobility of capital & labour

NOTES

1 Philip Abrams, *The Origins of British Sociology* (Chicago: University of Chicago Press, 1968).
2 Beatrice Webb, *My Apprenticeship* (London: Longmans, 1926), p. 170.
3 T. S. Simey and M. B. Simey, *Charles Booth: Social Scientist* (London: Oxford University Press, 1960), p. 252.
4 Charles Booth, *Labour and Life of the People of London*, vol. 1: *East London* (London: Williams and Norgate, 1889), p. 25.
5 Mary Booth, *Charles Booth: A Memoir* (London: Macmillan, 1916), p. 16.
6 M. Booth, *A Memoir*, p. 16.
7 Charles Booth, 'Occupations of the People of the United Kingdom, 1801–81', *Journal of the Royal Statistical Society*, 49 (1886), 350.
8 Booth, 'Occupations', p. 438.
9 Booth 'Occupations', p. 444.
10 The role of Mary Booth in the production of *The Life and Labour of the People of London*, and Charles Booth's other projects, has not been properly recognised. This is in part due to her own insistence, and to the way she diminished her contribution in the *Memoir* of Charles Booth's life which she published just after his death in 1916. In reality, Charles and Mary Booth were true collaborators in social research. They

discussed the research, its philosophical underpinnings, its policy implications, and its various methodologies regularly from its inception. Mary Booth carried out large sections of research, particularly in the review and summarising of related literature. Two examples will suffice: when Marx's *Capital* was published in English she took on the task of reading and summarising it so that she and Charles might discuss it and its implications; and when Charles Booth moved part of his staff into research on the aged poor, Mary Booth collected and analysed information on the pension schemes established in other countries and the state of the elderly populations. Mary Booth also edited all of Booth's writing and wrote or re-wrote significant sections. She studiously avoided any recognition of this, but examination of the original manuscripts often show that when Charles Booth's often lacklustre prose becomes suddenly lively and colourful it is because Mary Booth has written or re-written it. There are other discussions of Mary Booth in Simey, *Charles Booth* and in B. Norman-Butler, *Victorian Aspirations: the life and labour of Charles Booth and Mary Booth* (London: Allen & Unwin, 1972).

11 Passfield Papers, (Papers of Beatrice Webb) Archive of the British Library of Political and Economical Sciences, London.
12 Booth Collection, Archive of the British Library of Political and Economic Sciences, London.
13 Simey and Simey, *Charles Booth*, p. 79.
14 Letters, quoted in Norman Mackenzie and Jeanne MacKenzie, *The Diary of Beatrice Webb: Volume 1* (London: Virago, 1982), p. 55.
15 Quoted in MacKenzie and Mackenzie, *Diary*, p. 56.
16 Quoted in MacKenzie and MacKenzie, *Diary*, p. 166.
17 *Mansion House Report on Distress* (London: The Corporation of London, 1886), p. 13.
18 Booth to B. Potter, 27 August 1886, Passfield Papers (Papers of Beatrice Webb), Archive of the British Library of Political and Economic Sciences, London.
19 Booth to B. Potter, 27 August, 1886, Passfield Papers.
20 Booth Collection, Archive of the University of London, Institute of Historical Research, London. Senate House, I/1308 (iii).
21 Passfield Papers, 5 September, 1866; see appendix for complete text.
22 Passfield Papers.
23 Passfield Papers.
24 Passfield Papers.
25 Passfield Papers.
26 William Kruskal and Frederick Mosteller, 'Representative Sampling IV: The History of the Concept in Statistics. 1895–1939', *International Statistical Review*, 48 (1980), 170.
27 Quoted in Adam Kuper and Jessica Kuper (eds.), *Social Science Encyclopaedia* (London: Routledge, 1985), p. 722.
28 Booth, *Labour and Life*, I, p. 25.
29 Charles Booth, 'The Inhabitants of Tower Hamlets (School Board Division), Their Condition and Occupations', *Journal of the Royal Statistical Society*, 50 (1887), 327.
30 Jane Lewis, 'Parents, Children, School Fees and the London School Board', *History of Education*, 11 (1982), 291.
31 Lewis, 'Parents', p. 292.

32 D. Rubenstein, 'School Attendance in London, 1870–1906', *Occasional Papers in Social History* (Hull), 1 (1969).

33 E. J. Tabrum, quoted in Lewis, 'Parents'.

34 *School Board Chronicle* (December, 1872). Drawn from report in School Board Chronicle of annual meeting, discussed in Lewis, 'Parents'.

35 Lewis, 'Parents', p. 297.

36 T. D. Morgan, 'Truant Schools of the School Board of London', MA thesis, University of London, 1956.

37 J. Pritchard, in *School Board Chronicle* (October, 1885).

38 R. Massey, in *School Board Chronicle* (May, 1886).

39 Massey, in *School Board Chronicle*.

40 Lewis, 'Parents'; Morgan, 'Truant Schools'; SBL Records 1886–1901.

41 C. Battson, in *School Board Chronicle* (October, 1885).

42 MacKenzie and Mackenzie, *Diary*, p. 205.

43 Booth, *Labour and Life*, I, p. 26.

44 Booth, *Life and Labour* (2nd edn, 1892), I, p. 25.

45 SBL Records, 1903.

46 SBL Records, 1888.

47 Morgan, 'Truant Schools', p. 97.

48 M. Booth, *Memoir*, p. 16

49 Booth, 'Inhabitants of Tower Hamlets', p. 276.

50 Simey and Simey, *Charles Booth*, p. 187.

51 John Brown, 'Charles Booth and Labour Colonies. 1889–1905', *Economic History Review*, 21 (1968), 345–59; Michael Cullen, 'Charles Booth's Poverty Survey: Some New Approaches', in *The Search for Wealth and Stability: Essays in Economics and Social History Presented to M. W. Flinn*, ed. T. C. Smout (London: Macmillian, 1979).

52 Beatrice Webb, 'Methods of Investigation', *Sociological Papers*, 3 (1907), 348.

53 H. Llewellyn Smith, 'Memorandum on the Unemployed', 23 Jan. 1895, CAB 37/38; PRO.

54 Booth, *Life and Labour*, II, p. 16.

55 Booth, *Life and Labour*, II, p. 2.

56 Booth to Potter, 10 Sept., 1886, Passfield Papers.

57 Booth to Potter, 21 Sept., 1886, Passfield Papers.

CHAPTER FOUR

Hull-House Maps and Papers: *social science as women's work in the 1890s*

KATHRYN KISH SKLAR

In examining the contribution made by early women social scientists in the United States, this chapter focuses on the experience of Florence Kelley, a leading member of that group. Between 1892 and 1894 Kelley was closely involved in the production of *Hull-House Maps and Papers: A Presentation of Nationalities and Wages in a Congested District of Chicago, Together with Comments and Essays on Problems Growing out of the Social Conditions* (1895).[1] Not only did she arrange its publication but she authored two of its papers and supervised the creation of its pathbreaking maps. The result was the single most important work by American women social scientists before 1900.

In November, 1882, Kelley, then a recent Cornell graduate, published a pronouncement on the need for women to work as social scientists. Contained in an article, 'Need Our Working Women Despair?', which analysed the plight of wage-earning and professional women, Kelley's statement reflected her society's sex-segregated division of labour, but it also showed how women could turn that division to their advantage. 'In the field of sociology there is brain work waiting for women which men cannot do' she wrote, emphasising the compassionate character of recent social science.

While the science of man was a science of wealth, rest and self-interest, there was slight inducement for women to touch it. The new social science has humane interest, and can never be complete without help from women.

Women were a necessary and integral part of the 'brain work' of social science, she insisted.

It is the science of human relations. These must be studied as they exist, with patient care; but exact tabulation of facts is the beginning only; afterward comes the work of interpretation. That can be complete only when accomplished by the whole human

111

consciousness, i.e., by that two-fold nature, masculine and feminine, which expresses itself as a whole in human relations. Any attempt made by a part of the race to explain phenomena produced by complementary beings must be inadequate.[2]

Here Kelley expressed a complex truth about the relationship between American women and social science in the second half of the nineteenth century: while social science expertise in many ways made the men and women who used it more equal, it also deepened the distinctions between them. That is, it emphasised the 'masculine and feminine' components of human identity.

Ten years later as she was working on the components of *Hull House Maps and Papers*, Kelley stood preeminent among a generation of college-trained women social scientists who worked not in universities but in women's reform organisations. The power and influence of this group of women outside academic life derived significantly from their ability to maintain their own social-science oriented institutions, conduct their own social science studies, and advance their own social science goals. They only occasionally marched in the same processions as the (mostly male) social scientists of academia; generally they carried their own banners and kept in step with their own music.

Historians have only recently begun to study American women social scientists who were not affiliated to universities — that is to say, women who used social science methods before 1900. The first to broach the topic was William Leach in his 1980 book, *True Love and Perfect Union: The Feminist Reform of Sex and Society*, which focused on the decades preceding 1880. In 1982 Margaret Rossiter's book, *Women Scientists in America: Struggles and Strategies to 1940*, and Rosalind Rosenberg's *Beyond Separate Spheres: Intellectual Roots of Modern Feminism*, reminded us that women social scientists in the early decades of the twentieth century established small but important beachheads in the new social science disciplines then taking shape within universities. Mary Jo Deegan's *Jane Addams and the Men of the Chicago School, 1892–1918* (1988) reclaimed Jane Addams as a sociologist occupying a central place in that discipline around 1900, despite her lack of university affiliation. Ellen Fitzpatrick's fine new book, *Endless Crusade: Women Social Scientists and Progressive Reform*, focuses on Edith Abbott, Katharine Bement Davis, Frances Kellor, Sophonisba Breckinridge, and 'how academic social science helped influence Progressive social reform'.[3] These women inherited many of the same constraints that dominated the lives of their non-academic predecessors. For them, social science served as the same two-edged sword. On the one hand it supplied them with language and analytic tools equal to those of their male peers.

On the other hand it deepened their identification with female-specific topics and issues.

In this respect Kelley's experience, along with that of colleagues – Jane Addams, Julia Lathrop, Grace Abbott, Lillian Wald and others born before 1880 who affiliated with the Social Settlement Movement – is paradigmatic for women reformers in the Progressive Era generally. The more capable they became in addressing social problems, the more closely they became affiliated with female-specific social problems. *Hull-House Maps and Papers*, published in 1895, exemplified this process. Five of its ten articles focused on what might be called female-specific issues: sweatshop labour; Cook County charities; child labour; labour organisations for working women; a description of the work of Hull House residents. Of the remaining five articles, one dealt with 'Receipts and Expenditures of Cloakmakers in Chicago, Compared with Those of That Trade in New York,' and three described different ethnic groups in the settlement neighborhood. But the most significant of these exceptions were an article analysing the volume's maps and of course the maps themselves, based on data collected by agents employed by the US Department of Labor under the direction of Florence Kelley. Yet in a larger sense the entirety of *Hull-House Maps and Papers* was the product of female social science, since it was collectively produced by the residents of a female institution. Thus, a full understanding of the volume requires us to consider the origins of gender-specific social science in the United States. Two dimensions of gender relations in early social science seem especially crucial to such an effort: its institutional setting and its moral values.

Historical writings on women and early social science have overlooked the institutional connections between 'traditional' women's organisations and emerging social science in the 1860s. In that decade social science readily and enthusiastically incorporated women's institutions and women's issues. Women were not only present at the birth of American social science; they came with its territory. We know that Caroline Dall (1822–1912), author of *The College, the Market, and the Court* (1867), was a co-founder of the American Social Science Association, and that by 1874 six of the thirteen members of the ASSA board were women.[4] William Leach has described the multitude of women's social science associations that sprang into being in the 1870s and 80s, and the general compatibility of social science and feminism in that era.[5] Yet the centrality of women in the American Social Science Association in the 1870s had earlier roots. It came from women's benevolent and charitable institutions, which since the

1830s had employed rational approaches to solving social distress. For example, in their efforts to improve education for free black girls in the 1840s, members of the Philadelphia Female Anti-Slavery Society systematically visited all black schools in the city before determining to launch their own new school.[6] Initially, these modest efforts at rationalised benevolence carried no meaning beyond the moral or social goals they served; the technique itself was not empowered or valued. After 1870, social science techniques *were* empowered and valued, and so too were women's efforts to use them to solve social problems.

A good example of the way that women and women's interests were institutionally incorporated into American social science in its early years can be seen in the prominence of women in three of the five divisions of The American Social Science Association in the 1880s: 'education', 'public health', and 'social economy'. (The other two were 'jurisprudence' and 'finance'.) 'Social economy' was decisively female-dominated. Franklin Sanborn, head of the Division in 1887, characterised 'social economy' as 'the feminine gender of Political Economy' because it was 'very receptive of particulars' and dealt with 'Social welfare'.[7] Women responded to this friendliness in social science by forming their own organisations as well as by joining those led by men. As William Leach has shown, in New York in the early 1870s women formed the New York City Sociological Club, the Women's Progressive Association, and the Ladies' Social Science Association.[8]

Kelley's experience as a Cornell undergraduate exemplified the difficulty women had in eluding gendered features of social science. Raised in an elite Philadelphia family of mixed Quaker and Unitarian backgrounds, the daughter of William Durrah Kelley, who served fifteen consecutive terms in the US House of Representatives between 1860 and 1890, she was reading governmental reports at the age of ten and began using the Library of Congress at the age of twelve. In 1878 in the fall of her Junior year, Kelley co-founded the Cornell Social Science Club; her signature was the first to endorse the club's constitution. 'We students have formed a Social Science club which vows its intention of discussing "all live questions social, moral, and political"', she wrote to her father:

I have the honor to be secretary thereof and there are three or four professors who come very regularly; and, once in a while, take part in the debate. You would have been much pleased, I think, with the rational tone of the whole performance.[9]

According to the club's minutes, its purpose was 'to give a broader culture to its members by making them familiar with the vital questions of the day'. But the gendered approach to those questions can be seen in the fact that, as the club's only female member, Kelley served as its secretary; and she sponsored the only woman to speak before the club during her years at Cornell. (The guest lecturer was Mrs Clara Neymann of New York City who spoke on 'Rationalism in Germany' at the club's first meeting.)[10] Reflecting her orientation toward female-specific issues at Cornell, Kelley's honours thesis, 'Some Aspects of the Legal History of the Child since Blackstone', brilliantly analysed recent social, legislative, and judicial changes that permitted the state to intervene in family life to protect the interests of children.[11]

The institutional sources of gendered social science deepened in the late 1880s and early 1890s, when women avoided the political repression experienced by male social scientists in those years. Located in universities, many leading male social scientists had nowhere else to go when they were attacked for political bias by powerful persons in those institutions. Henry Carter Adams at Cornell in 1886, Richard T. Ely at Wisconsin in 1893, and Edward W. Bemis at the University of Chicago in 1894 were among the many university social science faculty who were either fired or threatened with firing for advocating 'radical' ideas. Richard Ely typified the accomodationist response to this threat when he recanted his radicalism during a trial staged by the University of Wisconsin Board of Regents in 1894. He declared himself 'a conservative rather than a radical', and withdrew from the American Institute of Christian Sociology, which he had helped found in 1893.[12] 'Objectivity' took precedence over advocacy as the most basic value of the new university disciplines.

While this purging of opinion was taking place among university social scientists, the Social Settlement Movement grew by leaps and bounds, attracting women and men who continued the older social science heritage that combined a 'hands on' approach to social welfare work with advocacy for social change. In 1891 there were six social settlements in the United States; in 1897, seventy four; by 1910, over four hundred.[13] Most male settlement leaders were ministers. While most settlements (including Hull House) included residents of both sexes, almost all were clearly identifiable as 'male' or 'female' by the gender of their Chief Resident. The settlement movement offered more to women than it did to men because women lacked the ministerial and professorial alternatives available to their male colleagues. Women's settlements and other women's organisations enabled a generation of college-trained women to forge lifelong commitments to social science based reform organisations that were independent of the political climate in universities.[14] These same organisations also channelled women's energies deeper in gender-specific topics and issues.

Florence Kelley's own career exemplifies this process in fascinating ways.

Confined within gendered limits, she and her colleagues constructed an effective bridge to the 'whole human consciousness' by focusing on working-class women and using them as a means of constructing a class analysis of contemporary society. In this way they used gender as a surrogate for class. Thus, Florence Kelley, as the Chief Factory Inspector of the State of Illinois in the years when *Hull-House Maps and Papers* was published, was appointed primarily because of her expertise in combatting the spread of sweatshop labour in Chicago, a phenomenon associated with wage-earning women and children. She extended that expertise to critique of the working conditions of men, but her political-social-rhetorical base was female.[15]

Hull-House Maps and Papers exemplified this base. In it Kelley and her colleagues combined female-specific issues with social science methods to move themselves closer to the center of political power. The main power of Social Science in their hands was its ability to explain the causes of social ills. Kelley's co-authored essay on child labour, for example, summarised data about the industrial employment of children in the US: 'it is not where labor is scarce, but where competition for work is keenest, that the percent of children is largest in the total number employed'.[16] Her causal explanation led to policy suggestions. For example, she concluded: 'there has been and can be no improvement in wages while tenement-house manufacture is tolerated'. Thus, like men, women used social science to gain leverage for particular policies in the public domain. Yet while women participated in social science 'discourse' as equals with men, they worked within their own institutions, and maintained their own legislative programme.

Important as this institutional perspective is on the history of early women social scientists in the United States, however, it is not the whole story. It explains why women were active within American social science, but it cannot explain why Kelley and her group put social science methods to such effective use in shaping the transition from the 'liberal' state of the early nineteenth century to the regulatory 'positive' state of the early twentieth century. It explains their presence within social science, but not their power in the polity.

One important source of their power, which has been under-appreciated in our understanding of social science in general and of women social scientists in particular, was the moral emphasis within early social science in the United States. Entrenched traditions of limited government in the US meant that social science was not only an important arm of public policy but also a crucial means of overturning the fundamental premises of the liberal, *laissez-faire* state. In England, France, and Germany social science served as an important arm of public policy in the late nineteenth and early twentieth centuries, but in none of those nations was government *qua* government so suspect as it was in the United States. Therefore, in the United States more than elsewhere in the industrialising west, social science acquired something of the character of a moral crusade against Social Darwinist *laissez-faire* public policies. The gendered aspects of early social science were constructed within this strongly moral context.

A good example of the moral roots of American social science in the 1860s was Franklin Sanborn, chief founder in 1865 of the American Social Science Association and the Association's secretary from 1873 until 1897. In 1859 Sanborn had been a major financial supporter of John Brown's raid on Harpers Ferry in 1859.[17] Throughout his long career Sanborn linked antebellum moral values with a degree of state activism unknown in the antebellum era. In the pages of the *Journal of Social Science* he persistently urged 'that civilization itself is an affair... mutuality of help among individuals', and denounced 'The chimera of non-interference by government', which 'has been conjured up so many times to thwart wise statesmanship and a decent public policy'.[18]

Sanborn's ally in this moral view of the activist state was Richard T. Ely, who founded the American Economic Association in 1885 for the express purpose of discrediting Social Darwinist theories and *laissez-faire* public policies. At the AEA's founding, Ely appealed to religious values.

We wish to accomplish certain practical results in the social and financial world, and believing that our work lies in the direction of practical Christianity, we appeal to the church, the chief of the social forces in this country, to help us, to support us, and to make our work a complete success, which it can by no possibility to be without her assistance.[19]

Ely did not have women in mind when he voiced this religious appeal, but his emphasis on 'practical Christianity' inevitably encouraged women to join him. Early AEA members included about fifty-five women – slightly less than 10 per cent of the whole, but a much larger proportion than could be found in analogous professional organisations in law or the ministry. (Interestingly enough, women protested against institutional sex seg-regation at AEA conventions, in the 1880s boycotting a separate reception arranged for female members when they were excluded from the association's main reception.)[20]

The transition from a liberal to an activist state in the United States was bumpier and fraught with more difficulties than was the case in England or Europe, and the moral commitment of women social scientists gave an essential boost to that transition. Their ability to construct moral arguments on behalf of less privileged social groups – immigrants, workers exposed to industrial hazards, women and men working more than ten hours a day, poor families generally, and child labourers – was central to the creation of the 'welfare state'. Their task was not only to justify particular gender-specific social programmes, but to justify the validity of *any* social initiative by the state.[21]

This Kelley and her colleagues did with great persistence and skill, utilising their politically autonomous institutions to emphasise the need for state initiatives with regard to women and children. As we will see, this moral stance was emphatically evident in *Hull-House Maps and Papers*. 'Objectivity' did not constrain their language. Of course, some of their moralism was misplaced, some exaggerated, and some downright hurtful.[22] But we need to understand it as flowing from the intersection of their own institutions, the values inherent in American social science, and intractable traditions of limited government in the United States.

As Kelley's 1882 manifesto about women and social science demon-strated, her generation of college-trained women were in a position to make larger contributions to social change than their mothers and grandmothers had been able to achieve through women's traditions of voluntary associations. Those traditions, which had taken shape in the economic, social and intellectual contexts of the 1830s–50s, were ineffective in the face of the scale of social problems introduced in the 1870s and 80s.[23] Economically, rapid industrialisation was generating struggles between capital and labour on an unprecedented national scale, accompanied by unprecedented bloodshed. Socially, millions of immigrants from eastern and southern Europe were beginning to reconstitute the American working class. Intellectually, the 'humane' social science of the American Social Science Association, which since its founding in 1865 had been sustained by older values of radical individualism, now was challenged by evolutionary modes of thought that seemed to undermine human agency. Social Darwinism and its *laissez-faire* consequences for public policy mocked these older earnest notions of social intervention on behalf of the poor or needy. These economic, social and intellectual changes demanded new, more systematic, approaches to social problems.[24]

In 1883 Lester Ward's *Dynamic Sociology* marked the beginning of a new era in which Sanborn's radical individualism was replaced within reform-oriented social science theory by a more organic view of social relations and the impact of 'mind' on social progress. Evolutionary modes of thought, previously the enemy of state intervention, now were harnessed to it. Radical antebellum reformers had a love–hate relationship with government – loving its potential for ensuring individual rights, but hating its ability to sustain corrupt social hierarchies. This dualism dissolved in the 1880s, when organic views of society blurred the distinction between state and social order, rendering the relation between the two as being as 'natural' as that between church and society. For many social scientists in the 1890s the question became: how could the power invested in social institutions like church and state best be brought to serve the interests of social progress – especially in the American political context, where traditions of limited government inhibited state action?[25] Needing more skills to answer such questions than she could acquire through voluntary associations or during her undergraduate training at Cornell, Florence Kelley applied for graduate study to the University of Pennsylvania, but was rejected on the grounds of her sex. Instead, she travelled in Europe after her family assigned her the task of accompanying her older brother while he recovered from alcoholism. There she encountered a Cornell acquaintance, M. Carey Thomas, who advised her to study at the University of Zurich, where women were not only admitted but – unlike Oxford or Cambridge – actually awarded degrees.[26]

Joined in Zurich by her mother and younger brother in 1883–4, Kelley studied government and law. Duplicating the experience of Richard T. Ely, W. E. B. Du Bois and other early social scientists who studied in Germany, she found in German evolutionary thought ideas that countered Social Darwinism much more effectively than British empiricism. Indeed, through her conversion to socialism she gained a wholly new perspective on social problems that never would have been possible had she studied at the University of Pennsylvania. Aware of 'baffling human problems' at home and abroad, she wrote in a brief autobiography,

here in Zurich among students from many lands, was the philosophy of Socialism, its assurance flooding the minds of youth and the wage-earners with hope that, within the inevitable development of modern industry, was the coming solution.[27]

Kelley's conversion to socialism was solidified by her marriage to a Jewish socialist medical student from Poland, Lazare Wishnewetzky. After her marriage she began translating the writings of Marx and Engels, her most important work being that of Engels's *Condition of the Working Class in England in 1844*, a study that placed early factory reports and other forms of British social science into evolutionary context. Alienated from her family and former friends, but thoroughly immersed in new 'materialist' perspectives on social science, and committed to her new life, she gave birth to three children in three years.[28]

Florence Kelley returned to New York with her family in 1886, and, with Lazare, joined the Socialist Labor Party. Her insistent advocacy of the writings of Marx and Engels, combined with her forceful manner at meetings not usually attended by women, earned her expulsion from the Party in 1887. Thereupon, she returned to her earlier interest in promoting the welfare of children through state intervention. By 1889 she had become the nation's most serious and systematic critic of efforts by state bureaus of labour statistics to collect data on and recommend legislation against child labour. Apart from the US Census, which before 1890 was dismantled after every decadal census and assumed no responsibility for the advancement of social science, state bureaus of labour statistics were the only governmental agencies gathering social data in the United States. Yet these bureaus were often ineffective because they were caught in the political cross-fire between state legislatures and organised labour. In June, 1889, in Hartford, at the Seventh Annual Convention of Commissioners of State Bureaus of Labor, Florence Kelley presented a thorough critique of their moral timidity and methodological inadequacy. Meanwhile Lazare's medical practice faltered and he began physically abusing her. Sometime around Christmas 1891, she borrowed money from a neighbouring governess and fled with the children to Chicago.[29]

There Kelley joined a group of talented women reformers at Hull House, founded four years earlier by Jane Addams and Ellen Gates Starr as a social settlement in the nineteenth ward of Chicago, to do social work and further social reform in the district. In this female institution her training as a social scientist finally took root in fertile ground. Kelley's children boarded with the family of reformer Henry Demarest Lloyd and his wife Jessie Bross Lloyd in suburban Winnetka. The settlement offered her a radically different but extremely satisfying alternative to married family life. She wrote her mother:

We are all well, and the chicks are happy. I have fifty dollars a month and my board and shall have more soon as I can collect my wits enough to write. I have charge of the Bureau of Labor of Hull House here and am working in the lines which I have always loved. I do not know what more to tell you except this, that in the few weeks of my stay here I have won for the children and myself many and dear friends whose generous hospitality astonishes me.[30]

Her opportunities for social observation were magnificent. As she wrote to Engels, 'I am learning more in a week of the actual conditions of proletarian life in America than any previous year':

We have a colony of efficient and intelligent women living in a working men's quarter with the house used for all sorts of purposes by about a thousand persons a week. The last form of its activity is the formation of unions of which we have three, the cloak-makers, the shirt makers, and the book makers.[31]

Here as never before was the chance for 'brain work' by women in 'the new social science'.

Kelley's first major employment as a Hull House resident came in May, 1892, when she was appointed as a Special Agent of the Illinois Bureau of Labor Statistics to 'investigate the sweating system in Chicago with its attendant child labor'.[32] She had suggested herself for such work soon after her arrival, but the post took some time to develop. 'Miss Addams is wirepulling with fair prospect of success of a position here in the bureau of labor statistics for me', she had written to her mother in mid-March.[33] Popular furore over sweatshop labour — launched by a woman journalist's exposé, and sustained by an investigation by the Chicago Trades and Labor Assembly — created the need for such a report, and Kelley convinced the bureau that she was the person to research and write it.[34]

Soon after her appointment Kelley proudly informed Engels of her new status in a letter that enclosed the 'schedule' used to record data at the household and shop level. 'For a full schedule, I receive the munificent compensation of fifty cents', she wrote. 'This is piece work for the government with no regular salary. It remains to be seen how many I can fill in a month.' She was expected to supervise '1000 schedules to be filled in by "sweaters' victims" in the clothing trades'. Among these were 'Poles, Bohemians, Neapolitans, Sicilians, and Russian Hebrews'.

The work consists in shop visitation followed by house to house visitation and I find my polyglot acquisitions invaluable. The fact of living directly among the wage earners is also an immense help.[35]

Crucial in getting her the special agent position in the first place, her location at Hull House was also critical in her successful completion of this important 'brain work'.

A year later Kelley began work on what were to become the maps of *Hull-House Maps and Papers*. Authored and compiled by residents of the settlement, and published in 1895 as part of The Library of Economics and Politics, under the general editorship of Richard T. Ely, Professor of Economics at the University of Wisconsin, the book's essays called attention to the innovative work of the burgeoning new settlement movement. Uneven in quality and reflecting the diverse talents of settlement residents, in many ways the articles convey more reliable information about the day-to-day life of the settlement than about the larger city. Some residents jokingly called the volume 'the jumble book'.[36] Nevertheless, the volume's maps were unique in contemporary American social science, and they deserve to be better known.

These maps were the American equivalent of Charles Booth's stunning 'Descriptive Map of London Poverty', published in five parts in 1891 with volume 2 of *Life and Labour of the People in London* – a study that eventually reached seventeen volumes.[37] Until the publication of the multi-volume *Pittsburgh Survey* in 1909, *HHM&P* represented the state of the art of social science analysis of working-class urban life in the United States.[38]

In many ways *HHM&P* imitated Booth's volumes. Both works contained maps that vividly depicted social conditions, both were collectively produced. Both were framed by moral approaches to social problems, and both expected their analysis to shape public policy. Both gave special attention to questions about labour, ethnicity, and geography. And, perhaps most significantly, both were undertaken on a voluntary basis by non-governmental agencies. These similarities reveal the multiplicity of shared Anglo-American traditions that informed the two works.

Yet differences between *HHM&P* and *Life and Labour of the People of London* point to revealing dissimilarities in the American and British contexts, which in turn lead us back to the female identity of the American authors. Most obvious were the different scales of the two works, and the degree to which their authors were committed to social science as a handmaiden to social change.

Booth's was the lifetime project of an independently wealthy, gifted amateur whose main energies went into his business career. Though his palatial family residence, Gracedieu Manor, placed him among the wealthiest rank of English society, Booth had a life-long fascination with the lives of the poor. He began his project by outlining his rigorous methods in papers presented to the Royal Statistical Society, which later became the base of his operations. He quickly attracted loyal assistants, seven of whom were employed on the essays for volume 2, published in 1889. Three of these were residents of Toynbee Hall, the original social settlement and the prototype for all others, including Hull House, even though Toynbee Hall excluded women. Booth's most talented assistant was his wife's younger cousin, Beatrice Potter (later Beatrice Webb), who like Florence Kelley was seeking work commensurate with her talents. Booth made her 'aware that every conclusion derived from observation or experiment had to be qualified as well as verified by the relevant statistics'.[39] Although Booth was the presiding genius behind the inquiry, its collective nature was especially visible in the production of the maps accompanying volume 2, published in 1891. For these he utilised the services of School Board Visitors, who classified every block in London by estimating the average income of families on it. Some specific households were visited in parts of East London, but the scale of the project forced him to rely on more general estimates. These were then reviewed by agents of the Charity Organisation Society. His goals were, above all, to compile accurate information.[40]

The Hull House volume, by contrast, was a much smaller production by women who saw social action rather than social surveys as their chief life work. As Jane Addams wrote in the introduction to *HHM&P*, the energies of Hull House residents 'have been chiefly directed, not towards sociological investigation, but to constructive work'.[41] Indeed, it was Florence Kelley's employment as the paid agent of the US Bureau of Labor that generated the volume's chief claim to fame – its extensive and detailed maps of Chicago's Nineteenth Ward.

Pathbreaking maps characterised both studies. This was no accident, for maps, with their incisive depiction of the interactions between population and geography, were especially appropriate tools for analysing the problems of late-nineteenth-century cities. Maps evoked the physical dimensions of those problems and their spatial scale, exposing the realities of social problems more concretely and more convincingly than prose descriptions or statistical charts. Through their omniscient perspective on social problems, maps empowered the observer in ways that prose or statistics could not match. Through their exacting detail the maps of *HHM&P* also depicted moral relationships – the concentration of certain ethnic groups in certain blocks; the relationship between poverty and race; between the isolated brothel district and the rest of the ward; between the very poor who lived in crowded, airless rooms in the rear of tenements and those with more resources in the front; between the observer and the observed. If in many respects social science replaced religion as the interpreter of moral priorities, maps best exemplified this substitution. They conveyed more than information. They also communicated moral imperatives. If this was true of maps generally, it was doubly true of the magnificent scale of the five Booth and two *HHM&P* maps, which measured twenty-four by twenty-two inches and forty-five by fourteen inches respectively.

Revealingly, whereas Booth's maps resulted from a master plan for mapping poverty throughout London, *HHM&P*'s maps were a spin-off of Florence Kelley's very practical need for an income capable of supporting her and her children while she campaigned against sweatshop labor in Chicago. She described her routine to Henry Demarest Lloyd in November, 1892, with only a passing reference to the work for Carroll Wright and the US Department of Labor that would eventually produce the remarkable maps of *Hull-House Maps and Papers*:

> I have swarmed off from Hull House into a flat nearby with my mother and my bairns ... I am teaching in the Polk Street Night School Monday to Friday evening inclusive. By day I am a 'temporary agent' in the employ of the Department of Labor – Carroll D. Wright – and, on Dec. 4 (Sunday) I go to Geneva [Illinois], Dec. 11th to Madison to tout for Hull House under the auspices of Mr. Ely, and Dec. 17th and 18th to Oak Park to speak on Hull House and the Sweating System on Sat. and Sunday eves. Me Voila! There is only a limited amount of me at best; and, such as it is, it works twelve hours on weekdays for 'grub and debts' and on Sundays it goes out of town to tell the outlying public how life looks in the nineteenth. By way of consoling the small fry for these absences I take one with me. Puss [Margaret, her daughter] is going to Geneva and Ko [Nicholas, her son] to Madison with me.[42]

Although Booth resided briefly in working-class London neighbourhoods, and although he utilised the aid of settlement residents, his work was not undertaken in the heat of the battle for social change. Kelley's was.

Did this lend any advantages to Kelley's work? The obvious disadvantage lay with her inability to survey the entire city and document the extent of its poverty as Booth had done for London, showing that about 30 per cent of the entire London population lived in poverty. Kelley's work was also constrained by limits imposed by her employer, the US Department of Labor. Yet these limits could be turned to her advantage. Her work as a 'special agent' for Carroll Wright in the winter of 1892–3, lay in selecting the location of the Chicago portion of *The Slums of Baltimore, Chicago, New York, and Philadelphia* (1894). She convinced Wright that his study should focus exclusively on the Nineteenth Ward, where Hull House was located.[43] This decision enabled her to study a small area in minute detail. The labour for that study arrived in the spring and summer of 1893 in the form of four government 'schedule men' and their piles of printed questionnaires.[44]

Kelley seized that opportunity to produce the unprecedented maps of *HHM&P*. The four agents worked full time between 6 April and 15 July, visiting 'each house, tenement, and room in the Nineteenth Ward', and collecting data about tenements and their inhabitants, which they then gave to Florence Kelley. Before she sent the information on to Wright, however, 'one of the Hull-House residents' – almost certainly Agnes Holbrook – copied 'the nationality of each individual, his wages when employed, and the number of weeks he was idle during the year beginning April 1,

1892'.[45] Hull House residents then transferred the nationality and wage information in graphic form onto maps of the ward.

This created vivid spatial depictions of the range and distribution of ethnicities and weekly incomes throughout the district. Coloured keys attached to the maps explained the symbols, fifteen for the 'Nationalities Map', six for the 'Wages Map'. First used in public health maps in the 1840s, after 1850 such colour-coding became increasingly feasible through the development of lithographic techniques. Yet not until the 1860s was it widely used – and still primarily for the depiction of urban sanitary conditions.[46] Thus Booth's application of this technique to measure poverty and its extension to nationalities and wages in the Hull House maps represented a distinct departure. (Though Kelley and Holbrook seem to have contemplated an 'unemployment' map, and collected data for it, one was never produced.)

While the government enumerators collected a vast array of data in response to the sixty-four questions posed on their schedules for each household, and Carroll Wright used that data to produce dozens of tables in the *Slums* volume, the 'Nationalities Map' and the 'Wages Map' utilised only two types of data, but by displaying spatial relationships these maps told more than all of Wright's charts combined. For they revealed systematic patterns that informed many of the empirical details collected by the agents. As Agnes Holbrook put it:

The partial representation here offered is in more graphic and minute form: and the view of each house and lot in the charts, suggesting just how members of various nationalities are grouped and disposed, and just what rates of wages are received in the different streets and sections, may have its real as well as its picturesque value.[47]

These large maps are unique for their period, and, apart from Booth's, we have none to compare them with. But Booth's do not map ethnicity, and they do not contain information at the household level.

In her 'Map Notes and Comments' Holbrook paid tribute to 'Mr. Charles Booth's maps of London [which] have served as warm encouragement'. Although the small area of the Hull House maps was dwarfed by 'the vast area covered by Mr. Booth's incomparable studies', Holbrook thought 'the two works have much in common'. She thought that the 'aim and spirit' were similar, but that the 'greater minuteness' of the Chicago survey would entitle it to a rank of its own, both as a 'Photographic reproduction' and 'as an illustration of a method of research'.[48]

Holbrook told the reader a great deal about their method, for the maps would, she hoped, be of value, not only to the people of Chicago who desire correct and accurate information concerning the foreign and populous parts of the town, but to the constantly increasing body of sociological students more widely scattered.

Conscious of this scholarly audience, she defined their methods. 'The facts set forward are as trustworthy as personal inquiry and intelligent effort could make them', she said. Not only was each house, tenement and room visited

but in many cases the reports obtained from one person were corroborated by many others and statements from different workers at the same trades and occupations, as to wages and unemployed seasons, served as mutual confirmation.[49]

Referring to Florence Kelley, Holbrook continued: 'experience in similar investigation and long residence in the neighborhood enable the expert in charge to get at all particulars with more accuracy than could have attended the most conscientious efforts of a novice'. From Holbrook's perspective of a few months' sojourn at Hull House, Kelley's year and a half residence there may indeed have seemed a 'long residence'. In any case, HHM&P was most definitely a collaborative effort.

Holbrook discussed some of the methodological choices they had made. Where a building contained residents of more than one ethnicity, the map makers allocated space proportionate to the number of individuals in the Nationalities Map, and to the number of families in the Wage Map. Thus the basic unit for the Nationalities Map was the individual, while for the Wages Map it was the family. Yet, oddly enough, the map-makers defined as a 'family' every self-supporting individual — 'every boarder, and each member of the family who pays board' — classifying him or her as a separate wage-earner and therefore a separate 'family'.[50] In spite of this atomistic categorisation system, Holbrook recognised the collective process of the family wage economy:

In this neighborhood generally a wife and children are sources of income as well as avenues of expenses; and the women wash, do 'home finishing' on ready-made clothing, or pick and sell rags' the boys run errands and 'shine;' the girls work in factories, get places as cash-girls, or sell papers on the streets; and the very babies sew buttons on knee-pants and shirt-waists, each bringing in a trifle to fill out the scanty income. The theory that 'every man supports his own family' is as idle in a district like this as the fiction that 'every one can get work if he wants it.'[51]

Yet in spite of this important conceptual leap that recognised the family economy, she nevertheless excluded the wages of any board-paying family member from the family economy.

Whether based on individuals or families, these calculations did not indicate population density. Density (as well as the presence of boarding house) could be inferred where one house was represented as containing 'Negroes, Italians, Chinamen, Russians, Poles, Germans, Swiss, French-Canadians, Irish, and Americans', but one had to read Holbrook's notes to learn that 'sixty men sleep every night in one basement room at No. 133 Ewing Street', or that the Negro and Italian districts were the most densely populated, or that 'almost everybody' kept boarders in the most densely populated Eastern portion of the ward.[52] However, the map did reveal that in tenements containing more than one nationality, Italians or Russian Jews usually occupied the rear, and that Jews and Italians rarely inhabited the same buildings.

The Nineteenth Ward included a red-light district, the substantial scale of which was abundantly clear on the wage map, which contained a special colour code – white – for brothels. The research classified as brothels only those places that defined themselves as such, 'the many doubtful "dressmakers" were classified according to their own statements.'[53] Matching these residences with the Nationalities Map reveals that most of these prostitutes were American-born women. Holbrook's noted that 'few of the girls' were Chicago-born, most having migrated from central and eastern states. Some, however, were Irish, and some black. Holbrook noted that 'in some houses the whites and blacks are mixed'[54]

The maps were not without problems. Native-born white Americans were represented on the Nationalities Map in white, indicating the presence of American-born children of American-born parents, as well as American-born children of foreign-born parents who, culturally speaking, were actually part of their ethnic communities. Despite or perhaps because of her pride in the maps, Holbrook readily acknowledged some methodological limitations. 'Carelessness and indifference on the part of those questioned' doubtless led to errors. Change and irregularity of employment probably generated inaccuracies. During the period of the investigation buildings and tenants changed in ways that could not be reflected in the schedules. Families moved constantly,

finding more comfortable apartments when they are able to pay for them, drifting into poorer quarters in these times of illness, enforced idleness, or 'bad luck'. Tenants evicted for non-payment of rent form a floating population of some magnitude, and a kodak view of such a shifting scene must necessarily be blurred and imperfect here and there,

Yet in spite of these limitations, she thought that the 'charts paint faithfully the character of the region'.[55]

In notes designed 'to make the maps intelligible' rather than to furnish independent data, Holbrook described life within the 'third of a square mile' they embraced. Her own values were clear, and she did not pretend to objectivity. She noted the presence of 'a criminal district which ranks as one of the most openly and flagrantly vicious in the civilized world', and an area that was 'the poorest, and probably the most crowded section of Chicago'. The main thoroughfares were 'semi-business streets', which contained

a rather cheap collection of tobacco-stands, saloons, old-iron establishments, and sordid looking fancy-shops, as well as several factories, and occasional small dwelling-houses tucked in like babies under the arms of industry.[56]

Bent figures stitching at basement windows testified to the presence of sweatshops. Signs abounded in Bohemian, German, Russian, and Italian advertising furnished rooms for rent, wine shops, dressmakers, calciminers (for wall whitening), and cobblers, 'while the omnipresent midwife is announced in polyglot on every hand'. The schedules revealed the presence of eighty-one saloons in this tiny area, 'besides a number of "delicatessen", "restauranten", and cigar-stands where some liquor is sold'.[57]

Most of the ward's population lived in rear tenements accessible through alleys. There 'the densest crowds of the most wretched and destitute congregate'. There urban problems were most acute.

Little idea can be given of the filthy and rotten tenements the dingy courts and tumble-down sheds, the foul stables and dilapidated outhouses, the broken sewer-pipes, the piles of garbage fairly alive with diseased odors, and of the numbers of children in every room, eating and sleeping in every window-sill pouring in and out of every door, and seeming literally to pave every scrap of 'yard'... surging in and out of passage-ways, and up and down outside staircases, like a veritable stream of life.[58]

Tuberculosis was widespread, child mortality was high, and many babies looked 'starved and wan'.

While Holbrook paid homage to Charles Booth's example, she and other authors in *HHM&P* conveyed much more distinctly than the Booth authors their hope of effecting social change. Holbrook insisted that 'Hull-House offers these facts more with the hope of stimulating inquiry and action, and evolving new thoughts and methods, than with the idea of recommending its own manner of effort'. The searchlight of inquiry 'must be steady and persistent if it is to accomplish definite results', she continued, but

merely to state symptoms and go no farther would be idle; but to state symptoms in order to ascertain the nature of disease, and apply, it may be, its cure, is not only scientific, but in the highest sense humanitarian.[59]

Hull-House Maps and Papers was more than a contribution to knowledge; it was a part of its authors' quest for social change.

Florence Kelley and other women in the Social Settlement Movement occupied an especially fortunate niche in the expanding and partially overlapping worlds of social science and social reform in the 1890s'. The splendid maps of *HHM&P* could not have been produced without the institutional resources of Hull House. It drew together the diverse talents of the map's originators — Florence Kelley's knowledge of social science techniques employed by state bureaus of labour statistics; Agnes Holbrook's appreciation of the value of transcribing social data into graphic form; and the availability of other residents (in addition to Holbrook) to do that transcribing.

Within their privileged setting in the midst of the social environment they studied, Hull House residents continued earlier 'humane' social science traditions that joined an appreciation for empirical details to a moral vision of social change. That link was evident in the essays of *Hull-House Maps and Papers*.

The first two of these were hard-hitting attacks on oppressive labour practices, 'The Sweating-System' by Florence Kelley and 'Wage-Earning Children' by Kelley and Alzina P. Stevens. These articles marked Kelley's progress as a social reformer as well as a social scientist, for they reflected her appointment by Governor John P. Altgeld as Illinois's first Chief Factory Inspector. With a staff of twelve that included Alzina Stevens, an experienced labour organiser who began her working life at the age of thirteen in New England textile mills, Kelley was charged with the enforcement of a pathbreaking eight-hour-day law for women and child workers that she herself had drafted. Enacted in 1893, partly through middle-class support mobilised by Jane Addams, that law was the fruit of Kelley's early investigations for the Illinois Bureau of Labor Statistics and the US Department of Labor. The merger of her perspectives as a social scientist and social reformer were visible in her persistent efforts to link social patterns with legislative actions. For example, she wrote that

The condition of the sweaters' victim is a conclusive refutation of the ubiquitous argument that poverty is the result of crime, vice, intemperance, sloth, and unthrift; for the Jewish sweaters' victims are probably more temperate, hard-working, and avaricious than any equally large body of wage-earners in America.

Yet, she continued, 'the reward of work at their trade is grinding poverty, ending only in death or escape to some more hopeful occupation'. These conditions led her to conclude that 'there has been and can be no improvement in wages while tenement-house manufacture is tolerated'.[60]

The same link between social data and social action characterised her co-authored essay on child labour. It summarised patterns of the industrial employment of children as revealed in US Census data nationally and in Illinois, concluding that 'it is not where labor is scarce, but where competition for work is keenest, that the per cent of children is largest in the total number employed'.[61] Drawing connections between child labour and oppressive working conditions for adults, the authors pointed out that long years of hard physical labour often disabled fathers by the age of forty, that periodic unemployment among adult men, and the 'loss of a limb which is regarded as a regular risk in the building-trades and among railroad hands' all led to increases in child labour. Revealing the moral grounds of their argument, they insisted upon 'the sacred right of children to school-life and healthful leisure', and viewed 'the prohibition of child-labor [as] a humanitarian measure, to be adopted in the interest of the children themselves'. This could be accomplished, they wrote, 'by means of scholarships' in grammar schools. 'Ample help to the poorest of the working children', they insisted, would 'make our public schools not class institutions, but in deed and in truth the schools of the people, by the people, for the people'.[62]

Revealingly, this ringing affirmation of civic morality was absent from four essays in *Hull-House Maps and Papers*. One – 'Receipts and Expenditures of Cloakmakers in Chicago, Compared with Those of that Trade in New York' – was written by a novice, Isabel Eaton, who resided at Hull House for only three months. She was testing her social science skills, and did not yet feel confident enough to make policy claims for her findings. Eaton collected information from 'certain leading workingmen of unquestionable trustworthiness within these trades', and analysed it to show that 'the Chicago cloakmaker thus has the advantage of the New Yorker', both with regard to wages and expenditures, but that for both 'there is something very seriously wrong in the proportion of rent and wages in the cloakmaking trade'.[63] Proving more about settlements as a testing ground for budding female social scientists than about problems in the garment trade, the essay implicitly criticised long hours, chronic indebtedness and low wages, but offered no remedies.

In three other essays the link between social science and public policy was also notable by its absence: Charles Zeublin, 'The Chicago Ghetto'; Josefa Humpal Seman, 'The Bohemian People in Chicago'; and Alessandro Mastro-Valerio, 'The Italian Colony in Chicago'. Of these, Zeublin's was the most scholarly. Trained as a minister, he founded the Northwestern University Settlement in 1893, and taught at the University of Chicago Extension School from 1892 to 1908. Like the other two essays on ethnic groups, Zeublin's was more descriptive than analytic. Following an historical introduction, he utilised subject headings – 'industrial', 'social', 'educational', and 'religious' – to summarise conditions, concluding that 'the evils of the Ghetto' were caused by 'the environment, including the wretched houses, narrow streets, and the conditions of employment, over which the Jews have little or no control', but that through their social and educational institutions Jews were exerting control over their environment.[64]

Essays on Bohemians and Italians reflected even less concern for public policy. Self-help among the former seemed to have rendered public policy irrelevant. Bohemian building and loan associations had 'disbursed over four millions of dollars, which is all invested in property by the working people', and twenty-three unions, mainly 'auxiliary to American labor unions' offer protection to skilled male workers. Working women were totally unorganised, however. Other descriptive categories, 'social life', 'family life', 'religion', and 'citizenship' mirrored themes discussed in Zeublin's essay on Jews and Mastro-Valerio's on Italians. The shortest of these three, Mastro-Valerio's, contained ample rhetorical flourishes, but made only one policy recommendation and it reflected the soul of a poet more than the analysis of a social scientist:

In my opinion the only means for the regeneration of the Italian immigrants from the state in which they nowadays find themselves in the crowded districts of the American cities, is to send them to farming. All other means are mere palliatives.[65]

Thus, not all *HHM&P* essays linked social science findings with public policy recommendations. These three authors were not part of the women's social science tradition that did so much to shape Florence Kelley's approach to the Nineteenth Ward. Their inclusion in the volume demonstrated the settlement's desire to include other perspectives than their own, and to let the ward's ethnic groups speak for themselves.

Three remaining articles, like the volume's first three, demonstrated the ability of women to use social understanding as a moral and political lever for social change. Part of that ability derived from women's capacity to bring new ideas to topics long associated with women's responsibilities and sensibilities, as could be seen in two essays – the 'Cook Country Charities', by Julia C. Lathrop, and 'Art and Labor', by Ellen Gates Starr, co-founder of Hull House. However, Jane Addams' article, 'The Settlement as a Factor in the Labor Movement', shows that more was happening here than the 'domestication of American politics'.[66] Women were not only using new methods in their approach to arenas long familiar with their activism; they were also entering new fields of action.

This facility on their part was partly due to the vitality of their participation in American traditions that linked social understanding with social action, but it was also due to the fact that American men were steering clear of these new fields, leaving them wide open for women to exploit. Florence Kelley's appointment as Chief Factory Inspector for Illinois was made within a set of gendered power relations in which no man equalled her competence both as a social investigator and as a formulator of public policy. Partly this was due to her remarkable combination of talents and experience, but it was also due to the persistence of the American traditions of limited government, the lack of a civil service bureauracy in the United States that might have trained men for such work, the dominance of most public sector jobs by political machines, and the tendency for organised labour to rely on non-political methods to achieve their goals.[67] Middle-class men also formed settlements and generated important social data, but most talented male social scientists were shifting their institutional location from voluntary agencies such as Chautauqua Literary and Scientific Circle and the American Social Science Association to the newly-emerging modern research universities.[68] An unusual, reform-minded governor such as John P. Altgeld knew only a very small pool of qualified applicants for such an appointment. Not surprisingly, the best-qualified was a woman.

Similarly, neither social scientists, nor civil servants, nor organised labour, nor politicians were competing with Julia Lathrop's construction of a reform agenda for Cook County Charities. Her article began with a forceful summary of the volume's maps.

As the study of these maps reveals an overwhelming proportion of foreigners, and an average wage-rate so low as to render thrift, even if it existed, an ineffective insurance against emergencies, we are led at once to inquire what happens when the power of self-help is lost.[69]

County institutions revealed 'to the philanthropist and the sociologist alike' the 'ultimate facts' about populations who have 'touched bottom', people for whom there were no other alternatives. As a member of the Illinois State Board of Charities, Lathrop knew well the county institutions — the infirmary, the insane asylum, the hospital, the detention hospital, and the county relief agency — their records, and their inmates. Her fascination with social data and her discovery of topics for further study often revealed a feminist perspective. 'the women's wards are never crowded as are the men's', she wrote:

By some curious law of pauperism and male irresponsibility, whose careful study offers an interminable task to any loving collector of data, men are in a great majority in poorhouses.[70]

Her recommendations for policy changes are also reflected her sensitivity to gender-related realities. She criticised the painful separation of husbands and wives when aged couples enter the infirmary as their last residence; the 'unscientific' cooking methods in all the institutions; the discharge of many patients from Cook County Hospital who were not yet strong enough to work or were 'without money or home': the lack of a training-school for nurses for the insane. But her strongest rebuke was reserved for the system of political patronage that dominated the county relief agencies and made them immune to reform.

The methods of this office, with its records kept as each changing administration chooses, its doles subject to every sort of small political influence, and its failure to co-operate with private charities, are not such as science can approve.

Her enumeration of needed reforms was expressed in terms of profound sympathy with those forced to turn to public agencies, as in her description of the crowds seeking outdoor relief in the winter of 1893–9:

It was a solid, pressing crowd of hundreds of shabby men and shawled or hooded women, coming from all parts of a great city whose area is over one hundred and eighty-six square miles, standing hour after hour with market-baskets high about their heads, held in check by policemen, polyglot, but having the common language of their persistency, their weariness, their chill and hunger. This crowd stood daily, unsheltered from the weather, before 130 South Clinton Street. Now and again a woman was crushed, – in one instance it is reported was killed, and the ambulance was called to take her away.[71]

Lathrop concluded 'that the charities of Cook County will never properly perform their duties until politics are divorced from them' (p. 161).

Turning to nourishment for the soul rather than the body, Ellen Gates Starr's essay, 'Art and Labor', shared Lathrop's moral outrage at dehumanising social conditions. She insisted that 'art and all good fruit of life to be the right of all'. She urged settlements and schools to 'demand time and means for supplying' the need for art, and warned that if 'we turn the fair earth into a prison-house for men with hard and loveless labor, art will die'.[72]

Jane Addams' essay, 'The Settlement as a Factor in the Labor Movement', rounded out the volume's presentation of an alternative social vision based on 'humane' social science. Focusing on sweatshops in the garment industry around Hull House as an example of modern labour problems, Addams explained why sweatshops existed and how they could be eliminated. 'Subdivision of labor and low wage have gone so far', she wrote, 'that the woman who does home finishing alone cannot possibly gain by it a living wage':

The residents of Hull-House have carefully investigated many cases, and are ready to assert that the Italian widow who finishes the cheapest goods, although she sews from six in the morning until eleven at night, can only get enough to keep her children clothed and fed; while for her rent and fuel she must always depend upon charity or the hospitality of her countrymen.[73]

This 'scientific' assessment of the Italian widow's wages was only one aspect of the settlement's understanding 'that in industrial affairs lack of organization tends to the helplessness of the isolated worker, and is a menace to the entire community'. This being the case, she concluded, the settlement 'is bound to pledge itself to industrial organization' and enter 'the labor movement'. Addams feelingly described Hull House work with labour unions, two women's unions being founded at the settlement, but she also noted that the labour movement entailed more than union organisation. A century earlier, she wrote, the masses endorsed political rights. Now they demand 'a share in the results of industry' in the form of greater leisure and higher wages. The settlement could play a useful role, she thought, in accentuating 'the ultimate ethical aims of the movement', since among business interests as well as workers 'there is a constant temptation towards a class warfare'.[74]

Class warfare raged in its most ferocious modern manifestation in the United States between 1890 and 1920. In no other Western democracy were the interactions between capital and labour so unmediated. Elsewhere through civil service bureauracies, labour parties, or traditions of active government, men used the tools of social science to promote what they saw as the welfare of the whole society. But political traditions of limited government, the absence of civil service bureaucracies, and the lack of a labour party in the United States created few such opportunities for men, increasing the risk of class war on the one hand and, on the other, opening up opportunities for women reformers. Women like Jane Addams, Florence Kelley, and Julia Lathrop were able to make the most of those opportunities because they could draw on a social science tradition that informed their practical approach and validated their ethical solutions to social problems.

Hull-House Maps and Papers concluded with an appendix, 'Outline Sketch Descriptive of Hull House'. There Addams itemised the settlement's myriad daily, weekly, and monthly activities, which during an average week attracted 2,000 visitors and 100 teachers, lecturers, or aides. As in the Hull House Maps and their featured place in the volume as a whole, this essay emphasised geographical location as the key to their enterprise.

This centre or 'settlement,' to be effective, must contain an element of permanency, so that the neighborhood may feel that the interest and fortunes of the residents are identical with their own. The settlement must have an enthusiasm for the possibilities of its locality, and an ability to bring into it and develop from it those lines of thought and action which make for the 'higher life'.[75]

Florence Kelley echoed that geographic sentiment when she wrote in 1898:

You must suffer from the dirty streets, the universal ugliness, the lack of oxygen in the air you daily breathe, the endless struggle with soot and dust and insufficient water supply, the hanging from a strap of the overcrowded street car at the end of your day's work...if you are to speak as one having authority and not as the scribes in these matters of the common, daily life and experience.[76]

Thus, as practised at Hull House, 'social science' was rooted in geography and the human relations that geography shaped.

Much of the settlement's work was too practical to be called 'social science'. A nursery for the babies of working mothers, girls and boys clubs for constructive after-school activity, and Sunday concerts could not qualify as such. Revealingly, however, social science appeared in the settlement's activities as a vehicle for adult discussions of social issues. A framework of social investigation and social inquiry provided the context for sometimes raucous debates on class relations. The Working People's Social Science Club was one such context; others included the Arnold Toynbee Club and the Chicago Question Club. A French visitor to the first of these called it 'a club where social science gladly uses the language of anarchy'. The membership was cosmopolitan, she said, 'plenty of those Russian Jews'. She was shocked at the 'rage and rancor' hurled by the working-class audience at the evening's speaker, a University of Chicago professor, and surprised that 'Miss Addams allow[ed] the guests to be so ill treated'. But she was impressed by the respect Addams elicited from the rough-and-ready working men, who strictly observed the six-minute limit she suggested for the length of their remarks.[77] One of those Russian Jews was Abraham Bisno, union organiser in the garment industry, who remembered how at a Hull House talk 'one of the great preachers of the Episcopalian Church', whose 'indictment of the order of things was as vigorous as that of any socialist', urged his listeners to place their hope in God. Bisno denounced this doctrine as a hypocritical shield to protect the interests of the clergy who were in league with the capitalists to benefit by the unequal distribution of wealth [and] the oppression of labor.

Some in the audience objected to his behaviour, but when he asked Miss Starr's opinion, she replied, 'Our meetings are free, and it is our intent that everybody attending should speak his mind honestly and freely'.[78] Addams later acknowledged that 'it was doubtless owing largely to this club that Hull House contracted its early reputation for radicalism'.[79] Social science smoothed the edges of that radicalism. In a variety of ways, some profound, some superficial, it helped Hull House bridge the gap between its own middle-class realities and those of its working-class constituencies. It also demonstrated the competence of Hull House residents on topics that embraced 'masculine' portions of 'the whole human consciousness'.

The multiple achievements of *HHM&P*, like those of the settlement itself, could never have been accomplished without institutional autonomy. Addams attracted sufficient financial backing from those who trusted her form of 'practical Christianity' to permit her to ignore critics who thought she went too far.[80] Salaried university professors had no such luxury, yet necessary as it was to the process by which its residents composed the maps and essays of *HHM&P*, the settlement's autonomy did not put it in a position to publish the volume unassisted. In this and other ways the power of Hull House residents derived from their contact with male allies as well as from their own independent institution. To exercise power of the sort represented in *HHM&P*, women reformers in the Progressive Era needed to control their own institutions, but they also needed to tap in to the power invested in male-dominated institutions.

Richard Ely was a natural ally for the publication of *HHM&P*. He and Florence Kelley had been corresponding since 1890, and in 1892 she had stayed at the Ely home in Madison. Thereafter her letters usually ended on a personal note – 'please give my kind regards to Mrs. Ely'.[81] Moreover, Ely's publication series, 'Library of Economics and Politics', published by Thomas Crowell of Boston, would bring the Hull House volume to the attention of interested readers. Other volumes that preceded *HHM&P* in the series included William Scott, *Repudiation of State Debts in the United States* (1893); Ely's own *Socialism and Social Reform* (1894); and *American Charities* by Amos Warner (1894).[82]

The agreement apparently dated from May, 1894, when Ely told Kelley that the volume would 'be in the market' in September. In June she gave up plans to publish her two essays with a German periodical that paid 'liberally and promptly', but by October the book was still delayed. That month Jane Addams entered into its editorial work, writing to Ely that she agreed with his criticism of Miss Eaton's paper. 'Mrs. Kelley and I have gone over it very carefully' with the result that 'it is now clearer'. She also expressed anxiety that the book's information would be outdated by the time of publication if further delays occurred.[83]

We have letters every week asking about it. Prof. Small told me the other day that he could not 'get on' any longer without it, and we feel that the matter will be so old and out of date if we wait much longer. Mrs. Kelley's office is already making great changes in the condition of the sweater shops in the neighborhood, the Jewish population is rapidly moving Northward, and all the conditions are of course, more of less, unlike what they were July 1st, 1893, when the data for the maps was finished.[84]

She wondered if it would help to have Robert Woods, of Andover House, Boston, see Mr. Crowell.

Delays were the least of their problems in November, however, when Ely conveyed Crowell's suggestion that the maps be reduced in size. Kelley responded fiercely, revealing how much the maps meant to her:

But the disappointment over the delay is trivial in comparison with the dismay which I felt when you suggested cutting the maps. This I positively decline to permit.

The charts are mine to the extent that I not only furnished the data for them but hold the sole permission from the U.S. Department of Labor to publish them. I have never contemplated, and do not now contemplate, any form of publication except as two linen-backed maps or charts, folding in pockets in the cover of the book, similar to Mr. Booth's charts.

If Crowell and Co. do not contemplate this, it will be well to stop work at once, as I can consent to no use of my charts in any other form.[85]

After Ely wrote to Addams that he had lost patience with Kelley, Addams explained that Kelley's anger was sparked by 'accumulated annoyances' from her work as Factory Inspector. She assured Ely that she realised it would have been impossible to get the book published without his aid, and that he would 'have no further annoyance in regard to the book' from Hull House. A week later Addams wrote Ely yet another soothing letter after the page proofs had been returned to Crowell.[86] Kelley may have upset Ely, but she got her way – the maps were published with linen backs in pockets in the book's cover. A cheaper edition was available without linen back, but there too the maps appeared in full.

Reviews of the book saluted its close look at one of the nation's most impoverished urban neighbourhoods. A New York newspaper was typical. It emphasised the example set by the Hull House report 'of how to go about dealing with the problem of congested areas, what to investigate, what to ascertain and how both to investigate and ascertain'. Congratulating the residents for copying Booth, whose 'monumental example' might well 'discourage, if not appall imitation', the review identified the volume's most fundamental characteristic as 'precision'.

It is quantitative – it counts noses; in other words, it is scientific. Hence it gives a firm point of departure for study: discussion need not be all in the air; there is a base-line, or a bench-mark.[87]

The most complete review appeared in the *Atlantic Monthly*, which noted that the 'industrial conditions of city life' had previously come to '"the reading public" mainly through the medium of fiction and the treatment of fact which pictures and the magazines render easily digestible'. The maps of the Hull House volume presented information of new complexity, which the reviewer did not try to summarise, concluding that 'the maps render possible an easy apprehension of the nature and condition of the community in which Hull-House is doing its work', but that 'the details of what they reveal must be seen upon the maps themselves'. This periodical recommended the volume as giving 'a very adequate conception of the work done by the American Settlement which has probably had the widest opportunities and activities', and noted the growing familiarity of middle-class people with settlement work: 'Happily, the time is past when everybody needs to be told just what these enterprises are'.[88]

Samuel Lindsay, reviewing *HHM&P* and two other works in Ely's series in the *Annals of the American Academy* found the volume 'interesting and valuable', and the maps, which 'teachers of social science and settlement workers will do well to study', of 'equal excellence' with those of Charles Booth. Yet while the maps seemed to be valued by 'the reading public', their expense meant that the book was not a profitable publication for Crowell, and it was not reprinted after the first 1,000 copies were sold.

Mary Jo Deegan has analysed the neglect of *HHM&P* by university sociologists, as well as their imitation of its methods.[89] In many ways the book's neglect was in keeping with its birth. Dedicated more to social action than to the collection of data, its chief authors, Addams and Kelley, had many more urgent matters demanding their attention than the reception or subsequent treatment of their book. Kelley may have felt that her own obligation was completed when she succeeded in getting the maps printed to her specifications. In 1898 she moved to New York, where she became General Secretary of the National Consumers League, a position she held until her death in 1932. Under Kelley's directorship, the NCL became the single most successful lobbying agency on behalf of legislative protections for working women and children – lobbying based on social data, carefully collected and analysed.[90] In New York Kelley continued until

1926 to live collectively with other women at Lillian Wald's Henry Street Settlement.

Almost a century after its publication, however, it is clear that *HHM&P* deserves more attention that it has received – from historians and sociologists alike. It demonstrates an important link between social science and governmental action – a link that ultimately aided the birth of what we now call the welfare state. Precocious for what it anticipated about the future of social inquiry, and valuable for what it revealed about the history of American social science, it set new standards for social investigations. Those standards arose from the most profound appreciation for the importance of geography as the basis for social analysis. They also sprang from the gendered features of contemporary social science.

NOTES

1 [Residents of Hull House], *Hull-House Maps and Papers: A Presentation of Nationalities and Wages in a Congested District of Chicago, Together with Comments and Essays on Problems Growing out of the Social Conditions* (Boston: Thomas Crowell & Co., 1895).

2 Florence Kelley, 'Need our Working Women Despair?', *The International Review*, 13 (Nov. 1882), 517–27. *The International Review* was a New York periodical in which her father published frequently.

3 William Leach, *True Love and Perfect Union: The Feminist Reform of Sex and society* (New York: Basic Books, 1980); Margaret W. Rossiter, *Women Scientists in America: Struggles and Strategies to 1940* (Baltimore: Johns Hopkins Press, 1982); Rosalind Rosenberg, *Beyond Separate Spheres: Intellectual Roots of Modern Feminism* (New Haven: Yale University Press, 1982); Mary Jo Deegan, *Jane Addams and the Men of the Chicago School, 1892–1918* (New Brunswick, NJ: Transactions Books, 1988); Ellen Fitzpatrick, *Endless Crusade: Women Social Scientists and Progressive Reform* (New York: Oxford University Press, 1990).

4 Leach, *True Love*, p. 315; Caroline H. Dall, *The College, the Market and the Court, or, Woman's Relation to Education, Labor and Law* (Boston: 1867).

5 Leach, *True Love*, pp. 292–347.

6 Carolyn Williams, 'The Philadelphia Female Anti-Slavery Society, 1833–1873', PhD. thesis, University of California, Los Angeles, 1991, ch. 5. See also Lori D. Ginsberg, *Women and the Work of Benevolence: Morality, Politics and Class in the Nineteenth Century United States* (New Haven: Yale University Press, 1990). Women's institutions enabled women to interact with men and men's institutions from positions of collective strength. Within their own institutions women also developed their own leadership, formulated their own goals, and controlled the distribution of their own resources.

7 *Journal of Social Science*, 16 (Dec. 1882), 98, quoted in Thomas Haskell, *The Emergence of Professional Social Science: The American Social Science Association and the Nineteenth-Century Crisis of Authority* (Urbana Ill: University of Illinois Press, 1977), p. 137. Limited in its purview as it might be, the Social Economy Division of the American

Social Science Association became the chief arm of the Association's efforts to influence public polity. In 1881 Sanford said that the Association's work of agitation and indoctrination' sprang out of 'our department of social economy'. *Journal of Social Science* (Nov., 1881), 33.

8 Leach, *True Love*, pp. 317, 139.

9 Florence Kelley to William Durrah Kelley, Ithaca, 2 Dec., 1878, Nickolas Kelley Papers, Box 66, 'FK Papers, WDK Letters from His Daughter, 1865–1888'.

10 Social Science Club Records, 30 October, 1878, Cornell University Archives. One of the club's co-founders, George Schumann, published a radical German-language weekly in San Francisco before coming to Cornell. After graduating in 1881, he published *The Radical Review* in Chicago for two years. Deceased Alumni Records, Cornell University.

11 See, Florence Kelley, *Notes of Sixty Years: The Autobiography of Florence Kelley*, ed. Kathryn Kish Sklar (Chicago: Charles Kerr, 1986), pp. 1–57.

12 Mary O. Furner, *Advocacy and Objectivity: A Crisis in the Professionalization of American Social Science, 1865–1905* (Lexington: University of Kentucky Press, 1975), pp. 150–158.

13 Allen F. Davis, *Spearheads for Reform: The Social Settlements and the Progressive Movement, 1890–1914* (New York: Oxford University Press, 1967), p. 12.

14 For the history of women on university faculties, see Barbara Miller Solomon, *In the Company of Educated Women: A History of Women and Higher Education in America* (New Haven: Yale University Press, 1985), pp. 57, 133–9, 189, 210. After 1900 women continued to make important contributions to the development of social surveys in the United States. For example, by creating the Russell Sage Foundation, Margaret Olivia Sage launched the single most important institutional support for American social surveys after 1900. In 1910 the Russell Sage Foundation published, as part of its sponsorship of the Pittsburgh Survey, Margaret Byington's *Homestead: The Households of a Mill Town*, which contained the most detailed maps of the six-volume survey, and today is probably the survey's most frequently-read volume. See John M. Glenn, Lillian Brandt, and F. Emerson Andrews, *Russell Sage Foundation, 1907–1946* (Russell Sage Foundation, 1947), pp. 3–12, and passim for Margaret Sage's initiative in its founding and the Foundation's research agenda before 1946. See also map 5, p. 248.

The settlement movement's significance for American women reformers was highlighted by that movement's failure to serve the same population in England. There prominent women reformers did not form lifelong affiliations with the movement; instead, many married male reformers and worked within male-dominated movements, such as Fabian Socialism or the Labour or Liberal Parties. Although the American Settlement Movement was dominated by women, this was not the case in England. Many talented British women made important contributions to social reform and the history of social surveys through the settlement movement: Florence Bell, Violet Butler, Maude Davies, Eglantyne Jebb, and Maud Pember Reeves, to name a few. Women's settlements in England, beginning with the Women's University Settlement in Southwark (1887), and followed by St Hilda's, Bethal Green, Lady Margaret Hall, Liverpool Victoria, Birmingham, Passmore Edwards and others offered women important opportunities for social activism. Yet differences in the social, political, and economic structures in the two societies meant that settlements served different purposes, and one of those differences lay in the degree to which the society's most politically-powerful reformers affiliated with the movement.

I am grateful to Michael Rose for generously sharing his current research on women in the British settlement movement. For the absence of the sustained presence of prominent women reformers in the British social settlement movement, see Martha Vicinus, *Independent Women: Work and Community for Single Women, 1850–1920* (Chicago: University of Chicago Press, 1985). For an example of how the Labour Party provided the single best umbrella for Beatrice Webb, Margaret Llewelyn Davies, Margaret Bonfield, and other contemporary English equivalents of Florence Kelley, see their contributions to Marion Phillips (ed.), *Women and the Labour Party by Various Women Writers* (New York: Heubsch, 1918). For the relationship between the British Civil Service and British social settlements, see Standish Meacham, *Toynbee Hall and Social Reform, 1880–1914: The Search for Community* (New Haven: Yale University Press, 1987).

15 Kathryn Kish Sklar, 'Hull House as a Community of Women Reformers in the 1890's', *Signs: Journal of Women in Culture and Society*, 10 (Summer, 1985), 657–77.

16 Florence Kelley, 'The Sweating System', in *Hull-House Maps and Papers*, pp. 41 and 50.

17 Benjamin Blakely Hickok, 'The Political and Literary Careers of F. B. Sanborn', PhD thesis, Michigan State University, 1953, pp. 135–245; Haskell, *The Emergence of Professional Social Science*, pp. 49, 129, 216; William R. Brock, *Investigation and Responsibility: Public Responsibility in the United States, 1865–1900* (Cambridge: Cambridge University Press, 1984), pp. 1–57.

18 *Journal of Social Science*, (Nov., 1886,), 7 and 10.

19 Quoted in James Dombrowski, *The Early Days of Christian Socialism in America* (New York: Columbia University Press, 1936), p. 51. See also John R. Everett, *Religion in Economics: A Study of John Bates Clark, Richard T. Ely, Simon N. Patten* (New York: King's Crown Press, 1946); and Dorothy Ross, 'Socialism and American Liberalism: Academic Thought in the 1880's', *Perspectives in American History*, 11 (1977–8), 5–80.

20 Richard T. Ely, *Ground Under Our Feet: An Autobiography* (New York: Macmillan, 1938), p. 147; *Publications of the American Economic Association, Vol. I, Constitution and List of Officers and Members of the American Economic Association, Supplement*, American Economic Association, July, 1889, p. 27. This volume listed a total of 604 members; 55 were women. Nine of those fifty-five female members were affiliated with Mount Holyoke College. British social science embraced similar trends. Frances Power Cobbe, social reformer who later became an advocate of women's rights, led the way within the British Social Science Association. In an 1861 publication she quoted an address by Lord Shaftesbury that commented on 'the value and peculiar nature of the assistance' women gave to social science:

Men may do what must be done on a larger scale; but, the instant the work becomes individual, and personal, the instant it requires tact and feeling, from that instant it passes into the hands of women. It is essentially their province, in which may be exercised all their moral powers, and all their intellectual faculties. It will give their full share in the vast operations the world is yet to see.

Frances Power Cobbe, 'Social Science Congresses and Women's Part in Them',

Macmillan's Magazine, (Dec. 1961), 94. I am grateful to Eileen Yeo for this reference. For more on British women and social science, see her forthcoming book on the topic.

21 See Fitzpatrick, *Endless Crusade*, for examples of important policy initiatives by women social scientists that were bolstered by moral imperatives. An enormous body of historical writings, embracing a wide range of historiographic issues contributes to our understanding of why the transition from the 'liberal' to the 'positive' state was so difficult in the United States. However, very little has been written on how social science helped ease that transition. While social science provided an important discourse among civil servants, politicians and social scientists elsewhere, such discourse was especially crucial in the United States where the 'liberal' or *laissez-faire* state remained stronger longer. Social science was not a magic remedy that healed all socio-economic or political problems in the US – for women or men reformers. Yet for both it offered a crucial means of justifying state activism.

Good examples of this were the state bureaus of labour statistics created in the 1860s and 70s by most state governments in industrialising regions. In his 1984 book, *Investigation and Responsibility: Public Responsibility in the United States, 1865–1900*, William Brock quoted Carroll D. Wright, the founder of American social statistics, to demonstrate the almost sacred value he attributed to the work of the state bureaus.

No matter for what reasons they were appointed, no matter how inexperienced in the work of investigation and of compilation and presentation of statistical material, no matter from what party they came and whether in sympathy with capital or labor, and even if holding fairly radical socialistic views; the men have, almost without exception, at once comprehended the sacredness of the duty assigned to them, and served the public faithfully and honestly, being content to collect and publish facts without regard to individual bias or individual political sentiments.

Carroll D. Wright, 'The Value and Influence of Labor Statistics', *Bulletin of the Bureau of Labor*, 54 (1904), 1,087, quoted in William Brock, *Investigation and Responsibility: Public Responsibility in the United States, 1865–1900* (Cambridge: Cambridge University Press, 1984), p. 154.

Historians usually mention four major aspects of the American polity that diminished the extent to which class could serve as an effective vehicle for political action. All four of these factors created political gaps – that is, they generated political vacuums in the United States in places where, in England, France, and Germany, elites, labour activists, and politicians were interacting more effectively to generate new, positive actions by the state to address social problems. I have argued elsewhere that these gaps created special opportunities for women in the United States. See Kathryn Kish Sklar, 'Women's Political Culture, Men's Political Culture, and the Creation of the Welfare State in the United States', in Sonya Michel and Seth Koven (eds), *Gender and Welfare States* (New York: Routledge, 1991).

(A) The simultaneous development of political democracy and industrialisation in the United States meant that before 1850 popular political values and elite-driven economic goals both endorsed 'liberal' or *laissez-faire* policies. In no other nation did universal white male suffrage emerge simultaneously with industrial capitalism. Elsewhere – in England, France and Germany – industrialisation occurred among a disfranchised populace whose political consciousness was shaped by the goal of acquiring state power in order to bend it to their own purposes. Not so in the United States, where in the antebellum era, working-class men wanted to prevent elites from using the state for their own ends; elites benefited from the unregulated interaction of capital and labour.

(B) In England, France, and Germany traditions of positive government combined with traditions of elite governance to produce formidable civil service bureaucracies, which led the way in formulating solutions for the problems created by industrialisation and urbanisation in the late nineteenth and early twentieth centuries. In the United States, civil service bureaucrats were never (and are not yet) effectively severed from patronage politics. This severely limited their ability to advocate positive governmental action to solve social problems, and it diminished the degree to which it preempted the work of using social science to justify positive government.

(C) Massive immigration into the United States between 1880 and 1920 transformed the American working class into a predominantly foreign-born class. This meant that working class politics revolved around an ethnic rather than a class fulcrum; and it diminished middle-class sympathy for working class social problems.

(D) Organised labour, under the leadership of Samuel Compers and the AFofL, quickly learned that American political structures, especially the ability of courts to overrule legislative enactments, rendered governmental institutions ineffective in labour's struggle to advance the interests of working people.

For the lack of 'positive' or administrative capacities in American government, see Stephen Skowronek, *Building a New American State: The Expansion of National Administrative Capacities, 1877–1920* (Cambridge: Cambridge University Press, 1982). For the American lack of a civil service equivalent to England's, see Ari Hoogenboom, *Outlawing the Spoils: A History of the Civil Service Reform Movement, 1865–1883* (Urbana: University of Illinois Press, 1961). For the dominance of political machines, see Morton Keller, *Affairs of State: Public Life in Late-Nineteenth Century America* (Cambridge MA: Harvard University Press, 1977). For the absence of a labour party in the US, see David Montgomery, *The Fall of the House of Labor* (Cambridge: Cambridge University Press, 1987).

22 Linda Gordon offers telling criticism of the tendency of white middle-class women reformers to view their working class 'clients' as 'the other', especially in comparison with black women equivalents in 'Race and Class in Women's Welfare Activism, 1890–1945', *Journal of American History* (forthcoming).

23 See Ginzberg, *Women and the Work of Benevolence*; and Anne Firor Scott's forthcoming history of women's voluntary organisations, *Natural Allies*.

24 Industrial strife and immigration are discussed in Herbert G. Gutman, *Work, Culture and Society in Industrializing America* (New York: Knopf, 1976). One of the best discussions of Social Darwinism remains Richard Hofstadter, *Social Darwinism in American Thought* (rev. edn, Boston: Beacon, 1955).

25 See Brock, *Investigation and Responsibility*, pp. 1–57.

26 See Kelley, *Notes of Sixty Years*, p. 68.

27 Ely, *Ground Under Our Feet*, p. 36; Jurgen Herbst, *The German Historical School in*

American Scholarship: A Study in the Transfer of Culture (Ithaca: Cornell University Press, 1965), pp. 1–22. Kelley, *Notes of Sixty Years*, pp. 71–72.

28 Kelley, *Notes of Sixty Years*, pp. 61–74.

29 The best discussion of state bureaus of labour statistics is Brock, *Investigation and Responsibility*, pp. 148–84. Kelley's critique was printed in *Fifth Annual Report of the Bureau of Labor Statistics of the State of Connecticut*, (Hartford: Case, Lockwood & Brainard, 1889), pp. 43–5.

30 Florence Kelley to Caroline Kelley, 24 Feb., 1892, Nicholas Kelley Papers, New York Public Library.

31 Florence Kelley to Friedrich Engels, Hull House, 7 April, 1892, Archive, Institute of Marxism-Leninism, Moscow, 8489 a & b. Also quoted in Dorothy Rose Blumberg, *Florence Kelley: The Making of a Social Pioneer* (New York: Augustus M. Kelley, 1966), p. 127.

32 Florence Kelley to Caroline Kelley, Hull House, March 16, 1892, Nicholas Kelley Papers.

33 Florence Kelley to Caroline Kelley, March 16, 1892.

34 The stories by Nell Nelson appeared in *The Times* of Chicago, a pro-labour paper. Women garment workers called a meeting attended by representatives of twenty-six women's organisations in October, 1888. Clipping 24 Oct., 1888, Thomas J. Morgan Collection, University of Illinois, Urbana. See Sklar, 'Hull House as a Community of Women Reformers'; and Meredith Tax, *The Rising of the Women: Feminist Solidarity and Class Conflict, 1880–1917* (New York: Monthly Review Press, 1980), pp. 65–93.

35 Florence Kelley to Friedrich Engels, Hull House, 27 May, 1892. Reprinted in Blumberg, *Florence Kelley*, p. 128.

36 Allen F. Davis, *American Heroine: The Life and Legend of Jane Addams* (New York: Oxford University Press, 1973), p. 100.

37 T. S. Simey and M. B, Simey, *Charles Booth, Social Scientist* (New York: Oxford University Press, 1960), pp. 115 and 128. Publication dates of the early volumes were: vol. 1, 1889; vol. 2 with Map of Poverty, 1891; vols. 3 and 4, 1896.

38 The earliest thematic maps in the United States were also problem-solving instruments. Sanitary survey maps for New York City in the 1860s, showing household variables such as privy facilities, utilised the advances that lithography made possible. So the basic technological steps were in place twenty years before *HHM&P*. See Jon A. Peterson, 'The Impact of Sanitary Reform upon American Urban Planning, 1840–1890', in Donald A. Krueckeberg (ed.), *Introduction to Planning History in the United States* (New Brunswick: Center for Urban Policy Research, Rutgers University, 1983), pp. 13–39; and Arthur H. Robinson, *Early Thematic Mapping in the History of Cartography* (Chicago: University of Chicago Press, 1982), pp. 24, 143, 193.

The major studies containing thematic maps by social reformers between *HHM&P* and the Pittsburgh Survey were Robert A. Woods (ed.), *The City Wilderness: A Settlement Study* (Boston: Patterson Smith, 1898); and Robert A. Woods (ed.), *Americans in Process: A Settlement Study by Residents and Assocites of the South End House* (Boston: Houghton, Mifflin and Co., 1903). The maps in the 1898 volume were extremely minimal and rudimentary compared to *HHM&P*, but improved colour-coded maps appeared in the 1903 study. Based on Booth's method of block rather than household analysis, the maps depicted 'Nationalities in the North End', (plate 5 in this volume) 'Nationalities in the West End', 'Buildings in the North End', 'Buildings in the West End', 'Industrial Grades in the West End', and 'Industrial Grades in the North End'.

Neither these nor the maps in the six volumes of *The Pittsburgh Survey*, published between 1909 and 1911, approached the sophistication and detail of the maps in *HHM&P*. See for example, Paul U. Kellogg, 'Community and Workshop', in Paul U. Kellogg (ed.), *Wage-Earning Pittsburgh, The Pittsburgh Survey*, (New York: Russell Sage Foundation, 1914), pp. 3–30. Depicting the whole city on one page, these maps give a general portrait of 'Congestion', 'Growth', 'Hospitals', and 'Health'. Six versions of the latter depicted 'Comparative Mortality by Ward Groups, 1903–1907': 'Tuberculosis', 'Pneumonia', 'Diarrhoeal Diseases', 'Other Violence (than suicide)', 'Typhoid Fever', and 'All Causes'. The most detailed maps in the Pittsburg Survey can be found in Margaret Byington, *Homestead: The Households of a Mill Town* (New York: Russell Sage Foundation, 1911). One, following p. 132, shows the 'location of 22 courts studied; number of children under 14 in each; location of churches and saloons; absence of playgrounds'.

All Pittsburg Survey maps were drawn by Shelby Harrison, co-compiler of A. Eaton and S. M. Harrison, *A Bibliography of Social Surveys: Reports of Fact-Finding Studies made as a Basis for Social Action: Arranged by Subjects and Localities: Reports to January 1st 1928* (New York: Russell Sage Foundation, 1930).

39 Simey and Simey, *Charles Booth*, p. 102.
40 Simey and Simey, *Charles Booth*, p. 113.
41 'Prefatory Note', *HHM&P*, pp. vii & viii.
42 Florence Kelley to Henry Demarest Lloyd, 327 W. Harrison St., 28 Nov., 1892, Henry Demarest Lloyd Papers, State Historical Society of Wisconsin.
43 Carroll D. Wright, Commissioner of Labor, *Seventh Annual Report, The Slums of Baltimore, Chicago, New York, and Philadelphia* (Washington: Government Printing Office, 1894).
44 Agnes Sinclair Holbrook, 'Map Notes and Comments', *HHM&P*, p. 7.
45 Holbrook, 'Map Notes', *HHM&P*, p. 7. There Holbrook clarified the classification methods of each map:

In recording the nationality of each person, his age, and in the case of children under ten years of age the nationality of his parents and his attendance at school were taken into account. All under ten years of age who were not pupils in the public school, and who were not of American extraction, were classified with their parents as foreigners. In estimating the average weekly wage for the year, first the number of unemployed weeks in early individual case was subtracted from the number of weeks in the year, the difference multiplied by the weekly wage when employed, and the result divided by fifty-two; then the amounts received by the various members of each family, thus determined, were added together, giving the average weekly income of the family throughout the year.

46 Robinson, *Early Thematic Mapping*, pp. 24, 143, and 193.
47 Holbrook, 'Map Notes', *HHM&P*, p. 9.

48 Holbrook, 'Map Notes', *HHM&P*, p. 11.
49 Holbrook, 'Map Notes', *HHM&P*, pp. 11–12.
50 Holbrook, 'Map Notes', *HHM&P*, p. 20.
51 Holbrook, 'Map Notes', *HHM&P*, p. 20.
52 Holbrook, 'Map Notes', *HHM&P*, pp. 8, 20.
53 Holbrook, 'Map Notes', *HHM&P*, p. 23.
54 Holbrook, 'Map Notes', *HHM&P*, p. 23.
55 Holbrook, 'Map Notes', *HHM&P*, p. 13.
56 Holbrook, 'Map Notes', *HHM&P*, pp. 3–4.
57 Holbrook, 'Map Notes', *HHM&P*, p. 4.
58 Holbrook, 'Map Notes', *HHM&P*, pp. 5–6.
59 Holbrook, 'Map Notes', *HHM&P*, p. 14.
60 Florence Kelley, 'The Sweating System', *HHM&P*, p. 41.
61 Kelley, 'Sweating System', *HHM&P*, p. 50.
62 Florence Kelley and Alzina Stevens, 'Wage-Earning Children', *HHM&P*, pp. 61, 72, 74–5.
63 Isabel Eaton, 'Receipts and Expenditures of Cloakmakers in Chicago, Compared with Those of That Trade in New York', *HHM&P*, pp. 84 and 88.
64 Charles Zeublin, 'The Chicago Ghetto', *HHM&P*, pp. 110.
65 Josepha Humpal Zeman, 'The Bohemian People in Chicago', *HHM&P*, pp. 119–20, 134.
66 In 'The Domestication of Politics: Women and American Political Society, 1780–1920', *American Historical Review*, 89 (June 1984), 620–48. Paula Baker's otherwise fine article uses a model of separate spheres to explain women's political culture rather than a model that emphasises the interaction and change over time between women's political culture and the larger political culture.
67 See note 21 above.
68 This process is described in Dorothy Ross, 'The Development of the Social Sciences', and Edward Shils, 'The Order of Learning in the United States: The Ascendancy of the University', in Alexandra Oleson and John Voss (eds.), *The Organization of Knowledge in Modern America, 1860–1920* (Baltimore: Johns Hopkins University Press, 1979), pp. 107–38 and 19–47. See also Martin Bulmer, *The Chicago School of Sociology: Institutionalization, Diversity, and the Rise of Sociological Research* (Chicago: University of Chicago Press, 1984), pp. 1–44.
69 Julia Lathrop, 'Cook County Charities', *HHM&P*, p. 143.
70 Lathrop, 'Cook County Charities', *HHM&P*, p. 146.
71 Lathrop, 'Cook County Charities', *HHM&P*, p. 158.
72 Ellen Gates Starr, 'Art and Labor', *HHM&P*, pp. 178–9.
73 Jane Addams, 'The Settlement as a Factor in the Labor Movement', *HHM&P*, pp. 185–6.
74 Addams, 'Settlement as a Factor in the Labor Movement', *HHM&P*, pp. 188–204.
75 Jane Addams, 'Appendix, Full House: A Social Settlement', *HHM&P*.
76 Florence Kelley, 'Hull House', *New England Magazine*, 18, 5 (July, 1898), 550–66, *quote* p. 550.

77 Mme. Marie-Therese Blanc, *The Condition of Woman in the United States* (Boston: Robert Bros., 1896), pp. 74–82.

78 Abraham Bisno, *Union Pioneer: An Autobiographical Account of Bisno's Early Life and the Beginnings of Unionism in the Women's Garment Industry* (Madison: University of Wisconsin Press, 1967), p. 120.

79 Jane Addams, *Twenty Years at Hull House* (New York: Macmillan, 1910), p. 183.

80 See Kathryn Kish Sklar, 'Who Funded Hull House?', in Kathleen McCarthy (ed.), *Lady Bountiful Revisited: Women, Philanthropy and Power* (New Brunswick, NJ: Rutgers University Press, 1990).

81 For example, Kelley used this phrase in letters to Ely dated 5 Oct., 1892, and 20 Aug., 1893. Richard T. Ely Papers, State Historical Society of Wisconsin, Madison.

82 Other titles in the series included: E. W. Bemis, *Municipal Monopolies* (1899); John R. Commons, *Proportional Representation* (1902); Frank H. Dixon, *State Railroad Control* (1896); Frederic C. Howe, *Taxation and Taxes in the United States* (1896); Edward Ingle, *Southern Side Lights* (1896); Lauros G. McConachie, *Congressional Committees* (1898); Charles B. Spahr, *An Essay on the Present Distribution of Wealth in the United States* (1896); William P. Trent, *Southern Statesmen of the Old Regime* (1897); W. F. Willoughby, *Workingmen's Insurance* (1898); F. H. Wines, *Punishment and Reformation* (1923).

83 Jane Addams to Richard Ely, Chicago, 31 Oct., 1894, Ely Papers.

84 Jane Addams to Richard Ely, 31 Oct., 1894.

85 Florence Kelley to Richard Ely, Office of Factory Inspector, Chicago, 14 Nov., 1894, Ely Papers.

86 Jane Addams to Richard Ely, 27 Nov., 1894, and 4 Dec., 1894, Ely Papers.

87 Unidentified news clipping [*New York Times*, March 1896], Hull House Scrapbook, 1896, *Jane Addams Papers*, Mary Lynn McCree Bryan *et al.* (eds.), (Sanford, North Carolina, 1985, microfilm, reel 73).

88 'Settlers in the City Wilderness', *Atlantic Monthly*, 77, 459 (January, 1896), 118–23; Samuel McCune Lindsay, 'Hull House Maps and papers', *Annals of the American Academy of Political and Social Science*, 8 (June 1896), 389–90.

89 Deegan, *Jane Addams and the Men of the Chicago School*, esp. pp. 63–6.

90 See Josephine Goldmark, *Impatient Crusader: The Life of Florence Kelley* (Urbana: University of Illinois Press, 1953).

CHAPTER FIVE

The place of social investigation, social theory and social work in the approach to late Victorian and Edwardian social problems: the case of Beatrice Webb and Helen Bosanquet

JANE LEWIS

While it is fully acknowledged that women played a major role in the philanthropic world of the late nineteenth century,[1] the part they played as social investigators has often been overlooked. The development of the social survey in Britain, for example, tends to be charted from Booth to Rowntree, to Bowley, with passing mention of the assistance Beatrice Webb rendered to Booth, but with little attention to the independent efforts of Helen Bosanquet and, later in the 1900s, of the Fabian Women's Group and of individuals such as M. E. Loane, Violet Butler and Eglantyne Jebb.[2]

This neglect may be due to the fact that female social investigation failed to develop along the quantitative paths pursued by the men. For women social investigators were rooted for the most part in the world of philanthropy and their interests were tied firmly to social work and to social action. Philanthropy provided late Victorian middle-class women with their only bridge to the public world of work and citizenship,[3] albeit, as it transpired, a social world in which the edges between public and private were effectively blurred. It was because the poor working-class family was the essential object of study and because the position of the working-class mother was commonly acknowledged to be 'pivotal' that female investigators could legitimately claim an interest in the field. As Denise Riley has commented: 'Women became both agents and objects of reform in unprecedented ways with the ascent of the social'.[4] However, whereas male social investigators moved onto either the world of policy-making or of professional social science in the university, women tended to remain in the world of social work.

Beatrice Webb and Helen Bosanquet both came out of the world of philanthropy and were both committed to social action. After graduating from Cambridge, Helen Dendy worked as a paid secretary of the Shoreditch

District Committee of the Charity Organisation Society from 1890 until her marriage in 1894. Beatrice Potter joined the COS in 1883 as an unpaid Visitor and worked as a rent collector in one of Octavia Hill's housing management schemes (while also keeping house for her widowed father), until she began working on Booth's survey of London. Helen Bosanquet remained committed to the predominantly female world of voluntary social work within the COS, writing a number of articles on social problems and books which drew on her social observation of the poor and which were intended to be used in the training of social workers. She also edited the *Charity Organisation Society Review* until 1912. Beatrice, however, became profoundly disillusioned with the philosophy of social work and was determined to move into what she clearly perceived as the male world of social investigation. Booth's survey allowed her to take a first step in this direction. Booth was a close family friend and himself an amateur in the world of social science. After Beatrice married Sidney Webb in 1892, they pursued together they 'life history of institutions' rather than social surveys. But just as social surveyors steadily attached greater importance to the development of quantitative techniques, so Beatrice followed Sidney in attaching more importance to documentary evidence than to data obtained from either interviews or social observation, which she later openly denigrated as feminine skills.[5]

The first theme of this chapter is therefore to suggest that Beatrice Webb and Helen Bosanquet differed profoundly in the way they negotiated that part of the social sphere to which women were permitted access. However, both women continued to share a commitment to social action, Beatrice through first social investigation and later historical and political analysis, and Helen through voluntary social work. Helen believed social work held the key to achieving social change, largely because of the importance both she and her husband Bernard (a professor of philosophy at the University of Aberdeen) attached to the reformation of individual character.

The Bosanquets and the Webbs were at the centre of Edwardian intellectual debate,[6] in which, as José Harris has recently observed, questions of social policy were central for perhaps the only time in British history.[7] In particular they differed profoundly on the role they saw for a centralised state bureaucracy. But both the Bosanquets and the Webbs were convinced of the importance of speaking the language of social *science* and were determined to eschew sentimentality. When Bernard Bosanquet delivered a lecture on individualism and socialism to the Fabian Society, he declared first that while he was aware that he had been invited because he was critical of the Fabian Society, if he had been addressing 'an audience of plutocratic sympathies then I should have had the pleasure of speaking much more than I shall tonight in the language of the Fabian Essays'.[8] He went on to deny any antithesis between individualism and socialism, emphasising instead the distinction between moral socialism and economic individualism on the one hand and moral individualism and economic socialism on the other, further stressing that it was the moral antithesis that dominated. The COS was, after all, able to contemplate with relative equanimity moving its School of Sociology under the umbrella of the Webbs' London School of Economics and Political Science in 1912, although this move effectively ended the integration of social work into social theory that the Bosanquets and other female social workers (for example at the Women's University Settlement) held dear. Further-more, both the Bosanquets and certainly Beatrice Webb shared a sense of moral purpose. Just as the Bosanquets stressed the idea of love working through charity, so Beatrice Webb wrote in 1901 that the ends of life were love, truth, beauty and honour and reiterated in 1907 that she and Sidney were striving for a world in which love shone through knowledge.[9]

The Bosanquets' view by no means characterised those of the COS as a whole; indeed, McBriar has described them as moderates.[10] Certainly Bernard Bosanquet's deep philosophical commitment to developing the theory and practice of social work matched that of his wife, and served to distance him from those described by Octavia Hill as the 'hard and dry' men of the COS. Perhaps as important in distinguishing the Bosanquets from their fellow members of the COS was the coherence and sophistication of their ideas. After listening to a talk by Bernard Bosanquet in 1898, Lord Thring freely admitted that it was 'above his head'.[11] Nevertheless, it was the views of the Bosanquets that informed many of the public positions taken by the COS including the Majority Report of the 1909 Royal Commission on the Poor Laws, which was drafted mainly by Helen Bosanquet. Similarly, the Webbs did not represent the unified view of the Fabian society, although they were probably its most influential voices. Beatrice Webb also sat on the Royal Commission on the Poor Laws and (together with Sidney) drafted the Minority Report. There were great similarities in the policy recommendations of the two reports. However, the Royal Commission captured the way in which the Webbs and the Bosanquets were at once antagonistic and yet had much in common. The fundamental difference between the drafters of the two reports was over means rather than ends. As Collini has pointed out, for Helen and Bernard Bosanquet the reform of the individual was both the means and the end.[12]

The Webbs on the other hand, firmly differentiated between the two. Social scientific methods could be applied to means, but should not be permitted to dictate ends. In short, their approach to the analysis of social problems was quite different.

This chapter will show that behind this difference lay contrasting views as to the relative importance of social facts and social theory. Whereas Helen Bosanquet had no hesitation in deducing modes of social action from the philosophical position she shared with her husband, who was a leading proponent of Idealism, Beatrice Webb experienced considerably more difficulty in establishing the relationship between the facts she derived from her social investigation and social theory.

BEATRICE WEBB: (I) FROM SOCIAL WORK TO SOCIAL INVESTIGATION

In 1883 the twenty-five year-old Beatrice Potter, who had been carrying out an ambitious programme of private study in addition to keeping house for her father, wrote that she hoped that Charity Organisation Society work would 'fit in well with my human study. One learns very little about human nature from Society.'[13] However, she did not find charitable social work to her taste. Work for the COS and then as a rent collector involved above all what Octavia Hill called detailed, practical work.[14] Beatrice found that it took all her energy and dulled her mind.[15] Furthermore, she developed serious doubts about the principles and practice of social work. Nevertheless, her decision to leave social work behind for good in 1888 was not easy, not least because both she and those around her saw it as preeminently women's work.

Throughout the 1880s, Beatrice Webb's diary made continual reference to her limited faculties and her doubts as to her ability to undertake intellectual work, fearing that her ambitions to move into the world of social investigation were merely the product of vanity.[16] Beatrice freely acknowledged male mental superiority and agreed with her mentor, Herbert Spencer, that women needed instruction above all in household duties.[17] Ideal woman, in her estimation, was inspired by religious feeling and sympathy to do her duty by her family, and to work selflessly for others.[18] The model of social work practice developed by Octavia Hill in the 1860s and 1870s stressed that sympathy was both central to womanly feeling and the key to successful work among the poor. Acknowledging this in 1883, Beatrice concluded that the impetus to cold-blooded inquiry must be 'shaken off sternly'.[19]

While charitable work deliberately appealed to womanly sympathies, its female leaders were dominated by what *Macmillan's* magazine called in 1889, a race of 'glorified spinsters'.[20] Beatrice herself engaged most fully in COS and rent collection work in the aftermath of her affair with Chamberlain she referred to the work as a 'narcotic'.[21] But she neither wished nor approved of women substituting service to others for service to the family. Her fellow rent collector, Ella Pycroft, a Devonshire doctor's daughter, wrote to Beatrice of the way in which her work successfully stopped her 'looking forward':

Mercifully for me, I never look forward now, – except to the chance of making the arrears less next week, and that hope generally fails me. I think it is no use blinding the fact that nothing can make up to us women for the loss of humanities – I know nothing will ever to me; one may bury one's cares for a time under a load of work, but they are always ready to come up again.[22]

Beatrice commented that both Ella Pycroft and Octavia Hill would have been 'much more' if happily married.[23] Her conviction that women need the comfort and connections of homelife and children were reinforced by those with whom she mixed socially. At a dinner with Frederic Harrison, the positivist, in 1886, she agreed that unmarried life could not be happy for women, but 'disagreed on the usefulness of it'. Harrison maintained that marriage was essential to the development of women's character, but Beatrice argued that 'if unmarried women kept their feelings alive, did not choke them with routine idleness, practical work or with intellectualism, though they must suffer pain, they were often for that very reason more sympathetic than married women'.[24] This conversation, recorded at length in her diary, must have been profoundly discouraging to Beatrice who was at that time struggling to commit herself to the life of a 'glorified spinster'.

As well as experiencing ambivalent feelings about her involvement in social work for personal reasons, Beatrice Potter also began to call into question both the principles and practice of the work she was doing. In the chapter of her autobiography which is devoted to the COS and written more with the benefit of hindsight and less from diary entries than any other in the book, she acknowledged the value of the principles on which the COS was founded: patient and persistent personal service, the acceptance of personal responsibility for the ulterior consequences of charitable assistance and the application of the scientific method to each case.[25] But there was an edge to her choice of verb in her description of COS workers as 'yearning to serve'. At worst the result could be, she thought, 'pharisaical self-congratulation'.[26]

As early as 1883, she experienced difficulty in applying the principles of the COS. After visiting an opium eater and his wife and three children she pondered in her diary: 'One is tempted to a feeling of righteous indignation against the man, but did he make himself? And is he not on the whole more pitiable?'[27] Nevertheless, it seems that in this instance she must have toed the COS line and refused the family relief, for in 1886, while reflecting on the difficulty of applying COS principles in 'hard cases', Ella Pycroft recalled Beatrice's account of the opium eater as a model of correct practice.[28] Certainly, Beatrice was not tempted in the direction of more old-fashioned almsgiving. In the manner of a good Spencerian, she worried lest no matter how it was practised, charitable relief would favour the weak to the detriment of the strong. 'But', she wondered,

can these considerations have any weight when we come face to face with individual misery, and do these economic facts bear any proportion in importance to the moral facts with which charity is concerned? Does not the advisability of charity depend on the moral qualities which are developed in the relation of giver and receiver...?[29]

Thus she perceived a possible tension between the moral animus of charitable endeavour and the prescriptions of classical political economy. In particular she became critical of the distinction the COS made between those deserving and those undeserving of charitable help (the undeserving being those of poor character, such as the drunkard or the opium eater).[30] She noted that the deserving were often people whom it was impossible to help effectively. Helen Bosanquet's efforts in 1893 to get the COS to drop this distinction in favour of deciding merely whether the applicant was 'helpable'[31] – defined in terms of whether he or she was likely to be able to attain self-support – did nothing to obviate Beatrice Potter's point that many of those in poverty through ill-fortune might still not qualify for assistance. Beatrice found difficulty in seeing how such principles could be 'made consistent with the duty persistently inculcated of personal friendship with the poor'.[32] Her perception of a double tension at the level of principle and at the level of practice was acute. Even those workers, like Ella Pycroft, who did not question the principles of scientific charity, experienced conflicts in their practice, especially when confronted by 'hard cases'.

It seemed to Beatrice Potter that the work of the COS Visitor or of the rent collector was 'an utter failure'.[33] She was disgusted by the 'collected brutality' of the very poor, whose members she regularly evicted from the buildings she was responsible for. In 1886 she recorded that 'the East End life, with its dirt, drunkenness and immorality, absence of combined effort or common interest saddens me, weighs down my spirit'.[34] At this point, not only did she despair of social work producing social change, but she also appeared to have little faith in the possibility of moral improvement among the poorest of London's population.

By 1888, she was involved in work on her old friend Charles Booth's social survey of London, which she found much more intellectually satisfying, providing as it did an opportunity to locate the problems of individuals within a large canvas, to classify, to search for causes beyond (but still including) that of individual character and, most important, to suggest solutions. She had been consistently shocked at the lack of interest on the part of leading women social workers in record keeping and in rigorously examining the nature of their work.[35] In short, by the late 1880s, she was convinced that a solution to social problems was to be sought through social investigation rather than through work with individuals. In entering the world of social investigation, she also made the decision to leave the women's world of practical social work. During her study of dock labour for Booth, she found that she relished the work of data collection, interviewing mainly men and collaborating with male investigators. The significance of the break in personal terms was signalled by her decision not only to become a social investigator but, in defiance of the opinions of both Booth and the economist Alfred Marshall, to investigate the 'male' topic of cooperation, rather than the more acceptable one of women's work. Even after her marriage to Sidney in 1892, her diary entries reveal the extent to which her identity continued to derive from her chosen career of social investigation, as she both worried about not pulling her weight in the partnership and expressed her determination to claim equality of recognition for her research.[36]

BEATRICE WEBB: (II) METHODS OF SOCIAL INVESTIGATION

Beatrice spent considerable time in the late 1880s thinking about how she might attempt the task of social investigation. She recorded in her autobiography that Herbert Spencer had been the first to teach her the value of facts, even though later she came to deplore the way in which he used them.[37] She abhorred the way in which Spencer deduced 'social laws from the laws of another science' and then proceeded to select facts to illustrate the laws he propounded. In 1885, she wrote: 'He irritates me by trying to palm off illustrations as data; by transcribing biological laws into the terms of social facts, and then reasoning from them as social laws'.[38] When a year later Samuel Barnett, founder of the Toynbee Hall Settlement, stated that it was his belief that ideas had more influence than facts, because ideas influenced character and the development of character was the key to life, Beatrice noted that she believed in ideas, but in ideas following facts.[39] She went on to plan an article on social diagnosis to show how far social action had been influenced by fact. She believed that the historical record could be made to show how social sentiment had been formed by descriptions of social facts, which in turn had given rise to political action. Ironically, this was an argument which owed as much to conviction as to evidence.

From her belief as to the correct relationship between ideas and facts came Beatrice Webb's conviction as to in the necessity for investigating the life history of institutions. She felt that Booth's methods resulted in a valuable snapshot of social problems but did not provide a means of investigating processes or of establishing causality.[40] She believed that charting social processes using scientific methods of research represented a step towards the development of a fully-fledged science of society.[41] This grand aim required meticulous attention to the collection of the facts, conjecture as the cause and effect, and verification by renewed observations of the material.

In 1900, during the early stages of the Webbs' massive study of local government, Beatrice recorded first her growing confidence in the possibility of developing a genuine social science and then, shortly afterwards, her fear that after all they would prove but chroniclers and compilers.[42] Increasingly, the Webbs insisted that the solution to the problem of bias lay in the collection of all the facts, a herculean task. They defied any attempt to establish which facts might be 'relevant' out of a conviction that patterns would emerge from them, literally that they would speak for themselves. This tendency had two important results. First, it led to more emphasis being placed on documentary research than on social observation or interviewing, which arguably had a particularly adverse effect on Beatrice's contribution, and second, both partners experienced considerable difficulty in establishing a precise relationship between theory and their empirical data. As T. H. Marshall noted in his Introduction to the Webbs' volume on *Methods of Social Study* (1932), which collected together their thought on social research, in the end the relationship between the Webb's central beliefs about the ideal structure of a social democracy and their data remained unacknowledged and untested.[43]

During the period of her transition to the role of social investigator in the mid and late 1880s, Beatrice showed less preoccupation with the acquisition of facts, from which 'truth' would emerge, and a greater concern about building up a picture of a social problem that incorporated the views

of all the major actors. During this period she conducted a lively debate in
her diary over the appropriate mix of research tools and ways of deciding
the scope of any particular study. Working for Booth on dock labour, she
recorded that 'the difficulty lies in keeping off the by-ways, mastering
the LEADING FACTS thoroughly and not attempting to study all the
excrescences'.[44] Similarly, during her study of the cooperative movement,
she remarked that the facts provided her with 'a bunch of keys' in terms
of important events, societies, technical terms and personalities which she
could then use to gain the confidence of interviewees and thereby move the
research onto another plane.[45] At this point in her career documentary
evidence seems to have been but one element in the research process and
by no means the most important one.

Most important in determining her success as a social investigator was
her capacity to undertake social observation. Her delight in first-hand
observation, particularly when it involved disguise (as in her investigation
of the tailoring trade in the 1880s), is obvious from the pages of her diary.
As Nord has remarked, disguise permitted a dramatic and sympathetic
identification with the people she observed.[46] The preface to her book on
the cooperative movement reveals the extent to which her attendance at
meetings of cooperators enabled her to make the imaginative leap that was
required to see that cooperatives were as much about consumption as
production.[47] Her study, with Sidney, of trade unions also involved her in
a considerable amount of observation of the working of trade union
committees and she began their joint study of local government in much
the same way, writing in her diary in 1899 that sitting in on council and
committee meetings had enabled her to get a sense of the 'tangle' of local
government.[48] She also attached considerable value to the method of
interviewing. Early on she realised her capacity for eliciting information,
contrasting her skill in this regard with that of Charles Booth.[49] Later on she
made a similar observation, this time favourably comparing her technique
with that of Sidney, who was too shy to ask questions effectively.[50] Social
observation and interviewing were the methods which aroused Beatrice
Webb's curiosity and provided her with her best insights. In contrast, fact
gathering from documentary sources drove her to distraction. Working on
her study of cooperation, she complained about the 'treadmill of disputed
facts, in themselves utterly uninteresting and appallingly dry', but noted,
'however, it is satisfactory to feel that one will never be beaten for lack of
industry'.[51] By the time she came to work with Sidney on the massive
amount of material they collected for their study of trade unions, she
declared herself to be sick 'of these ugly details of time work and piece

work'.[52] The local government study also relied almost entirely on documentary evidence and became above all a matter of 'getting the facts disentangled and marshalled one after another'.[53] Beatrice found herself unable to stick at the work of note-taking for more than a few hours at a time and was often forced to retire with a sick headache. Indeed, in many respects she found this work as boring as practical social work. Her devotion to it was a species of duty; there is in her diary entries a feeling, worthy of Octavia Hill, that the diligent and exhaustive search for documentary evidence represented 'right action', from which good prescriptions were bound to emerge.

But in practice Beatrice and Sidney found it difficult to make links between their life histories of institutions and theories of social democracy. Beatrice's understanding of process was derived almost entirely from Spencerian evolutionary ideas and therefore involved implicit notions of progress. For Beatrice, the terms history, evolution, kinetic and comparative method were virtually interchangeable, although in comparison with an audience of sociologists in 1906, who, like Spencer, experienced no difficulty in ascertaining 'laws of development' which would enable them 'to see in a general way the future course of history', Beatrice's understanding was sophisticated and her claims modest.[54] Nevertheless, the evolutionary approach the Webbs adopted for their study of trade unions in the 1890s, for example, was more narrowly administrative and tended, as Marshall later observed, to be divorced from the economic and political fabric.[55] Furthermore, as Beatrice admitted in her diary, the Webbs' theory of industrial democracy did not emerge from their book charting the history of trade unions. Rather, it had to be 'found'.[56] Similarly in the course of their research on local government, Beatrice spoke first of their work in 'arranging and re-arranging the evidence and arranging our facts in endless ways so as to find coincidences and perhaps causes', but also of the need for a 'brilliant and dogmatic theoretical part quite apart from the concrete narrative'.[57] At this same time (1903), Beatrice confessed her bewilderment as to the precise relation between their (or rather Sidney's) practical administrative work − on the London County Council, which was informed by particular social and political ideas − and their scientific work, in which they endeavoured to discover truth.[58] It was a tension that refused to go away and which was to permeate their Minority Report on the Poor Laws.

HELEN BOSANQUET: FROM SOCIAL THEORY TO SOCIAL WORK

Like other leading members of the Charity Organisation Society in the 1880s and early 1890s, and unlike Beatrice Webb, Helen Bosanquet believed firmly in the importance of ideas over facts. Writing during World War I, Bernard Bosanquet went to considerable lengths to argue both the ease and the importance of making links between philosophical principles and practical social work.[59] Indeed, both the Bosanquets mounted a series of attacks on the Webbian approach to social investigation and the importance attached to fact gathering. The Bosanquets believed that only through a thorough understanding of the mainsprings of human behaviour could a successful solution to social problems be found. The emphasis they placed on the development and reformation of individual character led them to favour social work as the ideal vehicle for achieving social change. All Helen Bosanquet's writings were directed towards practical social workers and were intended to provide them with rationale for their work.

The Bosanquets believed the restorative power of character to be the only sure way of tackling the problem of poverty. They emphasised that anyone, rich or poor could lack character, but as Helen argued in writing published before her marriage, the failings of the poor were additionally problematic because they were likely to become a public charge.[60] To change character would effect much more fundamental improvement than changing economic conditions; no misfortune, no matter how distressing was irredeemable until the individual's will was broken. Helen Bosanquet put the case at length in The Strength of the People (1903), where she argued that a man's circumstances depended on what he himself was and that it was therefore 'man himself who must be changed if his circumstances are to be avoided'.[61] It was not clear, for example, that giving the poor more money would help matters, unless the people were also educated to use the money wisely. For this to happen, a long process of education to persuade people to aspire to 'a higher standard' was required.

Mental struggle was considered crucial to the formation of character and purpose. Mind and will were the makings of character and both the Bosanquets argued that a science of society had to be a science of mind. Not surprisingly they (Helen particularly) turned to the emerging discipline of psychology for assistance in this task. From her reading of the work of G. H. Stout, a psychologist and colleague of Bernard Bosanquet's at St Andrews, Helen suggested that man could be distinguished from the lower animals by his progressive wants, which were developed by his recognition and pursuit of 'interests', initially within the family unit. However, there were those who failed to develop progressive wants, being satisfied merely with the lower pleasures of eating, drinking and sleeping. In such people bad habits played the same role as instincts in animals and prevented them breaking 'the elementary cycle of appetites'. Their behaviour could be changed only by dint of training and education.[62]

The family occupied a special place in the Bosanquet's thinking and its importance was elaborated by Helen in *The Family* (1906). The primary locus of self development was believed to be the family unit, where 'natural' affection between husbands and wives, and parents and children could be fostered until homes became 'nurseries of citizenship'.[63] When stable families combined 'young and old in one strong bond of mutual helpfulness', and children learned the meaning of responsibility, mutual service, trust and affection, there would be very few social problems.[64]

While individual character was thus held to be the most important determinant of the individual's circumstances, the Bosanquets stressed that this did not mean that an individual in distress was to be left to himself to work out his own salvation. Rather, it was crucial that the fortunate offer help to the unfortunate. Given the importance the Bosanquets attached to changing bad habits and helping the individual to develop the kind of interests which would enable him to raise his standard of life, they favoured individual social work as the best method of improving welfare. Achieving social change by changing individual will was necessarily going to be an inordinately slow process; change could only take place when the individual was ready for it. This further suggested to them that as crude an agent as the state would not prove able to secure effective change. Moreover, there was always the fear that the state would end up usurping the individual in the pursuit of his interests, for example in regard to his struggle to provide a better life for his children, thereby setting back the whole process of true social reform. The special importance attached to family obligations explains the particular relevance of the attack led by Helen Bosanquet and other Charity Organisation Society leaders to the introduction of school meals in 1906 and to old age pensions in 1908. The Bosanquets were not fundamentally opposed to any and all state intervention, but rather stressed the danger it posed to the exercise of individual will and effort.

Charitable social work on the other hand provided a much surer way of stimulating the kind of interests that would organise the life and develop the character of the individual. The Bosanquets believed that charitable work would increase the common good through mutual service based on reason and love. Social workers needed to combine principle, order and organisation with passion and wisdom. As Helen Bosanquet put it in 1900, it was easy for potential COS workers to learn the categories 'not likely to benefit, left to the clergy, poor law case, necessary information refused', but it was more difficult to learn how to keep a case out of one of these classes altogether.[65] The Bosanquets stressed the importance both of adopting a holistic approach and of seeking a complete understanding of the individual in relation to his environment, as a necessary preliminary to working out the best method of enabling him to become independent. The key to achieving this in practical social work was believed to be individual casework, a method that relied on scientific principles and social investigation of the individual's circumstances, as well as love and sympathy.

Most of Helen Bosanquet's published work was designed to help social workers understand the importance of learning why it was that individuals in need of help saw things the way they did and held the values they did, as preliminary step to working with them over a period of time to change both beliefs and behaviour. Helen Bosanquet did not follow Beatrice Webb in her effort to develop a new methodology for social science, although she acknowledged the importance of sociology. Indeed, Bernard argued strongly that the material for social work training was not to be found in the texts of the classical economists, whose views historians have often assumed to have been the most influential.[66] Helen Bosanquet also devoted considerable attention to assessing the value of statistics and (more positively) psychology. But she did not believe that theory would emerge from facts.

Ross McKibbin has described Helen Bosanquet's analysis of social issues as being like that of another leading Edwardian woman social investigator, Margery Loane (a district nurse by profession), essentially anecdotal and episodic.[67] Helen's first book-length study, *Rich and Poor* (1896), relied heavily on the power of the single illustration, using the speech patterns of the working class. In all probability the examples were real and drawn from her experience in the early 1890s as a paid district secretary for the COS. But their use assumed a certain music hall quality, playing patronisingly on the ignorance of those whose behaviour she believed required correction. The use of direct quotation was designed to show the perceptions of the poor, which according to Helen Bosanquet's thinking had to be understood before workers could comprehend the possible consequences of the aid they offered. She agreed with Beatrice Webb as to the importance of social observation, but felt that this merely confirmed the idea that circumstance was modified by the character.[68] Contrasting the behaviour of children in five families she observed across the back garden of her Hoxton house in the early 1890s, she commented on the children of number 1: 'they live with exactly the same surroundings, and might go to the same school; it is wholesome home atmosphere which is wanting'.[69] But her observations were by no means unsympathetic, especially in respect of the position of working class wives. She was sympathetic to cultural difference without being in the least susceptible to cultural relativism. She recognised the difficulty of budgeting on an irregular income and of avoiding the temptation of credit for example, and in her first book wrote of their 'patient endurance, unceasing sacrifice and terrible devotion'.[70] Indeed her sympathy and understanding of the position of the residuum was considerably greater than that of Beatrice Webb, who was overcome by disgust about life in the East End. Helen Bosanquet always made a point of writing about the 'sunny side' of working class life and of drawing the reader's attention to the good qualities possessed by the poor, which she felt might either be overlooked or misunderstood by a middle-class social worker.[71] Like Beatrice Webb, Helen Bosanquet adhered to a belief in progress, but in her case it was grounded in a belief in the capacity of the very poor for moral improvement.

Helen Bosanquet was very critical of the methods of social investigation used by Booth, Rowntree and the Webbs, because she felt that they neglected mind and motive. She believed that the world of facts must have an idea, a principle, and an order which had to be discovered first and which was fundamentally opposed to the notion that empirical data could be shuffled and reshuffled to produce a variety of explanatory frameworks. She maintained that the work of Booth, Rowntree and the Fabians appealed to the emotions on the basis of bad statistics.[72] Her point that statistical material was not necessarily value free in the way that early practitioners, Beatrice Webb included, assumed was valid. Similarly, her criticism of the Webbs' whole method of abstracting facts on slips of paper because it was 'open to the grave objection that the excerpts are very effectively separated from their context' was prescient. T. H. Marshall made a very similar point in his introduction to the Webbs' *Methods of Social Study*.[73]

Helen Bosanquet was of course convinced that her own methods were beyond reproach. Her major books began by asserting the importance of character and then used psychology (as a science of mind) to prop up a much larger moral and social theory than it had been intended to support. While her descriptions of working-class life were often both perceptive and sympathetic, the prescriptions following from her analysis relied on the imposition of a preexisting framework of moral and social philosophy which to all intents and purposes assumed the status of 'natural law'. Beatrice Webb's criticism of Herbert Spencer's tendency to mix induction and deduction and to give hypothetical laws of behaviour the status of social facts could also have been levied at Helen Bosanquet, who did not feel it necessary to conduct any rigorous investigation of the causes of poverty. She felt it sufficient to set out her theory of progressive wants, short circuited in the case of some by want of character, and then to draw on illustrations of human behaviour derived from what Octavia Hill would have called a 'thorough knowledge of the poor'.

Furthermore, considerable tensions arose between her prescriptions for social work practice and the theory that informed them. She insisted that casework represented an opportunity to develop relationships between rich and poor based on love and sympathy. Yet the poor were to submit to careful investigation of their circumstances and were to be encouraged to change their habits. Helen Bosanquet made an effort to impress on social workers the importance of recognising legitimate sources of pleasure among the working class that were alien to the middle-class observer – for example, the delight taken by working class fathers in the company of babies and small children – and of building upon such admirable qualities.[74] But inevitably the idea of working with the poor translated in practice to something rather more didactic. Nevertheless, she always made the basis of her thinking explicit and in terms of social work practice her insistence on the importance of character became an injunction to work with, and in modern parlance, 'empower' the individual. This is not how historians have commonly portrayed the practice of the COS, and in the field it is entirely possible that more COS workers were concerned about the evils of the state relief than were prepared to undertake long term work with the very poor on the basis of love and friendship. However, as Vincent and Plant have recently suggested, the Bosanquets' theory of social work showed more respect for human dignity than more modern theories of pathology and adjustment.[75]

ACHIEVING SOCIAL CHANGE: BEATRICE WEBB, HELEN BOSANQUET AND THE ROYAL COMMISSION ON THE POOR LAWS

While it is no longer usual for historians to label the Minority Report of the Webbs progressive and the Majority reactionary, it is still the case that the former tends to be praised for its greater coherence and, with the benefit of hindsight, for the importance it attached to abolishing the Poor Law.[76] But it is possible, nevertheless, to see the Minority Report as comprised of what were essentially a series of administrative solutions of profoundly limited vision. The Majority Report on the other hand, while more rambling and equally as unworkable in terms of practical politics, did embody the social theory worked out by the Bosanquets during the 1890s and 1900s and was arguably in the end a better integrated and even a more humane document.

The invitation to sit on the Royal Commission seems to have posed more problems for Beatrice Webb than for Helen Bosanquet. While Beatrice had left the women's world of social work for the less womanly work of social investigation, she continued to harbour considerable anxieties about undertaking any work that involved her on the public stage. Her diary of the 1890s often refers to feelings of dread and revulsion at the idea of women speaking in public, an objection apparently shared by Sidney.[77] Helen Bosanquet had considerably less ambivalence than Beatrice about women taking part in public life, believing firmly that women should seize the opportunity to widen their interests.

Beatrice's relations with her fellow Commissioners were, from the first, unhappy; as she freely confessed in her diary she had no idea how to behave on a committee. She feared being masculine and yet of 'playing the personal note'.[78] She had never been inclined to keep her own counsel as Helen Bosanquet apparently did to great effect, and undoubtedly appeared extremely high-handed in her chosen persona of social investigator par excellence. In 1905, she wrote that it would need all her self-control to stop her becoming 'self-conscious in my desire to get sound investigation', and in 1906 she stated her belief that 'no member wants a systematic investigation but myself'.[79] Indeed her impatience with the talents of her fellow commissioners meant that she altogether missed the crucial role being played in the drafting of the Majority Report by Helen Bosanquet, to whom she referred but rarely, and only then as 'the little woman'.[80]

Beatrice Webb felt that she and Booth, also a Commissioner, were alone in their commitment to proper social investigation. But despite her insistence on setting in train no fewer than four separate pieces of research funded by herself, Beatrice experienced considerable difficulty in reconciling pure research with the demands of political strategy. In 1908, she wrote to Sidney:

with seeming impartiality and moderation every word of that Report [the Minority] has to tell in the direction of Breaking-up the Poor Law, the argument has to be repeated in any conceivable form so that the reader cannot escape from it. It must be a real work of Art; we can dismiss Science. It will be High Jinks doing it and we will get to work at once. The more saturated it is with argument the less will they be able to adapt any part of it without the conclusions – but the argument must be cunningly wrought – so as to seem a mere recital of facts. The Wood shall absorb the Trees.[81]

This revealing passage not only forecast the nature of the finished report accurately, but also exposed its lack of any firm theoretical foundation.

Knowing the solution they wished to promote, Beatrice set about discovering the principles to underpin it and collecting facts to support them. In the Preface to their book on English Poor Law Policy, published in 1910, the Webbs described their by then customary method of recording factual information on separate slips of paper, and shuffling and reshuffling them until a pattern emerged. In fact the memorandum in which Beatrice presented her analysis of the change in the principles of the Central Poor Law Authority was drafted well before the research was completed. At the beginning of 1908, Beatrice wrote in her diary that having fortunately 'discovered' the shift in principles of administering poor relief, they were now 'manufacturing the heavy artillery of fact that is to drive both principles and scheme home'.[82] Helen Bosanquet was undoubtedly justified in her scathing criticism of Beatrice Webb's reading of Poor Law history; it was at this point that she made her famous suggestion that some of the slips of paper must surely have fallen under the table.[83]

In terms of promoting a particular political strategy all this need not have been harmful, and indeed may have been justified. But the Minority Report lacked firm grounding and, in the end, exhibited little regard for the poor themselves. Putting the case for the Majority, Beatrice defended her Report as a rational document, acceptable to all party opinion:

The Minority scheme is not Socialistic, however, in the sense in which Socialism is usually interpreted; that is it does not involve or even lead to the nationalisation of production, distribution and exchange. On the contrary, it is just as applicable and just as necessary to an Individualist as to a Socialist State – it is a sort of mains drainage system.[84]

Apart from confirming that the report had little by way of any theoretical underpinnings, Beatrice's use of the 'drainage' metaphor was telling. In her autobiography she recorded critically that her earliest recollection of any reference to the position of labour was her father's reference to workers as abstraction, 'like water'.[85] In her work of social investigation in the late 1880s, her reliance on social observation served in large measure to prevent her from making judgements that were unsympathetic or unrealistic. But the Minority Report put forward a scheme that showed a devotion to rational administration and little but the old distrust and contempt for the residuum (which Booth also shared) in its draconian proposals for forcing recalcitrant labour into a useful life.

Helen Bosanquet appeared equally as reactionary in her determination to hang on to a destitution authority, her rationale being that it required a single authority to treat the applicant for relief and his family as a unit. Booth sided with Helen Bosanquet in his desire to retain a destitution authority, although he had little sympathy with the Bosanquets' determination to 'know' and work with the poor. As Vincent has noted, unlike the Webbs, the Bosanquets wanted casework recognised as a specialism in its own right.[86] They envisaged a reformed destitution authority employing nothing less than an army of trained social workers devoted to helping the family back to independence and self maintenance. One of the chief criticisms levied at the Webbs by the Bosanquets was that the Minority's scheme threatened to break up the family as well as the Poor Law.

The idea of a new public assistance authority becoming 'in loco parentis' to the destitute and practising advanced 'social therapeutics'[87] through the medium of casework was just as politically impractical as the Webbs' scheme to abolish the poor law altogether. The Webbs' scheme was administratively extremely complicated; the Bosanquets' extremely costly. The Bosanquets envisaged 'every family in contact with the poor law ... under careful and friendly scrutiny with a view to its restoration to independent citizenship'.[88]Bernard Bosanquet emphasised that in dealing with the destitute 'you offer everything – the whole matériel and guidance of life'. The social work to be done was described in terms resembling a religious crusade: 'an army of social healers to be trained and organised ... disciplined and animated with a single spirit and purpose'.[89] In practice the possibilities for social control would doubtless have proved as chilling as the Webbs' plan for disciplining the residuum, but this was not the intent, at least. Faith in social work was firmly grounded, as it always had been, in the Bosanquets' belief in primacy of mind and will. Changing character, not machinery, was the important thing.

It was during her work on the Poor Law Commission that Beatrice Webb wrote to Sidney stating her belief that they were working for a world that would be 'reorganised on love shining through knowledge'.[90] But no attempt was made to unite moral ends with methods of social investigation designed to pinpoint the best administrative means. Helen Bosanquet had no such qualms, means and ends were united by a social theory that attached supreme importance to individual development. World War I tested the convictions of both women. Beatrice Webb was more seriously affected, suffering a major breakdown. In 1925, she wrote that looking back she realised 'how permanent are the evil impulses and instincts in man –

how little you can count on changing some of these – for instance the appeal to wealth and power – by any change in machinery'.[91] Helen Bosanquet also recognised that the task facing them was large when she wrote that the very world of ideas as to what actions are right and wrong required reconstruction.[92] But it is perhaps a measure of their surer foundation that her faith in her prescriptions endured when Beatrice's did not.

Given the gendered nature of the work of late Victorian and Edwardian social investigation, it is not surprising that Beatrice's bold decision to leave the female world of social work caused her more profound problems in relating to the public world and in forging an identity of her own. Both women were sustained in their course of action by political philosophies that provided clear and competing ideas as to how social change was to be achieved. The differences in their analyses of social problems were central to Edwardian debates about social policies and were underpinned by the profound difference in their approach to social problems, and particularly in the way in which they conceived of the relationship between social facts and social theory. In many respects they were arguably both more conscious of the importance of this relationship and more open in debating it than were the male investigators of the day. Booth was of course ill by the time of the Royal Commission on the Poor Laws, but his position was conspicuously less well worked out than either that of Beatrice Webb or Helen Bosanquet.

NOTES

The author wishes to thank the Nuffield Foundation for their generous support of this research. I am particularly grateful to Seth Koven for his illuminating comments on this paper.

1 Frank Prochaska, *Women and Philanthropy in Nineteenth-Century England* (Oxford: Clarendon Press, 1980).

2 M. S. Pember-Reeves, *Round about a Pound a Week* (London: G. Bell, 1915); M. E. Loane wrote numerous studies, one of her most influential was *The Queen's Poor* (London: Edward Arnold 1910); Violet Butler, *Social Conditions in Oxford* (London: Sidgewick and Johnson, 1912); Eglantyne Jebb, *Cambridge: A Brief Study of Social Questions* (London: Macmillan, 1906).

3 Anne Summers, 'A Home from Home: Women's Philanthropic Work in the Nineteenth Century', in *Fit Work for Women*, edited by Sandra Burman (London: Croom Helm, 1979).

4 Denise Riley, *Am I That Name?* (Minneapolis: University of Minnesota Press, 1988, p. 51).

5 'How to Study Social Questions', BBC Radio Talks 1929, Passfield Papers, VI item 80, BCPES.

6 A. M. McBriar, *An Edwardian Mixed Doubles. The Bosanquets versus the Webbs. A Study in British Social Policy 1890–1929* (Oxford: Clarendon, 1987).

7 Jose Harris, 'The Webbs, The COS and the Ratan Tata Foundation, Social Policy from the Perspective of 1912', in M. Bulmer, J. Lewis and D. Piachaud, *The Goals of Social Policy*, (London: Unwin Hyman, 1989).

8 Bernard Bosanquet, 'The Antithesis between Individualism and Socialism Philosophically Considered', *Charity Organisation Review* (Sept. 1890), 357.

9 Norman Mackenzie (ed.), *The Letters of Sidney and Beatrice Webb*, vol. ii, *Partnership, 1892–1912* (Cambridge; Cambridge University Press and LSE, 1978), p. 260, Beatrice to Sidney, 14 June, 1907.

10 McBriar, *Edwardian Mixed Doubles*, p. 368.

11 Discussion of Bernard Bosanquet's 'Idealism in Social Work', *Charity Organisation Review* (March 1898), 166.

12 Stefan Collini, 'Hobhouse, Bosanquet and the State: Philosophical Idealism and Political Argument in England 1880–1914', *Past and Present*, no. 72 (August 1976), 92.

13 Beatrice Webb's Diary, TS, BLPES (hereafter BWD), 30 April, 1883 f. 300.

14 Octavia Hill Papers, Marylebone Public Library, D. Misc. 84/5, especially *Letters to My Fellow Workers*, 1878–90.

15 Beatrice Webb, *My Apprenticeship* (1926; Cambridge: Cambridge University Press, 1979), pp. 261–265.

16 BWD, 10 Dec, 1886, f. 755.

17 BWD, 5 August, 1881, f. 172.

18 BWD, 2 Feb., 1881, f. 156.

19 BWD, 27 Dec., 1883, f. 348.

20 BWD, 21 Feb., 1889, f. 1009.

21 *My Apprenticeship*, p. 282.

22 Passfield Papers II (i) II, BLPES, item 154, Ella Pycroft to Beatrice Webb, 1 July, 1886.

23 BWD, 28 May, 1886, f. 669; and 9 Oct., 1886, f. 717.

24 BWD, 28 May, 1886, f. 666.

25 *My Apprenticeship*, p. 201.

26 BWD, 18 May, 1883, f. 308.

27 BWD, 20 May, 1883, f. 311.

28 Passfield Papers II (i) II, item 155, Pycroft to Beatrice Webb, 15 July, 1886.

29 BWD, 18 May, 1883, f. 308.

30 *My Apprenticeship*, pp. 202, 267, 278.

31 Helen Dendy, 'Thorough Charity', *Charity Organisation Review* (June 1893), 277.

32 *My Apprenticeship*, p. 202.

33 *My Apprenticeship*, p. 277.

34 BWD, 7 Nov., 1886, f. 743, 745.

35 *My Apprenticeship*, p. 202.

36 BWD, 30 July, 1893, f. 1286; 21 Sept., 1894, f. 1335; 21 Oct., 1901, f. 2097; 8 June, 1904, f. 2292–3.

37 *My Apprenticeship*, p. 193.

38 *My Apprenticeship*, p. 286.
39 *My Apprenticeship*, p. 286.
40 *My Apprenticeship*, pp. 245, 248.
41 Mrs Sidney Webb, 'Methods of Investigation', *Sociological Papers 1906* (London: Macmillans, 1907), pp. 345–51.
42 BWD, 31 Jan, 1900, f. 1986; 28 May, 1900, f. 2002.
43 T. H. Marshall, Introduction to Sidney and Beatrice Webb, *Methods of Social Study* (1932; Cambridge: Cambridge University Press, 1975) p. xxxv.
44 *My Apprenticeship*, p. 256.
45 *My Apprenticeship*, p. 358.
46 Deborah Epstein Nord, *The Apprenticeship of Beatrice Webb* (London: Allen and Unwin, 1930), p. xi.
47 Beatrice Potter, *The Cooperative Movement in Great Britain* (London: Allen and Unwin, 1930).
48 BWD, 16 May, 1899, f. 1961.
49 *My Apprenticeship*, p. 317.
50 BWD, 24 April, 1899, f. 1958.
51 *My Apprenticeship*, p. 357.
52 *My Apprenticeship*, p. 413.
53 BWD, 2 Jan., 1901, f. 2055; and 15 June, 1903, f. 2217.
54 Mrs Sidney Webb, '*Methods of Investigation*', pp. 352–3.
55 Marshall, Introduction to *Methods of Social Study*, p. xxxv.
56 BWD, 1 May, 1897, f. 1488.
57 BWD, 30 Jan, 1902, f. 2117; and 3 Nov., 1903, f. 2243.
58 BWD, 25 Feb., 1903, f. 2189.
59 Bernard Bosanquet, 'The Philosophy of Casework', *Charity Organisation Review* (March 1916), 17–33.
60 Helen Dendy, 'The Industrial Residuum', in Bernard Bosanquet (ed.), *Aspects of Social Reform* (London: Macmillan, 1895), p. 83.
61 Helen Bosanquet, *The Strength of the People. A Study in Social Economics* (1902; London: Macmillan, 1903), pp. 51 and 55.
62 Bosanquet, *The Strength of the People*, pp. 8–9.
63 Bernard Bosanquet, 'Duties of Citizenship', in Bosanquet, *Aspects*, p. 10.
64 Helen Bosanquet, *The Family* (London: Macmillan, 1906), p. 99.
65 Helen Bosanquet 'Methods of Training', *Charity Organisation Review* (August 1900), reprinted in Marjorie Smith, *Professional Education for Social Workers in Britain* (London: Allen and Unwin, 1953), p. 91.
66 McBriar stresses the influence of classical political economy on Helen Bosanquet, *Edwardian Mixed Doubles*, p. 13; C. L. Mowat, *The Charity Organisation Society, 1869–1913* (London: Methuen, 1961), also emphasises economic influences.
67 Ross McKibbin, 'Social Class and Social Observation in Edwardian England', *Transactions of the Royal Historical Society*, 28 (1978), 175–99.
68 Helen Bosanquet, *The Standard of Life and Other Studies* (London: Macmillan, 1898), pp. 31–4.
69 Helen Dendy, 'The Children of Working London', in Bosanquet, *Aspects*, p. 32.

70 Mrs Bernard Bosanquet, *Rich and Poor* (London: Macmillan, 1896), pp. 102 and 107.
71 Bosanquet, *Rich and Poor*, p. 120.
72 Helen Bosanquet, *The Poverty Line* (COS, 1903). Of the Fabian publications, *Facts for Londoners* was subjected to particularly scathing attack by the COS; see C. S. Loch, 'Returns as an Instrument in Social Science', in Bosanquet, *Aspects*, pp. 268–88.
73 Helen Bosanquet, 'The Historical Basis of the Poor Law', *Economic Journal*, 20 (June 1910) 185; Marshall, Introduction to *Methods of Social Study*, p. xxxv.
74 Bosanquet, *Rich and Poor*, p. 120.
75 A. Vincent and R. Plant, *Philosophy, Politics and Citizenship* (Oxford: Blackwell, 1984), p. 181.
76 For example, Kitty Muggeridge and Ruth Adam, *Beatrice Webb. A Life 1958–1943* (London: Secker and Warburg), p. 182.
77 BWD, 27 Nov., 1987, f. 894; and Mackenzie (ed.), *The Letters of Sidney and Beatrice Webb*. vol. ii, p. 5, 18 April, 1893, Beatrice Webb to Edward Pease.
78 Beatrice Webb, *Our Partnership*, ed. B. Drake and M. I. Cole (1948; Cambridge: Cambridge University Press, 1975), p. 377.
79 *Our Partnership*, p. 323; and BWD, 12 March, 1906, f. 2388.
80 *Our Partnership*, p. 392.
81 Mackenzie (ed.), *Letters of Sidney and Beatrice Webb*, vol. ii, p. 313, 2 May, 1908, Beatrice to Sidney.
82 BWD, 30 Jan., 1908, f. 2528. Alan J. Kidd, 'Historians or Polemicists? How the Webbs wrote their History of the Poor Laws', *Economic History Review*, 40 (August, 1987), pp. 400–17 has shown how a mixture of polemic and scholarly research also permeated the Webb's history of the poor laws written during the 1920s.
83 Bosanquet, 'Historical Basis of the Poor Law', p. 185.
84 Mrs Sidney Webb, 'The Prevention of Destitution', *The Royal Commission on the Poor Laws and Relief of Distress, A Course of Nine Lectures*, Sheffield Weekly News Reprints (Sheffield: W. C. Leng and Co., 1909), p. 17.
85 *My Apprenticeship*, p. 42.
86 A. W. Vincent, 'The Poor Law Reports of 1909 and the Social Theory of the COS', *Victorian Studies*, 27 (1984), 343–63.
87 Bernard Bosanquet, 'The Majority Report', *Sociological Review*, 2 (1909), 112.
88 'The Majority Report', p. 115; and Bernard Bosanquet, 'Charity Organisation and the Majority', *International Journal of Ethics*, 20 (1910), 405.
89 Bosanquet, 'The Majority Report', p. 115.
90 Mackenzie (ed.), *Letters of Sidney and Beatrice Webb*. vol. ii, p. 260, 14 June, 1907, Beatrice to Sidney.
91 BWD, 5 Dec., 1925, f. 4231.
92 Helen Bosanquet, 'Reconstructions of What?' *The Hibbert Journal*, June 1909, Bosanquet Papers, Trunk J, Box G, Newcastle University Library.

CHAPTER SIX

W. E. B. Du Bois as a social investigator: The Philadelphia Negro, 1899

MARTIN BULMER

The present period in the development of sociological study is a trying one; it is the period of observation, research and comparison – work always wearisome, often aimless without well-settled principles and guiding lines, and subject always to the persistent criticism: What, after all, has been accomplished? To this the most positive answer which years of research and speculation have been able to return is that the phenomena of society are worth the most careful and systematic study, and whether or not this study may eventually lead to a systematic body of knowledge deserving the name of science, it cannot in any case fail to give the world a mass of truth worth the knowing.

Being then in a period of observation and comparison, we must confess to ourselves that the sociologists of few nations have so good an opportunity for observing the growth and evolution of society as those in the United States. The rapid rise of a young country, the vast social changes, the wonderful economic development, the bold political experiments, and the contact of varying moral standards – all these make the American students crucial tests of social action, microcosmic reproductions of long centuries of world history and rapid – even violent – repetitions of great social problems. Here is a field for the sociologists – a field rich, but little worked, and full of great possibilities. European scholars envy our opportunities and it must be said to our credit that great interest in the observation of social phenomena has been aroused in the last decade – an interest of which much is ephemeral and superficial, but which opens the way for broad scholarship and scientific effort.

In one field, however – and a field perhaps larger than any other domain of social phenomena, there does not seem to have been awakened as yet a fitting realization of the opportunities for scientific inquiry. This is the group of social phenomena arising from the presence in this land of eight million persons of African descent.[1]

The writer was W. E. B. Du Bois, the year 1898. The tone of his remarks have a remarkably modern ring to them, and suggest a sophisticated understanding of the possible contribution of empirical social science before that contribution was well established. He had just completed the field work for his study *The Philadelphia Negro*, published in 1899. Yet Du Bois' work in Philadelphia and his subsequent attempts to develop a research programme at Atlanta University failed to have significant impact, and twelve years later, in 1910, he himself abandoned empirical social science for political activism and journalism. This episode forms part of the American social survey tradition, and is instructive both in its own right and by comparison with the position of women discussed by Kathryn Sklar in relation to Florence Kelley, in chapter 4.

William Edward Burghardt Du Bois was born in Great Barrington, Massachusetts in 1868, into a free black family. He was descended through his mother's side from an African slave, Tom Burghardt, who had been brought to New England early in the eighteenth century by a Dutch family. His father's family was of mixed white and black descent; his father abandoned his mother when he was small, and he – an only child – was brought up by her, who worked as a maid. Growing up in Great Barrington in a community where the colour line was not rigidly enforced, the young Du Bois learnt protestant, Yankee, values and to look down on ethnic immigrants from Central and Eastern Europe. Du Bois, however, was one of very few black people in a predominantly white community, which had a determining influence on his education. When he graduated from the local high school, he was the first black student to do so. Shortly thereafter his mother died. Four members of the white elite of the town stepped in, and arranged for Du Bois' study at college to be financially supported. Du Bois himself hoped to attend Harvard, but they arranged for him to be admitted to Fisk University in Nashville, the leading black college in the South, which he entered in 1885 and graduated from in 1888, having studied classics and liberal arts and edited the college newspaper. During the summer vacations he taught in black schools in the rural south.

In 1888 Du Bois achieved his ambition of being admitted to Harvard, financing his studies with a mixture of scholarships and vacation earnings. There he took undergraduate courses for two years, graduating with honours in philosophy and giving the class oration in 1890. This was followed by two years of graduate study working towards the PhD, taking courses in history and political science and starting work on a dissertation on the African slave trade which he submitted in 1895.[2] Although he took a course in sociology at Harvard from Edward Cummings, a professor of ethics with interests in this subject, it apparently made little impression. His dissertation is much more a straight historical monograph. A far more formative influence was the two years which Du Bois spent studying in Germany between 1892 and 1894, financed by the Slater Fund for the Education of Negroes, chaired by former President Rutherford B. Hayes.

At the University of Berlin, he took courses in economic history and sociology, including a course by the young Max Weber, and was

particularly influenced by Gustav Schmoller. With Schmoller, Du Bois did
research on the pattern of plantation economics and peonage in the South.
Schmoller favoured the use of induction to accumulate historical and
descriptive material. Social scientific facts, accumulated by careful inductive
analysis, could produce systematic causal explanations of social phenomena.
Schmoller, however, was also deeply involved in issues of social policy
through the *Verein für Sozialpolitik* and believed that social science could
contribute to social intervention. He insisted, however, on the distinction
between fact and value, and instilled this in his students. Du Bois quoted
his mentor as having said in a seminar: 'My school tries as far as possible
to leave the *Sollen* [should be] for a later stage and study the *Geschehen* [is]
as other sciences have done'.[3]

Du Bois' early studies, up to 1910, bear the influence of Schmoller: the
careful attention to empirical detail as a means of making inductive
generalisations, the use of empirical inquiry to illuminate issues of social
policy, an underlying interest in social justice and an historical approach.
'Schmoller ... drew Du Bois away from history into a type of political
economy which could easily be converted into sociology, and, at a more
general level, encouraged him to a career devoted to scholarship.'[4] As Du
Bois himself later recalled, he reacted against grand theories and appeals to
abstract principles. 'I determined to put science into sociology through a
study of the condition and problems of my own group. I was going to
study the facts, any and all the facts, concerning the American Negro and
his plight, and by measurement and comparison and research, work up to
any valid generalization which I could.'[5]

These details about Du Bois' early development are more relevant to
understanding his pioneering use of the social survey method than in the
case of, say, residents at the Hull-House, because as a scholar Du Bois
lacked the support of those around him and was essentially solitary,
working on his own and relying almost entirely upon his own resources.
To some extent this was a matter of temperament, but it mainly reflected
the social isolation which he experienced after 1888 as a black student in
a white world. At Harvard he mixed little with his white peers and
experienced loneliness. He found more congenial social contacts while in
Germany but still relied to a great extent upon his own resources. A diary
entry on his twenty-fifth birthday found him singing 'Jesus, Lover of my
Soul' and 'America' alone in his Berlin room and ruminating about his
future responsibility to advance the scientific study of the black race, the
search for scientific truth, the 'cold and indisputable' research that was
necessary to advance the interests of all black people. 'These are my plans:

to make a name in science, to make a name in literature and thus to raise my race.'[6]

The Trustees of the Slater Fund would not extend Du Bois' award to remain in Berlin for the third year necessary to obtain the PhD degree there. Schmoller petitioned for Du Bois to be admitted to the degree with less than the requisite number of semesters of study, but was not successful. Du Bois returned to the United States to work on completing his PhD for Harvard. Immediately he began teaching at Wilberforce University, an African Methodist church school in Ohio, where he stayed for two years, wrote up his PhD for for publication, married and clashed with the school authorities over various matters. An approach in 1896 to conduct a study of the black community in Philadelphia was therefore welcome and one which he accepted with alacrity.

The offer came from the Provost of the University of Pennsylvania, Charles C. Harrison, who wrote that the aim was to conduct an extensive study 'of the social condition of the Coloured People in the Seventh Ward of Philadelphia ... We want to know precisely how this class of people live; what occupations they follow; from what occupations they are excluded; how many of their children go to school; and to ascertain every fact which will throw light on this social problem'.[7] The instigator of the idea of the study was Susan P. Wharton, a member of the family which established the Wharton School and a Quaker member of the executive committee of the Philadelphia College Settlement, long interested in philanthropy for the black population. Wharton herself, Harrison and many of Philadelphia's wealthier families themselves lived in the Seventh Ward and had had an opportunity to observe social conditions at first hand. The meeting to plan the idea of the study took place at Wharton's house, only a few blocks from the black ghetto and the College Settlement House.[8] She asked the provost 'for the cooperation of the University in a plan for the better understanding of the coloured people, especially of their position in the city ... [we] are interested in a plan to obtain a body of reliable information as to the obstacles to be encountered by the coloured people in their endeavour to be self-supporting'.[9] One may speculate that the influence of the *Hull-House Maps and Papers* may not have been inconsiderable in suggesting a model for such a study.

Du Bois' name as a possible scholar to undertake the task was apparently suggested by Pennsylvania sociology professor Samuel McCune Lindsay. Du Bois was offered and accepted the one-year appointment at a salary of US $800 and moved with his young wife to the city in the summer of 1896, living in a one-room apartment above a cafeteria run by the College

Settlement. Du Bois later described its location as 'in the worst part of the Seventh Ward. We lived there a year,[10] in the midst of an atmosphere of dirt, drunkenness, poverty and crime. Murder sat on our doorsteps, police were our government and philanthropy dropped in with periodic advice.'[11]

For fifteen months, Du Bois immersed himself in the detailed empirical study of the Seventh Ward, the largest concentration of black people in a city which at that time had a black population of 45,000, the largest anywhere in the North. His experience of carrying out the study was different from that of Charles Booth or Florence Kelley, for he worked on his own with little support from others. Although nominally attached to the university with the position of 'Assistant Instructor', he had a one-year appointment which was not renewed, no office there, his name did not appear in the university catalogue, he taught no students, and he had only peripheral contact with members of the sociology department. His time was spent entirely in the black district, his principal social contacts, perforce, were with black rather than white Philadelphians. Colour distanced him too from the white philanthropists who had initiated the study, and meant that his contact with them was not on a regular basis. (A decade later Du Bois was in regular collaboration with Mary White Ovington, a white New York social worker with Settlement House connections and strong interests in the condition of black people. They both helped to establish the National Association for the Advancement of Coloured People in 1909, an organisation in which both white women and black men were prominent.[12]) The contrast between the Seventh Ward study and Hull House was marked. Florence Kelley was a resident of Hull House and full participant, W. E. B. Du Bois resided above a cafeteria belonging to the Philadelphia Settlement and was not a participant in the work of the Settlement.

This, it is true, was partly a matter of his own choice. Du Bois' study was a study of the *black* community and for many years his main social contacts, out of necessity and to some extent out of choice, were with other black people.[13] More important, his conception of science was a more rigorous one than that of Florence Kelley, and it precluded too close identification with philanthropy and social intervention. His task was to carry out the study. That task he fulfilled, and the empirical research required he did himself without the assistance of settlement house residents or a recruited research team.

The resulting monograph, a classic of American social science, was more limited in scale than the studies of Booth or Kelley, but gained in scope and penetration what it lost in extensiveness. *The Philadelphia Negro* was a study in depth of the social conditions of the 4,000 black people living in the Seventh Ward. After a historical introduction, it described their geographical distribution in the ward, the demographic, occupational and family structure, educational and housing conditions, and relations between the black and the white communities. Social and political organisation, the incidence of crime and the causes of pauperism and alcoholism were also examined. The emphasis upon social problems, however, was considerably less than in either *Life and Labour* or the *Hull-House Maps and Papers*, reflecting the fact that *The Philadelphia Negro* was a sociological community study as much as an examination of a social problem, or rather an approach to the latter through the former. It was intended to be a work of social science as well as an examination of social conditions. Indeed one of W. E. B. Du Bois' aims was to provide a detailed portrayal of life for black people in the Seventh Ward, and to show that black Philadelphians were a product of their social environment.

The design and execution of *The Philadelphia Negro* was clearly influenced by recent social surveys which had been carried out in Britain and the United States, particularly by Booth's London survey. Although there are a few references to Booth in the monograph, in general there is very little in the way of citation of other literature, so one's inferences are necessarily somewhat speculative. The short bibliography (pp. 419–23) is mainly devoted to material about and by black Philadelphians, but there are twenty-eight more general references. Three of these are to publications of Du Bois himself, thirteen are historical works about slavery or the history of Pennsylvania, five are publications of the Society of Friends (Quakers) about slavery, only seven are contemporary data sources or studies relevant to his subject. They include the US Census as a source of data, Richmond Mayo Smith's *Statistics and Sociology*, Carroll D. Wrights's 1894 report *Slums of Great Cities*, three Atlanta University monographs from 1896–8 on the condition of the black population, and only three monographs. These are the *First and Second Sociological Canvasses* of the Federation of Churches and Christian Workers in New York City, edited by Walter Laidlaw, from 1896–7, the *Hull-House Maps and Papers* from 1895, and Booth's *Life and Labour* in the 1892 edition. This list points to Carroll Wright and Richmond Mayo-Smith as influences on the statistical side, and the Booth and Hull House studies as models for the investigations as a whole.

This conclusion is supported by Du Bois' use of maps. The colour map reproduced in plate 4 of this volume appears to be closely modelled upon those in the *Hull-House Maps and Papers*. Part of the household map of 'The Distribution of the Negro Inhabitants throughout the Ward, and their social condition'[14] is reproduced in plate 4. It shows the black population of the ward classified house by house into one of four social classes in a manner combining the mapping techniques of Booth and Hull House. Du Bois' use of maps was sparing, but it was clear what were his contemporary models.

In his *Autobiography*, Du Bois recalled that he produced a clear plan of research when initially approach by the university, but that he had no particular methodological predilections:

I started with no 'research methods' and I asked little advice as to procedure. The problem lay before me. Study it. I studied it personally and not by proxy. I sent out no canvassers. I went myself. Personally I visited and talked with 5,000 persons. What I could, I set down in orderly sequence on schedules which I made out and submitted to the University for criticism. Other information I stored in in my memory or wrote out as memoranda. I went through the Philadelphia libraries for data, and gained access in many instances to private libraries of coloured folk and got individual information. I mapped the district, classifying it by conditions; I compiled two centuries of the history of the negro in Philadelphia and in the Seventh Ward.[15]

This account owes something to hindsight, for Du Bois clearly did have ideas about how to collect data which were not simply derived from his studies in Berlin nor constructed from common sense.

Two features of the study were particularly important. A systematic attempt was made to gather and collate data about the black population of the Seventh Ward from various sources. A principal source was a house-to-house canvas carried out by Du Bois himself throughout the ward, using schedules that he filled in. He constructed a family schedule and an individual schedule with questions about age, sex, conjugal condition, birthplace, literacy, occupation, earnings, ill health and association membership. The schedules contained simple questions about particular topics, but with explanatory notes which indicated a considerable degree of thought had gone into their preparation. For example, the family schedule included the questions 14 and 15: Occupations since 1 October 1891? *and* Present occupation? The rubric accompanying these two questions was as follows:

This is an important inquiry. Simple as it appears, it is always difficult in census work to get satisfactory replies to the question. Inaccuracy and insufficiency of statement are the most prominent evils to be avoided;
For instance, *remember*: We want to know not what a man 'works in' but what he does. We want to *distinguish between*: the owner or director of a business and one who works at it; between waiters and head waiters; between cooks in private families and in hotels; between coachmen, hackmen and draymen; between merchants and pedlers and those who keep stands.[16]

These detailed guidelines for the inquiry in the Seventh Ward read as if they may have been derived from the practice of the United States Census.

The second innovation was in conducting personal interviews himself with the black inhabitants of the Seventh Ward. Like Rowntree, Du Bois concluded that there was no substitute for direct questioning of the population to gather social data, using a systematic method of recording data. Like Rowntree, he carried out a complete enumeration of all households. Unlike Rowntree, he did all the interviewing himself. He described it in his monograph:

[i]n the fall of 1896 a house-to-house visitation was made of all the Negro families of this ward. The visitor went in person to each residence and called for the head of the family. The housewife usually responded, the husband now and then, and sometimes an older daughter or other member of the family. The fact that the University was making an investigation of this character was known and discussed in the ward, but its exact scope and character was not known. The mere announcement of the purpose secured, in all but about twelve cases, immediate admission. Seated then in the parlor, kitchen or living room, the visitor began the questioning, using his discretion as to the order in which they were put, and omitting or adding questions as the circumstances suggested. Now and then the purpose of a particular query was explained, and usually the object of the whole inquiry indicated. General discussion often arose as to the condition of the Negroes, which were instructive. For ten minutes to an hour was spent in each home, the average time being fifteen to twenty-five minutes.[17]

Du Bois was aware of the limitations of the study. Non-response was a problem in only a few cases. Of the twelve cases where no data was obtained, the majority were brothels but a few were 'homes of respectable people who resented the investigation as unwarranted and unnecessary'.[18] To assuage concern, the Family Schedule ended with the following caveat, which has a curiously modern ring to it:

Finally, remember that the information given is confidential; the University of Pennsylvania will strictly guard it as such, and allow no-one to have access to the schedules for other than scientific purposes. We ask, under these conditions, careful, accurate and truthful answers.[19]

But the reception that he received was not always of the warmest. As he recalled in his autobiography, his respondents did not receive him with open arms, and had a natural dislike of being studied as a 'stranger species'. It was a learning experience for the intellectual Du Bois. 'They set me groping. I concluded that I did not know so much as I might about my own people ... I became painfully aware that merely being born in a group, does not necessarily make one possessed of complete knowledge concerning it'.[20] One may surmise that the social distance between Du Bois and some of his respondents was considerable. Only two years before, colleagues at Wilberforce University in Ohio has been disconcerted by Du Bois appearing in high silk hat, gloves and walking stick, which combined with his dapper Vandyke beard, created a distinctive impression.[21] No doubt his dress was adjusted for the Seventh Ward, but this distinguished young member of the 'talented tenth' did not fit naturally into the milieu which he was studying. This made what he achieved all the more remarkable.

He himself recognised in the monograph that the quality of the data collected in the household interviews might have been contaminated by various factors, and he attempted to compensate for it.

Usually the answers [to the visitor's questions] were prompt and candid, and gave no suspicion of previous preparation. In some cases there was evident falsification or evasion. In such cases the visitor made free use of his best judgement and either inserted no answer at all, or one which seemed approximately true. In some cases the families visited were not at home, and a second or third visit was paid. In other cases, and especially in the case of the large class of lodgers, the testimony of landlords and neighbours often had to be taken. No one can make an inquiry of this sort and not be painfully conscious of a large margin of error from omissions, errors of judgement and deliberate deception. Of such errors this study has, without doubt, its full share. Only one fact was particularly favourable and that is the proverbial good nature and candour of the Negro. With a more cautious and suspicious people, much less could have been obtained. Naturally some questions were answered better than others; the chief difficulty arising in regard to the questions of age and income. The ages given for people forty and over [born prior to the abolition of slavery – MB] have a large margin of error, owing to ignorance of the real birthday. The question of income was naturally a delicate one, and often had to be gotten at indirectly.[22]

The methods of research used attempted to take account of the imperfections of the various sources, but placed particular weight upon the information gathered by Du Bois himself from a complete enumeration of black families in the Seventh District. Du Bois also made brief comparative studies of black Philadelphians in other parts of the city to compare his results with those that might be obtained in other areas. His empirical methods thus proceeded along careful lines which anticipated several standard features of twentieth-century social research. What is remarkable is how well worked-out they were at this period, when systematic social investigation using the survey method was in its infancy. Nor was the study purely descriptive, incorporating analyses of family structure, social stratification within the black community, the causation of crime and the effects of colour prejudice. Many of the black residents of the Seventh Ward came from rural Virginia, and at the same time as researching the monograph, Du Bois carried out a study of the skills, attitudes and habits which they brought with them to the North, which was published in 1898.[23]

The book begins with a clear statement of why the Negro problem in Philadelphia is of interest.

Here is a large group of people ... who do not form part of the larger social group. This is not altogether unusual; there are other unassimilated groups: Jews, Italians, even Americans; and yet in the case of the Negroes, the segregation is more conspicuous, patent to the eye, and so intertwined with a long historical evolution, with peculiarly pressing social problems of poverty, ignorance, crime and labour, that the Negro problem far surpasses in scientific interest and social gravity most of the other race and class questions'.[24]

Two chapters provide an historical introduction about black people in Philadelphia but the study is not primarily historical. Six chapters describe the characteristics of the black population of the Seventh Ward demographically, in terms of conjugal condition, birthplace, education and illiteracy, occupation and health. There then follow several chapters on Philadelphia Negroes as a social group, dealing with the negro family, black churches and other social organisations, the negro criminal and pauperism and alcoholism as problems in the community. A final group of chapters consider the physical and social environment, including housing and social stratification within the black community (on which Du Bois laid considerable emphasis in his introduction), race contacts and negro suffrage. In the final chapter, 'a word of general advice in the line of social reform is added',[25] though it is notable for the detached tone in which policy issues were addressed.

Instances only of the analysis offered may be given here. The chapter on the family presented data on black family structure in the Seventh Ward derived from Du Bois' survey. He had data on 2,441 families, containing 7,751 members; in addition, 1,924 lodgers lived in these families, a total population of 9,675. He analysed family incomes, some data on property ownership, and commented on the social disorganisation of family life consequent upon the experience of slavery, low incomes and high rents. Among the poor, temporary cohabitation was not uncommon; among the families with comfortable incomes, taking in of lodgers was common as means of meeting the rent. The analysis is a mixture of descriptive sociology and identification of social problems – for example the presence of adult strangers as lodgers in households with unsupervised young children – with an emphasis upon the former.

In the chapter on contact between the races, Du Bois provided an analysis of the effects of colour prejudice upon black Philadelphians, observing that while it did not account for the greater part of Negro problems, it was a far more powerful social force than most Philadelphians realised. He distinguished its effects upon ability to secure and to keep work, upon income and expenditure, upon children, and upon social intercourse with other racial groups. The effects of prejudice in each of these areas were illustrated with detailed cases collected during field work. This chapter was more analytical than several of the more descriptive ones, pointing out the obstacles under which black Americans laboured, and the role of white public opinion in maintaining this state of affairs.

Du Bois' capacity for analysis of a problem in the light of his data is evident in his discussion of stratification within the black community. Du Bois paid explicit attention to this, as he did in his rural study of Farmville, Virginia, within the framework of a sociological rather than a social policy problematic.

There is always a strong tendency on the part of the community to consider the Negroes as composing one practically homogeneous mass. This view has of course a certain justification: the people of Negro descent in this land have had a common history, suffer today common disabilities, and contribute to one general set of social problems. And yet if the foregoing statistics have emphasized any one fact it is that wide variation in antecedents, wealth, intelligence and general efficiency have already been differentiated within this group. These differences are not, to be sure, so great or so patent as those among the whites today, and yet they undoubtedly equal the difference among the masses of the people in certain sections of the land fifty or one hundred years ago; and there is no surer way of misunderstanding the Negro or being misunderstood by him than by ignoring manifest differences of condition and power in the 40,000 black people in Philadelphia.
And yet well-meaning people continually do this. They regale the thugs and whoremongers and gamblers of Seventh and Lombard streets with congratulations on what the Negroes have done in a quarter century and pity for their disabilities; and they scold the caterers of Addison Street for the pickpockets and paupers of the race. A judge of the city courts, who for years had daily met a throng of lazy and debased Negro criminals, comes from the bench to talk to the Negroes about their criminals; he warns them first of all to leave the slums and either forgets or does not know that the fathers of the audience he is speaking to, left the slums when he was a boy and the people before him are as distinctly differentiated from the criminals he has met, as honest laborers anywhere differ from thieves. Nothing more exasperates the better class of Negroes than this tendency to ignore utterly their existence.[26]

Du Bois was not just making a point about the treatment of black Philadelphians, for he immediately followed with an analysis of the social structure of the black community. He distinguished four groups within the black people of the seventh ward. The first were 'families of undoubted respectability earning sufficient income to live well; not engaged in menial service of any kind'. These were 'the aristocracy of the Negro population in education, wealth and general social efficiency'. He estimated that they comprised about 11 per cent of the black population of the Seventh Ward. He emphasised that this group kept to itself socially, and it would be almost impossible for a white person to meet members of the class. The second were 'the respectable working class', in comfortable circumstances in a good home with steady work. These were the mass of the servant class, the porters and waiters, and the best of labourers'. He estimated from his survey data that they comprised 56 per cent of the black population of the ward.
The third were the poor, persons not earning enough to keep them at

all times above want. They were honest, though not always energetic or thrifty. According to his survey, just over 30 per cent of families fell into this category of the poor or very poor. The fourth were the lowest class of criminals, prostitutes and loafers, the 'submerged tenth'. Du Bois estimated that on the basis of his canvas about 6 per cent of the population of the ward fell into this category; the proportion might rise slightly if one made allowance for defective data.[27] Du Bois also made a separate classification of his data in terms of income, and compared the incidence of poverty in black Philadelphia with its distribution in London according to Booth. Figure 6.1 shows the results presented, which as Du Bois observes, depend heavily upon how the 'comfortable' are treated. The line between that group and the 'poor' is less stable than in London because their economic status is less fixed.

In good times perhaps 50 percent of the Negroes could well be designated comfortable but in times of financial stress vast numbers of this class fall below the line into the poor and go to swell the number of paupers, and in many cases criminals. Indeed, this whole division of incomes of different classes is, among the Negroes, much less stable than among the whites, just as it used to be less stable among the whites of fifty years ago than it is among those of today'.[28]

How is one to assess the contribution of *The Philadelphia Negro*? It made no conceptual breakthrough comparable to Booth's or Rowntree's conceptualisation of poverty. It was not a study of a whole city or town, but of the black population of one section of a city; in that respect it was less comprehensive in its coverage than Booth or Rowntree. The monograph was, however, a pioneering social survey which studied that black population comprehensively and systematically. It was unique in its intensity of study, and there was nothing comparable being produced at the time from Columbia under Giddings or Chicago under Small. It was one of the first sociological urban community studies, employing a conception of social structure and addressing a wide range of sociological issues both descriptively and analytically. The description is more apparent, but underlying the description were theoretical notions which informed the analysis, ideas about the role of social environment in the determination of social outcomes which were quite novel for the period.[29] For example, in his analysis of the causes of crime in the black community, he suggested a connection between the experience of racial prejudice and involvement in crime. But the connection was not simple or direct.

The boy who is refused promotion in his job as porter does not go out and snatch somebody's pocketbook. Conversely the loafers at Twelfth and Kater streets, and the thugs in the county prison are not usually graduates of high schools who have been refused work. The connections are much more subtle and dangerous; it is the atmosphere of rebellion and

Average earnings per wk	No. of families	%	Comparison		
$5 & less	420 { 192	8.9	Very poor		
	228	9.6	Poor		
$5-10	1088	47.8	Fair		
$10-15	581	25.5	Comfortable		
$15-20	91	4.0	Good Circumstances		
$20 & over	96	4.2	Well-to-do		
TOTAL	2276	100.00%			

It is difficult to compare this with other groups because of the varying meaning of the terms poor, well-to-do, and the like. Nevertheless, a comparison with Booth's diagram of London will, if not carried too far, be interesting:

Poverty in London and Among the Negroes of the Seventh Ward of Philadelphia.

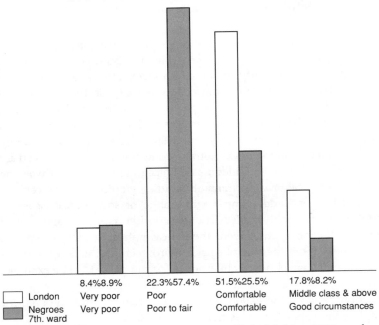

	8.4%8.9%	22.3%57.4%	51.5%25.5%	17.8%8.2%
□ London	Very poor	Poor	Comfortable	Middle class & above
▨ Negroes 7th. ward	Very poor	Poor to fair	Comfortable	Good circumstances

Figure 6.1   Poverty among negroes in Philadelphia, 1896, and a comparison with Booth's findings in London. From W. E. B. Du Bois, *The Philadelphia Negro*, p. 171. The Booth data is taken from *Life and Labour of the People*, II, p. 21.

discontent that unrewarded merit and reasonable but unsatisfied ambition make. The social environment of excuse, listless despair, careless indulgence and lack of inspiration to work is the growing force that turns black boys and girls into gamblers, prostitutes and rascals. And this social environment has been built up slowly out of the disappointments of deserving men and the sloth of the unawakened.[30]

The extent to which Du Bois' study was a pioneering one has not been recognised to the extent that it should be. The omissions are of two kinds. On the one hand the sheer failure to mention *The Philadelphia Negro* in discussions of the history of the early social survey is remarkable. Out of eleven publications between 1911 and 1952 which reviewed the use of the social survey in sociology, only one mentions Du Bois.[31] One is struck by the lack of impact which the study had at the time and its lack of emulators. It is extraordinary, for example, that even in the city in which it was carried out, it was 'the one important study of lower-class life in Philadelphia done before the 1960's ... it did not stimulate further analysis along similar lines, at least not in Philadelphia'.[32] This neglect of a classic study owed a great deal to the fact that Du Bois was black, and that American sociologists in the period between 1890 and 1910 were not particularly interested in studying black America.[33] Robert Park did not begin teaching at the University of Chicago until 1913.

Yet contemporary evidence of Du Bois' stature is provided by his contacts with Max Weber. On his visit to the United States in 1904[34], to attend the St Louis Congress of Arts and Sciences, where he presented a paper on German social structure, Weber met Du Bois in Atlanta; he had either known Du Bois in Berlin or heard of him from Schmoller[35] and had been in correspondence with him.[36] He arranged for Du Bois to contribute an article on the situation of the negro in the United States to the *Archiv*, which was published in 1906.[37] The preceding article to that by Du Bois in the journal was by Georg Simmel, the article immediately following by Robert Michels. He was in good company.

Du Bois' race meant that when the study was completed, he had no chance of an appointment at one of the leading American universities, all of which were all-white.[38] Baltzell observes that had the monograph been published in the 1960s, Du Bois would have been besieged with job offers from leading departments. This was not so in the 1890s. In his presentation to the American Academy of Arts and Sciences in 1898, shortly after research for *The Philadelphia Negro* was finished but before it was published, he called for a research programme located in a black college 'which is not merely a teaching body, but a centre of sociological research, in close connection and cooperation with Harvard, Columbia, Johns Hopkins and the University of Pennsylvania'.[39] There was no response. After the completion of the study Du Bois moved to Atlanta University, a black university, where he continued a research programme on black Americans over the next decade, with creditable results considering the lack of resources from which he suffered there.

The Philadelphia Negro was reviewed in a number of magazines and in the *American Historical Journal*.[40] It was not reviewed in the *American Journal of Sociology*. Du Bois received almost no acknowledgement among (white) sociologists. The sociology of race relations, when it first became substantially established, developed at the University of Chicago a decade later under W. I. Thomas and Robert Park, assisted by black sociologist Charles S. Johnson.[41] Du Bois struggled purposefully at Atlanta University to develop a research programme, but with relatively little success. He observed in 1904:

We can go to the South Sea Islands half way around the world and beat and shoot a weak people longing for freedom into the slavery of American colour prejudice at the cost of hundreds of millions, and yet at Atlanta University we beg annually and beg in vain for the paltry sum of $500 simply to aid us in replacing gross and vindictive ignorance of race conditions with enlightening knowledge and systematic observation.[42]

Despite these obstacles, he organised a programme of research, enlisted the help of part-time, unpaid assistants throughout the South, and published sixteen monographs between 1898 and 1914.[43] Their quality, however, was not as high as that of *The Philadelphia Negro*, inevitably given the demands on Du Bois' time from teaching. This also reflected the funding difficulties.

The total cost of the thirteen publications [published in the Atlanta series up to that date, he wrote in 1909] has been about $14,000 or a little over $1,000 a year. The growing demands of the work, the vast field to be covered and the delicacy and equipment needed in such work call for far greater resources. We need, for workers, laboratory and publications, a fund of $6,000 a year, if this work is going to adequately fulfil its promise. Last year a small temporary grant from the Carnegie Institution in Washington greatly helped us, and this year our work was saved from suspension by an appropriation from the John F. Slater Fund.[44]

For a decade following 1898, Du Bois was a most serious scholar, with an excellent scientific understanding and first-class academic credentials, intensely committed to academic work, establishing the first major black department of sociology in the country. He was also an essayist and commentator on the position of black people in the United States, a member of the 'talented tenth' and antagonist of Booker Washington in arguments over the best strategy for black people to follow. His public clashes with Washington no doubt contributed to his inability to secure research funding, since white philanthropists supporting black Americans relied heavily upon Washington for advice.[45] During the first decade of the century, these political interests became more salient and Du Bois' concerns shifted.[46] In 1909 Du Bois was one of the founders of the National Association for the Advancement of Coloured People (NAACP), and in 1910 he left academic life permanently to become editor of the NAACP magazine, *The Crisis*. He did not leave his academic interests entirely behind. In *The Crisis* he used facts, observation and historical material in articles where appropriate, but the magazine was aimed at a mass audience in political and emotional terms as well as providing analysis of the social situation of black people. For Du Bois it was a marked change of direction. This abandonment of a scholarly career at the age of forty-two was a response to the isolation and neglect from which Du Bois' work suffered, and his feeling that it was very difficult to make a significant impact upon American race relations as a black academic.

'Two considerations', he wrote in old age, 'broke in upon my academic work and eventually disrupted it: First, one could not be a calm, cool and detached scientist while Negroes were lynched, murdered and starved; and secondly, there was no such definite demand for scientific work of the sort that I was doing as I had confidently assumed would be easily forthcoming'.[47] Among these experiences was the writing of a pioneering monograph which was almost completely ignored by his academic peers, yet which we can now recognise as an important part of the social survey tradition and a classical sociological monograph.

It is necessary to keep this phase of Du Bois' career in perspective. In his later writings, particularly his autobiographies, Du Bois had become somewhat disenchanted not only with academic social science but even with many aspects of American society, and the past was reinterpreted through presentist concerns. Du Bois' career as a writer and propagandist after 1910, moreover, meant also that he tended to be seen in the 1920s and 1930s by social scientists more in that role as political activist than as the historian and social scientist he had been between the ages of twenty-two and forty-two. Nevertheless, there can be little doubt that one important factor in Du Bois' abandonment of social science was the indifference with which his work was received in the white scholarly world. It is this experience which sets him apart from other early survey researchers, for although their findings by no means commanded universal assent, they did command attention and publicity when they were published. Du Bois was denied that attention, because he was black, because the condition of black Americans was not a matter of major political or scholarly concern around 1898, and because a racially stratified system of higher education gave him no significant opportunities for sustained interaction with his white peers in the academic community.

NOTES

1 W. E. B. Du Bois, 'The Study of the Negro Problems', *Annals of the American Academy of Political and Social Science*, 9 (January, 1898), 1–2.

2 W. E. B. Du Bois, *The Suppression of the African Slave Trade to the United States of America 1638–1870* (New York: Longmans Green, 1896), the first monograph in the Harvard Historical Studies series, based on his Harvard PhD thesis submitted in 1895.

3 Quoted in D. S. Green and E. D. Driver, 'Introduction', in Green and Driver (eds.), *W. E. B. Du Bois on Sociology and the Black Community* (Chicago: University of Chicago Press, 1978), p. 7.

4 F. L. Broderick, *W. E. B. Du Bois: Negro Leader in a Time of Crisis* (Stanford: Stanford University Press, 1959), p. 27.

5 W. E. B. Du Bois, *Dusk of Dawn* (New York: Harcourt, Brace, 1940), p. 51.

6 W. E. B. Du Bois writing in his diary, quoted in M. Marable, *W. E. B. Du Bois: Black Radical Democrat* (Boston: Twayne, 1986), p. 19.

7 Quoted in Marable, *Du Bois*, p. 25.

8 E. Digby Baltzell, 'Introduction', to W. E. B. Du Bois, *The Philadelphia Negro; A Social Study* (first published by the Univeristy of Pennsylvania 1899; New York: Schocken, 1967), p. xviii.

9 Quoted in E. M. Rudwick, *W. E. B. Du Bois: Voice of the Black Protest Movement* (Philadelphia: University of Pennsylvania Press, 1960), p. 30.

10 In fact, for a total of fifteen months, from the beginning of August 1896 until the end of December 1897, with a break of two months in the summer of 1897 when he was carrying out for the US Commissioner of Labor the study of Farmville, Virginia, cited in n 23.

11 W. E. B. Du Bois, 'My Evolving Program for Negro Freedom', in Rayford W. Logan (ed.), *What the Negro Wants* (Chapel Hill: University of North Carolina Press, 1944), p. 38.

12 See Nancy J. Weiss, *The National Urban League, 1910–1940* (New York: Oxford University Press, 1974), pp. 20–8, 48–60. In 1911 Ovington published a study, *Half a Man: The Status of the Negro in (New York* New York: 1911) which followed the example of *The Philadelphia Negro*. She and Du Bois apparently first met in 1903, when Miss Ovington became interested in the condition of black Americans, as a result of the reputation which he established with *The Philadelphia Negro* and by his essays *The Souls of Black Folk* (Chicago: A. C. McClurg, 1903). See 'Introduction' by Charles Flint Kellogg to the 1969 edition of *Half A Man* (New York: Hill and Wang), p. xiv.

13 'These efforts to withdraw from almost all contacts with white people he used to consolidate an identity for himself. He wanted to know and to embrace who and what

he was and what his own life and society were. Most of all, however, he had, in order to save and use his talent, to learn and think of himself as a gifted scholar, writer and social scientist.' Allison Davis, 'Du Bois and the Problem of the Black Masses' (W. E. B. Du Bois Institute for the Study of the American Black, mimeo, n.d.).

14 *The Philadelphia Negro*, between pages 60 and 61. (page 1 in 1899 edition).

15 W. E. B. Du Bois, The *Autobiography of W. E. B. Du Bois* (New York: International Publishers, 1968), p. 198.

16 Du Bois, *The Philadelphia Negro*, p. 402.

17 *The Philadelphia Negro*, pp. 62–3.

18 *The Philadelphia Negro*, p. 62, note 12.

19 *The Philadelphia Negro*, p. 403.

20 Du Bois, *Autobiography*, p. 198.

21 Marable, *Du Bois*, p. 22.

22 Du Bois, *The Philadelphia Negro*, p. 63.

23 W. E. B. Du Bois, 'The Negroes of Farmville, Virginia: a Social Study', *Bulletin of the Department of Labor*, 3 (January, 1898), 1–38, reprinted in abridged form in D. S. Green and E. D. Driver (eds.), *W. E. B. Du Bois on Sociology and the Black Community* (Chicago: University of Chicago Press, 1978), pp. 165–95.

24 'The Negroes of Farmville, Virginia', p. 5.

25 'The Negroes of Farmville, Virginia', p. 9.

26 'The Negroes of Farmville, Virginia', p. 310.

27 'The Negroes of Farmville, Virginia', pp. 309–19.

28 'The Negroes of Farmville, Virginia', p. 172.

29 Baltzell, 'Introduction', p. xxiv–xxv. Du Bois explicitly referred in his introduction to the need to study the environment in which black people lived, including the physical environment and 'the far mightier social environment – the surrounding world of custom, wish, whim and thought which envelops the group and powerfully influences its social development' (*The Philadelphia Negro*, p. 5).

30 Du Bois, *The Philadelphia Negro*, p. 351.

31 D. S. Green and E. D. Driver, 'W. E. B. Du Bois: A Case in the Sociology of Sociological Negation', *Phylon*, 37, 4 (December, 1976), 322. See also E. M. Rudwick, 'Note on a Forgotten Black Sociologist: W. E. B. Du Bois and the Sociological Profession', *The American Sociologist*, 4 (November, 1969), 303–6. The monograph is not mentioned, for example, in Park and Burgess' *Introduction to the Science of Sociology* of 1921.

32 Allen F. Davis, 'Introduction', in A. F. Davis and M. H. Haller (eds.), *The Peoples of Philadelphia: A History of Ethnic Groups and Lower Class Life 1790–1940* (Philadelphia: Temple University Press, 1973), p. 4.

33 In contrast to studies of white ethnic minorities. For an example, see Peter Roberts, *Anthracite Coal Communities* (New York, 1904), a study of coal-mining settlements in western Pennsylvania. Roberts was a student of W. G. Sumner at Yale, and addresses ethnic differences in the villages. The book is permeated with explicit assertions about the superiority of Anglo-Saxons and the inferiority of Slavic immigrants to the United States.

34 On Weber's American visit see Marianne Weber, *Max Weber: A Biography* (English

translation, New York: Wiley, 1975), pp. 279–304. On Weber's interest in race and nationality, see E. M. Manasse, 'Max Weber on Race', *Social Research*, 14, 2 (1947), 191–221, and John Stone, 'Race Relations and the Sociological Tradition', in J. Stone (ed.), *Race, Ethnicity and Social Change* (North Scituate, Mass.: Duxbury Press, 1977), pp. 67–8.

35 Manasse, 'Max Weber on Race', p. 197, n. 15.

36 Du Bois, *Dusk of Dawn* (New York: Harcourt Brace and Co., 1940), p. 67.

37 W. E. B. Du Bois, 'Die Negerfrage in den Vereinigten Staten', *Archiv für Sozialwissenschaft und Sozialpolitik*, 22 (1906), 31–79.

38 See M. Weinberg, *A Chance to Learn: A History of Race and Education in the United States* (Cambridge: Cambridge University Press, 1977), pp. 263–336.

39 Du Bois, 'The Study of the Negro Problems', p. 20.

40 Rudwick, *W. E. B. Du Bois*, pp. 33–4.

41 W. I. Thomas was writing earlier about race and ethnic differences and their explanation, but the work on race did not really take off until Park's arrival in 1913. The first major piece of research on black Americans, as distinct from white European immigrants, was the research for the Chicago Commission on Race Relations, *The Negro in Chicago* (Chicago: University of Chicago Press 1923). For more details, see M. Bulmer, 'Charles S. Johnson, Robert E. Park and the Research Methods of the Chicago Commission of Race Relations 1920–1922: An Early Experiment in Applied Social Research', *Ethnic and Racial Studies*, 4 (July, 1981), 289–306.

42 W. E. B. Du Bois, 'The Atlanta Conferences', *Voice of the Negro*, 1 (March, 1904), 86.

43 The Atlanta studies of which Du Bois was the principal author were: *Some Efforts of Negroes for Social Betterment* (1898); *The Negro in Business* (1899); *The College-Bred Negro* (1900); *The Negro Common School* (1901); *The Negro Artisan* (1902); *The Negro Church* (1903); *Some Notes on Negro Crime, Particularly in Georgia* (1904); *A Select Bibliography of the American Negro* (1905); *Health and Physique of the Negro American* (1906); *Economic Cooperation among Negro Americans* (1907); *The Negro American Family* (1909); *Efforts for Social Betterment among Negro Americans* (1909); *The College-Bred Negro American* (1910); *The Common School and the Negro American* (1911); *The Negro American Artisan* (1912); *Morals and Manners among Negro Americans* (1914), all published by the Atlanta University Press.

44 W. E. B. Du Bois, preface to *The Negro American Family* (Atlanta: Atlanta University Press, 1909), p. 5.

45 The course of their conflict, which first became apparent in 1902 and 1903 when Du Bois published a critical review of *Up From Slavery* and his chapter 'On Mr Booker T. Washington and Others', in *The Souls of Black Folk*, which contained measured criticism of Washington's strategy for black advancement, is described in Louis R. Harlan, *Booker T. Washington: The Wizard of Tuskegee, 1900–1915* (New York: Oxford University Press, 1983), esp. pp. 50–1. Before 1902 they appear to have maintained mutually respectful relations, Washington indeed attempting to bring Du Bois to Tuskegee to direct research with a job offer around 1900.

46 See Arnold Ramapersad, *The Art and Imagination of W. E. B. Du Bois* (Cambridge, MA: Harvard University Press, 1976).

47 Du Bois, *Autobiography*, p. 222.

CHAPTER SEVEN

Concepts of poverty in the British social surveys from Charles Booth to Arthur Bowley

E. P. HENNOCK

I

In an article published in 1976 I tried to restore Charles Booth's survey of poverty in London to its own historical period, the late 1880s.[1] The target of that article was that mythical social investigator usually known as Booth-and-Rowntree. The widespread assumption that one could speak of their two surveys, one initiated twelve years after the other, as if they were much the same had led to a number of misapprehensions about the content of Booth's work and its purpose.

Booth had been primarily interested in enumeration and description. (I, p. 6) In order to enumerate it was necessary to classify and it was for his system of classification that he was most commonly remembered. His division of the population into classes A–H remained for a long time a convenient set of terms in social description. This classification was basic to Booth's strategy as a social investigator; it provides the key to any understanding of the significance of his figures. Booth's well-known and much quoted discovery that roughly 30 per cent of the population of London were living in poverty acquires a different significance from what is often thought when we note that Booth considered those whom he classified as 'poor' (Classes C and D) as lacking comfort but as neither ill-nourished nor ill-clad according to any standard that he thought could reasonably be applied (I, p. 131). In 1897 he was still stressing that the poor in Class D (low but regular earnings) on the whole had enough to eat and that they led healthy though rather restricted lives (IX, p. 430). Only the 'very poor' (Class B) he considered to be 'in want', a situation into which he placed no more than 8·4 per cent of London's population. Even of them only a percentage would be 'in distress'.[2]

The validity of such statements must in turn depend on the methods of

189

investigation used. Booth relied for his systematic information on the memory and note-books of School Board Visitors, i.e. school attendance officers, and he cross-checked their information with the help of clergy and charitable workers who claimed to be familiar with the household in question. There was, however, no house-to-house visiting, nor were School Board Visitors asked to obtain any information specially for the survey. Booth relied solely on what knowledge had come to them in their normal course of work. This work included inquiries into earnings in connection with requests for the remission of school fees for impoverished families. The reliability of this information, even when it was available, was open to grave doubt, as was pointed out to Booth when he presented his first interim report to the Royal Statistical Society, and as he had himself admitted when planning his operations. 'At the end it is only an opinion and I hesitate to make it the basis for our classification', he had written. He did however ask for it to be recorded. Earning figures are recorded in less than 20 per cent of cases. In the absence of this kind of knowledge the classification was based 'on the general appearance of a home'.[3]

What Booth was counting were impressions, carefully cross-checked with other impressions insofar as these were available. One of his collaborators was to describe the Poverty Survey very accurately as 'a statistical record of impressions of degrees of poverty', a view echoed by another collaborator, who added that it was 'the great triumph of Mr. Booth's inquiry that he had succeeded in this difficult and delicate task'.[4]

This chapter is concerned with Booth only insofar as it is necessary to establish the relation between his work and that of Rowntree. Rowntree undoubtedly thought of himself as a follower of Booth. His personal copy of *Life and Labour*, a wedding present from the office staff of his firm, was copiously marked and annotated in the volumes dealing with poverty.[5] The wedding had been in December 1897; within nine months he had begun to prepare his own survey of poverty in York.[6]

Like Booth, Rowntree provided a classification of the population, or rather in his case of the working-class population, and described the conditions of life in the different classes. Like Booth, he divided the population into classes according to degrees of poverty and comfort, but, as he pointed out, the difference of method employed makes a comparison of the two classifications misleading.[7]

There are two differences of method to which I want to draw attention. Booth had conducted his work on the assumption that the information required was already known to someone other than the householder himself. Rowntree quickly learnt that he could not proceed on that assumption, and he employed a special investigator to undertake house-to-house visits. Freed from reliance on the School Board Visitors, whose knowledge extended only to families with children of school age, he embarked on a survey of the total working-class population, which he defined as those households that kept no domestic servant (p. 35).[8] Booth had worked from a sample amounting to roughly half the population but selected on a basis over which he had no control and which was not random. He drew attention to this limitation and argued that his figures were likely somewhat to overstate the actual amount of poverty (I, pp. 4–5). Rowntree's figures could in this respect be taken without reservation.

The second difference is more radical. Whereas Booth's classification was based largely on what he called 'conditions of poverty' (I, p. 33), Rowntree's was based on a systematic attempt to arrive at an estimate of household income. With the exception of his class A, which rather confusingly described a way of life (I, p. 131), Booth had classified families by 'their apparent status as to means' (I, p. 24). The income figures for a moderate family that he quoted to explain what he meant by such classification as 'very poor', 'poor', etc., were for illustrative purposes only 'I, p. 33). As already indicated, the methods at his disposal enabled him to obtain income figures for no more than a very small proportion of households. (See n. 3.) Yet it was this passage that was most often quoted then as now. I would guess that the error of assuming that Booth had actually been able to classify his households by their income, an error not uncommon among recent writers, was one that was widely shared by Booth's contemporaries. Not by Rowntree, however, as is clearly shown by his comment in the margin next to the crucial passage. Rowntree was determined to obtain the necessary information on household income. Since his investigator was visiting every house, he had tried to do this by direct questioning, but he had been unsuccessful. He discovered that wives often did not know and husbands could not be relied upon to tell. When in 1936 he mounted a second survey, he had learnt from his experience and never even asked. What it was possible to obtain was information on occupation and workplace, and it was on this basis that he estimated earnings, using his knowledge of standard wage rates for skilled labour and of other wage rates paid in his own works, by the corporation, and by other large employers of his acquaintance.[9]

Income as estimated by these means together with household composition formed the basis of Rowntree's four-fold classification of the working-class according to the weekly income for a moderate family of two adults and between two and four children (see table 7.1).

It should be noted that the income brackets are very unevenly stepped. Why had he chosen these particular income brackets for his classification? Two of the most plausible answers to that question can definitely be ruled out. He had not done so because he attached any intrinsic significance to these divisions. Indeed he explained that he regarded all forms of income classification as arbitrary (p. 27). Nor did he regard them as particularly useful. Quite the contrary. The purpose of the classification had been to describe the standard of life enjoyed in each of the classes, but he confessed that for his purpose Class C was useless on account of the wide range of incomes that were comprehended within it (pp. 60–1). Since Class C accounted for one third of the population under review (see table 7.1) this greatly impaired the utility of the classification adopted. The real reason for Rowntree's choice is more banal. These were the income levels which Booth had used, not to classify his population, but to illustrate the income that his classes might be expected to have (I, pp. 33, 133).

We therefore find Rowntree taking Booth's notional income levels and classifying the population of York on that basis, using the household income figures that he had obtained in the roundabout way as already described. Although, as he pointed out, a direct comparison of the two sets of figures would be misleading, the aim of his investigation was so far obviously the same. Nor does the similarity end there. Just as Booth had set out not merely to show the numerical relations of his classes to each other but also to describe the general conditions under which each class lived (I, p. 6), so Rowntree proceeded to do the same in chapter 3 on 'The Standard of Life'.

Rowntree's work is not much remembered for his income classification. Social commentators continued to refer to Booth's classes long after the publication of Rowntree's work. What Rowntree is remembered for is his distinction between *primary poverty*, characterised by family income insufficient for the maintenance of mere physical efficiency, and *secondary poverty*, characterised by family income that would have been sufficient but for the fact that some of it is absorbed by other expenditure either useful or wasteful. This was his great conceptual innovation, and it is expounded immediately following the classification by income, in chapters 4 and 5 of the book.

It is a very puzzling matter that there is hardly any connection between what Rowntree wrote about his classes A–D and what he wrote about primary poverty. Although it is possible to calculate that out of the total of 11,465 households in primary poverty 809 must have come from either class B or class C, there is no way of telling how many came from each.

Table 7.1 *Rowntree's four-fold classification of working class incomes.*

Class	Weekly income	Nos. of households	Nos. of persons
Class A	under 18 shillings	656	1,957
Class B	18 shillings and under 21 shillings	983	4,492
Class C	21 shillings and under 30 shillings	3,822	15,710
Class D	over 30 shillings	6,099	24,595

Source: Poverty, pp. 31, 32, 47, 60, 65.

Table 7.2 *Booth's and Rowntree's classification compared*

Booth's classification	Booth's notional and Rowntree's estimated income categories	Rowntree's classification
A (not a matter of poverty)	–	–
B very poor	Under 18 shillings	A
C irregular earning	18s and under 21 shillings	B
D low wages	21s and under 30 shillings	C
E regular standard earnings	over 30 shillings	D
F higher class labour		

There are only two tenuous links between the two sets of investigation. A table (p. 45) breaks down the composition of class A on lines similar to a later table (p. 120) that lists the causes of primary poverty. This makes the lack of similar tables for classes B and C doubly frustrating. The other cross-reference concerns the statement that the 549 families in primary poverty due to the death or incapacity of the chief wage-earner 'are with few exceptions included in class A' (p. 122). He himself never said so, but it is possible to calculate that there were forty-two such exceptions.

Thus as far as Rowntree was concerned the two investigations, that into the economic and social condition of the wage-earning class in York in chapters 2 and 3, and that into poverty, its extent and its causes, which occupied chapters 4 and 5, seem to have been largely insulated from each other even when they drew on the same body of evidence.

The remarkable fact is, however, that they did not always even draw on the same body of evidence. If there is little connection between the classification by income and the investigation of primary poverty, there is no connection at all with the investigation of the total extent of poverty in the city. Rowntree produced a figure of 27·84 as the percentage of the population of York in poverty. Except that it was obtained by an investigation of all working-class households, not merely of those with school-children, that figure was obtained by methods as crude as those of Booth. In both cases it is the result of counting impressions. Although Rowntree had taken great pains to obtain information on family income which he regarded as reasonably reliable, he reached his conclusion on the total amount of poverty in York by ignoring it. He chose instead to judge by the appearance of the household and occasionally checked on this by talking to the neighbours (pp. 115–17).

In a detailed and valuable exposition of Rowntree's work, J. H. Veit-Wilson has recently also drawn attention to this strange fact. As he put it, 'the precise criteria used by Rowntree's investigators to determine which members of York's working class were or were not poor *did not include income* ...; they were *behavioural* and *visible*'. He has suggested that Rowntree defined poverty not as lack of income but as a life-style.[10] In practice this is certainly what he did, but not because he had really accepted such a definition of poverty. He distinctly contemplated the possibility that to rely on appearance could lead to error and gave an example of a clean and tidy family which would be overlooked. In practice he believed that such errors would largely be cancelled out by other families who lived in 'apparent poverty' despite an adequate income (pp. 116–17). Booth had made much the same point. He had had to be content to rely on impressions even though he explicitly defined poverty with the help of a notional income figure as illustration, believing like Rowntree that errors were likely to be insignificant (I, p. 33; II, pp. 19–20).

That similarity to Booth provides the real explanation for Rowntree's strange neglect of his income data when estimating the total number in poverty. Had he wished to measure total poverty in cash terms Rowntree could have done so, as Veit-Wilson rightly points out, since he had information on the earnings of every working-class household in York.[11] But this is no proof that Rowntree's *definition* of poverty, not merely his *method*, excluded considerations of income. There is another and better reason why he chose to pay no attention to his information on household income. The principal object of Rowntree's investigation, as he explained in the introduction to his work, was to discover how far Booth's conclusions for London were applicable to smaller urban populations. Comparison was what mattered to Rowntree first and foremost; all other questions were secondary (p. vi).[12] It was therefore essential to identify poverty in the same way as Booth had done. There were undoubtedly many difficulties in the way of using information on household income to construct a measurable concept of poverty, as he was to discover in subsequent years. The point to bear in mind, however, is that in 1899 he had a very good prior reason for not wishing to attempt anything of the sort. At that stage for him as for Booth before him, poverty was in practice what informed observers recognised as such.

The distinction between the two sub-categories, primary and secondary poverty, is another matter. Here lay Rowntree's important *innovation*. We need to ask ourselves what it was for.

II

I propose to distinguish once again between innovation in method and innovation in aims, and to argue that we are here dealing with the first but not the second. Rowntree's *aim* in distinguishing between primary and secondary poverty, was to tackle a problem with which his generation was only too familiar. But he was the first to find a convincing *method* of doing so.

The problem was that of distinguishing between poverty due to insufficient means and poverty due to wasteful expenditure. To put it in other words, 'How many were really poor and how many just wasteful?' The issue had been familiar to Charles Booth. It was the question that he had been asked by Leone Levi, when he had presented the first results of his survey to the Royal Statistical Society in 1887. He had responded by tabulating the opinions of nine School Board Visitors on the 4,000 East London families with whose circumstances they were reasonably familiar. Two tables of Causes of Poverty had been included in his second paper to the Society and reproduced in the first volume of *Life and Labour*.[13] I have discussed these tables in a previous article and have argued that Booth's category, 'questions of habit', as used there was in fact designed to distinguish mismanagement of income in its obvious form, i.e. by excessive expenditure on drink and bad housekeeping, from other causes of poverty. The further subdivision of the remaining causes into 'questions of circumstances' and 'questions of employment' distinguished matters (illness and large family) that were peculiar to individual family circumstances and at he moment largely unavoidable, from matters connected with employment and, in Booth's opinion, capable of being affected by his proposals for reducing the overstocking of the London labour market.[14]

These issues were not, however, central to Booth's purpose. He deprecated the reliability of the tables 'unless they could be supported by other evidence' (I, p. 147). Since he knew that he had no means of obtaining such evidence, he countered any further objection by a sturdy assertion of common sense and in the opening chapter of his second volume declared that he proposed to take people as he found them, i.e. to call it poverty if it looked like poverty and to go on counting (II, pp. 18–20). What was central for Booth in his study of poverty was to ascertain the total numbers, 'who from whatever cause do live under conditions of poverty or destitution'. He was responding in his own particular way to a sense of crisis that had overtaken all social observers in the 1880s. Was it true, he asked, as many seemed to be assuming, that the brutalised poor, the hordes of barbarians, were a danger to civilisation in London? While others were debating remedies, he suggested that a sensible response was more likely to follow if the size of the problem was first understood. By counting 'the lowest class of occasional labourers, loafers and semi-criminals' (class A) separately from the 'poor' and 'very poor', he came up with figures to discredit the prophets of doom. 'The hordes of barbarians' did not exist. What existed was 'a disgrace but not a danger' (I, p. 39).

He was just as much concerned to safeguard the distinction between poverty and working-class comfort. If the barbarians of class A were not to be confused with the poor, neither were the 'true working classes', whose desire for a larger share of wealth was, in his view, of a different character. The moral he wished to convey was clearly spelt out to his readers. 'To confound these essentially distinct problems is to make the solution of both impossible; it is not by welding distress and aspirations that any good can be done' (I, p. 155). Thus it was the categorising as much as the enumerating that brought the reassurance, for the totals were the result of a method of investigation that put the emphasis on sub-dividing rather than aggregating phenomena.[15]

Once the sense of immediate crisis had passed what was left were the further questions, which had been asked before the scare and which were to survive its passing. These were concerned with the means towards social progress and could be answered only on the basis of an adequate theory of causation. If poverty was to be reduced, the causes of poverty had to be removed. It was a matter of fundamental importance to know whether to concentrate thought and endeavour on increasing the income or on reducing the wasteful consumption of the poor. In this sense questions of causation were questions of strategy for reformers. Rowntree's aim was therefore not new nor was he the first to proffer an answer. It was a matter on which assertions were constantly being made, as Leone Levi had done at the meeting of the Royal Statistical Society or as the mentors of the Charity Organisation Society were repeatedly to do.[16] Booth in his characteristic way had found a means of quantifying those of the School Board Visitors, but assertions they remained unless they could be supported by other evidence. What was needed was not the counting of assertions but an uncontrovertible means of making the crucial distinction.

There is little doubt that it was a crucial distinction in Rowntree's eyes. In his introduction he had set out the questions to which he wished to find an answer. Dominating all else was the question of how far the general conclusions reached by Booth for London were applicable to smaller urban populations. However, the others were

1. the total extent and depth of poverty in the city;
2. how much of it was due to insufficiency of income and how much to improvidence;
3. how many families were sunk in a poverty so acute that they suffered from chronic insufficiency of food and clothing;
4. the possibility of estimating the effect of this on physical deterioration and the death-rate. (p. vi)

He set out to answer the second question in terms of the relative numbers of persons affected, and did this by first devising a method of answering the third question, i.e. of counting the number of families 'whose total earnings were insufficient to obtain the minimum necessaries for the maintainance of merely physical efficiency'. Such families he described as being in primary poverty (p. 86). As is well-known, this method consisted of measuring the minimum expenditure necessary for the maintenance of physical efficiency, drawing on recent studies of nutrition for the measurement of food-requirements of a man engaged in moderate labour, turning them into a diet that could be costed, and then adding an estimated sum for rent, fuel, clothing and other household sundries. By comparing these requirements with the family incomes that he had collected, he was able to calculate the numbers of families and consequently of persons who lived in what he called primary poverty. By subtracting that number from his total of families in poverty he obtained the number of those in secondary poverty, defined as 'families whose total earning would be sufficient for the maintainance of merely physical efficiency were it not that some portion of it is absorbed by other expenditure, either useful or wasteful' (pp. 115–16). He gave both the number of families and of persons, and the proportion of the population to whom this applied.

Unfortunately these strategies do not provide the answers to the two questions which he had set himself. The methods available to him do not quite meet the aim that he had in view. Secondary poverty as he calculated it could be due to other causes than improvidence. As he was careful to point out when he explained his method, it could be due to expenditure 'either useful or wasteful.' 'Expenditure needful for the development of the mental, moral or social sides of human nature' and 'expenditure for sick clubs and insurance' all fell on the wrong side of a poverty line designed to calculate minimum necessary expenditure for the maintenance of merely physical health (p. 87).[17] Nor was that the only mismatch. 'Families sunk in a poverty so acute that they suffered from chronic insufficiency of food and clothing', to quote the wording of the third question, were not limited to those in primary poverty, as once again he acknowledged when explaining the implications of his method in detail (pp. 114, 134).

What comments should one make about these inconsistencies between the task he set out in the Introduction and what he achieved in the body of the book? For J. H. Veit-Wilson, who has also noticed them, they serve to exonerate a long list of authors who have misreported Rowntree's work and he explains these and other inconsistencies by reminding us that Rowntree was no academic scholar.[18] It is true that *Poverty: a Study of Town Life* abounds with inconsistencies in a way that the social surveys of an academic such as Bowley do not, but I prefer to regard them as useful clues for the process of historical detection. We should bear in mind that the distinction between insufficiency of income and improvidence enshrined in the Introduction was of long standing and had an obvious practical implication. it is not hard to understand that Rowntree wished to address himself to it. The same cannot be said for that between primary and secondary poverty. It was the outcome of designing a practical and acceptable method of inquiry and it suffers from all the limitations of that design. In several crucial places Rowntree himself betrays an uneasy awareness that he was not quite managing to do what he wished, yet without ever confronting these inconsistencies and coming to terms with them. The result is confusing, as anyone who has ever undertaken a close reading of the text will know.

Thus what are we to make of the much quoted figures of 9·91 per cent of the population of York in primary poverty and 17·93 per cent in secondary poverty, and the absolute numbers of families and individuals from which these percentages were derived?[19] The questions in the introduction to the book seem to leave no doubt that he intended the value of his survey to lie in the provision of reliable numbers and proportions. Yet in the body of the book there is much to suggest that this is exactly what it was not reasonable to expect from his method of investigation, and that the value of his calculations lay elsewhere. He went out of his way to emphasise that by a single-minded concentration on mere physical efficiency he excluded not only wasteful but also useful expenditure, and gave his readers a heart-rending sketch of the social decencies that would be excluded thereby (p. 133–4). He furthermore selected a diet even plainer than that sanctioned in the workhouse (pp. 98–9). He was obviously trying to set a minimum, so clearly inadequate by conventional standards, that no one would be inclined to dismiss it as being over-generous.

That must mean that Rowntree's poverty line was not intended to provide a reasonable measure. On the contrary, it provided so unreasonable a measure that its value for establishing the actual proportion of anything that related realistically to the lives of the poor is very dubious, not only to us but to Rowntree himself. In fact he provided two additional and quite different sets of figures for the proportion of primary and secondary poverty, taking in each case a somewhat less drastic view of the minimum. 'The point at which "primary" passes into "secondary" poverty', he wrote, 'is largely a matter of opinion, depending on the standard of well-being which is considered necessary' (pp. 111–12, 141).

The only sensible thing that can be said about Rowntree's measure of persons in primary poverty is that it indicated an absolute minimum figure. In summing up he did on one occasion refer to the result as 'no less that 7230 persons', but if this was intended to make an important point, the effect was lost when on the very next page he quoted the number of those in secondary poverty without this qualification and produced a table accordingly (pp. 297–298).

In 1976 I suggested in a footnote to my article on Charles Booth that in his approach to primary poverty Rowntree had freed himself from Booth's pre-occupation with classifying and enumerating.[20] His own words would suggest that I was wrong. The language of numbers and proportions dominates the book throughout. Yet the only way to make sense of his procedure is to view it, as he himself does not seem to have done, as a means to calculate the mere minimum required so as to subject a widely held belief to scientific falsification. We cannot tell 'how much was due to insufficiency of income and how much to improvidence'. But in the case of no less than 7,230 persons it was certainly not due to improvidence. We do not know how many families suffered from chronic insufficiency. But no less than 1,465 must certainly have done so. The importance lies not in the numbers but in the logic.

Yet without a high enough set of numbers the outcome could easily appear merely trivial. Hence the constant reminder how unsuited the method actually was for the production of realistic figures and the provision of alternative and much more impressive proportions.

The ambiguities left unresolved even in the Summary and Conclusion of the book could certainly be misleading. *The Times* had paid more attention to Rowntree's figures than to his reservations when it drew its own moral from his work: 'Mr. Rowntree admits that some 18% of the people who are in dire poverty might be fairly comfortable but for the habits of drinking and betting. Few of their friends speak pointedly and directly to them of these vices and their consequences.'[21] It is true that Rowntree believed that when all reservations and adjustments had been made there still remained a considerable amount of poverty to which the strictures of *The Times* were not inappropriate. But this is not the way in which his figures could be used.

III

To draw attention to the mismatch between Rowntree's stated intentions and his actual achievement is of course no way to do full justice to the latter. In the end Rowntree's work is not to be understood primarily in relation to what he took over from Booth. The internal inconsistencies are important exactly because they reveal Rowntree breaking free from the approach of his predecessor and establishing himself as a true pioneer. The idea of a poverty line obtained by the calculation of necessary expenditure, though subsequently modified and reinterpreted, was to dominate poverty surveys from then onwards.

What is new is the emphasis on physical efficiency, an emphasis nowhere to be found in Booth's concept of poverty. The inefficiency of Booth's Class B, most of whose work he considered to be 'inefficiently done, both badly and slowly', was primarily a mental and moral condition and only occasionally a physical one (I, pp. 149–51, 154). It was far removed from the sort of concept with which Rowntree was to operate.

The invention of the poverty line was therefore important for no less than three reasons. It contributed to a long-standing argument and disposed of it at least in its more extreme form. Secondly it provided a new way of seeing poverty in relation to the national interest. Thirdly it attempted to stake out a limited area within which the investigation of poverty could achieve a new degree of certainty. We have looked at the first of these points, and shall now turn to the other two.

The new perspective on poverty was provided by linking physical efficiency explicitly with the industrial future of the country. This lent to the facts of poverty an importance and 'an urgency ... not easy to exaggerate in consequence of the stress and keenness of international competition.' 'The highest commercial success will be impossible so long as large numbers even of the most sober and industrious of the labouring classes receive but three-fourths of the necessary amount of food', i.e. 'the food required for moderate work' (pp. 220–1, 256, 259–61). The impact that he made was largely due to the way in which he presented poverty as a threat to the national interest at a time when fears about international competitiveness had become common.[22] The reputation that *Poverty* acquired as a text for reformers has little to do with any programme of reform to be found in its pages. It has to do with the conclusions that people drew from it. In this case the conclusion was intended from the beginning, for it underlay the very strategy of the investigation.

Rowntree's success was well deserved. He had found a way to respond to a common anxiety of his day by devising a suitable method of inquiry. His father had already tried to use the concept of physical efficiency with its relevance to 'the conditions of industrial competition' for the purpose of social reform. But it was the son who discovered how to make the concept operational by drawing on recent developments in nutritional science.[23] There is of course more to a minimally efficient diet than the calculation of calories, proteins, fats and carbohydrates. Most of the factors that went into the calculation of the poverty line rested on a range of assumptions that were not physiological but cultural, accepting many of the conventions of the England of his day. Bowley put it well in 1924 when he described Rowntree's calculations as appearing to have a scientific basis and as far as knowledge of nutriment at that time went being accurate, adding, 'it is in fact conventional rather than absolute'.[24] Those who want to know in detail how Rowntree moved in and out between the physiological and cultural will find the process described by Karel Williams.[25] But the matter is of no great importance except on the mistaken assumption that this was the crucial distinction that he was trying to make in constructing the poverty line. It is to be hoped that this widely held assumption has not survived its recent refutation by Veit-Wilson.

For Rowntree the crucial distinction was different. It was that between expenditure necessary 'for the development of the mental, moral and social sides of human nature', and expenditure necessary 'for the maintenance of merely physical efficiency' (pp. 86–7). The first he refused to calculate. The second he calculated in such a way as to avoid being accused of including unnecessary expenditure by even the harshest of critics. This was the sense in which he strove to identify the absolute minimum and he succeeded fairly well in defending himself against criticism from that side.[26]

He thereby established a privileged area where agreement could be achieved. Mere physical efficiency was not all there was to life, as he repeatedly explained, and to consider it in isolation was a most artificial exercise. But despite repeated attempts by Helen Bosanquet and Charles Loch to challenge the appropriateness of his procedures he managed to establish the point that it was an *essential part of life, and that the number of those below that level was a significant* number. Even the two sets of alternative figures were useful in this context. They demonstrated with how little adjustment to the strict minimum almost half or more than three-quarters of the poor could fall short of this essential aspect of life, essential not only to themselves but to the nation. Could it be that he had found the original proportions which his strict definition had produced – little more than a third of the poor – not quite as striking as he had hoped?

Beyond that privileged area lay all the rest of life, the ethical considerations as distinct from the economic ones, as he was to describe the contrast in 1910.[27] In 1913, by now acutely aware of the pressure on him to come up with a less artificial poverty line but still unable to see how, he fell back on a careful restatement of his original approach. In trying to estimate how much to allow for matters other than the maintainance of physical efficiency 'we enter a region of controversy, where personal opinion must take the place of scientific data'.[28] Like all restatements in a different mental climate, it was misleading. There had always been more to the poverty line than scientific data; there had always been personal opinion, the harsh opinion of the sceptics who had to be won over.

IV

Rowntree's chapter 4 had seemed to be a straightforward attempt to provide relative proportions but on closer inspection has turned out to contain an argument in which the actual proportions play a very secondary role. Much the same might be said of chapter 5, 'The Immediate Causes of Poverty in York', particularly the first and largest part which dealt with the immediate causes of primary poverty.

That just over half of primary poverty should have been due to the low wages earned by the family's chief bread winner even though in regular employment was startling, particularly when we remember the attention that had previously been paid to irregular or casual earnings as a major cause of poverty.[29] But we need to remember that Rowntree was actually dealing here with subdivisions of very small numbers. It was the concept of the poverty cycle that transformed the 640 households counted in the actual survey into a larger and far more significant phenomenon. It was this that enabled Rowntree to claim that 'every labourer who has as many as three children must pass through a time probably lasting about ten years, when...he and his family will be *underfed*' (original emphasis). In his description of the 'five alternating periods of want and comparative plenty' which characterised the life of the labourer he went out of his way to demonstrate the significance of these periods of want for the physical and mental retardation of the race. He thereby turned what might otherwise have been regarded as a mitigating factor into the opposite, a serious threat to the national interest (pp. 130–8, quotation from p. 135). Booth had known about the alternating periods and had described them (IX, pp. 421–5). It was when Rowntree brought the idea to bear on his own specific discoveries and preoccupations that it turned into an important concept for the study of poverty.

That 'the wages paid for unskilled labour in York are insufficient to provide food, shelter and clothing adequate to maintain a family of moderate size in a state of bare physical efficiency' (p. 133) strikes us as perhaps the most important of Rowntree's discoveries. Not him, however, at least not at the time! He never even mentioned it in his Summary and Conclusion, where the immediate causes of poverty were totally ignored.

There is no close or straightforward connection between what Rowntree had written on this subject in 1901 and the interest in minimum wage policies that formed part of the agenda of Liberal Radicalism ten years later. Rowntree himself had other priorities after 1901. In particular he wanted to drive home the significance for urban England as a whole of the total amount of poverty in York and spent some time trying to find ways of underpinning his view that York was typical.[30] Thereafter he concentrated on betting and gambling, a subject more closely connected with secondary than with primary poverty, and edited a book on the subject in 1905.[31] When after 1906 he began to think about another poverty survey it was within the context of the question of land tenure, to whose importance he had already drawn attention in 1901.[32] It was the plight of the landless labourer that became the focus of his attention, and it was in the context of his work for the Liberal Radical Land Campaign that he finally developed the implications of low wages for a policy of social reform. *Land and Labour, Lessons from Belgium*, published in 1910, did no more than commend the minimum to 'thoughtful employers' (pp. 398–9). But in 1913 he published a study of the standard of living of the English rural labourer, which echoed the language of his urban study of 1901, declaring that 'the wage paid by farmers to agricultural labourers is, in the vast majority of cases, insufficient to keep a family of average size in a state of merely physical efficiency'.[33] A few months later the Report of the Liberal Land Enquiry Committee, in which he played a prominent part and which provided Lloyd George with the intellectual case for his Land Campaign of 1913–14, came out in favour of 'wages tribunals to fix minimum wages to enable the labourer to keep himself and an average family in a state of physical efficiency and to pay a commercial rent for his cottage'. Such a minimum wage policy for rural labourers was adopted by the Liberal Government and formed part of its abortive programme in 1914. The urban part of the Land Enquiry Committee's report made very similar recommendations but the Government's eye was firmly fixed on the rural labourer where the political advantages lay.[34]

These proposals could cite the wages boards set up under the Trade Boards Act of 1909 as a precedent. The Act had resulted from a campaign against sweated trades, but neither the campaign nor the government's response to it provided any evidence that even prominent social reformers had been much influenced by Rowntree's discoveries on wages. The best comment on this matter was made by R. H. Tawney, when he pointed out in 1913 that Rowntree's discovery had 'deprived the word "sweating" of much of its sensationalism, while adding to its significance'. It had made a nonsense of the concentration on a limited group of special trades, for 'if wages inadequate to support physical existence are criteria of sweating, then a very large proportion of all unorganized workers must be sweated'.[35]

All this would suggest that any connection between Rowntree's *Poverty* and the minimum wage policies advocated in 1913–14 is tenuous indeed. This underlines what is for us the really important point. The poverty line of 1899 had not been devised for the purpose of prescribing a minimum wage. Its artificial nature made it most unsuitable for the purpose, as became increasingly clear once Rowntree and others became interested in prescribing norms. In 1913 he drew attention to the difference between the income envisaged for the purpose of the primary poverty line and the notion of a reasonable living wage, but had to confess that he knew no generally acceptable way of proceeding from the one to the other.[36] By 1918 the same set of imperatives had driven him to do just that and he produced a calculation of human needs with which to underpin proposals for minimum wage legislation.[37] The expedients to which he was driven in the process have recently been the subject of severe critical comment. It is apparent that for such purposes methods originally designed with very different aims in view were of doubtful value.[38]

This new interest in base lines for minimum wages or for a minimum income by such means as family allowances, important though it was, did not signal the general abandonment of Rowntree's creation of 1899, the poverty line.[39] While the social reformers moved in one direction, away from the concepts of 1899 and towards prescription, the practitioners of the social survey moved in the opposite direction. They held on to the concept of the poverty line as originally established but increasingly emphasised its artificial nature and found a new justification for its use. That development was largely due to Arthur Bowley.

Before turning to Bowley's contribution let me sum up my principal conclusions about Booth and Rowntree.

Booth's concept of poverty has to be seen in the context of his wider classification of the population. It reflected his determination to distinguish those social categories that were the objects of anxiety in the 1880s from other sections of the population, and to establish the relative size of each. The methods available to him led him to rely on the enumeration of impressions gathered from expert witnesses. His approach to social investigation was collaborative and eclectic.

Rowntree must be considered a major innovator in the methods of investigation. He exercised a much closer control over the process of inquiry than Booth had done. One major innovation was systematically to investigate household income. The other was his distinction between primary and secondary poverty.

In his aims he was less innovative than in his methods. His primary aim was to replicate in York what Booth had done in London. This emphasis on comparability inhibited him from exploiting his methodological innovations to the full. It accounts in particular for the similarity between his concept of poverty and that of Booth.

The distinction between primary and secondary poverty should be regarded as a new method to resolve the long-standing debate about the causes of poverty. In this case the matching of new methods to old aims was only partly successful. By emphasising physical efficiency he was, however, able to present poverty in a new light, relating it directly to the national interest. Moreover, by distinguishing economic from ethical considerations he attempted to stake out a limited area in which the enumeration of poverty could achieve a degree of certainty such as had not existed before.

Finally his analysis of the causes of primary poverty gained greatly in significance through his use of the poverty cycle. By means of this concept he converted a static into a dynamic view of the impact of primary poverty on the family.

v

Bowley's most important contribution to the social survey was the use of random sampling. By making household studies quicker and cheaper he was able to break out of the straightjacket that had confined both Booth and Rowntree to the investigation of a single city. His study of several towns of carefully contrasting types, chosen with reference to the Board of Trade's nation-wide inquiries into manual workers' earnings and into local variations in the cost of living, stood in a paradoxical relation to that of his predecessor. It was Rowntree who drew attention to the importance of studying the conditions of urban life right across provincial England, but it was Bowley who developed the methods of investigation that finally made it possible to do so.[40]

In 1912 he undertook a pilot study of working-class households in Reading based on a 5 per cent sample, and followed this up in 1913 by similar studies of Northampton, Warrington and Stanley, a mining town in County Durham. All four were published together in 1915 as *Livelihood and Poverty*. An investigation of Bolton in 1914 on a 10 per cent sample but otherwise by identical methods was published in 1920.[41]

This multiplication of surveys within a short time and by identical methods made strict comparison possible. In what Bowley chose to investigate and therefore to compare his debt to Rowntree is very obvious. Like Rowntree he investigated household income as well as housing-conditions, inquiring about rent levels, housing types and degrees of overcrowding. Like Rowntree he was concerned to use his knowledge of income, rents and prices to establish the proportion of the working-class population below a poverty line.

To this he added an inquiry into household composition by age, sex and earning-power with particular reference to the ratio of dependants to earners in each household. 'In discussions relating to minimum wages, it is frequently assumed that the earnings of a grown man ought to be at least sufficient to support a wife and two children', he explained. He set out to test that assumption and demonstrated that it applied at most to 36·2 per cent of adult wage earners in his towns (p. 31).

Apart from this one innovation the similarities testify to Rowntree's influence, but Bowley's methods of compiling his income data were in important respects different from those of his predecessor. He was far more ready to sacrifice accuracy to speed and simplicity and content to ignore all sorts of ancillary income and income fluctuations that Rowntree had taken into account. Rowntree had prided himself on the care with which he had collected his information, knowing that nothing less than absolute meticulousness would serve to convince the inevitable hostile critics of the significance of his results.[42] He was shocked when he realised on a careful reading of Bowley's second study of the same towns undertaken by the same methods how credulous Bowley had been in accepting figures of wage-income volunteered by the housewife.[43]

The investigation of income was chiefly a means to calculate the number of families in poverty. Here too Bowley demonstrated an independence of approach. In the first place he showed no interest at all in mere impressions of poverty. Poverty for Bowley was what Rowntree had called primary poverty, i.e. the consequence of 'receiving a total income insufficient for the maintenance of physical health' (p. 36).[44] Poverty as something recognisable by the observer received no mention in the book, and the preoccupation with the relation between 'that which is seen and that which is not seen' which Rowntree had taken over from Booth was quietly abandoned.[45] In future, investigators of poverty were to be on the defensive over the rather different relation between the income that is declared and that which is not declared.

Although Bowley took over Rowntree's concept of primary poverty he modified it in two ways. He retained the fundamental distinction between expenditure necessary for the maintenance of merely physical efficiency and expenditure needful for the development of the mental, moral and social sides of human nature, and like Rowntree he firmly excluded the latter. What he did not retain was Rowntree's decision to disregard the conventional standards of working-class diet and instead to use an entirely vegetarian diet in his calculation of minimum costs. Rowntree had felt it necessary to do this to guard himself against objections, however unreasonable, that he was being unduly generous. Working more than a decade later, Bowley was less sensitive to such objections. He was well aware that Rowntree had respected conventional standards of rent and clothing and that the exclusion of meat was inconsistent. He argued that within the permitted categories the assumptions should be as realistic as possible and made a small allowance to cover the additional cost of 2 lbs. of meat per week per adult. He also thought it realistic to distinguish more sharply between the need of children of different ages than Rowntree had done (pp. 79–81). His New Poverty Standard therefore accepted Rowntree's basic principle. His modifications were for the sake of consistency and no more.

It is of course the basic principle itself, with its blind disregard of the social nature of man in estimating a necessary minimum standard, that makes the whole concept of primary poverty as Rowntree had expounded it appear so unrealistic. Bowley was well aware of what he called the 'abstract and arbitrary' nature of the primary poverty concept.

In *Livelihood and Poverty* his main response was the same as Rowntree's in 1901. Since it was unrealistic to expect anyone to behave as the primary poverty model expected of them, it would be reasonable to apply the standard with some latitude (p. 37). But tucked away in a later chapter written to defend his methods against criticism he had begun the process of distancing himself from Rowntree's assumptions. The New Poverty Standard 'does not profess to measure a minimum necessary for efficiency' – a statement on which he does not expand in any way and which could have referred to several very different reservations – yet it makes an intelligible line by which we can divide the population and by the use of which we can compare towns' (p. 177).

He developed both ideas at greater length in another book, more academic in its approach and more forthright in its judgement, that was published in the same year. Efficiency, he explained was as vague a word as heat and fine weather. He had 'still to be convinced that the scale of diet made familiar by Mr. Rowntree has that definiteness which is so often assumed by people who quote his results'. He regarded it rather 'as a useful arbitrary measurement of a low scale of living... It makes a useful and intelligible line even if it is not possible to accept it as the Poverty Line, which divides the poor from those who have a competence'. 'All we can at present get is a carefully devised descriptive scale corresponding to some arbitrary standard which we recognise as undesirably low.' Bowley's criticisms may be summed up under two heads. He doubted the close connection between food intake and work output and he thought that the concept of hard work was too vague to lead to calculations of calorie requirements within the narrow limits of the kind needed. The more he distrusted the arbitrary character of his poverty standard and the vagueness of its basis, the more he emphasised its value as an instrument of comparison. 'It is very useful to have a definite measure for testing progress and comparing societies.'[46]

These points were repeated in 1923 in the second edition of the book, and acknowledged in 1924 when he embarked on his second study of the same five towns that he had investigated in 1912–14. The method of measurement was to be the same, adjusted for price changes, but the object of this arbitrary and artificial 'Poverty Standard' had become explicitly to obtain a comparison over time. *Has Poverty Diminished?* does not offer any new approach to the problem of identifying and measuring poverty. The concept of poverty to which it refers is one whose illegitimacy is hardly in doubt, and which is justified in technical terms alone. 'Whether or no the standard so defined is the best that can be devised for any one date, there is no doubt that it affords an adequate basis for studying the changes which have taken place.'[47]

To allow the generally accepted concept of poverty to drop out of sight and to concentrate on that fraction of it for which Rowntree had designed a form of measurement is strange enough, but understandable when we remember that Bowley was a mathematician accustomed to dealing with measurable abstractions. But to call this quantity 'poverty' *tout court* was taking crassness rather far. Replacing the concept of poverty by that of measurable poverty required a powerful justification. That justification was the importance of the comparative approach.

VI

It is hard to know how acceptable this highly technical redefinition of the term 'poverty' really was when *Livelihood and Poverty* first appeared. The year 1915 was not a time when a book of this kind attracted much attention. What attention it did attract concentrated on the new technique of random sampling and on the surprising fact that among his four towns it was Reading that suffered from the greatest poverty.[48] *Livelihood and Poverty* might well have sunk from view and its quirky redefinition of poverty with it, had Bowley not repeated his investigation in 1924. It was *Has Poverty Diminished?* that made him more widely known as an investigator of poverty, for it dealt with a subject of great contemporary interest, the difference between the pre-war and the post-war world.

Just before the war the poverty survey was primarily about poverty as a nation-wide phenomenon, urban in Bowley's work, rural in Rowntree's. The relation between national uniformity and local diversity was what loomed largest. The experience of the war changed the perception of the problem and therefore the agenda for investigation. Prices and income changed drastically under the impact of war and post-war conditions. But it was far from obvious how these changes combined to affect the distribution of poverty and how permanent they would prove to be. No one was better placed to appreciate this than Bowley, who in the immediate post-war years produced a string of publications on the movement of prices and wages since 1914. He had long been familiar, through this earlier work on the movement of real wages since the eighteenth century, with the practice of using defective evidence to construct arbitrary but consistent series of index numbers for the purpose of comparison over time.[49]

Has poverty diminished? can therefore be understood in terms of Bowley's recent preoccupations. But it also redefined the aim of the poverty survey in line with a major preoccupation of the time. If what mattered most was a comparison between the pre- and post-war situation, an arbitrary standard would meet the need provided that it could always be calculated in precisely the same way.[50] Bowley's calculations showed a considerable improvement over 1912–14. Even on the most pessimistic assumptions the proportion of families in poverty had been reduced by almost half. The principal reasons for the improvement were a rise in the wages of the unskilled and a fall in family size and therefore in the number of dependents.[51]

For our present purpose even more striking than these results is the hold that Bowley's approach to the aims of the social survey and his concept of poverty came to acquire. This was no doubt due in part to his influential position as Professor of Statistics at the London School of Economics from 1919 to 1936, at a time when the social survey, originally pioneered by wealthy private individuals, became institutionalised as an acceptable activity of universities. But it was chiefly due to the fact that in a period of rapid economic change the question of the rate and direction of that change remained of general interest well beyond the confines of universities.

How else can one explain the substantial financial support from diverse sources that enabled the London School of Economics in 1928 to launch the *New Survey of London Life and Labour*? This venture ran to nine volumes and was intended to repeat every aspect of the survey on which Charles Booth had embarked just over forty years before. As Sir Hubert Llewellyn Smith, the director of the project, explained, the object was to use Booth's work as 'a basis for answering the insistent questions which are on all men's minds. In what direction are we moving? Is poverty diminishing or increasing? Are the conditions of life and labour in London becoming better or worse?'[52]

Llewellyn Smith had been one of Booth's original collaborators and in the project piety was inextricably mixed with an interest in comparison.

Since Booth had had to base his classification on merely notional income levels and to rely on the opinion of school attendance officers checked against that of other experts, Llewellyn Smith decided to do the same. The result was an elaborate street survey and a new set of poverty maps conducted in the mental equivalent of historical fancy dress. Avoiding all attempts at random sampling or direct inquiries into household income, school attendance officers were wheeled on as alleged experts. Since the abolition of school fees they no longer had any reason to inquire into family resources as part of their work, unlike their predecessors forty years before. Even so they were asked to classify all families with school children according to a system as close to Booth's as altered circumstances would allow. Their suggestions were then checked against information from public assistance officials and others with special knowledge in Booth's time-honoured way (III, pp. 97–114).

To supplement this attempt to study the London of 1928 by the methods of 1888, Bowley was commissioned to do a parallel survey. His contribution may be described as using the methods of 1912. He drew a random sample and used a questionnaire with questions on income and household composition. His biggest problem was to fix a poverty line. Ever since 1899 that had involved calculating the cost of diets and adding an allowance for clothing, household sundries and rent. Bowley's solution was to impose the same procedure on Booth's data by any means available however strained. These consisted of taking Booth's notional income at the line that divided total poverty from comfort and updating it by a price index. Booth had also published specimen budgets from thirty families drawn from his various classes. These were turned by a highly complicated and ingenious series of calculations into 1928 income equivalents.

Bowley claimed that the result was very close to his own poverty standard. He admitted that the poverty line in question reflected the world of 1912–14 and would have been regarded as unacceptably low by 1928. But it was still too high for a comparison with Booth's figures, even when every questionable assumption had been granted.[53] Basically Bowley was trying to obtain a comparison with his own previous surveys while at the same time producing some rough equivalent to Booth's figures.

How rough may be appreciated in the light of the following considerations. We know that the budgets recorded by his class C and D informants revealed a higher expenditure than 21 shillings per week. It is also obvious that the way of life of most families in classes B, C and D did not lend itself to such regular record-keeping and that his informants were therefore highly uncharacteristic of their class. In addition it is impossible to know how many of the families allocated to the various classes actually had the notional income assigned to that class. Bowley's procedure disregarded every one of these facts.

I am less concerned with the accuracy of the figures than with the significance of the concepts and shall leave the investigators responsible for these two contributions to the study of poverty in London at the end of the 1920s to make their own comments on what they had achieved. 'Admittedly a poverty line which leaves no margin for any expenditure on amenities beyond satisfying the barest physical necessities does not correspond to modern ideas as to the true connotation of the word "poor"', wrote Llewellyn Smith (III, p. 130). 'The opinion as to what constitutes poverty has changed in fifty years and it is desirable to draw up a future definition for future use. To do this from the material collected for the Survey and to give any resulting measurement was found to be impractical in the absence of budgets of expenditure and of any accepted definition.' So wrote Bowley in 1936. By that date he felt that something should be done to modify the poverty line. It was not much, however. He contented himself with upgrading the minimum food expenditure on children under fourteen years in the light of the recent conversion of nutritionists to a high milk diet and to the importance of fresh fruit and vegetables as a source of vitamins. This raised the percentage of London working class children in families with an income below the poverty level from 6 to 12 per cent.[54]

Bowley regarded his contribution to the *New Survey of London Life and Labour* as his most important work.[55] The challenge that he had taken on in what was his third and last social survey lay not in the collection of the information, for which he employed what by then were well-established methods. It is found in the ingenuity that he brought to the comparison of that information with the totally different kind of evidence found in Booth's survey of forty years before. Snatching at an illustrative figure here, a set of household budgets there, a table of estimates somewhere else, he converted a scattered and diverse body of quantities into something to be aligned with Rowntree's tables of families in primary poverty, and then in turn with his own figures for 1912–1914 and 1924.

As one watches the dexterity with which he transformed three such different concepts of poverty, each created in a context and for purposes far removed from one another, into a single statistical series, one is left uncertain whether to admire or protest. It is like watching a conjuror stuffing his coloured handkerchiefs into the magic tube and pulling out a single multicoloured scarf. One is dazzled as much by the audacity as by the skill.[56] This dazzling performance has brought some confusion in its wake. Those of us who have tried to tackle this confusion and correct the myths that have gathered round the concepts of poverty employed by Booth and the early Rowntree, may be likened to stage-hands clearing up after the conjuror's performance, who find that the differently coloured handkerchiefs are separate after all.

NOTES

1 E. P. Hennock, 'Poverty and Social Theory in England: The Experience of the 1880s', *Social History*, 1, 1 (January, 1976), 67–91. The first edition of Booth's survey was entitled *Labour and Life of the People*, vol. I, *East London* (London: Macmillan, 1889); vol. II., *London* (London: Macmillan, 1891). The title by which the work is commonly known and which will be used throughout, *Life and Labour of the People in London*, was adopted for the second edition in 1892. For the material published in 1889 and 1891 references are to the first edition. For subsequent material, references are to the volume and page numbers of the second and third editions, either of which can be consulted.

2 See Hennock, 'Poverty and Social Theory', pp. 73–4 for details.

3 Charles Booth 'The Inhabitants of Tower Hamlets (School Board Division), their Condition and Occupations', *Journal of the Royal Statistical Society*, 50 (1887), 327–8, 395, (hereafter cited as *JRSS*, 50). C. Booth to B. Potter, 5 Sept. 1886, quoted in T. S. and M. B. Simey, *Charles Booth, Social Scientist* (Oxford: Clarendon Press, 1960), p. 84. See also 'Notes on Booth's definition of "Poverty"' in Simey and Simey, *Charles Booth* appendix 4. The figure of 20 per cent has been kindly supplied by Kevin Bales and is based on his unpublished research.

4 Clara Collett, 'Some Recollections of Charles Booth', *Social Services Review*, 1 (1927), 384. H. L. Smith, Memo on the Unemployed 23 Jan., 1895, PRO 37/38/10. I owe the latter reference to Kevin Bales. For further details, see Hennock, 'Poverty and Social Theory'.

5 It was the nine-volume second edition of 1897 that had just been published. It is now in the J. B. Morrell Library of the University of York, together with the *Third Series* (Religious influences) and the *Final Volume* of 1902, also annotated and marked. The last was a gift from Booth.

6 Rowntree, *The Poverty Line* (London: Henry Good, 1903) p. 14. Rowntree's description of the details of his survey methods and timing in that work is more careful than that given in *Poverty*, which seems to have been the source for the different date suggested in Asa Briggs, *Social Thought and Social Action – A Study of the Work of Seebohm Rowntree* (London: Longmans, 1961), p. 25, where the date mentioned is January 1899.

7 Rowntree, *Poverty: a Study of Town Life* (London: Macmillan, 1901), p. 27.

8 This method necessarily omitted domestic servants resident in their employers' homes.

9 The statement in Briggs, *Rowntree*, p. 28, that the investigators did not collect wage statistics would seem to be contradicted by *Poverty*, p. 26, which makes it clear that

they did so whenever they could. It is odd, however, that there was no column for earnings provided on the pages from the note-books of the investigators, as reproduced in *Poverty*, pp. 38–51. Rowntree, in commenting on the information omitted in the published version so as to preserve anonymity, does not suggest that complete columns had been omitted.

10 J. H. Veit-Wilson, 'Paradigms of Poverty: A Rehabilitation of B. S. Rowntree', *Journal of Social Policy*, 15 (1986), 76–7, 80, 92.

11 J. H. Veit-Wilson, 'Paradigms of Poverty: A Reply to Peter Townsend and Hugh McLachlan', *Journal of Social Policy*, 15 (1986), 505. See also Peter Townsend, 'Paradigms of Poverty: A Comment', *Journal of Social Policy*, 15 (1986), 497–8.

12 See E. P. Hennock, 'The Measurement of Urban Poverty: From the Metropolis to the Nation 1880–1920', *Economic History Review*, 2nd ser. 40 (1987), 208–27, for the way in which this comparison shifted the focus of poverty studies away from London. That article deals with aspects of the social surveys not dealt with in this chapter and may be regarded as complementary to it.

13 Booth, *JRSS* 50, 394; Booth, 'Conditions and Occupations of the People of East London and Hackney, 1887', *JRSS*, 51 (1888), 295 (hereafter cited as *JRSS* 51); Booth, I, 146–9.

14 Hennock, 'Poverty and Social Theory', pp. 80–4.

15 Hennock, 'Poverty and Social Theory', p. 75.

16 E.g. Bernard Bosanquet (ed.) *Aspects of the Social Problem* (London: Macmillan, 1895), pp. 78–80; Helen Bosanquet, *Rich and Poor* (London: Macmillan, 1896), ch. 3.

17 Rowntree used the terms physical efficiency and physical health indiscriminately.

18 Veit-Wilson, 'Paradigms of Poverty', pp. 71–3. Since many of the books listed there are textbooks in common use, it is to be hoped that his list of errors will obtain wide publicity among those responsible for teaching the subject.

19 They actually refer not to the total population of York but to the population excluding inmates of institutions and are inconsistent with other figures in the book. Anyone who wants to know what Rowntree actually managed to count should consult the table in Veit-Wilson, 'Paradigms of Poverty', p. 78.

20 Hennock, 'Poverty and Social Theory', p. 91n.

21 *The Times*, 23 August, 1902. In any case the 18 per cent in secondary poverty was a percentage not of those in poverty but of the total population of York.

22 For the development of these fears and the way in which the economic threat from Germany came to acquire the status of a commonly accepted fact after 1895, see E. P. Hennock, *British Social Reform and German Precedents: The Case of Social Insurance 1880–1914* (Oxford: Clarendon Press, 1987), pp. 15–17.

23 J. Rowntree and A. Sherwell, *The Temperance Problem and Social Reform* (London, 1899). See Karel Williams, *From Pauperism to Poverty* (London: Routledge and Kegan Paul, 1981), pp. 359–60 for a discussion of the relationship between the two works.

24 A. L. Bowley and M. H. Hogg, *Has Poverty Diminished?* (London: P. S. King, 1925), p. 13. Bowley's desire to modify some of the conventions while retaining the principle on which the poverty line was constructed had made him sensitive to the distinction. See below.

25 Williams, *From Pauperism to Poverty*, pp. 356–8.

26 Rowntree, *Poverty Line*. For criticisms, see H. Bosanquet, 'The Poverty Line', *Charity Organisation Review* (Jan. 1903), pp. 1–23; C. S. Loch, 'Memorandum relating to some Investigations as to the Number of 'Poor' in the Community'. *Report of Inter-Departmental Committee on Physical Deterioration, App. III* 1904, Cd.2175, XXXII.

27 B. S. Rowntree, *Land and Labour: The Lessons from Belgium* (London: Macmillan, 1910), p. 399.

28 B. S. Rowntree and M. Kendall, *How the Labourer Lives* (London: Nelson, 1913), p. 30.

29 Booth, I, 147, 151–5.

30 Hennock, 'Measurement of Urban Poverty', p. 215.

31 B. S. Rowntree (ed.), *Betting and Gambling. A National Evil* (London: Macmillan 1905).

32 Rowntree, *Poverty*, p. 145. For the timing of this new initiative and other details, see Briggs, *Rowntree*, pp. 67–78.

33 Rowntree and Kendall, *How the Labourer Lives*, pp. 31–2.

34 Land Enquiry Committee, *The Land*, vol. I. *Rural* (London: Hodder and Stoughton, 1913) p. 47; vol. II, *Urban* (London: Hodder and Stoughton, 1914), pp. 160–2; B. B. Gilbert, 'David Lloyd George, the Reform of British Land-Holding and the Budget of 1914', *Historical Journal*, 21 (1978), 117–41.

35 R. H. Tawney, *Poverty as an Industrial Problem* (London: Ratan Tata Foundation, 1914), pp. 14–15. For the making of the 1909 Act and its background, see F. J. Bayliss, *British Wages Councils* (Oxford: Blackwell, 1962); J. A. Schmiechen, *Sweated Industries and Sweated Labour* (London: Croom Helm, 1984); J. Morris, *Women Workers and the Sweated Trades: The Origin of Minimum Wages Legislation* (Aldershot: Gower, 1986).

36 Rowntree and Kendall, *How the Labourer Lives*, pp. 30–1.

37 B. S. Rowntree, *The Human Needs of Labour*, (London: Nelson, 1918; 2nd rev. edn, 1937).

38 Williams, *From Pauperism to Poverty*, pp. 364–8.

39 J. MacNicol, *The Movement for Family Allowances 1918–45: A Study in Social Policy Development* (London: Heineman, 1980), esp. chs. 1–3.

40 Hennock, 'Measurement of Urban Poverty', pp. 212–26. For biographical information on Bowley see *Dictionary of National Biography 1951–60* (Oxford: Oxford University Press, 1971); Agatha H. Bowley, *A Memoir of Professor Sir Arthur Bowley, 1869–1957 and his Family* (privately published, 1972); W. F. Maunder, *Sir Arthur Lyon Bowley, 1869–1957* (Exeter: University of Exeter Press, 1972) and the obituary in *JRSS*, 120 (1947), which includes a select bibliography.

41 A. L. Bowley, "Working-Class Households in Reading", *JRSS*, 76, (June, 1913), 672–701; A. L. Bowley and A. R. Burnett-Hurst, *Livelihood and Poverty* (London: Ratan Tata Foundation, 1915); and *Economic Conditions of Working-class Households in Bolton, 1914. A Supplementary Chapter to 'Livelihood and Poverty'* (London: Bell, 1920).

42 See his comment in Rowntree, *The Poverty line*, p. 13.

43 See the marginal comments in Rowntree's personal copy of A. L. Bowley and M. H. Hogg, *Has Poverty Diminished?* (London: King, 1925) pp. 31, 63, 97, 118, 124. The volume is in the J. B. Morrell Library of the University of York. Rowntree's personal copy of *Livelihood and Poverty* in the same library has been so heavily scored by subsequent readers that I have not found it possible to draw any conclusions from it as to Rowntree's reactions.

44 Bowley consistently used the phrase 'physical health' where Rowntree had referred to 'physical efficiency'.

45 Rowntree, *Poverty*, p. 135, n. 1.

46 A. L. Bowley, *The Nature and Purpose of the Measurement of Social Phenomena* (London: King, 1915), pp. 166–7, 170, 172, 174.

47 A. L. Bowley and M. H. Hogg, *Has Poverty Diminished? A Sequel to 'Livelihood and Poverty'* (London: King, 1925), p. 14.

48 See reviews in *JRSS*, 78 (1915), 455–6 (by A. D. Webb) and *Economic Journal*, 25 (1915), 427–30 (by Rowntree).

49 A. L. Bowley, 'The Measurement of Changes in the Cost of Living', *JRSS*, 82 (1919), 343–61; 'Cost of Living and Wage Determination', *Economic Journal*, 30 (1920), 114–7; *Prices and Wages in the United Kingdom 1914–1920* (Oxford: Clarendon Press, 1921); and 'The Relation between Wholesale and Retail Prices since the War', *Economica*, 2 (1922), 195–207. For his pre-war work on wage indices, see the fourteen articles by A. L. Bowley and H. G. Wood, 'The Statistics of Wages in the United Kingdom during the Last Hundred Years', *JRSS*, 61 (1898) – 69 (1906).

50 Bowley, *Measurement of Social Phenomena*, pp. 183–4.

51 Bowley and Hogg, *Has Poverty Diminished?* pp. 15–25 for further details.

52 *The New Survey of London Life and Labour*, 9 vols. (London: King, 1930–35). The quotation is from vol. I, p. 4.

53 He claimed to have pitched his line 'perhaps 5%' above Booth's. Vol. III, p. 435. The detailed calculations are in vol. III, appendix 2.

54 A. L. Bowley, 'The New Survey of London Life and Labour. Effect of Modifying the Poverty Line', *JRSS*, 99 (1936), 364–6. The quotation is on p. 364. It should be noted that the emphasis is on income. Additional free milk at school was not taken into account.

55 *Dictionary of National Biography 1951–1960*, p. 134.

56 He had done something very similar once before, when constructing the index of real wages in collaboration with H. G. Wood, which linked the diverse fragments of evidence since the late eighteenth century to the very different conceptions that informed the Board of Trade's wage census and cost of living survey in 1906 and 1908. See n. 49.

CHAPTER EIGHT

The part in relation to the whole: how to generalise? The prehistory of representative sampling

ALAIN DESROSIÈRES

> A German thinker offers a model which meets our needs; I refer to Leibniz and his system of monads. Each culture (or society) expresses the universal in its own way, as does each of the monads of Leibniz. And it is not impossible to think of a procedure (complicated and laborious it is true) allowing one to pass from one monad or culture to another through the intermediary of the universal taken as the sum integral of all known cultures, the monad-of-all monads, present on everyone's horizon.
>
> In passing, let us acknowledge and salute an achievement of genius; it is from the seventeenth century that what is doubtless the only serious attempt to reconcile individualism and holism has been passed on to us. Leibniz' monad is at the same time both a whole in itself and an individual in a system that is unified by its very differences. Let us call it the universal Whole.
>
> Louis Dumont, *Essays on Individualism*, p. 210.

Social research using probability samples only appeared for the first time at the end of the nineteenth century, and then in a very rudimentary form, more intuitive than formal, in the work of the Norwegian Kiaer. The first calculations of confidence intervals, by the English statistician A. L. Bowley date from 1906, while the detailed formalisation of methods of stratification was only worked out by Neyman in 1934.[1]

Research inquiries about small numbers of individuals had of course been carried on for much longer, and especially throughout the nineteenth century. Often these were carried out by people of substantial scientific culture – engineers from the 'Corps des Mines ou des Ponts' – for whom the principles of computation of probability necessary to intuit the method of survey sampling would not have represented an insuperable obstacle. Laplace used them as early as the end of the eighteenth century in order to estimate the size of the French population, but this pioneering work was not followed up for nearly a century.

217

The fact that systematic procedures of probabilistic sample selection are today not much more than half a century old shows that the initial discovery and the subsequent use of a technological innovation occurs within distinct cognitive and social conditions. Before inventing a solution to a problem, the problem itself must be identified as a problem, in this case the question of representativeness, in the sense of the term as used by statisticians.

One can not fail to recognise that this concern is expressed in terms of homotheticity, for the precise definition of certain elements of the part of the whole is very recent, more recent then than the national census (championed by Quetelet in the 1830s) and the monographic investigations (Le Play, at about the same period).[2] Looking at available work on the history of empirical social science, of statistics and of sampling,[3] one has the impression of passing directly from a period when the question of representativeness was practically never discussed (see for example the publications between 1914 and 1916, of the Statistique Générale de la France, on household budget inquiries by the statistician Duge de Bernonville or the sociologist Halbwachs) to another when the issue was unquestionably obvious, as in the debates of the International Institute of Statistics, first between 1895 and 1903, then from 1925 and 1934.

These debates, when they took place, were not about the requirement of representativeness as such, but developed along different lines at two periods. Between 1895 and 1903 the question was, on the one hand, whether it was legitimate to replace the whole by the part (comparison with censuses) and on the other if in proceeding in this way one did 'better' than with monographs in the manner of Le Play, still much admired in this period. As we shall see, this 'better' did not bear directly on the requirement of representativeness in the sense of *precise measurement*, but concerned the possibility of comprehending a *diverse population*. Later, between 1925 and 1934, the debate turned on the choice between 'random selection' and 'purposive selection'. Neyman's development of the theory of stratification aimed a fatal blow at 'purposive selection'.

The chronological summary given above draws on several studies on the history of social research. It shows how, between 1895 and 1935, the prevailing scientific norms about descriptions of the social world were radically transformed in respect of *generalisation* about a whole society from observations relating to a part of that society. This transformation raised and addressed the question: How to pass from a 'part' to the 'whole'?

The two methods of generalisation, that of *purposive* versus *random* selection, successively (and also simultaneously) in use in social investigations carried out over the last century and a half seem quite unlike each other, as if each had its sphere of validity, its own logic. The confrontation could only take place through mutual denunciation, of which several examples will be given below.

This apparent incompatibility can be better understood if it is set within the wider context of the general issues involved in conceptualising the links between the parts and the entirety of a society, as they have appeared to confront each other since the beginning of the nineteenth century, in the wake of those two social upheavals, the French Revolution and the rise of English economic liberalism. Studies of this transformation of relations between the parts and the whole of society include those of Polanyi, Dumont and Nisbet.[4] The research of Boltanski and Thévenot, which is devoted to a general investigation of different ways of constituting social wholes has also been an important inspiration of the present work.[5]

The contrast, set out by Louis Dumont, between 'holism' and 'individualism' is a good starting point. It is often used by historians and anthropologists, though their use of 'whole' is not adequate for our purpose. In the 'holistic' view which for Dumont characterises traditional societies before the two political and economic revolutionary upheavals, the social 'whole' has an existence prior to and superior to its constituent parts (and in particular to individuals). On the other hand, in the individualist world view, which is that of 'modern' societies, individuals, whether as citizens or as economic agents, are organised in different ways, without being totally subsumed within these larger groupings.

This dichotomous style of conceptualising on the one hand a social whole embracing all its members, and on the other hand the atomised individuals in modern society (a distinction one also finds in Toennies's contrast between 'Gemeinschaft' and 'Gesellschaft') does not however take account of another way of constituting the whole, which is precisely that of the statistician seeking to draw *a representative sample*. The 'social whole' of Dumont's holism and the exhaustiveness of approach of the statistician are two completely different ways of thinking about a totality. The contrast between them helps us to grasp what distinguishes the two implicit ways of generalising which underly monographs as opposed to sample surveys.[6]

The intellectual configurations outlined above confronted and combined with each other in various ways in the course of the nineteenth century in the work of the founding fathers of social science: Quetelet, Tocqueville, Marx, Toennies, Durkheim, Pareto ...[7] But they were certainly not acting as a 'deus ex machina' drawing in turn the thread of this or that empirical research technique. Rather they represented intellectual groupings each with their own internal coherence, but quite different when compared with each other. These differences are identifiable in the debates about methods of research in this period. Each thinker or each of the intellectual configurations implied not only a different way of thinking about how society should be run, but also the place of the social sciences in such management, and the place of probabilistic ideas in these sciences, from Quetelet to Fisher. This provides us with a thread to follow in studying the history of this aspect of social inquiry from before the appearance of the 'representative method', through the development of probabilistic reasoning during the debates of the International Institute of Statistics between 1895 and 1934, to the first use of the method and the debates between 'random selection' and 'purposive selection'.

THE RHETORIC OF THE EXAMPLE

One can reconstruct the philosophy of those inquiries which aimed to generalise from observations made without the modern constraint of representativeness from three cases which apparently are quite different from each other: the monographs of Le Play and his followers between 1830 and 1900; the English poverty studies of Booth and Rowntree between 1880 and 1900; and thirdly the work of the Durkheimian, Maurice Halbwachs, on working-class budgets between 1900 and 1940.

The common element in these different inquiries, otherwise very different, is that people questioned were chosen from a network of known people: families described as 'typical' by village leaders in the case of Le Play, people known to the School Board Visitors in the case of Booth, volunteer workers found through the intermediary of trade unions in the case of Halbwachs. Of course these selection methods were rightly stigmatised as likely to lead to 'bias' in the subsequent period, but, in the context where they were used, they were consistent with the aims of these inquiries, which on the whole were to describe the functioning (and malfunctioning) of working class communities subject to the vicissitudes of industrialisation. It was not yet a case of measuring social phenomena in order to prepare policy measures, as was to be the case after the development of the Welfare State, but rather to put together the elements with which to sketch out the typical personalities in a history being told or organised, in particular by means of classification. Classification in terms of 'typical' actors is one of the results of this type of inquiry, just as, in the following period, atomised individuals became the key actors (studied in terms of their voting behaviour or as buyers in studies of market behaviour), when it was necessary to count precisely.

It was not entirely the case that probabilistic ideas were completely absent from these inquiries and their interpretation. But this was rather a 'holistic' conception of probability, inspired by Quetelet and by the importance which he attached to the regularity of averages derived from large populations, whereby the dispersion and variable character of individual characteristics appeared to be reliably subsumed within the single figure representing the whole. This lace-like regularity strongly supported a conception of the social whole going beyond and subsuming the compared parts.[8]

This application of the law of large numbers to the stability of averages (for example, the annual rates of births, marriages, crimes or suicides) made a strong impression on the contemporaries of Quetelet and were the chief weapons of a macrosociology for which the 'social' had a reality external to and over and above individuals. This is the thread leading to Durkheim's *Suicide* and also, as we shall see, to Halbwachs' studies of the 'conscience ouvrière'.

It is because the probabilistic model of the law of large numbers directs attention towards the regularity of averages and not towards the dispersion of distributions, the variations of frequency of attributes, or dispersions that it cannot be regarded as the source of probability sampling. For, if the averages are stable, it is enough to find cases that are near to the average, which, on their own, are taken to be typical of the whole. Not only do they represent it but literally they are the totality, since in the holistic schema it is the totality which is primary, individuals being not more than *contingent manifestations*. The intellectual model of this notion of the average is provided by the theory of measurement error in astronomy or gunnery. The *ascension droite* of a star is only known through a series of contingent measures distributed according to a normal curve around a mean, which provide the best estimate of that average. Similarly, for Quetelet, contingent individuals are random manifestations of a 'divine design' which makes up superior reality.

Knowing that toward the end of the nineteenth century, this conception of statistics was still dominant (at least in France, for in England the first work of Galton and Pearson was beginning to appear), one can explain why in 1890 Emile Cheysson, a follower of Le Play, described and justified the 'monographic method',[9] just before the Norwegian statistician Kiaer put forward his very different 'representative method'.

The monograph ... is very careful to avoid the particular case and to search out the general case; the accidental case, the exception, the anomaly are ignored to focus upon the average, in search of typification. Typification is the essence of the monographic method. Without typification, it is not worth bothering; but with the construction of types, the method is able to illuminate social and economic investigations with bright intensity...

The observer...is guided in his choice by large synthetic statistics, by administrative inquiries, which cover the country with their network and map out the terrain across which the author of the monographs is going to range. With the help of the information thus placed at his disposal, he will know in advance the population which he wishes to study and can choose typifications with precision and without fear of error. Official statistics act as the advance guard, providing the averages which point the author of the monograph towards typification. In turn, the monograph by means of a detailed study verifies the general results of the inquiry. These two major procedures thus act as a check on each other, whilst each keeping their distinctive character.

While the methods of administrative inquiry spread out over the surface, the monographic method ploughs in depth. Official statistics, putting into the field an army of agents who are more or less zealous and experienced, accumulates a mass of facts grasped rather superficially and from a single point of view; they are poured pell-mell between the grindstones; the law of large numbers is relied upon to eliminate the most basic observational errors. The monographic method aims on the other hand at quality rather than quantity of observations; only carefully selected observers are used, at the same time artists and scientists, who take possession of a constructed typification, and work unceasingly at it until they have penetrated to its marrow.[10]

The core of these monographs was made up by the identification of the expenses and receipts of the family budget, carried out by a more or less prolonged stay by the investigator in the home. Even if, however, they were established in a uniform manner, as by Le Play, they were still not really destined to be *compared* in order to identify budget structures typical of different *milieux*, as in the work done by Halbwachs shortly afterwards. This was one of the criticisms which the latter directed against the studies of the Le Play school.[11] The question is thus: *what purpose do they serve?*

The earlier monographic inquiries seem to have been oriented basically toward the defence and exemplification of a certain conception of the family and of social relations. Arguments were advanced by Cheysson which bear on the needs of the administrator and the legislator wishing to understand the effects of their general and abstract measures upon the particular concrete cases of typical families. The *gestionnaire* concern was also associated with a moral preoccupation:

This knowledge is indispensable both to the moralist who wishes to influence social customs and the man of affairs who wishes to influence public action. The law is an arm with two sides: if it can exercise great power for the good, it can also do much harm in inexperienced hands.[12]

Such facts are evoked for the study of the apportionment of fiscal charges on those in the agricultural, commercial and industrial sectors, or for the effects of certain regulations restricting the work of women and children. The moral preoccupation is explicit, and there is no technique used or even suggested for linking in practice the several available monographs to the holistic picture of the state: the question of an ultimate social framework of categories within which all individuals would find a place is never raised.

The monographs of le Play and his disciples have been criticised and then forgotten for reasons both technical and political: on the one hand they offered no methodological guarantee about the choice of sample, and on the other they propped up a discourse hostile to the French Revolution, to universal suffrage and to the Code Civil, and sought to reestablish the social relations of the Ancien Régime. Nevertheless, the cognitive programme and the political programme were very coherent. Knowledge was the result of an intimate acquaintance of the investigator with the working-class family. The results were presented as useful not only to produce social knowledge, but also to create and sustain personal ties based on trust between member of higher and lower social classes.

Included most often in the advocacy of traditional family virtues, the monographs rarely served as the basis for structural comparisons, except in one case, that of non-monetary income, recorded as grants or 'aubaines': rights to use communal land, family gardens, natural resources. Not being dependent upon the market, these forms of remuneration maintained direct and personal links between members of different classes and therefore supposedly reflected the persistence of patriarchal social ties. Thus, in Eastern Europe, a society still largely rural and little industrialised, this element was stronger than in the West where towns and the market economy played a larger role.

The idea was that traditional social ties, overthrown by the economic and political transformations taking place in society, could not be understood except by prolonged contact between observer and observed. That this observation should take account of the entire significance of actions which the investigator could not isolate and code in *a priori* terms, is found in other modes of knowledge-creation which developed subsequently, and which embody other ways of generalising than that of representative sampling: ethnological descriptions of non-Western societies on the basis of long and patient periods of field work in the community by the investigator, psychoanalysis building a model of the structure of the unconscious on the basis of completely individual data, gathered in the course of personal exchanges of very long duration.

This same approach to knowledge, by which a case studied in great depth can on its own enable the construction of a 'generic man', and uncover the mechanisms underlying a 'common humanity', are found at the same period in the work of experimental psychologists, like the German, Wilhelm Wundt, who, in his laboratory, tried to identify such general traits. The idea of the dispersion of traits of the human psyche only appeared much later, thanks to the work of Pearson and Spearman.

One sees clearly, in the way Cheysson justifies the choice of his 'typical cases' with reference to averages calculated from the grand synthetic inquiries, that the theory of averages of Quetelet was able to provide, for nearly a century, an intellectual scheme allowing one to think at the same time about the variety between individuals and the common features of a species or of a social group:

With the help of the information thus placed at his disposal, the author of a monograph will know in advance the population which he wishes to study and can choose typifications with precision and without fear or error. Official statistics act as the advance guard, providing the averages which point towards typification.[13]

This was a means of signalling, in a manner of speaking, the method of 'purposive selection' which, between 1900 and 1930, constituted a sort of link between the two types of method, indirectly through *territory*, as will be explained below.

HALBWACHS: THE SOCIAL GROUP AND ITS MEMBERS

Halbwachs was a pupil of Durkheim but, more than that, from the time of his thesis on 'The Working Class and Standards of Living' (1912) he was concerned with techniques of inquiry and making observations of facts. Much more than the followers of Le Play, whose work he criticised sharply, he was aware of the *diversity* of cases observed and sought means of interpreting this diversity, as Durkheim had done in *Suicide*, thereby inventing modern quantitative sociology. By another route he was familiar with certain work on probability: his thèse complementaire (1913) concerned 'The Theory of the Average Man; An Essay on Quetelet and Moral Statistics', and he even wrote with Maurice Frechet in 1924 a small manual on probability. In this manual, the very compact discussion introduced about problems of sampling and inquiry (pp. 151–62) is headed 'the number of budgets'. It bears on the discovery of an 'economic' equilibrium between the number of people investigated and the more or less thorough character of the observations made, that is to say, a comparison between 'intensive' and 'extensive' methods and not at all about problems of *drawing a sample*, which he does not discuss.

What he kept of the 'law of large numbers' was the view that a collection of small, numerous, haphazard and various causes balanced each other to produce a supposed 'average' to reveal the essential truth according to the scheme of Quetelet. This was particularly so in the method termed 'extensive', then much in use in the United States, where certain samples exceeded 10,000 persons. But, as he rejected the intensive method of le Play which gave no indication of diversity and did not allow the *cross-tabulation of variables* suggesting *explanations*, he rejected also the extensive method of the Americans because, as a Durkheimian sociologist, he distrusted a microsociological interpretation of the law of large numbers.

In effect, he said, those favouring extensive methods have well understood that the responses obtained could involve errors, lack of precision or failures of recall. Nevertheless,

they thought that by multiplying the cases, they would obtain, by the operation of the law of large numbers, compensation and a growing reduction in these imperfections.[14]

But Halbwachs imagined that, like all other social facts, these omissions or imperfections have systematic macrosocial causes and were not random in the probabilistic sense. He had the intuition that there might be 'systematic bias':

it is observable that omissions do not happen by chance ... An omission is associated with a state of inattention in the subject and an obligation which he owes to fulfill a fairly great social duty ... If omissions are periodic, regular, it must be that the causes of inattention and the causes which explain these duties to fulfil are constant forces ... But the fact that omissions are periodic leads one to think that the forces which explain them, by virtue of the arrangement of social life, exercise themselves in their turn, and that their effects is in exact proportion to their constant intensity.[15]

He then turns to a detailed analysis of 'the effects of inquiry' linked to interaction, to the role of the investigator, showing that, in all cases, the errors would be unlikely to be random and independent one of another. In effect, in these extensive American inquiries, there is no budget diary kept, and the investigator asks *a posteriori* questions about the sample which, in the final analysis, are judgements resting on opinion:

The aim of science, here as elsewhere, is to replace formed principles and opinions, or vague and contradictory ideas, with precise knowledge, founded on fact; but here the facts are distorted in advance, seen through an opinion which blurs and obscures the contours of the data. One is caught in a circle of averages.

The whole of this critique of the American method is centred on the idea that the 'law of large numbers' is supposed to eliminate numerous errors, small and independent of each other, and not at all on the fact that this same 'law' could be used to justify a method of random selection of a sample in a diversified population *in reality* and not as a result of errors of observation. Here one is still closer to the model of Quetelet than to that of either Galton and Pearson.

Nevertheless, Halbwachs explicitly draws attention to the diversity of the population of workers, and it is precisely upon this subject that he opposes Le Play and his choice of 'typical cases' guided by averages. Halbwachs asks by what visible exterior trait one can characterise the average worker's family:

Many households do not know themselves whether their budget balances or not. In any case, they do not inform people of the fact. Now if this is not seen or known, or cannot be inferred, how can one overcome family solidarity. How to find and how to seek the average cases in this domain?

It is therefore necessary to observe directly, with the help of completed budget diaries, a range of families, in order to be able to study the effects of this or that factor; size of family, presence of children, etc. But this diversity and these variations remain macrosocial ones, in the tradition of Durkheim's analysis of suicide and the 'constant causes' of Quetelet. The German investigations used by Halbwachs seemed to him to be free of the disadvantages of the other inquiries: sufficiently small to allow a careful verification of budget diaries and large enough to study their variation.

The objective of this research, however, is quite as much to identify the traits of a common 'working class consciousness', whose relatively homogeneous character stems not from a divine essence as with Quetelet (Halbwachs was a materialist) but from common material conditions of existence, which a quasi-Darwinian adaptation leads to similar requirements both in practical life and in consciousness. It is because he was interested in this working-class consciousness that the problems of sampling did not present themselves in at all the same terms which they would do for those who, half a century later, would use such studies to promote national accounts.

Thus pleased that the German Metalworkers Union had been able to collect as many as 400 budgets, he noted:

It is obviously owing to working class solidarity and the influence which syndicalist organisations exercise over their members that this result has been achieved. (p. 138)

Elsewhere, commenting on certain budgets collected by Charles Booth in London for very poor families, he questioned the rigour with which the budget diaries had been collected in these extreme cases and concluded, icily, by asking if these most deprived sections were really part of the working class:

by reason of the state of destitution in which these households find themselves, perhaps a brief observation provides a fair picture of their chronic misery; but one cannot be sure. For the rest, in studying social classes this lowest social layer, which lacks a shared consciousness, is not the most interesting and perhaps can only be known superficially. (p. 470)

Despite everything which distinguishes the followers of Le Play from the Durkheimians, as much in the scientific as in their political projects, one can nevertheless identify certain common points between them. Wishing above all to rethink (much more subtly by the latter than the former) the nature of social ties destroyed by the revolutionary changes, their empirical inquiries aimed to identify the persistence of ancient forms or the birth of new forms of such ties, while appreciating in each case their moral import.

But this motivation for making empirical inquiries with a view to social reconstruction, common throughout the nineteenth century, including Quetelet, was not accompanied by any aim of *direct* social and political action, and did not as a result entail any requirement for *exhaustiveness* in a territorial or national sense. The assumed degree of generality of described *cases* was enough to support moral and political developments, which made no sort of reference to a defined territory (with the exception, if you will, of Le Play who compared in a very general way Eastern Europe with Western Europe).

The history of the gradual emergence of the notion of representativeness in its modern sense can be juxtaposed to that of the extension and transformation of the political and economic tools for dealing with problems of poverty, from the aristocratic or parochial charity of the eighteenth century to the diverse forms of the welfare state, which began to appear at the end of the nineteenth. At this point social statistics were changing their function. Previously, they were generally used to illustrate comprehensive analyses of a social world portrayed in holistic terms (the model of Quetelet) or in organicist terms (the model of Auguste Comte). Now they were becoming little by little an essential part of policies, otherwise highly varied, which sought to act at the level of individuals, and the idea of representativeness then took on a decisive importance, to evaluate the costs and benefits of the policies promulgated.

Among these, three successive developments were to play essential roles in bringing in the idea of representativeness in its modern form: the introduction of the laws providing for social security, in northern Europe from 1890 onwards; then – thanks to the railways – the development of national markets for consumer goods and in their wake market research, and finally the possibility of conducting national election campaigns – thanks to the radio – something which happened first in the United States between the wars.

REPRESENTATIVENESS AND THE NATIONALISATION OF SOCIAL STATISTICS

The common element in the transformations in each of these three areas is the transition from modes of local administration centred on personal relations (charity, small commerce, craftsmen, rural markets, electoral patronage) to other national ones in which locality as a setting for the daily reproduction of social ties diminishes in importance. The groundwork for this move to general equivalence and making uniform different areas[16] was laid, at least in France, by the organisation of *Départements*, the diffusion of the *Code Civil*, universal suffrage, compulsory military service, universal education in *l'école laique* (secular state schools), without mentioning the introduction of the metric system and the national timetabling of the railways. These were prior conditions for the development of two related concepts, of *exhaustiveness* and *representativeness*, completely absent, as we have seen, from the work of the followers of Le Play and Durkheim.[17]

Two studies by E. P. Hennock of the series of investigations of poverty conducted by Charles Booth, Seebohm Rowntree and Arthur Bowley, provide a good example of the links between these three transformations.[18] These were (1) the nationalisation of social statistics, (2) the diffusion of the 'representative method' and of random selection, and (3) the beginnings of the development of the Welfare State. A study of the debates in the International Statistical Institute from 1895 onwards also largely confirms the hypothesis.

The poor: how to describe them? what to do about them?

Throughout the nineteenth century, the history of British studies of poverty is linked to changing interpretations and explanations of the phenomenon and to the remedies proposed. Early in the century[19] 'reformists' carried out local investigations filled with recommendations about improving the morality of the working class. The approach differed from that of Le Play only in that the condemnation of the market economy is clearly less vigorous.

Around 1880, the economic crisis was at its height and the situation appeared to be particularly dramatic in London, above all in the East End.[20] A public discussion began about the circumstances of the section of the working class below a line considered to amount to extreme poverty. This recurrent debate, at all times and all places ridiculous because of the arbitrariness of the definition of the poverty line and of the methods used to measure it, is of historical interest at this point because it led to a typology of poverty, at the same time descriptive, explanatory and operational. For Booth derived from his measures of poverty policy measures for dealing with the problem: remove from London the indigent, in order to relieve the burden on those who were slightly less poor and who were in that condition for economic and macrosocial reasons (the crisis). The typology is in fact more complex (there are eight categories) and bears at the same time on the level and regularity of income. The data are based on the *impressions* of School Board Visitors and result in detailed statistics.

But their main importance for us lies in the association between the typology and the geographical results. Up to that point the problems of poverty had been dealt with at the parish level. But the case of London was particularly dramatic and it seemed from Booth's researches that, contrary to what had been previously thought, the condition of the 'very poor' was scarcely better in London as a whole than in the East End alone; the issue of the geographical representativeness of the results by district led little by little to political conclusions. The recommendation that the very poor be ejected from the city assumed very definitely that the situation was most serious in London. Booth's inquiry was confined to London, and so generalisations in the manner of Le Play or even Halbwachs were not possible; to take action, it was going to need a *mock-up*, a *scale model* of the whole nation: the national sample survey would provide it.

A few years later, Rowntree undertook in York a similar inquiry to that of Booth in London. He was aware that Booth's methods could be improved, and gave much greater attention to the techniques of collecting the data. Yet he could not change them completely, for the essential aim was to be able to compare the proportion of the very poor in the two cities. And it appeared from his research that the size of this group was scarcely less in York than in London. This strengthened the argument that poverty would not be dealt with locally. The establishment of the first old age pensions in 1908 (a policy also proposed and researched by Charles Booth) was a move to take national control of the incipient social insurance, bringing to bear a macrosocial response to problems which could no longer be presented as arising from individual morality (working-class sobriety and bourgeois charity). Between Booth in the 1880 and Rowntree in the first decade of the new century the problems initially posed in local terms were henceforth national issues, but the tool which would provide this new national social statistics were lacking; this would be introduced by Arthur Bowley.

International competition and weighty statistics

The relationships between the technique of inquiry, the use which is expected of it and the means used changes radically not only because of the introduction of new social laws, but also because of the weight attached in the English context at this period to discussions of the rivalry between the great industrial powers and of the question of free trade. This led to several comparative inquiries between countries. Rowntree entered into communication with Halbwachs, who organised a study following his methods, published by the Statistique Générale de France in 1914.[21] Then, most strikingly, the British Board of Trade mounted a very major operation in different countries which, even if it did not use probabilistic methods, was the first of such breadth in Europe, involving so many countries. In France, data were collected from 5,605 working-class families, and the questionnaires were distributed by trade unions in some thirty cities.[22]

It was because the British Liberal Government needed arguments for its battle against protectionism that important public resources were mobilised for the Board of Trade, allowing inquiries to take place in a large number of towns and posing crucial questions for the future establishment of the necessary infrastructure for sample surveys: the organisation of a network of homogeneous investigators, taking account of specific local circumstances (type of housing, consumption habits, employment structure). One unintended by-product of this international comparison was the possibility of comparison between towns in a single country.[23]

The next step made possible by this ambitious operation was that Bowley could formulate in a plausible way the possible conditions for 'representative' inquiries (using the terminology of the period) and could organise a survey, of one in twenty of the population, in four towns chosen in such a way that two were of the 'mono-industrial' type and two others were 'multi-industrial'. He saw too that conditions of comprehensiveness and of representiveness were linked to a third consideration: *the obligation to respond* to a survey, a theme absent in all which went before. By doing this, Bowley shifts the process of interaction between the investigator and those studied away from the model of the confident familiarity based in the network of sociability, identified in earlier studies, to make participation in research become more like a kind of general civic duty, analogous to universal suffrage or conscription for military service.

At the same time, *error* and *precision* changed their nature. Just as Rowntree was particularly careful about methods of recording information, but ignorant of questions of sampling, Bowley was less careful about recording. Rowntree criticised him for (to cite one example) accepting replies on income level given by the *wives* of wage earners, in the absence of their husbands, which Rowntree himself refused to do. Above all, however, Bowley made estimates of imprecision, of the margin of error, a respectable objective. The confidence interval was recognised as such and was no longer concealed shamefacedly in bashful silence as some sort of *mistake*. There, again, technique and the law of large numbers took the place of moralising about the individual.

In the same line of inquiry Bowley no longer sought to identify poverty from impressions gained during visits, as Booth had done, but rested his analysis upon established quantitative variables. Nor did he seek to distinguish poverty due to 'bad habits' from poverty due to economic causes, excluding all explicit moral judgement from his investigations.

Moreover, and this is the culmination of everything that went before in terms of *professional identity*, he asserted the right *not* to be obliged to formulate some *solution* to the problems of poverty. At about the same time, Max Weber emphasised the distinction between science and politics, a quite new stance in the context of nineteenth-century thinking.

As economists and statisticians we are not concerned with palliatives or methods of expediency, but with a correct knowledge and true diagnosis of the extent of the evils, on which can be built reasoned and permanent remedies.[24]

A comparison of Booth, Rowntree and Bowley (following E. P. Hennock's discussion in chapter 7), who knew each other and referred to each other's work, shows clearly the coherence of the varied cognitive, technical and political features of the great changes in epistemology and methodology which were taking place around 1900. These went hand in hand: the beginnings of the Welfare State at the level of the national society, the nationalisation of production and of the interpretation of data, the substitution of neutral technical machinery for moral judgements, and above all the appearance of a new professional figure, *the government statistician*, distinct both from the man of letters of the nineteenth century, agonising about the dissolution of social ties, and the bureaucratic official directly responsible for dealing with social problems.

The Congress of the ISI: from exemplary monographs to systematic inquiry

This new role, 'the government statistician', appeared more and more clearly in the national statistical societies and above all in the International Statistical Institute, created in 1883, which brought together the most important government statisticians from different countries. Gradually the enlightened and eclectic amateurs of the nineteenth century were replaced by the technical professionals of statistics, in cultural outlook more and more mathematical and less and less historical or political.

It was in these circles that, starting in 1895, there began the discussion of the 'representative method'. This was started by the Norwegian Kiaer, who had organised in his country a first 'representative enumeration' in 1894 involving selections drawn from particular localities and then from among people in these localities, who were questioned about qualifications, income, expenditure, days out of work, marriage, and number of children.

The initiative of Kiaer was extensively discussed in the course of the four successive congresses of the ISI, between 1895 and 1903, and at the latter date the Berlin congress adopted a motion favouring the method, with the reservation that it should be clearly specified 'in which conditions the choice of observed units is made'. The report asked for was not presented until 1925, by the Dane Jensen. A motion (see appendix, p. 241) was then adopted, which did not, however, settle the argument between the two methods of 'random selection' versus 'purposive selection'. This latter method was not eliminated until after Neyman's work in 1934.

In the first phase, from 1895 to 1903, the probabilistic aspect of the new method, and the necessity of random selection of the cases selected was given little attention, and moreover during the 1894 inquiry Kiaer was not very particular on this point, the importance of which he was not yet aware. For example, after having carefully selected districts and streets, he left to the investigators the choice of houses to visit:

They should visit not only average homes from the social point of view but in general houses representing the different social or economic conditions found in the community.[25]

In fact, by insisting strongly, and for the first time in such a setting, on the idea of *representativeness*, Kiaer basically wanted to show that provided one took certain (rudimentary) precautions in the choice of sample one could obtain, for several *controllable* variables (because they were already covered in complete enumerations), results good enough to be able to assume that for other variables these results would also be 'good enough', without having to be very precise about the meaning of the latter expression. The essential feature of the idea of representativeness was truly in this notion: *the part replacing the whole*. In previous inquiries no one had thought to compare the part with the whole, because the *whole* was not thought of in the same terms. Quetelet, for example, considered that the average man summarised in himself a population, but it was upon these average traits and their regularity that attention was focused, and not on the population itself with its limits, its structures and its variations.

But for Kiaer such a concern with exhaustive description and representativeness in this new sense was certainly present, even if the technical tools were not yet available. The tools, necessary for *selecting* a *random* sample and calculating *confidence intervals* would not appear until they were presented by Bowley in 1906, outside the ISI (though he was to participate actively in the Congress of 1925 which relaunched the debate, with Jensen, March, Gini...)[26]

The technical debates at these meetings of statisticians have already been described in important previous work from the angle of the progressive integration of results of probability calculations and of mathematical statistics into the theory of sampling.[27] It has been shown that the decisive step from this point of view was the work of Neyman on stratification,[28] which sent 'purposive selection' to the graveyard. We shall not go over the same ground here, but rather examine how Kiaer introduced his method, and why he felt the need to compare this to the *monographic method* of Le Play, a comparison which would not have seemed relevant to the statisticians of the next century.

The justifications which Kiaer gave for his inquiry were indicative of the more general transformation from a period in which the links between social classes were still thought of in terms of orders and of places, and were thus incommensurable, to another where individuals of various social classes could judge themselves against a common national standard, in which the issue of *inequality*, not conceivable in the other system, became fundamental, and where the problems of poverty were no longer thought of in terms of charity and neighbourliness, but in terms of social laws voted by parliaments.

Kiaer observed that previous inquiries had been concerned with *workers* or *the poor* alone, since it was not yet conceivable that one could put different social classes side by side, within a larger whole. He was therefore one of the first to put the problem of 'social inequality' in such terms.

Furthermore, it is striking that the following should have been stated at the beginning of the first text bearing upon representativeness in social statistics, the work of a government statistician.

One thing above all has struck me, that detailed investigations about budgets, housing and other economic and social conditions which have been carried out concerning the working classes, have not been extended in a similar way to all classes in Society. It seems to me obvious that in considering even the worker question properly speaking, one should compare the economic, social and moral etc situation of the workers to that of the middle classes and the upper classes. In a country where the upper classes are very rich and the middle classes very well-to-do, the claims of the working classes relative to their income, their housing, etc are measured on a different scale than in a country (or a district) where the majority of people belonging to the upper classes are not rich and where the middle classes are in straightened circumstances.

From this proposition, which seems to me quite clear, it follows that in order properly to understand the conditions of the working class, it is also necessary to understand, beyond that, the analogous features of other social classes. But one must take a step further and say that, since society is not made up only of the working class, one ought not in social investigation to neglect paying attention to any class in the society.[29]

He explains immediately afterwards that this inquiry is going to perform a role in the creation of a superannuation fund and social insurance scheme, guaranteeing a social equalisation and a statistical treatment of varied risks:

From the beginning of this year [1896] there has operated and operates in our country a representative enumeration whose object is to clarify various questions concerning the project of creating a general superannuation fund and insurance against invalidity and old age. This enumeration operates under the auspices of a parliamentary committee charged with examining these questions and of which I am one of the members.[30]

Two years later, in 1897, in the course of a new discussion at the ISI, the argument turned on what this new 'representative method' showed compared to the 'typological method' then advocated in the heart of the ISI by statisticians who followed Le Play, such as Cheysson. Kiaer insisted in that discussion on the *territorial* aspect; that the representative sample was a miniature of the total territory ... showing, not just types, but also the 'variety of cases which are found in life'. While not yet tackling the question of random selection, he does insist upon the control of the results by matching tests with the nation's general statistics.

The terminology being used in our programme today, 'procedures in typological studies', does not conform to my own ideas. I shall have occasion to demonstrate the difference which exists between typological investigations and representative investigation.

By representative investigation I mean a partial investigation where observations are gathered in a large number of scattered localities, distributed right across a particular territory in such a way that the entirety of localities observed forms a miniature of the total territory. These localities should not be studied arbitrarily but following a rational grouping based on the general results of statistics; and the individual reports collected in each area ought to be arranged in such a way that their results can be controlled in several ways using general statistics.[31]

When he contrasted his method, allowing the description of the 'variety of cases' to that which only showed 'typical cases', he underlined a transformation quite parallel to that which Galton and Pearson would bring about in relation to the old statistics of the average as used by Quetelet: by bringing attention to focus upon the *variability of individual cases*, with the notions of variance, of correlation and of regression, the English eugenists moved statistics from the ground of the study of wholes summarised by a single average (holism) to analysis of the *distribution* of individual values *to be compared*. Kiaer continued:

The Institute has recommended the conduct of investigation using *selected types*. Without wishing to dispute the value of this kind of partial investigation, it has certain disadvantages compared to representative investigations. Even if one knows the proportions in which the different types enter into the total, one is far from reaching a plausible result for the whole; for the total includes, not only types, that is average proportions, but all the variation of cases that one finds in real life. It is therefore necessary, before the partial investigation can provide a true miniature of the whole, that one observes not only the types, but all kinds of phenomena. And that can be done, even if not completely, with the help of a good representative method which ignores neither the types nor the variations. (p. 181)

Then, trying to put himself between the two fundamentally different modes of knowledge, represented by individual monographs and by complete enumeration, he insisted in a surprising way that he thought his representative sampling could perform just as well as the producers of monographs did on *their territory* ('the blood, the flesh, the muscles') when, in the future, samples would be compared with complete enumerations (in matters of cost and precision) but surely not with monographs. This shows the significance of a mode of knowing resting on intuition of the totality of the person:

In discussing the reciprocal roles of the monographs and of partial statistics, we have said that the monographic method is concerned with objects that one can neither count, nor weigh, nor measure, while partial statistics is concerned with 'objects which by themselves could be counted in their entirety but which, by deliberate purpose, are only counted in part...'

... In general, I believe one can apply to partial investigations and above all to representative investigations the eloquent words which our esteemed colleague M. Bodio pronounced at

Berne concerning the work of our lamented Dr Engel on working class family budgets. 'Statistical monographs and complete enumeration are two ways of investigating social facts which are complementary to each other. Enumeration, by itself, can only give the general outline of phenomena, the silhouette, so to speak, of figures. The monographic method' – and here I would add partial investigation in general – 'allows the analysis to explore all the details of the economic and moral life of a people, giving the blood, the flesh and the muscles to the skeleton built from general statistics, and in its turn enumeration completes the ideas provided by the monographic method.'
With the addition of the words 'by partial investigation', I find in these words an excellent demonstration of the reciprocal roles of partial investigations and general statistics.[32]

He thus described his ideal tool, as being as rich as the monographic method and as precise as complete enumeration, so long as the *requirement of representativeness* (which he intuited but still lacked the technical equipment for) should be respected:

The scientific value of partial investigations depends much more upon their representative character than on the number of facts. It is often the case that the data which are easy to obtain are more representative of an elite than of ordinary people.[33]

The procedure used is verified *a posteriori* if the controllable variables are not too different between the sample and the census:

To the extent that partial investigation is shown to be correct in relation to the points which can be controlled, the results are probably also correct in relation to points which cannot be controlled with the help of general statistics.[34]

The idea that the probabilistic theorems formulated since the beginning of the nineteenth century would enable one to say more about the 'probable errors' which were involved in drawing random samples (and hence the significance of the deviations observed by Kiaer) occurred to no one at that time. Procedure was still anchored in a sound knowledge of *territory*, control being exercised only after the event. The break of the link with territory and the mathematisation of these procedures only came later.

The introduction of probabilistic schemes appeared timidly in only 1901 in a new discussion about Kiaer's method, when the German economist Bortkiewicz said that he had used 'formulae deduced from analogous cases by Poisson, to determine if the difference between two numbers occurred by chance or not' and established that in the cases presented by the Norwegian this was not the case and that *the deviations were significant*. Thus, the sample of Kiaer was not as representative as he thought. Bortkiewicz had delivered a rough blow to Kiaer. Oddly, however, in the ensuing debate, no one took up the argument of Bortkiewicz and we do not even know the reaction of Kiaer. Perhaps Bowley had wind of it, for five years later, 1906, he presented at a meeting of the Royal Statistical Society the first calculations of confidence intervals.[35]

How to reconcile 'what one knows already' with chance

The idea according to which one could guarantee the representativeness of a sample thanks to 'control variables' nevertheless coexisted for thirty years with the method called 'purposive selection'. This continued to emphasise a territorial division of the national area into a collection of districts, from which were selected a sub-group, not randomly, but in such a way that a certain number of essential variables (the control variables) would have the same values for this sub-group as for the entire territory.[36]

A remarkable use of this method was presented in 1928 by the Italian statistician Corrado Gini. Having to get rid of, due to overcrowding, the individual returns of the Italian Census of 1921, he had the idea of keeping part of them, relating to 29 districts (out of 214 in Italy as a whole) for which the averages of seven variables were close to those of the country as a whole (births, deaths, marriage, proportion of the population in agriculture, proportion of the population urbanised, average income, mean altitude of the district above sea level). The choice of the 29 districts best fitting these constraints was carried out as the outcome of a laborious trial-and-error process, which Gini himself criticised, showing that unless a very restrictive hypothesis about the linearity of correlations between controlled and uncontrolled variables was used, there was no reason why such a sample should be a good representation of Italy as a whole.

This entire discussion, which extended from Jensen's report in 1925 to Neyman's paper in 1934, turned in fact on the connection between random selection and 'what one knew already from other sources' (for example, the census). This led progressively from the 'control variables' of Kiaer to 'purposive selection', each of them being finally rejected in favour of the technique of *stratified* sampling according to *a priori* divisions of the population, supposed to summarise *what is known already*: that is to say, that there exist significant differences in averages between social classes and that the precision of global estimates is improved by *a priori* stratifying. This assumes that such nomenclatures, residues of previous knowledge, exist, have a certain continuity and solidity and inspire confidence – the same role as that played after 1950 by social class categories, the level of qualifications, the classification of municipalities, the types of family etc. The development of machinery for representative sampling thus passed on the one hand to the sphere of the mathematicians, bit by bit cleansed of the old 'control variables' (by Neyman), and on the other hand to a system of nomenclatures registering the characteristics of people in categories guaranteed by a State which was the custodian of the general interest and developed by a state statistical institution commanding confidence.

This point is highlighted in the report in 1925 by Jensen on the representative method. Observing that the method still attracted criticism because it only related to a part of the population, he asked whether it was sufficient, to assuage this sort of attack, that the statistical administration should inspire confidence. The fact that two kinds of problem, technical and socio-political, should be called to mind at the same time is an element in the reply which can be compared with the initial question (why was the representative method not used sooner than it was?):

This objection contains the real kernel, that the greatest importance must be attached to the existence of a state of mutual confidence between the institution which exercises the official statistical service and the population which both supplies the material for the statistics and for whose sake all the work is done. The official statistics ought of course to be exceedingly cautious of its reputation – 'it is not sufficient that Caesar's wife is virtuous, all the world must be convinced of her virtue', But it would hardly be warrantable purely out of regard to prestige, to prevent a development which in itself is acknowledged to be really justified. One does not omit to build a bridge with a special design because the public, in its ignorance, distrusts that design; one builds the bridge when the engineer can guarantee its bearing strength – people will then use the bridge in due course and rely on its solidity.[37]

Jensen's problem in this passage is to make clear the intimate relationship between the technical strength of the statistical object and its reputation; it is this apparent strength which gives such weight to government statistics.

The Welfare State, national markets, electoral forecasting

From about 1930 the State's use of the sampling method for the purposes of administering social problems was joined by two other representative techniques bearing on the entire national territory. These were both of particular relevance in the USA: the study of the market for consumer goods and electoral forecasting.

In these two instances, it was necessary that standardisation and the establishment of national equivalence tests be carried out in advance. For consumer goods large firms needed to be able to distribute standard products on a regular basis over the whole territory by means of a national transport network, and required that these products should be clearly identified;[38] it then became possible to carry out a national opinion poll to find out if consumers preferred Coca Cola or Pepsi Cola.

For election forecasting, it mattered that the candidates should be the same throughout the country (which was the case for American presidential elections but not for voting in French *arrondissements*) and that their image should be relatively diffused and unified. This began to happen, thanks to the radio. It was also necessary that the sampling frame should be as close to the electorate as possible: polls conducted by telephone led to accidents, as in 1936 when as a result of questioning the better-off voters who owned telephones, the victory of the Republican presidential candidate was wrongly predicted.

What is common to these different cases is that these inquiries are carried out for the results to be given to others, who use them for operational ends (administration, large firms, on radio stations or in newspapers). The representativeness is then the condition allowing the identification of the *cost* of this knowledge and its *relevance*, recognised both technically and socially. In each case it is also *individuals* who are concerned (recipients of benefit, consumers or voters) and no longer totalities such as the divine order of Quetelet, the patrimonial line of descent as in Le Play or working-class consciousness of Halbwachs.

The monad and the shoe laces

The passage from one mode of thinking to another with the help of which we have tried to interpret the appearance, at the beginning of this century, of a new conception of representativeness, has been interpreted in the past in many ways. One of these, of which Louis Dumont provides an echo in the text cited at the beginning, contrasted 'national cultures' supposedly incommensurable with each other (the German tradition) with a universal or at least universalistic 'civilisation' (the English tradition emphasises the economic version, the French the political version). Dumont indicates that in order to resolve this contradiction, Leibniz imagined a 'monadic system' in which 'each culture expressed *in its own way* the universal', an easy way of generalising.

This history of the idea of representativeness has brought us back to the question of *generalisation*: what is the part? what is the whole? We have seen that the two operations, the political and the cognitive, in order to delimit a relevant whole (the nation or the market, whatever may be defined as appropriate) and to define and make comparisons possible between elements in this whole (citizens or consumers, as appropriate) were indispensible in making possible the appearance of the modern idea and technical implementation of representativeness.[39]

The problem posed by the transformations in the notion of representativeness, and in particular the discussion of the period 1895–1935, is to know how to reconcile knowledge produced according to different principles. This is a problem to which the 'controlled variables' of Kiaer, the 'purposive selection' of Jensen and Gini, and the 'stratification' of Neyman tried in turn to respond. This points also to the theoretical problem, as old as the calculation of probabilities, of the choice between accepting and rejecting 'a priori laws'.

In the course of the 1925 debate, Lucien March, then aged sixty-six, who had seen many upheavals in statistical thought, evoked this problem in terms which seem both shrewd and archaic, for all these matters had since been formalised, that is, in a sense, set:

The system which best reconciles the method of selection with the units of measurement of the inquiry are not necessarily those which best correspond to the idea of representation. As we have observed, this assumes that the units show no difference amongst themselves. Now, the representative method has for its aim the highlighting of the differences. The hypothesis therefore seems to be compatible with the aim being pursued. From there, preferences for a better understood choice, more intelligently made. For example, certain people exclude extreme cases supposed to be abnormal, or else they make a choice of specimen using some criterion of what they judge essential.[40]

When March speaks of 'difference', underlining the apparent contradiction between the necessity of making equivalent the units of measurement and researching the differences among them, one could reply that later formalisations have satisfactorily resolved this problem. But his hesitations, to decide whether it was necessary to make a choice 'better understood, more intelligent', if it was necessary to eliminate the 'abnormal cases', reflects truly a problem which the statistician, *if he already knows his field of inquiry*, will always encounter.

This 'advance knowledge' is often acquired by direct contact, by familiarity (but not always, as one sees in the case of 'controlled variables' linked to general statistics). It is thus of the same order as Dumont's 'culture' or Toennies' 'community'. There is always for the observer the intuition of a global knowledge of the totality of a situation, a person or a group.

'One must put together what has been pulled apart' is sometimes said by the researcher about his analytic work. It is also the problem of generalisation: putting together the whole in its unity. To reach the totality starting from one of its parts: this fantasy never ceases to animate the scientist. In the most recent developments of opinion polling, techniques made possible by powerful computers permit the simulation of this reconstruction by generating a large number of sub-samples from the initial sample, and then studying the properties of this derivative distribution of statistics. This method has been christened 'bootstrap', for it evokes the dream of lifting oneself up literally by one's bootstraps from the ground, pulling on one's laces. This dream of reconstructing the world from one of its parts is not without analogy with the 'complicated and laborious procedure' suggested by Leibniz to move from a single culture to the universal. What has changed is the cognitive and political machinery.

APPENDIX

Resolution of the ISI on the Application of the Representative Method in Statistics, Rome 1925 (Report by Adolph Jensen)

Considering that it is necessary in many cases to draw general conclusions based upon partial investigations owing to the impossibility of procuring a complete statistical material;

Considering that even in such cases where complete material is available it may be sufficient to work up a portion of this material provided that this working up is done in a rational manner; and

Considering that the saving of labour, time and money which is possible by limiting the investigation to a portion of the material will often make it possible to make a much more intensive use of the information at hand and to enter far more deeply into the subject than is possible by a working up of the whole material;

I. With reference to the Resolution passed at the Session at Berlin in 1903, again calls attention to the very considerable advantages which can be obtained by applying the Representative method under the following conditions:-

(A) *Random Selection* A number of units are selected in such a way that exact equality of chance of inclusion is the dominant rule. Then precision is related to the number included which should be large enough to render significant additional deviations;

(B) *Purposive Selection* A number of groups of units are selected which together yield nearly the same characteristics as the totality. In order to have any knowledge of the precision of the estimate it is necessary than sufficient groups should be included to allow the variation between the characteristics of the groups to be measured. But since the precision often depends to a great extent on the discretion used in making the selection, the following controls are recommended:-

1. The selection on the same principle should be made twice or more; after their comparison, the sames can be merged. (This principle is also applicable to the Random Selection);

2. In repeated observations, the relation between the part and the whole should from time to time be examined more minutely;

II. Recommends that the investigation should be so arranged wherever possible, as to allow of a mathematical statement of the precision of the results, and that with these results should be given an indication of the extent of the error to which they are liable;

III. Repeats the wish expressed in the Resolution of 1903, that in the report on the results of every representative investigation an explicit account in detail of the method of selecting the sample adopted should be given.

NOTES

1 This chapter was presented to the 19th *Journées de statistique* at Lausanne, Switzerland, in May 1987, and has appeared in French in J. Mairesse (ed), *Estimation et sondages: cinq contributions à l'histoire de la statistique* (Paris: Economica, 1988), pp. 97–116. Original translation into English by Martin Bulmer, with further improvements by Simon Szreter. It forms part of research currently underway into the history of the empirical socials sciences, carried out in collaboration with Michaël Pollak, as members of the Groupe de Sociologie Politique et Morale in the Ecole des Hautes Etudes en Sciences Sociales. It owes much to comments made on an earlier version by Luc Boltanski and Laurent Thévenot.

2 Catherine Bodard Silver (ed.), *Frédéric Le Play on Family, Work and Social Change* (Chicago: University of Chicago Press, 1982), pp. 179–83, 58–75.

3 The main articles on the history of these techniques are: F. F. Stephan, 'History of the Uses of Modern Sampling Procedures', *Journal of the American Statistical Association*, 43 (1948), 12–39; You Poh Seng, 'Historical Survey of the Development of Sampling Theory and Practice', *Journal of the Royal Statistical society*, series A 114 (1951), 214–31; Wei-ching Chang, 'Statistical Theories and Sampling Practice', in D. Owen (ed.), *On the History of Statistics and Probability* (New York: Marcel Dekker), pp. 298–315; M. H. Hansen and W. G. Madow, 'Some Important Events in the Historical Development of Sample Surveys', in Owen, *History of Statistics*, pp. 76–102; W. Kruskal and F. Mosteller, 'Representative Sampling IV: The History of the Concept in Statistics 1895–1939', *International Statistical Review*, 48 (1980), 169–95; M. H. Hansen, 'Some History and Reminiscences of Survey Sampling', *Statistical Science*, 2 no. 2 (1987), 180–90; Ingram Olkin, 'A Conversation with Morris Hansen', *Statistical Science*, 2 no. 2 (1987), 162–79. If, on the one hand, each develops satisfactorily the increasingly precise formal definition of the actual idea of representativeness, none on the other hand, studies the history of the requirement of representativeness as such.

4 Karl Polanyi, *The Great Transformation* (1944); L. Dumont, *Essays on Individualism: Modern Ideology in Anthropological Perspective* (Chicago: University of Chicago Press, 1986); Robert A. Nisbet, *The Sociological Tradition* (New York: Basic Books, 1966).

5 L. Boltanski and L. Thévenot, *De la justification: les économies de la grandeur* (Paris: Gallimard, 1991).

6 L. Thévenot, 'La politique des statistiques: les origines sociales des enquêtes de mobilité sociale', *Annales, E.S.C.* no. 6, Nov–Dec. 1990, 1275–1300.

7 Nisbet, *Sociological Tradition*.

8 A. Desrosières, 'Histoires de formes: statistiques et sciences sociales avant 1940', *Revue Française de Sociologie*, 26 no. 2 (1985), 277–310.

9 A. Desrosières, 'L'Ingénieur d'état et le père de famille: Emile Cheysson et la statistique', *Annales des Mines*, Série Gérer et comprendre, no. 2 (1986), 66–80.

10 E. Cheysson (with A. Toque), *Les Budgets comparés de cent monographies de famille* (Rome: Botta, 1890), pp. 2, 3.

11 M. Halbwachs, *La Classe ouvrière et les niveaux de vie* (Paris: Alcan, 1912).

12 Cheysson, *Les Budgets comparés*, p. 6.

13 Cheysson, *Les Budgets comparés*, p. 2.

14 Halbwachs, *La Classe ouvrière*, p. 152.

15 Halbwachs, *La Classe ouvrière*, pp. 152–3.

16 Not necessarily in the daily reality of things and people as is suggested by certain apocalyptic descriptions in terms of 'normalisation' and 'surveillance', but at least in the manner of making an *inventory* of *seeing*.

17 Still today, the presence or absence of these two ideas in social science serves as a criterion for distinguishing two profoundly different ways of articulating these sciences with the management of the social world. The relevant criterion is not, as often is thought, their *quantitative* character, but the requirement of representativeness.

18 E. P. Hennock, 'Poverty and Social Theory in England: The Experience of the 1880s', *Social History*, 1 (Jan. 1976), 67–91; 'The Measurement of Poverty: From the Metropolis to the Nation, 1880–1920', *Economic History Review*, 2nd series 40 no. 2 (1987), 208–27

19 P. Abrams, *The Origins of British Sociology, 1834–1914* (Chicago: University of Chicago Press, 1968).

20 Hennock, 'Poverty and Social Theory; 'Measurement of Poverty'.

21 M. Halbwachs, 'Budgets de familles ouvrières et paysannes en France, en 1907', *Bulletin de la Statistique générale de la France*, 4 fasc. 1 (1914), 47–83.

22 Board of Trade, *Cost of Living in French Towns: Report of an Inquiry by the Board of Trade* (London: Carling and Son, 1909).

23 Hennock, 'Measurement of Poverty'.

24 A. L. Bowley, 'Presidential Address to the Economic Section of the British Association for the Advancement of Science', *Journal of the Royal Statistical Society*, 69, Part III. (1906), 540–58.

25 A. N. Kiaer, 'Observations et expériences concernant les dénombrements représentatifs', *Bulletin de l'Institut International de Statistique*, 9 (1985), 176–8.

26 Bowley, 'Presidential Address'.

27 See, for example, Seng, 'Historical Survey', and Kruskal and Mosteller, 'Representative Sampling IV'.

28 J. Neyman, 'On the Two Different Aspects of the Representative Method: The Method of Stratified Sampling and the Method of Purposive Selection', *Journal of the Royal Statistical Society*, 97 (1934), 558–606, followed by Discussion, pp. 607–25.

29 Kiaer, 'Observations et expériences', p. 177.

30 Kiaer, 'Observations et expériences', p. 177.

31 A. N. Kiaer, 'Sur les méthodes représentatives ou typologiques appliquées à la Statistique', *Bulletin de l'Institut International de Statistique*, in (1897), 180–5.

32 Kiaer, 'Observations et expériences', pp. 182–3.

33 Kiaer, 'Observations et expériences', p. 183.

34 Kiaer, 'Observations et expériences', p. 183

35 Bowley, 'Presidential Address'.

36 A trace of this idea persists when, at the beginning of big election roundups, the results of a certain village are announced which, in the past, has always voted 'the way France votes'.

37 A. Jensen, 'Report on the Representative Method in Statistics', *Bulletin de l'Institut International de Statistique*, 22 (1925), 374.

38 F. Eymard-Duvernay, 'La Qualification des produits', R. Salais and L. Thévenot (eds.), *Le Travail: marchés, règles, conventions* (Paris: INSEE-Economica, 1986).

39 We note in passing that under its banner, we distinguished nation from market, citizen from consumer. There two aspects of social ties which in fact are quite distinct were assimilated to one another to simplify the argument. (Boltanski and Thévenot, *Les Economies de la grandeur*).

40 L. March, 'Observations sur la méthode représentative et sur le projet et de rapport relatif à cette méthode', Annex D. *Bulletin de l'Institut International de Statistique*, 22 (1925), p. 449.

CHAPTER NINE

The Pittsburgh Survey and the Social Survey Movement: a sociological road not taken

STEVEN R. COHEN

INTRODUCTION

Several months before the Great War had begun in Europe, Frederick Jackson Turner delivered a commencement address to students at the University of Washington. Turner commented on some observations Talleyrand had made, while on a visit during Washington's administration, about the young American Republic:

Looking down from an eminence not far from Philadelphia upon a wilderness which is now the heart of that huge industrial society where population presses on the means of life, even the cold-blooded and cynical Talleyrand, gazing on those unpeopled hills and forests, kindled with the vision of coming clearings, the smiling farms and grazing herds that were to be, the populous towns that should be built, the newer and finer social organization that should there arise.[1]

But as Turner evoked the glorious promise of America, in the face of which even the great cynic Talleyrand had been moved, he shifted ground from the bucolic republican environment of the late eighteenth century to early twentieth-century urban America:

And then I remembered the hall in Harvard's museum of social ethics through which I pass to my lecture room when I speak on the history of the Westward movement. That hall is covered with an exhibit of the work in Pittsburgh steel mills, and of the congested tenements. Its charts and diagrams tell of the long hours of work, the death rate, the relation of typhoid to the slums, the gathering of the poor of all Southeastern Europe to make a civilization at that center of American industrial energy and vast capital that is a social tragedy.[2]

Thus stood Turner, informing his young audience of the new dangers to the Republic brought on by rapid industrialisation. Just as his audience would

245

appreciate the use of Talleyrand to detail the promise of the eighteenth century, so too would it appreciate his use of the *Pittsburgh Survey* to explore the challenge of the twentieth.

To many reformers, the *Pittsburgh Survey*, and other similar empirical social research, not only informed citizens of new political problems brought on by uncontrolled industrialisation; it also created a new scientific tool to help provide democratic control of that dynamic process. 'As we turn from the task of the first rough conquest of the continent', Turner told his audience, 'there lies before us a whole wealth of unexploited resources in the realm of the spirit. Arts and letters, science and better social creation, loyalty and political service to the commonweal'.[3] To minds shaped by the reform movements of the early twentieth century, the *Pittsburgh Survey* was the most notable example of a new scientific and democratic method to help transform American society from one in which free land had once provided the means for mass democracy and individual opportunity, to one in which science, the arts and 'a thousand other directions of activity', would now have to provide such opportunities. The *Pittsburgh Survey* was part of the Progressive effort to create a 'new era...[when] schools and universities [will] widen the intellectual horizon of the people, help to lay the foundations of a better industrial life, show them new goals for endeavour, inspire them with more varied and higher ideals'.[4]

Moreover, if, as Turner continued, 'legislation [was] taking the place of the free lands as the means of preserving the ideal of democracy', then a science of legislation would be needed to make that new arena of democratic experience a working reality. A politically informed social science, of which the *Pittsburgh Survey* was perhaps the most famous example, would provide the intellectual means of assisting governments, like that in the State of Wisconsin, in shaping the growth of the new industrial order in ways commensurate with American Democracy. Universities and social science would be to the new Industrial Republic of the twentieth century what land and frontier common sense and individual ingenuity had been to the Agricultural Republic of the Founding Fathers.

Sensitive to and schooled in socialist as well as traditional economic thought, these researchers tried to demonstrate a third way in which the 'social question' of the late nineteenth and early twentieth-centuries could be conceived of and then answered. Though in the end its theory would remain undeveloped, the *Pittsburgh Survey* ought to be understood as an attempt to demonstrate how social research and social planning might inform one another. To these early twentieth-century reformers at least, social science, in principle, could be enlisted in the democratic struggle to control the disturbing implications for individual liberty of economic concentration in early twentieth-century America.[5]

In what follows, I will argue that the empirical research and sociological analysis of the *Pittsburgh Survey* should not be considered a quaint piece of muckraking reportage that predates the arrival of 'legitimate' social science research, as many sociologists have long considered this work.[6] Rather, it should be viewed as a serious, albeit abortive, attempt, grounded in empirical research, to understand how industrial capitalism shapes urban development. In part, the contemporary view of this research stems from the fact that these researchers were rather open and partisan about their political goals. To people who regard science and partisan purpose as mutually exclusive activities, the *Pittsburgh Survey* must necessarily be something other than 'real' social science. Since this manner of excluding the *Pittsburgh Survey* from the category of 'social science' is itself an important part of the story of the *Pittsburgh Survey*, I will explore elements of the history of how this important piece of social research has come to be judged by academic social scientists, especially those at the University of Chicago.

What did this combination of empirical research, social theory and political partisanship mean in the days before World War I? And why did this as well as other social surveys later disappear from the methods of academic sociology and social science? This disappearance, recently analysed by Martin Bulmer as part of what he calls a 'discontinuity' in the history of social research, resulted from the rejection of the social survey as a legitimate tool of research by sociologists at the University of Chicago in the 1920s.[7] I will suggest that this 'discontinuity' occurred because the scientific and policy potential of the *Pittsburgh Survey* went untested by the social scientists at the one university where one might realistically have expected such an effort to have come from — the University of Wisconsin.

THE *PITTSBURGH SURVEY*

Between 2 January 1909 and 6 March 1909, the magazine *Charities and the Commons* — a national leader of reform opinion — published thirty-five articles containing new information about a wide variety of subjects in the heavily industrialised city of Pittsburgh: steelworkers, steelworkers' families, women workers, Slavs, Jews, blacks, Ruthenians, Russian Old Believers, programmes for civic improvement, aldermanic courts, lodging houses, slums, public health, education, factory inspection, work-related accidents, and still more.[8] These articles were part of a national reform

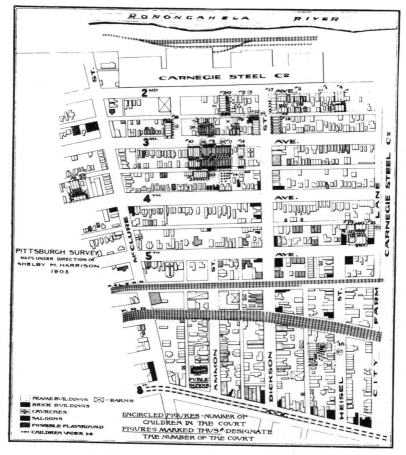

Map 5   A section of Pittsburgh.

campaign that focused on Pittsburgh to publicise what these reformers believed were intolerable urban conditions. The survey work had been organised originally by the New York based Charities Publication Committee – the organisation responsible for *Charities and the Commons* (edited by Paul Kellogg) – in conjunction with a request from the chief probation officer of the Juvenile Court of Allegheny County to conduct a study of the 'social conditions in Pittsburgh and vicinity'.[9]

The request from Pittsburgh had come at a time when Kellogg and his editor-in-chief, Edward Devine, were discussing the possibility that the Russell Sage Foundation might be interested in funding such a study. It was, and by the end of 1907, the survey had acquired US $27,000, most of it from the Sage Foundation. Seventy-four people went into the field for varying lengths of time and with different aspects of the study in mind: twenty-two of them simply provided assistance (like Judge Buffington of Pittsburgh, Max Eastman, and William Matthews, head of the Kingsley Settlement House which provided lodging for several of the researchers), ten others prepared reports independent of the *Charities* staff (many of whom were Pittsburgh notables who reported on such things as playgrounds and on the coalition of forces favouring civic reform), thirty-seven others did field work from one to nine months (this group included John R. Commons, Florence Kelley, Lewis Hine and Robert A. Woods), and, lastly, five people spent an entire year in the field and wrote what would later become the most detailed and integrated sections of the survey (Crystal Eastman, John A. Fitch, Margaret Byington, Elizabeth Butler and Paul Kellogg).[10] All of these activities, as well as the impressive photographic exhibitions of Lewis Hine, were meant to shape public opinion in Pittsburgh and thereby bring pressure to bear on local and national politicians.

As with other reform efforts of its day, the *Pittsburgh Survey* was part of the political arsenal used by urban reform groups against political machines. Among other things, the findings of the survey were used in a proposal made by the Civic Improvement Commission to reform the system of taxation in Allegheny County. The Commission also proposed, on the basis of the findings of the survey, to change how the school board and city council worked, and in the new city charter of 1911 the older twenty-seven wards were consolidated into a single urban constituency with nine councilmen elected at large. In these respects the *Pittsburgh Survey* was much like other efforts of urban elites at this time to wrest political control from the machines that had come to dominate ward politics in many large, industrialised cities.[11]

However, the uses to which the survey's findings and methods could be, and were in fact, put stretched beyond the movement of business elites in local politics in Pittsburgh. For instance, Victor Berger, leader of the Socialist Party in Wisconsin and the first socialist elected to the House of Representatives, asked John R. Commons, head of the industrial studies section of the *Pittsburgh Survey*, and Professor of Political Economy at the University of Wisconsin, to design a survey of Milwaukee much like the one had had done in Pittsburgh. The information officer of the Socialist Party in Wisconsin, for another, wrote to William Leiserson (who, like John Fitch, was a student of Commons and a colleague in Pittsburgh) asking advice about several aspects of municipal administration: home rule, municipal ownership of housing, direct legislation, taxation and proportional representation.[12] There were also allied national reform movements to which the findings and arguments developed in the *Pittsburgh Survey* contributed. Thus, Crystal Eastman's work on work-accidents and her critique of the existing legal theory of negligence as applied to industrial accidents were used by advocates of both workmen's compensation and employer liability legislation in Ohio, Connecticut and Pennsylvania.[13]

By 1914, all of this, as well as additional material, was published in a six-volume work entitled the *Pittsburgh Survey*. Two of these six volumes – *Wage Earning Pittsburgh* and *The Pittsburgh District* – are collections of the articles which had appeared in the series in *Charities and the Commons* in the early part of 1909. (Shortly after the field work began, Kellogg had the name of the magazine changed to *The Survey*). They include articles on topics as disparate as the reform movement in Pittsburgh, black steelworkers, and social outcasts. A third volume, *Women and the Trades*, is noteworthy because it is one of the earliest comprehensive surveys of the tasks women performed in a heavily industrialised city. Elizabeth Butler studied some 22,000 women workers in the non-ferrous trades: canning, laundry, confectionery, crackers, cigars, garments and printing, to name but a few. She was among the first to draw systematic and public attention to the facts that women were paid less than men for similar work, that they worked longer hours than the law permitted, and that their working conditions were unhealthy and dangerous. As with other topics of the survey, her research was undertaken intentionally to help in the national fight to secure legislation protecting workers from such abuses.

Some readers of the *Pittsburgh Survey* acquire their main impression from these parts of the survey, and conclude that the survey was scattered and conceptually unfocused. This characterisation suggests that the data gathering aspects of the survey were vastly superior to the analytical ones. To be sure, a certain disarray is evident in the organisation of the survey's findings. But as one goes deeper into the survey, a more conceptually unified research project emerges.

Support for this claim comes from the fact that the remaining three volumes of the survey – *Homestead: Households of a Mill Town*, *Work-accidents and the Law*, and *The Steel Workers* – fully one half of the entire survey – focus on a single theme: the impact of the steel industry on specific aspects of urban life. Crystal Eastman's study of work-accidents was, as I have noted, a groundbreaking study of the law of contracts as it was applied to relations between workers and their employers. Margaret Byington's study of the economic and social circumstances of ninety families of steelworkers provided still other essential information about how the steel industry shaped the everyday lives of these people. She investigated how the steel companies controlled the real estate and housing markets around the mills. Lastly, John Fitch studied steelworkers, the process of iron and steel production, and the steel corporations. It completes this triad of works on the economic foundation of the urban environment in Pittsburgh – the steel industry.[14]

Moreover, the editor of the *Pittsburgh Survey*, Paul Kellogg, explained in his preface to Fitch's study, *The Steel Workers*, that

> Steel is the basic industry in America ... Its products enter into every tool and structure and means of traffic in civilization ... Moreover, the largest employer of steel workers in Pittsburgh is the largest employer of labor in America today ... [*The Steel Workers*] depicts the industry which gives wealth and business pre-eminence to the region, which directly determines the well-being of a great company of wage earners and their families, and which influences all other lines of employment in and around Pittsburgh.[15]

Kellogg believed that Fitch's study dealt with the economic reality that underpinned many other urban developments which the *Pittsburgh Survey* considered. His remarks also suggest that the Byington, Eastman and Fitch studies – the major part of the *Pittsburgh Survey* – together formed a single, larger study of the great steel industry. Contrary to what one might think upon first looking at the great number of small, relatively unrelated studies in the survey, the primary researchers of the *Pittsburgh Survey* thought of their work not only as a description of life in an industrial center, but also as an analysis of the social forces that shaped the city's growth. As Kellogg remarked in the preface to Byington's study: 'Miss Byington's commission was to analyze these factors [sanitation, housing, and public education] as they enter jointly into the life of one of the small industrial communities ... characteristic of the Pittsburgh District ... Her book complements Mr. Fitch's volume on wages and the general labor conditions in the steel industry.'[16] By looking into the way Fitch studied the steel industry, one can investigate how these Progressive reformers understood the dynamics of capitalism and the impact of the economic system on urban growth and democratic institutions.

THE ANALYSIS OF DATA

Paul Kellogg asked John Commons to supervise the study of industrial conditions for the survey, and Commons in turn asked two of his graduate students – John Fitch and William Leiserson – to do most of the research. Fitch conducted research for *The Steel Workers* as part of his graduate

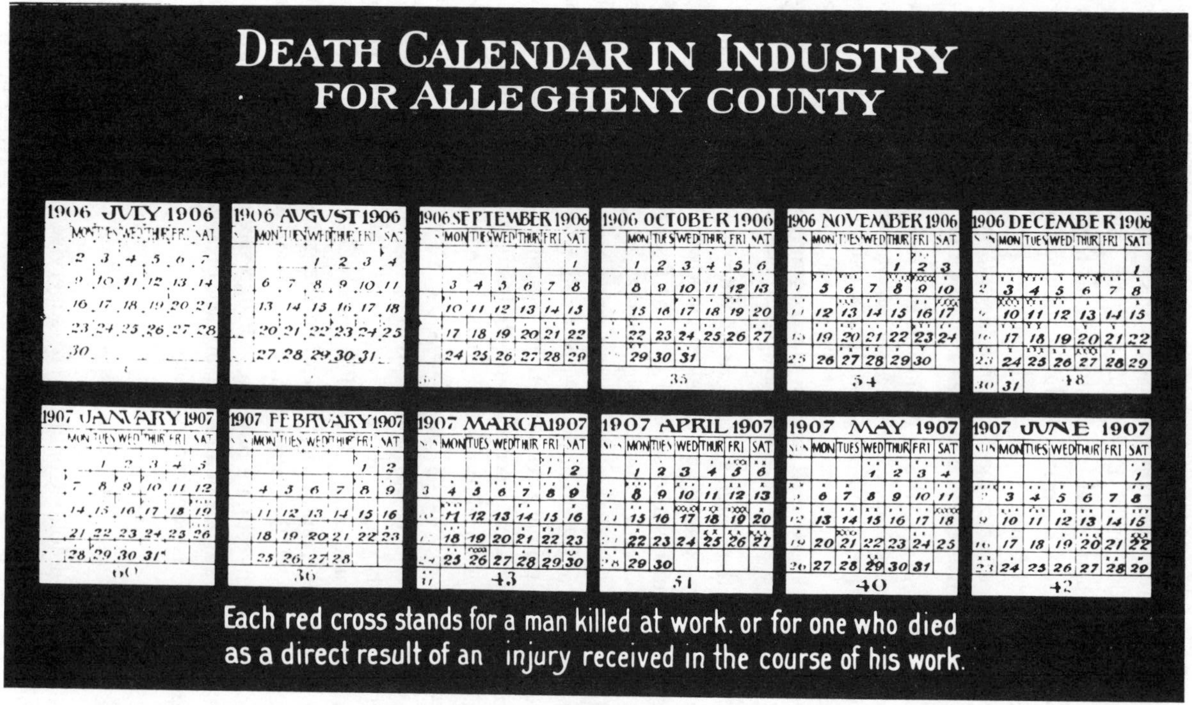

Map 6 'Death Calendar'.

training in political economy, and he must be considered as an immediate predecessor to what has since become known as the Commons School of Labor History. In addition to using various documentary sources in his work, Fitch conducted about a hundred intensive interviews with steel and ironworkers in many of the mills in the Pittsburgh District. I have located these field notes and have used them to compare what Fitch published about these men with the entire range of evidence he actually collected.[17] Such a comparison allows one to trace how Fitch reached his conclusions about the functioning and possible future development of industrial capitalism in the United States.

Central to Fitch's analysis of the steel industry was a basic proposition in political economy taken from the teachings of Commons: that only increases in productivity would create a realistic basis upon which the conflict of interests between labour and capital could possibly be resolved democratically.[18] In this view, an increasing material pie created the logical possibility that both labour and capital could benefit from economic growth (even if increases might not be divided equally). Given this view, Fitch was immediately confronted by an important empirical question: did the existing methods of production, which created the wealth to be shared by workers and capitalists, in fact undermine the political rights and living standards of workers, as many socialists argued, or did they extend them?

Evidence that Fitch was aware of the theoretical implications of this question comes from the work of one of his fellow researchers – Crystal Eastman. She described the socialist argument in *Work-Accidents and the Law*:

Better factory and railroad acts ... a law making every serious accident a direct and unmistakable expense to the business – these are the means of improving the employer's motive [for maintaining safe working conditions]. Yet with all these means, we shall not be able to make the protection of workmen his first interest, for clearly his first interest must be production. Herein lies the strong argument of the socialists ... legislation will, they maintain, make an employer stop for a moment to take thought for safety, but the force of competition will soon drive him on.[19]

Moreover, Eastman held the view that the socialist prediction could be avoided by taking democracy seriously. Though Fitch did not himself write the following words, it is no wild inference to suggest that he agreed with Eastman's comments:

the way is open for democracy to bring all these forces [factory and railway legislation] to bear upon the motives of the employer before accepting the conclusion that modern industry cannot be carried on under a competitive regime without the present wholesale destruction of the workers.[20]

Remarkably frank about the problem which lay before them, these Progressives understood that in order to disprove the socialist thesis, they would have to analyse industrial capitalism far more critically than many Progressives were then willing to do. And they would have to propose more far-reaching political solutions to the problems of twentieth-century industrial capitalism than President Wilson would be ever likely to support.[21]

Fitch did not formulate his research in a terribly self-conscious or systematic manner, making it difficult to know exactly how far and in which direction Fitch and his colleagues in Wisconsin wished to take their political economy in 1912. However, this undetermined theoretical situation ought to compel our attention to Fitch's work, precisely because it contains an embryonic argument about how modern capitalist industry can and ought to be shaped by democratic institutions. That this argument remained undeveloped is insufficient reason to judge that it had no theoretical potential. It may be more to the point to inquire into why social scientists chose not to develop whatever potential it did contain.

For example, given the premise of the political economy employed by Fitch and his colleagues – that labour and capital have a basic conflict of interest – it follows that if workers' rights and standard of living were in fact undermined by the very methods of production which created wealth, then one could conclude that a contradiction existed between the growth of the economy as a whole and the benefits which could be expected, in principle, to accrue to the great mass of the working population. If, however, it were shown that workers' rights and standard of living were undermined not by necessary conditions of production but by episodic factors like ignorance, sloth, greed, incompetence, and the like, then an expanding pie could still, in principle, become the basis of an increasing standard of living for all. Fitch's interviews with workers on various crews in the mills address this problem, even though Fitch did not present this research question or its many implications in any systematic fashion. Fitch's interviews were the data needed to begin the hard work of spelling out how the Wisconsin School's emerging theory of the economic and political process – and not the theory of the socialists – could become the basis of urban planning in Pittsburgh and throughout the nation generally, even if such was not the case at the moment.

Fitch spoke with workers on blast furnace crews, open-hearth crews, and Bessemer crews, as well as with workers from the rolling mills. Two of the many possible illustrations from Fitch's original field data show how complex the data were and how he used them to support a reading of the labour problem that was compatible with his ideological position.[22] The first illustration comes from Fitch's interviews with blast furnace men. In 1908, blast furnace production of pig iron was seven times greater than it had been in 1858. Fitch ascribed this enormous increase – a necessary increase if the rest of the iron and steel industry were also to develop – to growth in metallurgical knowledge, engineering skills, and work organisation. He also observed an improvement in the safety of the working conditions involved in this very hazardous job. At the same time, he cautioned his readers that, even with these improvements, safety lagged far behind the overall organisation of work: the 12 hour day and the 7 day work week were still considered by the steel manufacturers to be necessary. 'Although ... changes and improvements have reduced the labor cost and increased tonnage, they have not improved working conditions in proportion. Modern ... furnaces are held to require continuous operation and all the men are worked on an average schedule of twelve hours a day, seven days week ... 365 days a year.'[23] Fitch argued in *The Steel Workers*, however, that 'in spite of the technical necessities of continuous operation, it is not necessary that men should work continuously ... That [the twelve-hour day] is unnecessary ... is evidenced by the experience of other countries ... America has not a single blast furnace with an eight-hour day, but furnaces in the north of England have the eight-hour day in successful operation.'[24] In short, there was no technical necessity, contrary to what steel companies claimed, for working the men twelve hours a day, seven days a week. But what did this conclusion mean for other aspects of Fitch's analysis of the work process?

By reviewing Fitch's notes we may go over in some detail his judgement of what was or was not 'necessary' in the work of blast furnace crews. In one infamous case, that of a blast furnace explosion in which fourteen men were killed – one of them completely submerged by the molten charge – Fitch took the view of the engineering 'experts' in his published report:

In January, 1907 Number 2 furnace of the Liza group, owned by the Jones and Laughlin Steel Co., exploded without warning blowing out the whole side of the furnace and burning to death fourteen men ... Many engineers from all parts of the country came to Pittsburgh ... to examine ... the explosion ... All agreed that the accident could not have been foreseen and that the furnace was constructed according to the best known model.[25]

Significantly, Fitch did not say in his published report what the actual cause of this horrible accident had been – it simply could not have been 'foreseen'. But the 'expert' judgement of the engineers may not have been the same as that of many of the blast furnace men whose views were known to Fitch but not published. For instance, Fitch spoke with Mike Walsh, the head blower of the furnaces in the Eliza group, who told him that 'When no. 2 broke out last year no one would have thought it possible. [It] had just been tapped and so an explosion was not to be expected.' Walsh also told Fitch that no slips had occurred for over a year and that the plates and pipes were new. Since a mechanical failure had seemed unlikely, even to the 'experts', perhaps these facts might have suggested another explanation. For instance, were there any aspects of the way in which work was organised that might have led to fatal errors? Fitch had indeed learned of two other possible causes of this sort of accident from the workers he interviewed: either a misapplied blast of air or water coming into contact with the molten iron. Both are errors in the application of human labour and judgement. With respect to these possibilities, Walsh told Fitch:

The men are not much good after midnight on the long turn [17 hours into their shift] ... On the first cast Sunday morning and through the day [the men] use the tapping rod with force and determination ... but by the time they make the last cast Monday morning ... their strength is almost gone. They handle their tools listlessly. It requires a sharp vigilance on the part of the foreman to keep everything going right.

From these statements, it is hard to imagine that Fitch did not consider that this accident might have been the result of the fact that the men had been overworked. However, he would go only so far as to say in the published report that 'it is usually impossible to tell, in any accident case, just how much the negligence of the employe [sic] contributed to the occurrence ... [But] in blaming their employees for lapses of attention which have resulted in accidents, manufacturers may often be demanding a self-control and mental alertness such as few men can sustain throughout practically their entire working hours.'[26] Fitch seemed to analyse this accident as having only two *possible* basic causes: either that this accident had been the result of mechanical failure alone or that the accident was the combined result of overwork and the negligence of the workers themselves. He conceived of overwork and negligence as if they were not, or could not under certain conditions become, themselves the effects of a more basic cause – of the drive to maximise profits, for example. He chose not to test whether the drive to make sizeable profits forced the steel corporation to seek radically reduced labour costs, which in turn translated into unsafe working conditions which could not have been altered without undermining the profit margin of the corporation. This was the socialist hypothesis mentioned in Eastman's analysis and Fitch failed to discuss it directly.

A different reader of these interviews might have wondered whether profit-seeking drove the corporation to tolerate unsafe working conditions, as the socialist view implied, and whether, as a result of this factor, the so-called 'necessity' behind certain accidents was itself the result of employing certain methods of managing human labour – methods dictated not by technical 'necessities' of steel making, but by the capitalist constraints of profit-making. Given this reasoning, there would hardly have been clear justification for concluding, as the 'experts' had, that this accident could not have been 'foreseen'. As it was, Fitch took a relatively weak explanatory position. His ideological point of departure led him to conceive of what his informants told him in terms of adjustments to a system of production and distribution that were basically sound; and nothing the men said forced him to examine this underlying premise. He remained content with the conclusion of the engineering experts that the actual cause of this accident was something of a mystery, despite the fact that he had an alternative explanation that had still not been rejected. Fitch did not really believe he could tell what had caused the accident, and in his view, nobody else could either, even though it was important to point out that the manufacturers held a notion about accidents that did not help remedy the overall situation.

On logical grounds alone, however, Fitch could have argued either the socialist hypothesis or his own, since these data can affirm either one. Perhaps the fact that the survey research had not been designed in such a way as to test these mutually exclusive hypotheses made it possible for Fitch to interpret what he heard from workers in a manner compatible with the principles of political economy and democracy he believed in, even though, as I have pointed out, he was aware of the alternative, socialist explanation. It is therefore interesting to speculate at this point that, had some kind of falsification method of inquiry been in use at that time, Fitch could perhaps have avoided the logical error of assuming his conclusion.

In a second illustration, the question is not that of safety and so-called 'necessary' risks of work, but that of political freedom. Fitch had met an astute roller at the Braddock mills who explained to him that the job of leading the rolling mill operations was as much a job of controlling other workers as it was a job of great mechanical skill. 'A roller is of importance ... in bossing his gang of men. He must be a person capable of getting along with men. He must keep a clear head under all circumstances and be ready for any emergency in handling either men or the machinery.' This boss also believed the twelve-hour day, the speed-up, and low wages were effective ways of disciplining workers and of motivating them to meet the extreme demands of production. 'The eight-hour day is ideally the proper working day, [I] believe it is impossible. The common run of working men need the pressure to which they are subjected to make them keep strictly at work. The domineering tactics of the Steel Corporation are really good for them...High wages have a bad effect upon the men.'

This roller had left the union at the Braddock mills in 1902 for the chance to be a boss roller, and he told Fitch that his success depended upon the fact that the corporation had complete control over the men. This honesty makes his next remarks about the harshness of industrial conflict seem all the more compelling. 'Corporations are crowding the men down to the very last limit; freedom is practically taken away. It would be easier to start an organization of the Molly Maguires in the mill than a union.' Fitch's published view of such comments was that

if the treatment that the steel companies are now employing toward their workmen be indefinitely prolonged, it will be hard to predict the ultimate action of the workers... Revolutions, however, do not necessarily involve violence. And through either the trade union or the political movement... there is bound to be a revolution erelong that shall have as its goal the restoration of democracy to the steel workers.[27]

Fitch's notes contain a great variety of strongly held views about the political situation in the mills. It is interesting that he did not pursue the richness of argument and belief in the published report. This may have been in part because he did not believe it was for him to judge how to respond to the dismal conditions faced by other men. And it may have been in part because he wished to develop a politically neutral method for handling such intense labour-management conflicts.

Indeed, Fitch's ideological commitment to liberal democracy enabled him to resolve disturbing trends and inconsistencies in his data by asserting that the State, along with science, would offer some practical, democratic means of dealing with the economic and political conflicts detailed in his empirical data. Fitch's data revealed how serious and widespread such conflicts were in the steel mills in Pittsburgh. His theoretical training, moreover, led him to conceive of such conflict as arising quite naturally from the economic processes of capitalism; 'in all industries, the underlying cause of friction...[is] the economic conflict...between capital and labor'.[28] But he rejected the socialist proposition that one might have eventually to choose either increasing output and profits or a decent standard of living (including political freedom) for workers. Unlike men such as Eugene Debs, who had come in the 1890s to reject completely any competition between workers and capitalists, Fitch (and Commons before him) contested the socialist claim that only by socialising the means of production might one have both a high standard of living and political democracy. Fitch believed that the solution to the problem of industrial conflict lay not in replacing private property with some kind of direct political control of economic life, as socialists argued, but rather in making it possible for workers, employers and the consuming public to figure out how best to share the wealth that can be created by market processes.[29]

QUESTIONS OF INTERPRETATION

The *Pittsburgh Survey* appeared at a time in American history when bitter controversies over job control and the powers of the state in relation to new, vast industrial corporations had not yet been settled.[30] Progressives like those who worked on the *Pittsburgh Survey* were trying to bring their liberalism into line with the rather profound changes going on in the American economy. They were further to the left than Progressives like President Wilson, because in their view liberalism could not ignore, or leave to the business and professional classes, the difficult task of making democracy a living reality for workers – men, women, blacks, immigrants. Unlike the Progressivism of the New Freedom, their Progressivism included the idea that Congress could act as the authority needed to establish minimum standards and procedures of industrial work, below which companies would not be allowed to operate. Such standards might include not only safety and wage requirements, but procedural ones as well, like giving workers access to their firm's books and electing workers to sit on boards of directors.[31] More generally, their 'Social Liberalism' called for a national economic policy founded on the existing democratic polity, in which workers and owners would have wide access to the legislative process for the purpose of pressing their antagonistic claims about property rights and in which a legal method of defining the 'just' distribution of work and profits would be established.

Their hope was that they might make a national programme of the 'Wisconsin Idea'.[32] But though partially successful in Wisconsin, the Wisconsin Idea could not survive the rigors and realities of national party politics – the 'Southern' wing of the Democratic Party and the 'Business' faction of the Republican Party alone were insurmountable obstacles to winning political power. Only for a brief time, near the end of Franklin Roosevelt's first term some twenty years later, did national political conditions favour the Progressive ideas of Fitch's circle.[33] Surprisingly, however, their conception of a national economic policy is similar to what has become known over the last fifty years as the political formula of the labour parties and social democratic polities of Western Europe. What succeeded in becoming part of the ordinary politics of European polities in the last generation failed to take root in the United States – not because there were no proponents of that point of view, but because they were unsuccessful.

Clearly, Fitch and his colleagues were contributing ideas and data to the late nineteenth- and early twentieth-century effort to discredit social Darwinist and *laissez-faire* ideas. In my opinion, however, their ideas cannot be assimilated neatly into today's debate over the meaning of reform in the Progressive Era, in part because World War I cut short serious consideration of some of their ideas about industrial democracy. The extensive nationalisation that took place during the war within the institutional framework of the War Industries Board, the Bolshevik Revolution of 1917, and the post-war Red Scare, among other events, cut off serious discussion and analysis in the United States about the distribution of power in America and about different ways workers might play an active part in industrial development. Still, some contemporary historians portray the work of the *Pittsburgh Survey* as a self-serving or cynical response of an emerging class of welfare professionals to the *laissez-faire* Social Darwinism of pre-war days.[34] The survey researchers, like most reformers in the Progressive Era, were not, in this interpretation, really offering a challenge to the political or social status quo, despite their fervent denunciations of much of that order. They were trying to create a rationalised industrial order in which their professional expertise would be needed by industry and goverment.[35] Anything to the right of Debs, in this view, was self-serving apologetics for capitalism. In the view of one of the most influential revisionist historians of the 1960s.

... the liberal state ... [was] developed in the Progressive Era ... [by] the replacement of the ideological concepts of laissez faire ... [with] an ideal of a responsible social order in which all classes could look forward to some form of recognition and sharing in the benefits of an ever-expanding economy. Such a corporate order was, of course, to be based on what banker V. Everitt Macy called 'the industrial and commercial structure which is the indispensable shelter of us all'.[36]

But if some progressive reformers, like Commons, responded to the arguments of socialists with new theories of property rights under capitalism, and if other reformers later on, like Mary Van Kleeck, went so far as to suggest a nationally planned economy not unlike ones proposed by the major Social Democratic parties in Europe, then one must wonder whether the ideas, intentions and political activities of 'Progressivism' were simply too ambiguous, indefinite and unfulfilled to have brought about the specific illiberal or anti-democratic effects which some historians today attribute to them.[37] To many of the reformers who took part in the *Pittsburgh Survey*, the meaning of the 'industrial and commercial structure which is the indispensable shelter to us all' was not what it was to Macy. To write as if it were is to deny the ideological diversity and ambiguity from which the political volatility of the Progressive Era comes in the first place. However much certain reformist ideas and reform activities have contributed to the creation of the 'Corporate Liberal State', one cannot ignore other influences, well beyond the Progressive movement, which have had at least as much to do with this important development in twentieth century political life – such as two world wars, fascism, a world-wide economic depression, and a successful communist revolution.

Furthermore, some historians have taken certain remarks in the survey about immigrants, for example, as evidence of racist, and hence 'conservative', attitudes of so-called 'progressive' reformers.[38] But such conclusions do not follow. For though one can find pejorative statements in the *Pittsburgh Survey* about race, gender and ethnicity, so too can one find them in the writings of certain left-wing and socialist writers and organisations *of that day* – from socialists in Wisconsin and elsewhere in the United States, to anarchists in France and Russia and, indeed, in Marx himself.[39] Negative racial, religious and national images found in the survey were, to some extent, part of the rather dismal cultural climate at the turn of the century not only in the United States but also in Europe. It should not surprise us that many of the liberal factions of that day were not immune to such images. (In fact, insofar as the issues of feminism and anti-semitism are concerned, one could argue that the *Pittsburgh Survey* is superior to much of the common prejudice of that day.) Some scholars have confused the general historical context in which the *Pittsburgh Survey* was conducted with biases specific to the survey. Being politically radical or liberal at the turn of the century did not necessarily mean, as it does to so many today, being racially enlightened.

Some scholars also claim or assume that when reformers at the turn of the century used terms like 'social work' or 'social engineering' or 'scientific management' they had in mind some meaning which these terms have today.[40] To many contemporary historians and social scientists, both 'social work' and 'scientific management' imply some kind of cynical adjustment to existing social and economic realities. 'Social engineering is an exact designation for [the ideology of the survey reformers]. The Survey's staff conceived of society as a machine and of themselves as mechanics. So they attempted to measure social mechanisms in much the same fashion as scientific managers administered the machinery of business'.[41] But Fitch, to give but one contrary example, held that the focus of social work and of industrial management ought to be to solve problems of economic organisation and the distribution of political rights, not to provide individual therapy or to help people adapt to political and industrial realities.[42] As he said to a conference of social workers as late as 1920:

The worker [has] no right to a voice in industry. If he had such a right it would be difficult for him to exercise it because he has no access to facts concerning the industry, which are essential to intelligent action ... The books are closed to him ... These facts lead inevitably to the conclusion that the worker ... is not a citizen of the industrial commonwealth, but is rather an alien possessed of few rights and subject at any time to deportation without trial ... The status of workers must be altered – to meet the needs of all the people.[43]

Fitch also wrote a sympathetic introduction to the account of the famous and bitter steel strike of 1919 by William Z. Foster, one of the leaders of the Communist Party in the US:

... the book as a whole is so well done ... and ... the essential message that it conveys is so true, that it is a pleasure to write these words of introduction ... It sets forth as no other book has, and as no other writer could, the need of the workers in this great basic industry organization, and the extreme difficulty of achieving this essential right. It shows also in the sanity, good temper, and straightforward speech of the author what sort of leadership it is that the steel companies have decreed their workers shall not have.[44]

Even after the war, when Red-baiting and political retrenchment were the order of the day, Fitch and other left-leaning liberals took seriously the idea that a form of unionisation should be created in the United States that would accomplish here what Guild Socialism and Social Liberalism were at that time trying to create in Europe. (Leninism, of course, was just becomimg one of the many extremely contentious issues of the day among American liberals.)

The work of these Progressives demonstrates that there was a tendency within American liberalism critical of mainstream Progressivism, in part because they were more critical than most liberals about the sociological and economic conditions needed to maintain democratic institutions (and hence less moralistic), and in part because they had learned from the critical and political insights of socialists. It is hard to imagine this sort of thinking coming from the self-serving, opportunistically minded, social welfare 'expert' one finds in Progressive Era historiography. Being in favour of some kind of rationally planned economy at the turn of the century (and for a long time thereafter) did not necessarily mean that one accepted the emerging corporate structure of American industry; in fact it could also mean anything from Commons' notion of a politically regulated capitalist economy to some kind of centralised planning model.[45]

The political implications of rejecting the Social Darwinism of the 1890s were not only (or even most importantly) that some professions like social work would be needed to help government and industry organise industrial production based on vast amounts of capital and human labor. The logic of Fitch's argument in 1910 did not lead inexorably toward the conclusion that industrial problems should be worked out in the context of bureaucratically organised unions like those of the 1950s[46] Other ways of handling a nationally planned industrial and capitalist order were then being bitterly contested. Fitch's view was one important voice in the intense ideological discussion which has received less attention than it deserves, perhaps because it was a loser in the ideological contest.

This reading of the survey raises the following question about the sociology of the social reform and social science in the early twentieth century: what moved certain academic social scientists, and especially those interested in sociological questions, away from the notion that the study of social forces ought to give special weight to the idea that economic processes underlie many sociological processes – most especially that of urban development? To answer this question, histories of specific disciplines in specific universities are particularly helpful, for such studies help explain why certain specific implications of general ideas about society gained a national academic audience, while other *possible* implications of these general ideas either were not developed at all, or remained only local in influence. One might observe here an analogy with the many doctrinal and organisation disputes among socialists between 1848 and 1920 and find that much of the intellectual and political history in this period is rooted in conflict among groups which themselves were rooted in specific historical, institutional and political circumstances.[47] Similar attention ought to be given to the sociological history of Social Liberalism.

ON 'DISCONTINUITY' IN THE HISTORY OF SOCIAL RESEARCH

The disappearance of the social survey from the methods of established social science is discussed in detail in chapter 11 by Bulmer from the point of view of the development of the dominant Chicago School of Sociology between roughly 1915 and 1935. To Vivian Palmer, author in 1928 of the influential textbook on the Chicago style of sociology, *Field Studies in Sociology: A Student's Manual*, the sociological survey – as opposed to the social survey – was not concerned with reform and amelioration, but with 'the scientific discovery of how human societies function'.[48] An even more striking statement of this position is Robert Park's remark, to graduate students intent on reforming society, that while the world was full of crusaders their role as sociologists was to 'be that of the calm, detached scientist who investigates race relations with the same objectivity and detachment with which the zoologist dissects the potato bug'.[49] To Chicago sociologists, social reform and good science were independent endeavours.

In my opinion, however, the Chicago School praised its own work too excessively and dismissed the scientific and political potential of the social survey movement too easily. It is the case that many of the theoretical implications of the propositions and evidence presented in the *Pittsburgh Survey* were not consciously developed by Fitch or his colleagues. Some may even have been consciously ignored. But it does not thereby follow either that there was no underlying theory of urban development in the *Pittsburgh Survey* or – even more importantly – that the survey movement studies were incapable of being formalised in a way that would have made their efforts more solidly scientific in this sense. Why, for example, is the political economy underlying the *Pittsburgh Survey* less sociological than the social psychology underlying the more 'legitimate' work in *The Polish Peasant*?

The issue of 'discontinuity' may be clarified still further if one looks at the conditions at the University of Wisconsin which led in the direction of a social (or 'institutional') economics of society, rather than in the direction of a social psychology and social ecology of society. The leaders of the political economy department at the University of Wisconsin (sociology was not a separate department until 1917) were interested in developing ideas about the social aspects of economic processes (one of which was the evolution of cities), unlike the sociologists at the University of Chicago. Commons, for one, continued to develop his ideas about 'institutional' economics and the legal theory of capitalism. He also developed what has since become known as the Commons School of Labor History. However, there was no decision to develop or to test the theoretical potential of the urban studies like the one done in Pittsburgh.

The distinction, for example, drawn by sociologists at the University of Chicago, between social science and political partisanship would not likely have been an important factor in the decision to discontinue development of the social survey at the University of Wisconsin. Social scientists at the University of Wisconsin routinely did their work with the political and financial support of several very important political authorities – among them the Progressive Party and the Socialist Party – and their work was sought out by the State Government, controlled by Progressive forces, as part of routine state administration. This is the famous Wisconsin Idea, described by Charles McCarthy. Being a socialist at the University of Wisconsin, or taking socialist theory seriously, was not as much of a threat to one's academic career as it was at the Rockefeller-endowed University of Chicago. Public advocacy of ideas like the municipal ownership of utilities was not feared as much in Wisconsin as in Chicago.[50] The public voice of labour was more powerful in Wisconsin than in Illinois, especially after the defeat of Progressive politics in Illinois during the administration of Altgeld in the mid-1890s. It was in Madison, and not in Chicago, that social scientists could take seriously the idea that it was possible, in principle, to do serious research into controversial social issues and at the same time proposed remedies implied by that research, without necessarily sacrificing the scientific quality of that research. It is true that the theoretical beginnings presented in social surveys like the *Pittsburgh Survey* were not followed up at Wisconsin. But not because it was obvious to them that genuine social science cannot mix with controversial policy debates.

NOTES

I would like to thank Doreen Lomax, Kathryn Sklar, Herb Sloan, Allan Silver and especially Allan Horlick for their comments in earlier drafts of this article.

1 Frederick Jackson Turner, 'The West and American Ideals,; *The Washington Historical Quarterly*, 5 (October, 1914), 243–57.

2 Turner, 'The West', 241.

3 Turner, 'The West', 257.

4 Turner, 'The West', 257.

5 See Robert E. L. Faris, *Chicago Sociology, 1920–1932* (San Francisco: Chandler, 1967), pp. 8, 125; Lewis Coser, 'American Trends', in Tom Bottomore and Robert Nisbet (eds.), *A History of Sociological Analysis* (New York: Basic Books, 1978), p. 318.

6 For detailed information about The *Pittsburgh Survey*, see Steven R. Cohen 'Reconciling Industrial Conflict and Democracy: The *Pittsburgh Survey* and the Growth of Social Research in the United States', PhD thesis, Columbia University, 1981, and 'From Industrial Democracy to Professional Adjustment: The Development of Industrial Sociology in the United States, 1900–1955', *Theory and Society*, 12 (1983), 47–67.

7 On Bulmer's discussion of 'discontinuity', see Martin Bulmer, *The Chicago School of Sociology*, (Chicago: Univerisity of Chicago Press, 1984), pp. 64–80.

8 Paul U. Kellogg *et al.*, *The Pittsburgh District: Civic Frontage* (New York: Russell Sage, 1914), pp. 499–502.

9 Memorandum, Paul Underwood Kellogg to Edward Devine, 25 April, 1907, Kellogg Papers, Social Welfare History Archives (hereafter SWHA), University of Minnesota; and Alice Montgomery to Kellogg, 11 June, 1906, *Pittsburgh Survey* Folder, SWHA.

10 Kellogg, *Pittsburgh District: Civic Frontage*, pp. 499–501.

11 Samuel Hays, 'The Politics of Reform in Municipal Government in the Progressive Era', *Pacific Northwest Quarterly*, 55 (1965), 157–69; Roy Lubove, *The Progressives and the Slums* (Pittsburgh: University of Pittsburgh Press, 1962).

12 John R. Commons to Victor Berger, 11 April, 1910, American Association for Labor Legislation Papers, Wisconsin State Historical Society (hereafter WSHS); Carl Thompson to William Leiserson, no. date, Leiserson Papers, WSHS.

13 See Trisha Early, 'The Pittsburgh Survey', unpublished seminar paper, 6, 24, 41 and appendix B, Archives of Industrial Society, University of Pittsburgh, 1972; Commons to Berger, 11 April, 1910, American Association for Labor Legislation Papers, WSHS; Carl Thompson to Leiserson, no date, Leiserson Papers, WSHS; Shelby Harrison, *The Social Survey* (New York: Russell Sage Foundation, 1931), *passim*; Second Annual Meeting of the American Association for Labor Legislation, 1908, Labor Collection, WSHS; Isaac Rubinow, *Social Insurance* (New York: 1913), pp. 74–95; James H. Boyd, *The Law of Compensation for Injuries to Workmen* (Indianapolis: Bobbs-Merrill, 1913), p. 61; P. Techumseh Sherman, 'Before the Industrial Accidents Commission', State of Pennsylvania, nd., Labor Collection, WSHS; *Liability and Compensation Lectures* (Hartford: The Insurance Institute of Hartford, Inc., 1913), pp. 75, 169–206.

14 Elizabeth Butler, *Women and the Trades* (New York: Russell Sage Foundation, 1909); Crystal Eastman, *Work-Accidents and the Law* (New York: Russell Sage Foundation, 1910); Margaret Byington, *Homestead: Households of a Mill Town* (New York: Russell Sage Foundation, 1910); John Fitch, *The Steel Workers* (New York: Russell Sage Foundation, 1911); Kellogg, *Pittsburgh District: Civic Frontage*; Paul Kellogg et al., *Wage Earning Pittsburgh* (New York: Russell Sage Foundation, 1914).

15 Fitch, *The Steel Workers*, pp. v–vi.

16 Byington, *Households of a Mill Town*, p. vi.

17 Quotations from various interviews appear in this paper without endnotes. They are taken from Fitch's field notebooks, which are private papers in the possession of his grandson, Mr Charles Hill, who may be contacted through the author. Details about all the interviews may be found in Cohen, 'Reconciling Industrial Conflict and Democracy'.

18 Fitch, *The Steel Workers*, p. 75. Richard A. Gonce, 'The Development of John R. Commons' System of Thought', PhD thesis, University of Wisconsin, 1966; Ben B. Seligman, *Main Currents in Modern Economics: Economic Thought since 1870* (Chicago: Quadrangle Books, 1971), I, 159–77.

19 Eastman, *Work-Accidents and the Law*, p. 115.

20 Eastman, *Work-Accidents and the Law*, p. 115.

21 For instance, Wilson was not only opposed to labour's demand that unions be exempted from the anti-trust provisions of the Clayton Act, but in general he approached questions of social reconstruction politically and pragmatically rather than critically and programmatically in the sense developed in studies like the *Pittsburgh*

Survey. See Arthur S. Link, *Woodrow Wilson and the Progressive Era* (New York: Harper and Row, 1954), 69–70, 224–30.

22 For examples of how Fitch analysed workers' memories of the famous Homestead strike of 1892, see Steven R. Cohen, 'Steelworkers Rethink the Homestead Strike of 1892', *Pennsylvania History*, 48 (1981), 155–77.

23 Fitch, *The Steel Workers*, p. 30.

24 Fitch, *The Steel Workers*, pp. 177, 181.

25 Fitch, *The Steel Workers*, pp. 64–65.

26 Fitch, *The Steel Workers*, p. 67.

27 Fitch, *The Steel Workers*, p. 243.

28 Fitch, *The Steel Workers*, p. 75.

29 Though his views had not been fully developed at the time he conducted his research, Fitch did have an opportunity to state them some years later. See, John A. Fitch, *The Causes of Industrial Unrest* (New York: Harper and Brothers, 1924).

30 R. Jeffrey Lustig, *Corporate Liberalism: The Origins of Modern American Political Theory, 1890–1920* (Berkeley: University of California Press, 1982), p. 245, and *passim*; among more liberal scholars the period is also portrayed as extremely contentious, see Milton Derber, *The American Idea of Industrial Democracy, 1865–1965* (Chicago: University of Illinois Press, 1970), 92–199.

31 Fitch, *The Causes of Industrial Unrest*, pp. 401–19.

32 See Charles McCarthy, *The Wisconsin Idea* (New York, The Macmillan Co., 1912).

33 William E. Leuchtenberg, *Frankilin D. Roosevelt and the New Deal* (New York: Harper and Row, 1963), pp. 167–96.

34 John McClymer, *War and Welfare: Social Engineering in America, 1890–1925* (Westport, Ct.: Greenwood Press, 1980), pp. 1–68; James Weinstein, *The Corporate Ideal in the Liberal State: 1900–1918* (Boston: Beacon Press, 1968), pp. ix–xv, where Weinstein ignores any meaningful diversity among reformers seeking to restructure industry in the post-laissez-faire era.

35 McClymer, *War and Welfare*, pp. 216–221.

36 Weinstein, *The Corporate Ideal*, p. x.

37 A remarkable description and penetrating analysis of the ideological and political diversity of the period of 1916–1925 may be found in David Montgomery, *The Fall of the House of Labor: The Workplace, The State and American Labor Activism, 1865–1925* (New York: Cambridge University Press, 1987), pp. 411–64; see also John R. Commons, *Legal Foundations of Capitalism* (1924; Madison: University of Wisconsin, 1957); and Mary Van Kleeck, *Miners and Management* (New York: Russell Sage Foundation, 1934).

38 McClymer, *War and Welfare*, pp. 1–68. See also the many remarks of Herman and Julia R. Schwendinger, *Sociologists of the Chair* (New York: Basic Books, 1974)

39 Take, for example, Marx's manner of attacking Lassalle: 'as shown by the shape of his head and the growth of his hair, ... he is descended from the negroes who joined the flight of Moses from Egypt (unless his mother or grandmother on his father's side were crossed with a nigger). This union of Jew and German on a negro foundation was bound to produce something out of the ordinary. The importunity of the fellow is also negroid', quoted in David McLellan, *Karl Marx; His Life and Thought* (New York:

Harper and Row, 1973), 322; Daniel Bell, *Marxian Socialism in the United States* (Princeton: Princeton University Press, 1952), pp. 89, 100, 159, and *passim*; George Lichtheim, 'Socialism and the Jews', in *Collected Essays* (New York: Viking Press, 1973), pp. 413–457; Ray Ginger, *The Bending Cross* (New Brunswick: Rutgers University Press, 1949), pp. 19, 42–3, 63, 68, 92–3, 116, 215–16, 257–61, 345, 378, 396.

40 On the debate over such terms, see Morris Janowitz, 'Sociological Theory and Social Control', *American Journal of Sociology*, 81 (1975), 82–108; McClymner, *War and Welfare*, *passim*; Schwendinger, *The Sociologists of the Chair*; Vernon K. Dibble, review of *The Sociologists of the Chair*, in *History and Theory*, 15 (1976), 293–321; Mary Van Kleeck, *Miners and Management*, pp. 16–20, 213–22, 225.

41 McClymer, *War and Welfare*, p. 32.

42 See Frances Fox Piven and Richard A. Cloward, *Regulating the Poor; The Functions of Public Welfare* (New York: Random House, 1971); Roy Lubove, *The Professional Altruist* (Cambridge: Harvard University Press, 1965), 55–117, 144–9; David Montgomery, *The Fall of the House of Labor*, p. 459.

43 John Fitch, 'The Human Factor in Industry', address delivered to the Massachusetts Conference of Social Work, 10 November, 1920, Survey Associates Papers, SWHA.

44 William Z. Foster, *The Great Steel Strike and its Lessons* (New York: B. W. Huebsch, 1920), pp. viii–ix.

45 See Van Kleeck, *Miners and Management*, *passim*.

46 On the issues of bureaucracy versus democracy and Progressive politics see, James T. Kloppenberg, *Uncertain Victory; Social Democracy and Progressivism in European and American Thought, 1870–1920* (New York: Oxford University Press, 1986), pp. 199–400; Samuel Haber, *Efficiency and Uplift* (Chicago: University of Chicago Press, 1964).

47 Leszek Kolakowski, *Main Currents of Marxism* (New York: Oxford University Press, 1978); George Lichtheim, *A Short History of Socialism* (New York: Praeger, 1970); Franz Borkenau, *World Communism* (1939; Ann Arbor: University of Michigan, 1962).

48 Bulmer, *The Chicago School of Sociology*, p. 7.

49 Bulmer, *The Chicago School of Sociology*, p. 76.

50 See Mary O. Furner, *Advocacy and Objectivity* (Lexington: University of Kentucky, 1975); David Thelan, *The New Citizenship* (Columbia: University of Missouri, 1972).

CHAPTER TEN

The world of the academic quantifiers: the Columbia University Family and its connections

STEPHEN P. TURNER

By 1900, Columbia University was the leading center of academic statistical social science in the United States, a position of dominance it held until the twenties. The two figures who had positions of intellectual leadership in the 'Social Science' programme, Richmond Mayo-Smith and Franklin H. Giddings, were part of the same network of personal relationships and memberships in voluntary associations as the figures who were most closely identified with the idea of the social survey, such as Paul Kellogg. Many of the figures in the movement were trained at Columbia or had ties to the university. Columbia research often served as methodological inspiration for later social survey work or was inspired by the defects of the knowledge available to such organisations as the Charity Organisation Societies, the settlement houses, and other such organisations. In this process of intellectual exchange, the early elements of a distinctively 'sociological' conception of surveys and community studies emerged, as did a distinctive philosophical rationale for quantification in sociology. Several of the surveys of small communities that were exemplary for the emerging field of Rural Sociology, for example, were Columbia dissertations.

There is an unsurprising tendency on the part of anyone writing on the history of the social survey in the United States to think of the social survey movement itself, retrospectively, in terms of the definitions, claims of originality, and models developed by Paul Kellogg and Russell Sage Foundation, one of the major backers of community surveys. Kellogg, in his enthusiasm for the programme that emerged around the Pittsburgh survey, tended to fail to acknowledge the antecedents of the survey, especially in the doomed European tradition of Moral Statistics, of which Mayo-Smith was in a sense the last representative, and in the collection of statistics by State and subsequently national bureaux of 'Labor Statistics' after the civil war, and in the expansion of the collection of federal social statistics under the auspices of the census, which repeatedly expanded the range of its questions, and various federal commissions, such as the Tenement study, sponsored by the leading figure in the Labor Statistics movement, Carroll Wright, which was the original source of data for the Hull House maps discussed in chapter 4.

Columbia's early and intense commitment to quantitative social research reflected the broader appreciation of these roots that one would expect to find in an academic institution, and this is evident in the dissertations done by the students in the department who were to go on to become academic sociologists. As we shall see, the topics selected by Columbia sociologists for their own surveys reproduced the canon of reform topics established by the 1880s by the Massachusetts Bureau of Labor Statistics. Columbia's distinctive contribution, which is evident in the transition from the statistical thinking of Mayo-Smith to that of Giddings, was to define this work in terms of an explicit philosophy of science, derived from Karl Pearson, which was the basis for the distinctive strain of social research that became 'mainstream sociology' and came to be supported by the Social Science Research Council in the twenties and thirties. This new style of survey was in a certain sense the successor of the Kellogg-style survey supported by the Russell Sage Foundation. But there was no 'discontinuity'. If we consider the diversity of the research activities of the sociologists who were part of the larger Columbia family, of its graduates and their students in the interwar years, the picture is rather one of close personal patronage, and professional connections between a relatively small group of researchers whose careers and interests spanned a broad range, in which the Kelloggian social survey had an important, but subordinate place. Some of the research topics and styles that fell in this range, perhaps most of them, had an afterlife in academic sociology; but the Kelloggian survey, poorly adapted to the rhythms and constraints of academic life and part time, individualistic research, and orphaned as a result of the declining financial fortunes and changed interests of its main financial supporter, did not, though its variants were to be found as late as the fifties, for example in the Kansas City survey performed in connection with the University of Chicago.

This chapter will tell the story of the Columbia family and its connections in the milieu shared by Columbia social science and New York philanthropy, the source of much of the survey work done in the period 1905–25 and of course subsequently the source of much of the funding for later 'academic' survey research done under the auspices of the SSRC. The members of this 'family' had a role in settlement houses, reform survey work, foundations, the government, reform politics, and of course the emerging discipline of academic sociology. Because this story is largely a story of networks and connections and their intellectual consequences, and because the number of connections is large, it is necessary to limit the discussion to a few exemplary situations and relationships, and a few strands in the fabric of connections between academic social science and the movements of institutionalised reform.

THE BACKGROUND: REFORM STATISTICS AND REFORMIST ASSOCIATIONS

In the disciplines of both statistics and sociology, American universities took over topics that had a long prehistory in public discourse, a discourse that took place in part in the intellectual journals of the period after the Civil War, such as *The North America Review* and the *Century*, but which was sustained by a large set of interested organisations, both governmental and private, and a relatively well-defined set of public issues toward which these organisations were oriented. Typically these organisations, several of which were under the umbrella of the American Social Science Association, had an explicitly reformist character, and were organised around specific topics, such as prison reform. They generally took the form of a 'council' of some sort that included reformist luminaries, but the main work of the organisation, to hold meetings and often to produce a publication, was usually in the hands of a small number of activists. In time, the universities contributed to the leadership of these organisations, and overlapping membership on these boards constituted a kind of web that tied together a large number of intellectual activists, reformers, university professors and presidents, and governmental officials. The development of social science in the university for the most part followed the establishment of these organisations, so the original flow of personnel was from the organisations to the university.

The character of this network, which reached its peak in the early nineties, may be seen in the careers of its ubiquitous members. The 'statisticians' most frequently represented in this network of boards of directors were Carroll D. Wright and Francis Amasa Walker, each of whom rose through the ranks in the Union army, and ultimately became professors, civil servants, and college presidents.[1] Wright rose to the rank of colonel in the war, and became a state senator in 1871. In 1873 he took over the Massachusetts Bureau of Labor Statistics, which had been founded in 1869, and became US Commissioner of Labor in 1888, honorary professor of political science at Catholic University in 1895, president of Clark College and professor of Applied Sociology in 1902. He served as the original director of the Carnegie Institute's programmes on economics and sociology, in 1902.[2] Walker, son of an Amherst economist, had a similar career, playing a large role in the development of the census, ending as President of MIT.

Wright's great success was the Massachusetts Bureau, which became an international model of research and a pioneer both in methods and in the topics addressed. It was in the work of this bureau that the characteristically modern methods of survey analysis — machine tabulation, individual data cards, interviews based on printed schedules or questionnaires, concerns with sampling, the use of index numbers, and large numbers of respondents (sometimes in the tens of thousands) — were first combined. Under Wright and his predecessors, who controlled the bureau for the first four years after its founding in 1869, a wide range of reform topics was addressed. These went far beyond the census and far beyond the narrower questions of the economics of labor to an extensive examination of a wide range of topics relating to the life of workers. In the first report of the Massachusetts Bureau in 1869, the following 'very important subjects' were cited as matters for inquiry: 'the hours of labor, the wages, the savings, the manner of life at home and from home, the recreations, the culture, moral and mental, of the laborers, and the influence of the several kinds of labor upon their health and body and brain, not ignoring the subjects of cooperation, strikes, trades-unions, and the general relations of capital and labor, with such matter relating to the history of labor and labor legislation, here and abroad, as we might be able to gather'.[3] By 1870, this list had expanded to include research on housing, intemperance, and child labour, by 1871, poverty, Boston tenements, domestic and women's work, and so on. In the 1870s, pauperism, crime, the 'afflicted classes', the cost of living, nativity, convict labour, and other topics had been added.[4] Later, indeed by the 1890s, the work of these bureaus had largely narrowed to the economic and demographic interests of the present day employment surveys, with some interesting exceptions, such as the concern with child labour. As we shall see, the range of these early studies, and the topics themselves, were taken up again under academic auspices at Columbia.

Like Major John Wesley Powell, who created and headed the Bureau of Indian Ethnology and the US Geological Survey and who, like Walker, was politically sponsored by Garfield,[5] Wright and Walker were largely autodidacts, rather than university scholars. Both Wright and Walker were active participants in the reform movements and preacademic social science of their time: each served as an officer or board member of the American Social Science Association, the American Statistical Association, the Association for the Promotion of Profit-Sharing, and each of them participated in the American Economic Association. The pattern was not uncommon. Giddings was one of those who followed this path.

Giddings, born in 1855, had been forced to leave Union College for financial reasons in 1875, after completing two years of study. He became a newspaperman in Springfield, Massachusetts, an area which was a hotbed of organisations of this sort. Giddings was soon part of the discussions of the problems of employment, inflation, and monetary policy: among his earliest writings was a proposal for price-indexing contracts. By the close of his career as a newsman he was delivering papers to the meetings of economics societies and editing movement journals. The character of this milieu is difficult to recapture. The sheer number and variety of the organisations that were founded in the late nineteenth century is itself astonishing. They ranged from various anti-vice leagues and prohibitionist organisations to associations for 'scientific' exchange, such as the Connecticut Valley Economic Association, one of Giddings' first arenas.

The reform organisations served as the framework for a porous and absorptive intellectual community which was not dependent, at first, on the university or on any specific European inspirations: the community was an analogue to the socialist left in Europe, in that it provided an audience for the ideas of the day, a source of non-academic intellectual recruits, and a great deal of intellectual work, in the form of editing and writing, as well as a degree of practical engagement and experience that prevented the rise of doctrinaires. American sectionalism and federalism, especially the fact that the states, and in the case of poor relief, the counties, still possessed the bulk of legal and regulatory power over social and economic questions, meant that the focus of these organisations was localistic, and that national organisations served as means for sharing local experiences rather than as bearers of national programme. The experience of participation in these organisations left a mark on what was to follow, both at Columbia and at Chicago, where Robert Park had undergone a similar education. Giddings, like Park, was organisationally adept, talented at communicating ideas to a wider public, both journalistically and as a public speaker, and somewhat cynical about what Park called do-gooders. Having been raised as a child of a particularly strict congregationalist minister of the Christian reformist type that flourished after the success of the abolitionist movement, Giddings was also explicitly sceptical about many of the manifestations of these movements, including those that flourished under the leadership of the main competitor to Columbia social science, The Johns Hopkins

University family, of which Richard T. Ely was the personal and spiritual leader, and to whom such Chicago personalities as Small were devoted.[6] In the case of Giddings, this cynicism sometimes extended to aspects of the survey movement itself, as it did for Park. In time, these differences in temperament led to, or supported, other differences that separated Giddings from the survey movement. But the differences took the form they did in part because of the manner in which the academic environment at Columbia itself developed. This is a complex story, much of which precedes Giddings' entry onto the Columbia scene in the early nineties.

THE COLUMBIA IDEA

When John Burgess returned from Germany to Amherst College in 1874 as a professor, he sought to recreate on the American soil something analogous to the schooling in social science he had received in Europe. This experience, and the model of learning and especially *Forschung* that Burgess and many other Americans acquired, was the inspiration for the creation of programmes of graduate education in the expanding American universities of the post-Civil War era. Part of Burgess' German experience was with the statistics of Wappaus, a Göttingen Professor. Statistics was thus an essential element of Burgess' image of the social sciences from the start. When he was called to Columbia, he took with him an Amherst student who was to become a leader in statistics, Richmond Mayo-Smith, to be one of the four original members of the faculty of political science. By 1890 Mayo-Smith accounted for the largest body of statistical course work in the United States: four courses, all designed for the graduate social science students at Columbia.

In 1877, Mayo-Smith was twenty-four years old, a newly appointed assistant to Burgess. In 1883 he was appointed full professor of political economy. He began the teaching of statistics in 1883, with a course attended by three students.[7] His rationale for the course was fitted to Burgess's aim of producing civil servants, and to the Cameralism that Burgess espoused: statistical method, Mayo-Smith said, 'gives us a picture of actually existing society and is thus more fitted for guiding state action'.[8] The statistics in question were those collected by the government, and it was simply assumed in the discussions of statistics of the era that the employer of statisticians would be the government and that the government would collect the statistics.

Mayo-Smith had an interesting and complex relation to governmental statistics, reform and social science. On the one hand, the American statistical community in the United States was small, and he was quickly absorbed into the networks of reformers and reform intellectuals of which Burgess was already a part. Mayo-Smith was active in the American Statistical Association and the Charity Organisation Society of New York. Within these diverse movements and organisations there was a great deal of room for disagreement over such questions as immigration (one of Mayo-Smith's specialties), the trend of wages (a concern of his student Charles Spahr), as well as divorce, the topic of Willcox's dissertation of 1892, the first American statistical dissertation on a recognisably 'sociological' topic. Yet these communities were sufficiently small that the kinds of intellectual conflicts that inevitably arose could be managed personally, especially by a person like Mayo-Smith, an inveterate Club man at a time when such clubs as the Century in New York, of which he was a member, were foci of scientific and literary life. Mayo-Smith and Wright were on friendly terms, and Mayo-Smith was evidently well-liked in the Massachusetts Bureau: in 1887, Pidgin, one of the pioneers of machine tabulation, proposed that Mayo-Smith spend the summer with him at one of the Boston beaches to work with him on a book of practical statistics.[9]

ACADEMIC-PHILANTHROPIC RELATIONS IN NEW YORK

In 1891, Burgess and Mayo-Smith raised the subject of the need for a chair of sociology, meaning ethology, penology, charity, and poor-relief – subjects that Burgess' friend Sanborn had taught at Cornell in the late eighties as a special lecturer.[10] Seth Low, who had been a reform mayor of Brooklyn, persuaded the board to appoint Giddings, then thirty-six, who had in 1888 been appointed at Bryn Mawr as professor of political science (the position held previously by Woodrow Wilson), to commute to Columbia on Friday to give a joint seminar with Mayo-Smith. In 1894, Low offered to pay the salary of a professor of sociology, and Giddings was appointed. Giddings soon made his mark, and a programme in sociology developed quickly. Giddings himself exerted his influence in a special way. He ran a kind of beer-and-pretzels salon known as the FHG Club, to which his best students and a few others, such as Arthur and Paul Kellogg (editor of *The Survey*) and Charles Beard, were invited. Invitations were an honour for the students, and the experience was formative for many of those who participated: they acquired a common set of ideas about the prospects of sociology as a science, and a strong core of personal relationships to peers.[11]

The slogan 'the city is the laboratory of the social sciences', variously attributed to Mayo-Smith and Giddings, appeared in the earliest announcements of the new programme in sociology,[12] and both Giddings and Mayo-Smith put the idea into effect by initiating research projects using available data. In 1894, Mayo-Smith secured authorisation to use COS case records as research material.[13] Mayo-Smith and Giddings themselves served on a three-person committee that statistically examined 500 records, examining 'causes' of distress and tabulating methods of treatment. They recognised the inadequacies of the records for statistical purposes, 'and confessed that the benefit of such an investigation as they had made came principally to the students who had engaged in it'.[14] But the studies had some consequences: for example, they contributed in succeeding years to reforms of case record keeping and an attack on the doctrine of causality implicit in the old standard COS blank, which was replaced in 1907.[15]

The studies grew out of a complex body of personal relations to the wider philanthropic scene. In this respect, Giddings continued the practices of Mayo-Smith, whose primary 'public service' contribution had been to serve as a district officer of the Charity Organisation Society in New York. Giddings' student Tenney recounts that Giddings

found that one of the expectations connected with the chair of Sociology was that the occupant should serve on the councils of the University Settlement and the Charity Organization Society. For many years, therefore, after coming to Columbia, Professor Giddings was one of the directing minds guiding the policies of these institutions ... In part because of these connections, the lectures and seminars in Sociology and in Statistics from their inception were attended by many persons interested in what is now known as social work.[16]

Giddings eventually served not only on the COS and University Settlement House boards, but as President of Richmond Hill House, on the board of the State Charities Aid Association and even on the New York City Board of Education.[17]

The COS network was an incubator of the survey movement in that these networks provided the structure of patronage and community of intellect that made possible the enormous infusion of funds for surveys in the period after 1905. The Russell Sage Foundation was created as a direct outgrowth of the network established by the New York COS and the attitude toward research that flourished there. At the death of Russell Sage, a financier of enormous wealth and exceeding personal unsavouriness, his widow, on the advice of her attorneys, Robert W. de Forest and his brother Henry, and with the encouragement of other trusted persons, including Johns Hopkins President Daniel Coit Gilman, himself a Baltimore COS leader, established the foundation bearing Sage's name.[18] De Forest suggested modelling the finances of the organisation on the (Rockefeller) General Education Board, Carnegie Institute, and Borke Foundation, and to aspire to become for the nation such a 'center of charitable and philanthropic information as the Charity Organisation Society makes for the city', stressing 'research, study, teaching, publication', but not excluding other kinds of aid to activities leading to 'the permanent improvement of social conditions'.[19] Yet the contribution of Mayo-Smith and of Giddings (who was favourably inclined to the reformist aims, but suspicious of the foundations[20]) to the creation of the intellectual climate which made possible this channelling of funds into surveys is difficult to specify precisely. Personal ties, however, are quite readily traced. Mayo-Smith's student Spahr edited the reformist *Outlook*; and Giddings' students, as we shall see, were distributed widely around the foundations and the surveys themselves. The COS created in 1898 a tenement house commission, which included the architect and philanthropist I. N. Phelps Stokes, who was later to head a race-relations foundation, endowed by a relative, to which one of Giddings' students, T. J. Jones, was appointed as an executive.[21]

GIDDINGS AND HIS STUDENTS

Giddings had, by 1901, developed a complex conception of sociology as a quantifiable subject, and this conception was impressed relentlessly on his students. Giddings, as Sims recalled, 'had developed a true scientific approach ... [which] he communicated to his students. He was definitely trying to develop a quantitative instead of a purely qualitative sociology ... To find ways of measuring and weighing sociological data was his chief interest.'[22] But though the researches of Giddings' students reflected Giddings' theoretical ideas and the current state of his methodological thinking, the content of the research reflected the standard topics of the reform catalog, and these were the topics of research done by the MBLS as early as its first few years. Thus the research agenda itself directly reflected the reform agenda that grew up and gained coherence in the period 1866–1905.

The topics of the Columbia dissertations before World War I were strikingly similar to those done by the MBLS, including among others, studies of *The Enforcement of the Statutes of Laborers* (Putnam, 1908), *A History of California Labor Legislation* (Eaves, 1910), *Factory Legislation in Maine* (Whiting, 1908), *The Employment of Women in the Clothing Trade* (Willett, 1903), *The Negro at Work in New York City* (Haynes, 1912),

Minimum Wage Legislation in Australia (Collier, 1915), and *Dressmaking as a Trade for Women in Massachusetts* (Allison, 1916), which, like Parmelee's *Inebriety in Boston* (1909), even shared the locale; Ogburn's dissertation on the emergence of consistency between the states with respect to child labour legislation was based on material of a kind collected routinely as part of Labor Statistics reports under the heading of surveys of legislation; Chapin's study of the emergence of certain common education practices was analogous; T. J. Jones' study of a New York City block of tenements was a Giddingsonian approach to this topic. Giddings himself planned a study of workingmen's leisure in 1912–13, using the same kinds of questions asked by the MBLS studies of the same topics, and Gillin later published 'Wholesome Citizens and Spare Time'.[23]

But there was a distinctive intellectual orientation to this new research. Jones' study of a block of tenements, published in 1904, but based on field research that began in 1897, is illustrative of several features of this new model of sociological scholarship. Jones begins the study by observing that 'the rural character of the people swarming in our tenements' is largely unknown, and that 'even the missionary, the pastor, and the settlement worker have but an inadequate and erroneous idea of the peoples around them'.[24] Jones spoke from experience: he had 'at different times been engaged as a visitor for a church, for a settlement, and for an organization that searched independently for facts concerning life in the tenement districts, and ... found that the information gained in the first two instances too often contradicted that gained in the third'.[25] In fact, he had matriculated at Union Theological Seminary and Columbia, receiving an MA in sociology in 1899, the BD in 1900. He served as acting headworker of the University Settlement of New York City, editing its annual report of 1902, a collection of studies of urban conditions. He was also briefly employed by the Charity Organisation Society, the Federation of Churches of New York City, and by the Census Bureau.[26] He was thus well aware of the status of knowledge of the tenement dwellers, and Giddings' views were persuasive to him. The flaw in past research, he believed was 'a lack of unity of conception in regard to the matters to be learned'.[27] His own study, in contrast, he described as a self-conscious

attempt to study a New York City street according to a complete system of social principles. Even if the system were proved to be arbitrary, the work would be more valuable, the writer believes, than an unsystematic attempt, however long continued, for the reasons that the investigator has a basis for search and an order for arranging in his mind the innumerable impressions made by the unit considered. Without a system the study of a people is but a wild-goose chase, and this, indeed, is the nature of too many of the so-called sociological investigations now carried on. Read the results of these investigations and you feel that you have been through a mine more or less rich in information. You are possibly stirred to pity or to blame by the conditions described, and you may give your help accordingly; but when this task is accomplished the outcome of the investigation is simply a conglomerate mass of facts, practically useless for the future. According to the system used in this dissertation we shall gather facts which may be expected to substantiate or to overthrow certain theories as to the manner in which well-known social forces work themselves out. Thus we may hope for results of permanent value.[28]

This is of course the voice of Giddings as well.[29] Jones concerned himself with one of Giddings' pet, indeed primary, ideas, that 'concerted volition' took place differently among groups of different kinds, particularly groups of different ethnicities. This was tied in part to an anxiety that immigrants could not be assimilated into the kinds of social relations characteristic of American democracy. The Jews and Italians who predominated in Jones's block were particular objects of concern.

Jones described in great detail, in terms of Giddings' categories, the development and occurrence of 'like behavior,' 'motives of conduct' according to Giddings' categories of ideo-motor, ideo-emotional, dogmatic-emotional (Giddings' term for the puritanism he grew up with) and critically intellectual (of which no instances could be found in the block), and forms of 'concerted volition' or association. His 'method' was to perform a 'sociological census', to visit each family in the block, on Saturday morning. 'No more than twenty families were visited in a day, so as not to overburden the mind with facts'. Basic demographic data was collected on a blank; the observational results would be classified in a day or two in the next week: necessary because the system of classification was a system of ratings by the observer. 'Provided with blanks used by the Federation of Churches the investigator knocked at the door of a tenement. Generally a voice from within would call out, "Come in." Quite often a voice would ask, "What do you want?" And the visitor would answer, "I want to know how many persons are in this family," or in more difficult cases the answer was "I am taking a sociological census," with emphasis on the last word. The door opened in all but one case out of the two hundred and eleven'.[30] Jones was following in the footsteps of others. Indeed, he wrote 'These people have been visited by so many officers and agents that they have grown indifferent to all investigations. They take it as a matter of course'. But his own investigation 'was a surprise to them, and many were curious about it. The curiosity was soon lost, in the great majority of the cases, in the friendly relations that arose between the visitor and the family'.[31] Jones, a Welshman by birth, looked enough like a Jew to pass as one.

From the Hebrews a hearty welcome was gained by the ability to pronounce the Talmud in the original. The visitor's corrupt German and dark complexion were often taken by the Jew as a guarantee that he was one of their race.[32]

The Italians were more difficult, but his appearance helped there as well, and in 'one instance he was asked if he was an Italian priest'. To the Irish, 'he could claim to be a brother Celt', but the Irish did 'not care who knows about them'.[32] Knowledge of German and 'an admiration for the German character' sufficed in the case of the Germans.

In a typical case, the Cohens, Jones visited the family on a Saturday morning. The father, a tailor born in New York City, was not home, but his wife and two young children, and mother-in-law, were home. The mother-in-law had been born in Russia, married a Jew in Portugal, moved to England and then to 'America with a number of children, who', Jones wrote, 'are now well situated, one daughter being married to a fairly well-to-do Jew and living comfortably on Long Island'. Jones learned all this 'in an interesting conversation about' such topics as 'the progress of the Hebrew people', the movement from the lower to the upper East side, 'where the block was located, to the West side', the comparative morality of the ethnic groups, and the observations of the two women that the Irish were 'very thriftless and careless, spending much of their money in drink' but their observation that some of the children nevertheless 'grew up to be fine men and women'.[34] They also discussed their own religious practices: the mother tried to keep the Sabbath; the daughter 'no longer cared for Jewish customs...[and] ate what she wanted,...checked only by her mother's wishes'. The daughter took herself not to look like a Jew, and believed that *her* daughter was 'not anything like a Jew'.[35] These were, in short, Americanisation stories.

Jones, however, was concerned to classify the families in terms of his 'scheme of mental and moral types', so these discussions were the basis of ratings, which he explains, in this specimen case. The family was not 'impulsive', because the mother-in-law showed self-restraint on an occasion 'when the landlord abused her people'. Intellectually, the family had left the 'credulous' stage, as shown by the daughter's attitude toward 'Hebrew customs'. The mother's 'credulousness' in this instance was overweighed by her tolerance of her daughter and the acuteness of her own observations on this and other subjects. Unlike most of the residents of this block, this family did 'think for themselves'. Of the four types of character identified by Giddings, Jones thought it evident that the family had passed the threshold of the 'rationally conscientious' type, though 'not a high example'.[36] In addition, Jones recorded the various traits of character that were associated with social life, ascribing to this family compassion and generosity, and such traits as truthfulness, industriousness, frugality, cleanliness, and orderliness.[37] These classifications were applied to each family in the block, and the numbers in each of these categories and other Giddingsonian categories, leading to such results as

In 21 families mere persistence was found to be the dominant method of accommodation, and in 121 more families a subordinate method. In 149 families accommodation was the dominant, and in 51 families a subordinate method. In 27 families self-control was the dominant, and in 22 families a subordinate method.[38]

No cross tabulations were performed, but for each category the ethnic distribution was discussed.

One aim of the discussion was obviously to account for the susceptibility of each group to machine politics, and the distance of each group from full participation in 'Anglo-Saxon' political culture. As Jones put it, 'A dictator seems to be necessary to every successful organization on the upper East side'. Jewish 'individualism' was least susceptible to this pattern. Jewish organisations 'are not large; leadership is not strongly emphasised; argument, discussion, and disagreement are matters of course. The Irish, with their qualities of leadership and their strong social instincts, form societies in which the "machine system" is always to be observed'.[39] Jones, like Giddings, saw as a danger 'the infusion' into American life 'of foreign ideas and manners, and its tendency thereby to modify Anglo-Saxon habits'.[40]

GIDDINGS AS A METHODOLOGIST

Giddings of course did not invent community studies. In Small and Vincent's Chautauqua text of 1894, *An Introduction to the Science of Society*, the topic of variant forms of community life and various kinds of social relations within communities was the core of the book, which had a full complement of exemplary maps and discussions of the kinds of group life that are to be found in rural, small town, and urban society.[41] Many of the kinds of strategies that interested Giddings, such as grouping persons by dominant motives, were part of Small and Vincent's book. What Giddings added was a complex methodological rationale and an argument for the preferability of certain kinds of social knowledge, or more precisely an image of the evolution of social knowledge. The effects of this conception are evident only in modest ways in Jones' dissertation, and in fact Giddings seems to have been, in practice, rather tolerant of different methods. The community studies done under his influence tended to be descriptive, as Jones' was, rather than quantitative. But they shared with Jones' the use of his distinctive theoretical terminology.

The primary source of the methodological considerations that marked out Giddings from such contemporaries as Small and Vincent and from the social surveyors outside academia, was Karl Pearson's philosophy of science text, *The Grammar of Science*. What Giddings took from Pearson were two closely connected thoughts: first, that the stages which a body of thought passed through to become a science were the ideological, the observational, and the metrical;[42] second, that the highest metrical form which sociology was able to attain would be correlational analysis. Thus the business of sociology, for Giddings, was precisely the transformation of speculations tied together by a logical bond, such as his own sociological theory, which was a theory of forms of association, *into* a set of correlations. Giddings regarded this methodological work as his primary contribution. *Inductive Sociology*, published in 1901, was not, however, a critical success. Yet he stuck to the basic ideas in it, and improved them to fit with new developments in statistics.

In *Inductive Sociology* Giddings gives an example of what he takes to be a paradigmatic scientific demonstration of sociology – he generates, on speculative and logical grounds, the following proposition; only the population that has many, varied, and harmoniously combined interests is consistently progressive in its choices.[43] He metricises this by constructing an index number of heterogeneity (based on distributions of blacks and foreign-born in state populations, something easily derived from census data) and producing a categorisation of states based on this number. The distribution of the states indeed corresponds to our intuitive sense of the progressiveness of their politics.[44] He does not create an index number for this. Had he done so, he could have calculated a Pearsonian correlation.

The problem Giddings faced in actualising this model of scientific development, and to which he devoted an extraordinary amount of effort, was in creating 'indices'. The efforts are retrospectively quite odd. At first, Giddings produced long lists of things that are countable, that correspond to theoretical concepts, or which sort objects into categories that correspond to the kinds of categories used in nineteenth-century social theory and in public discourse about social questions. A glance at Giddings' early lists shows how difficult this problem in fact was. In *Inductive Sociology*, he tried to come up with indices for the following classificatory categories, among many others; 'emotional types', including 'choleric', 'sanguine', 'melancholic' and 'phlegmatic',[45] 'state of political cooperation' including under the subheading 'public' from 'Activity Violent, Military, Coercive' to 'Activity Peaceful, Legislative, and Administrative, but Dogmatic and Coercive' or 'Peaceful, Legislative, and Administrative, Deliberative, Reasonable, Educative'.[46] Most of these distinctions, he thought, could be made by observers, and as we have seen his students, such as T. J. Jones, reported systematic classifications of individuals into similar categories on the basis of 'observation'. F. Stuart Chapin later recalled that 'Giddings in his treatment of method in connection with seminars and in conferences with students was all for clarification of social observations'. But what he arrived at was 'more of a rating system'.[47] The drive to construct 'behavioural indices' was in any event already present in 1901; its roots were deeper.

The development of Giddings' methodological thinking is visible in the gradual evolution of the form of the empirical dissertations done under him. The earliest are 'observational' as T. J. Jones' tenement study had been; J. M. Williams (1906) simply returned to the small New York town in which he had grown up and performed a 'census', and examined the social and economic relations that bound the town to its countryside, a hop-producing region. This book, *An American Town* (1906), Giddings regarded as the 'best approximation' to a 'comprehensive sociological survey of a community'.[48] This general topic was the theme of a series of dissertation which took the form of community studies focused on the same 'theoretical' theme, the interlayering of various forms of association (which itself built on the topic of cooperation, especially as it had become extended in the 1890s to the notion of 'socialisation', by which Giddings meant the development of social ties and associations, of which cooperative associations were a particular type.)[49] There were many studies of this same general type performed at Columbia, including Warren Wilson's *Quaker Hill* (1907), E. S. Todd's *A Social Study of Clark County, Ohio* (1904), F. V. Soule's *An American Village Community* (1909), and Newell Sims' *A Hoosier Village* (1911), and others. J. L. Gillins' *The Dunkers* (1906) was concerned with a form of community association; Chaddock's *Ohio Before 1850* with the problem of individualism and the role of different groups in the westward migration to the creation of community institutions and frontier democracy.

In the twenties, these slowly gave way, proportionally at least, to correlational studies: T. J. Woofter's *Negro Migration* (1920) was the first to use multiple regression techniques; Luther Fry's *Diagnosing the Rural Church*, an ISRR study, and F. A. Ross' *School Attendance in 1920*, both published in 1924, represented the most complete realisations of Giddings' methodological ideas. In Ross one finds the regression equations familiar to readers of present structural equations modelling, and the same reasoning. But studies of small communities and their 'associations' remained a staple product of Columbia sociology throughout this period. These evolved as well. Chaddock's study of Ohio before 1850 was perhaps the most Giddingsonian of the early community studies, and pioneered the metricisation of his concerns. Wilson, who became the Presbyterians' researcher on country churches, produced sixteen 'community and church' studies, usually with the county as the unit of analysis. As early as Odum's dissertation, which involved fifty southern communities, the community had been used as the unit for aggregated data analysis. The fullest development of this came in the work of the Institute for Social and Religious Research, which published many volumes of correlational analyses, including a great deal of partialling, using 'indices' relating to community and church life.[50]

Contemporaries regarded all such studies as 'social surveys'. The ISRR evolved out of the failure of an attempt to perform a world religious survey, and is thus a lineal product of the 'survey' movement. Lynd's *Middletown* was done under ISRR auspices and with ISRR financing. Lynd's career, which included a BD from Union Seminary, home mission work in the west, Rockefeller patronage, and extensive foundation work in the inner circles of New York philanthropy and the SSRC, reads very much like the careers of various earlier Columbia students, with a few differences: Lynd was an old Princetonian and socially connected to New York philanthropy and Club life to a greater extent than any of them had been prior to becoming a 'social researcher.' Where *Middletown* differed from its predecessors was in the fact that the dissertations were one-person efforts, while Lynd, with the backing of the ISRR, had a staff of helpers, and in the fact that the guiding sociological hypothesis being examined – which was initially, and not surprisingly given the dominance of the ISRR by Giddings' students, a concern with the social correlates of religious life – disappeared in Lynd's write up, which was rejected by the ISRR and ultimately published through other Lynd connections. Its 'methods' were those of the earlier studies, and the academic sociologists who performed these studies were enraged by Lynd's claims of methodological priority, which were quite false.

THE SURVEY MOVEMENT AND THE ACADEMIC QUANTIFIERS

The later work of these students developed the ideas and practices they had learned at Columbia: Woofter on Blacks and migration, Woolston on prostitution, Gillin on criminology and penology, Gehlke on delinquency – it is a list which could be easily extended. Many other sociology departments produced survey researchers and statisticians; but the Columbia contribution was ubiquitous and relatively uniform. With these later studies, the methodological impulses that the movement for a scientific sociology had shared with the social survey movement took on new aims. Giddings' students in academic positions generally turned away from community studies, though these survived as a genre in rural sociology for much longer, and toward such topics as the measurement of social status, Chapin's concern. His students also continued to develop his methodological conception and revised his theoretical ideas, which often appeared without full acknowledgement in their writings.

The separation of academic sociology and its quantitative work from the Kelloggian model of the social survey was thus a gradual affair. The changes and the close connections between the various spheres of activity that contributed to the social survey may be seen in some of the careers of the members of the Columbia family. Ogburn, who was at the University of Washington before going to the National War Labor Board during the First World War, wrote the following in a 1919 letter of recommendation for Howard P. Woolston's career:

He has a good record of substantial achievement. His four-volume survey for the Factory Investigating Commission of New York is quite a splendid piece of work. He also drove home a [sic] excellent year's work with the Social Hygiene Society – making a survey of the whole U.S. He is now head of department of social, economic, and political science at the College of the City of New York, taking Clark's place who left to become president of some western state university. He studied under Tarde and Durkheim in France. Is thought highly of at the Univ. of Chicago as well as Columbia, having studied at both places. He was head worker in earlier years at Greenwich Settlement House. Is thought well of by the *Survey* group in New York, Paul Kellogg and others.[52]

Woolston had his first contact with sociology as a Divinity Student at Chicago, where he was briefly employed by Small. In his student years he worked at Harvard on a scheme to create a 'social museum' as part of the Peabody, and studied in Germany with Simmel. He spent the bulk of his academic career at Washington, which was the largest and most successful sociology department in the West in the interwar years, with a large faculty. In the twenties he chaired a multidisciplinary Committee on Community Research at the University, and proposed civic centre for Seattle designed to help serve to interpret the City to its citizens and others, with a 'sociological department' which would contain educational exhibits on such things as death rates sociologically subcategorised – a permanent form of the kind of exhibits that were part of the Springfield and Pittsburgh survey models.

This range of experiences was not atypical. A similar list of activities could be drawn up for the others in Woolston's cohort, such as Odum, Chapin, or Ogburn. The transitions from one employer to another were not absolute passages from one sphere to another. Connections were kept up, consulting work performed, and advisory roles continued to be played.[53] The range of activities of the members of the Columbia family expanded over time. T. J. Jones became a major figure in the promotion of practical education for Blacks in the South, and the strategies he promoted there were adopted by the British Colonial authorities in Africa, after a survey by the Phelps-Stokes African Education Commission.[54] Yet the topics as well as the focus on the community that were central concerns for the survey movement as it developed from the time of the Pittsburgh Survey to *Middletown* remained basic topics of concern to most of Giddings' students throughout their careers, which in several cases reached into the fifties. What was the relationship between the two bodies of work? What changed?

The students of Giddings prospered in academic sociology, and with the rise to prosperity of academic sociology, to an extent not generally recognised by historians of sociology, for whom the rise and fall of Chicago is the simpler and more dramatic story. There were six Columbia presidents of the American Sociological Society in the interwar era, Lichtenberger, Gillin, Ogburn, Odum, Chapin, and Hankins. They were each, in the language of the day, 'Giddings men', who shared a coherent methodological vision, and shared a great deal of Giddings' own theoretical vision and conception of the field. Odum edited *Social Forces*, and Hankins became the first *ASR* editor. The group almost totally controlled the sociology funded through the SSRC in its first five, and most successful, years. The Columbian group had an exceptional degree of social coherence. Giddings' FHG Club held reunion dinners at least into the twenties, and students would be recommended from one generation of Columbians to another as having been FHG Club members.[55] The ties were profitable in many ways. When Odum needed information on the situation in New York foundations, he could and did call on his graduate school peers, such as Ogburn, or even receive grants from those who had become foundation executives, such as T. J. Jones, who helped fund the Sea Islands research while at the Phelps Stokes foundation.[56] In short, the academic quantifiers in the Columbia family had the same roots as the survey movement, but they were broadly enough trained, and their methodological vision was sufficiently strong that they adapted — for example, to the changes in sources of funding and to the rise of quantitative psychology.

The survey movement represented by Kellogg, in contrast, could not adapt to the changed political climate of the twenties. The early survey model depended heavily on civic support and especially on voluntary participation. In the twenties, the simplicities of the pre-war reform idea no longer attracted the support of the professional classes, at least to the extent they had before. The paradoxes of patronage and dependence,[57] and the financial weakness of the Russell Sage Foundation, conspired against the survey idea. In his 1909 dissertation, Woolston wrote that his study was 'but a fragment of a complete investigation of neighborhood life' by which he meant one which dealt 'with housing conditions and home life, with business interests, social activities, political organization and general ethical tendencies'.[58] The study of fragments survived the ideal of comprehensiveness and the Behemoth efforts they entailed.

When the depression shifted power from the states to the federal government, academic sociology, with its broader methodological remit, particularly its capacity to deal with demographic change and with psychological aspects of social life, was better (though only slightly better) able to respond. Such pressing regional problems as the race problems of the south, the national problem of the migration of rural blacks to the urban north, and the general problem of the response to the newly visible Black presence, became central to the SSRC agenda. These topics were largely beyond the power of the local 'survey' to illuminate, and typically beyond the capacity of local establishments to face.

NOTES

1 Walker's father had himself been a member of a board which produced a survey-like study for Massachusetts (Charles F. Pidgin, *History of the Bureau of Statistics of Labor of Massachusetts and of Labor Legislation in that State from 1833 to 1876* (Boston: Wright & Potter, State Printers, 1876), p. 16).

2 Carroll Davison Wright: His Life and Statistical Works, L. L. Bernard Papers, Chicago, University of Chicago Library.

3 Quoted in Pidgin, *History of the Bureau of Statistics*, pp. 54–5.

4 Some of these researches were narrowly statistical. Most of them, however, included, and sometimes consisted of, what we would now call 'qualitative' material, including testimony by participants, folk-theorising by physicians and other persons with expertise, and the reproduction of responses to open-ended questions.

5 On Powell and the patronage of science in Washington in this period, see my 'The Survey in Nineteenth-Century American Geology: The Evolution of a Form of Patronage', *Minerva*, 25, 3 (1987), 282–330.

6 Giddings' contempt for Chicago sociology in general and Small in particular was intense, and this was communicated to and shared by his students. Yet Giddings himself remained personally on good terms with many of the sociologists who came out of the Chicago tradition. Even C. A. Ellwood, a Small student who often wrote for a liberal Protestant audience, had one of his explicitly religiously oriented books of the early twenties endorsed by Giddings.

7 Joseph Dorfman, 'The Department of Economics', in Gordon Hoxie, Sally F. Moore, Joseph Dorfman *et al.* (eds.), *A History of the Faculty of Political Science Columbia University* (Morningside Heights, NY: Columbia University Press, 1955), pp. 161–206; p. 173.

8 Dorfman, 'Department of Economics', p. 173.

9 Mayo-Smith to Mrs Mayo-Smith, 22 May, 1887, Mayo-Smith Papers.

10 The Teaching of Sociology at Cornell University, L. L. Bernard Papers, p. 2.

11 Charles Elmer Gehlke, L. L. Bernard Papers, p. 4.

12 Chaddock, Robert E., 'Social Statistics in the Faculty of Political Science', *Columbia University Quarterly*, 24 (1932), 431; Howard W. Odum, *American Sociology: The Story of Sociology in the United States through 1950* (New York: Greenwood Press, 1951), p. 61.

13 Kellogg facilitated the use of the records (J. S. Lowell and C. R. Lowell to Mayo-Smith, 22 March, 1894, Mayo-Smith Papers).

14 E. T. Devine, *When Social Work Was Young*, (New York: Macmillan, 1939), p. 35. One of the students who studied COS records was the author of one of the first Masters' theses done under Giddings, Elsie Clews Parsons, later to become famous as an anthropologist.

15 Gustav Kleene, 'The Statistical Study of Causes of Destitution', *Journal of the American Statistical Association*, 11 (1908), 284.

16 A. A. Tenney, Sociology at Columbia University, L. L. Bernard Papers, p. 7.

17 See Giddings to Odum, 11 Dec., 1924, Howard W. Odum Papers, Southern Historical Collection, Chapel Hill, University of North Carolina Library. Hankins even suggests 'that Giddings thought of himself as a potential Mayor of New York' (Frank H. Hankins, Oral History Collection, Columbia University).

18 John M. Glenn, Lillian Brandt and F. Emerson Andrews, *Russell Sage Foundations, 1907–1946*, vol. 1 (New York: Russell Sage Foundation, 1947), pp. 4–5.

19 Glenn *et al.*, *Russell Sage Foundation*, p. 8.

20 Giddings simply did not find the idea that the wealthy would serve the cause of genuine reform credible. He expressed his reservations on the subject in a paper, 'The Dangers of Charitable Trusts', published shortly after the establishment of the Russell Sage Foundation, at a time when his academic peers were applauding the prospective contributions of the fund to social change (Glenn *et al.*, *Russell Sage Foundation*, p. 17). The foundations were equally suspicious of Giddings; Lawrence Frank, an ISRR and Rockefeller insider, at the time of the negotiations for the Chicago Local Community Research Grant, insisted that they take care to avoid drilling 'their ideas into their students' heads' in the fashion of Giddings (Quoted in Martin Bulmer, *The Chicago School of Sociology: Institutionalization, Diversity, and the Rise of Sociological Research* (Chicago: University of Chicago Press, 1984), p. 142).

21 Devine, *When Social Work Was Young*, p. 73.

22 Quoted in Lowry Nelson, *Rural Sociology: Its Origins and Growth in the United States* (Minneapolis: University of Minnesota Press, 1969), p. 29.

23 The labour problem and its various solutions, such as profit-sharing, trade-unionism, and syndicalism, were interests of Giddings to the end of his life. (See 'An Intensive Sociology: A Project', *American Journal of Sociology*, 36 (1930), 13). One of the few

dissertations to which Giddings wrote an introduction was Louis Levine's *Syndicalism in France*, which had a high reputation among Giddings' students (Ogburn to Odum, 17 April, 1923, Odum Papers).

24 Thomas Jesse Jones, *The Sociology of a New York City Block* (New York: AMS Press, 1968), p. 7.

25 Jones, *City Block*, p. 7.

26 Jones, *City Block*, p. 135.

27 Jones, *City Block*, p. 7.

28 Jones, *City Block*, p. 8.

29 Virtually the same sequence from settlement canvassing to more 'scientific' description is found in H. B. Woolston's *A Study of the Population of Manhattanville* (Studies in History, Economics and Public Law 93 (1909) who cites Jones, Booth, Rowntree, and the Hull House and (Boston) South End House studies. Woolston's approach is more exclusively demographic than in Jones', but he treats this as a flaw, and embraces both the ideal of a comprehensive survey and the idea that the aim of the survey is to aid in the creation of a 'comprehensive scheme of betterment' (p. 5) which he thought would best be pursued through socialisation and the schools, but with an eye to local variation in neighbourhood communities. This enterprise is described in the theoretical vocabulary of Giddings as a product of like response to like stimuli (pp. 7–8).

30 Jones, *City Block*, p. 10.

31 Jones, *City Block*, p. 10.

32 Jones, *City Block*, p. 10.

33 Jones, *City Block*, p. 11.

34 Jones, *City Block*, p. 12.

35 Jones, *City Block*, p. 12.

36 Jones, *City Block*, pp. 14–15.

37 Somes of this was based on observation of the house and its contents. Thus drinking habits were indicated by the 'vichy bottle' in the houses of the Jews, the beer-bucket in that of the Irish. Jones, *City Block*, p. 15.

38 Jones, *City Block*, p. 60.

39 Jones, *City Block*, p. 129.

40 Jones, *City Block*, p. 129.

41 Albion Small and George E. Vincent, *An Introduction to the Science of Society* (New York: American Book Co., 1894).

42 An idea with obvious Comtean origins. As a Cambridge student, Pearson had come under the influence of a Comtean librarian.

43 Franklin Henry Giddings, *Inductive Sociology: A Syllabus of Methods, Analyses and Classifications, and Provisionally Formulated Laws* (New York: Macmillan, 1901), p. 181.

44 Giddings, *Inductive Sociology*, pp. 286–90.

45 Giddings, *Inductive Sociology*, p. 75.

46 Giddings, *Inductive Sociology*, p. 175.

47 P. W. Althouse, *The Intellectual Career of F. Stuart Chapin* (New York: Columbia University Press, 1980), p. 228. These systems, on which Chapin himself was put to work, were not so far removed, conceptually, from Chapin's own living-room scale of the late twenties. Some of the examples in *Field Work and Social Research* (New York:

Century, 1920), may be seen as an intermediate step (e.g. pp. 148–9). For other historically proximate sources, see Jean Converse, *Survey Research in the United States* (Berkeley: University of California Press, 1987, pp. 34, 426). It may be noted that Chapin was himself the product of a reform-oriented Brooklyn family which included a former mayor.

48 Franklin H. Giddings, 'Exploration and Survey', *Journal of Social Forces*, 3 (1925), 206.

49 'Socialisation' in this sense is the theme of the classical studies in rural sociology by Charles J. Galpin. See his *Rural Life* (New York: Century, 1920).

50 Giddings wrote the introduction to the 'methodological' volume in the series, Luther Fry's Columbia dissertation, (*Diagnosing the Rural Church: A Study in Method* (New York: George H. Doran, 1924)). In the thirties and later this kind of work was subject to severe criticism on much-overstated grounds as the problem of ecological correlation. The strategy has since revived. The Columbia people were well aware of the difficulties with interpreting partials, as is evident in the volume produced by Stuart Rice's Committee on Social Statistics of the American Statistical Association. See Ogburn, 'Statistical Studies of Marriage and the Family', in Stuart Rice (ed.), *Statistics in Social Studies*, (Philadelphia: University of Pennsylvania Press, 1930), p. 29. Nor were they unaware of the problems with what was to be claimed as the solution, the elaboration model. See F. A. Ross, 'The Use of Statistical Data and Techniques in Sociology', in L. L. Bernard (ed.), *The Fields and Methods of Sociology* (New York: Ray Long & Richard R. Smith, 1934), pp. 458–75; p. 469.

51 Suzzalo was himself an educationalist who had taught the first course in Educational Sociology at Columbia, and a prominent figure in foundation circles, especially the Carnegie Foundation.

52 Ogburn to Suzzalo, 10 April, 1919, Presidential Papers, University of Washington Archives, Seattle, Washington.

53 Odum, for example, had at the beginning of his career a position with a municipal bureau in Philadelphia, and continued his relationship with Philadelphia reform groups long after going to North Carolina. This was quite common.

54 The later part of the Jones story is told in Edward H. Berman, 'Educational Colonialism in Africa: the Role of American Foundations, 1910–1945', in Robert F. Arnove (ed.), *Philanthropy and Cultural Imperialism* (Boston: G. K. Hall, 1980), pp. 179–201.

55 Ogburn to Odum, 3 May, 1922. Odum Papers.

56 E.g. Ogburn to Odum, 18 January, 1924; Guy B. Johnson and Guion G. Johnson, *Research in Service to Society: The First Fifty Years of the Institute for Research in Social Science at the University of North Carolina* (Chapel Hill: University of North Carolina Press, 1980), pp. 50–1.

57 In a sense, surveys of the Kelloggian sort, which relied very heavily on local professionals for advice and participation, were in effect consensus building devices. The full realisation of the survey as a means of reforms required the support of the leading business and professional classes to make the survey relevant to the community and of course to carry the reforms out. The interests of these groups were ultimately in conflict with the ideas of movement figures like Kellogg, or at least potentially so.

58 Woolston, *Manhattanville*, p. 6.

CHAPTER ELEVEN

The decline of the Social Survey Movement and the rise of American empirical sociology

MARTIN BULMER

When the report of the President's Committee on *Recent Social Trends* was published in 1933, it contained almost no trace of evidence produced by the Social Survey Movement, despite the fact that Shelby M. Harrison was Secretary-Treasurer of the committee and one of its six members, and that by this period there had been over 2,000 social surveys carried out in the United States. The contributors to the content of the report were predominantly although not entirely academic social scientists, chosen by William Ogburn, Howard Odum and Charles Merriam, who dominated the work of the committee. Among outside contributors, foundation officials such as Lawrence K. Frank writing about childhood and youth were more in evidence than the proponents of the social survey in its early form. The evidence which contributors drew upon was of various kinds, including historical materials, official statistics, organisation records, and the results of social science field studies, but they did not include social survey data. The Pittsburgh and Springfield Surveys were not mentioned, nor was *The Philadelphia Negro*. Though only one case, *Recent Social Trends* was a major summary of the state of knowledge of American society around 1930 compiled by a group dominated by empirically-oriented social scientists. The ommission of any reference to the social survey is therefore all the more remarkable. And it brings to light a paradox and exposes a discontinuity in the history of American empirical social science which it is the aim of this chapter to explore.

PARALLELISM AND DISCONTINUITY

The paradox in the history of social investigation in the United States before 1930 is that the Social Survey Movement and surveys conducted in the manner of Booth such as the *Hull-House Maps and Papers* did not make

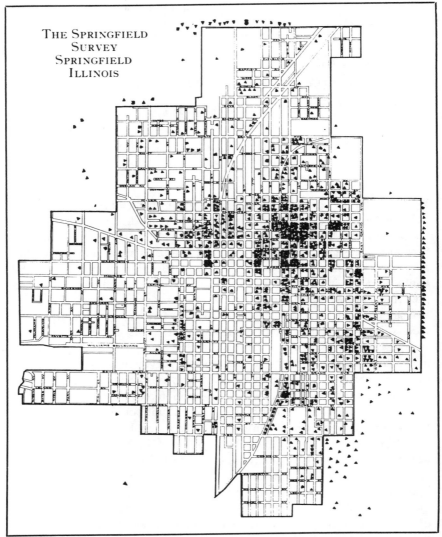

THE SPRINGFIELD
SURVEY
SPRINGFIELD
ILLINOIS

Map 7   Size and extent of the charities problem.

a significant impact upon the empirical social science which emerged
between 1900 and 1930. In sociology, political science and social
psychology, other methods of research were developed which by-passed
the social survey as it had emerged between 1890 and 1920. And there was
marked discontinuity between the early social surveys, the predominant

methods of research in sociology and political science during the interwar period, and the modern, post-1935 sample survey.

The origins of the modern sample survey, as Jean Converse has recently shown, lay in part in these academic developments – for example, in attitude measurement in psychology, in part in the more extensive application of probability sampling methods to human populations, and in part to the advent of studies of populations in the mass for commercial and media clients, to understand the workings of the armed forces, and to study political behaviour.[1] But the connection with the early social surveys was somewhat tenuous in the United States, whereas there was a much greater degree of continuity in Britain. Indeed, the modern sample survey has had such different origins and so differs from these origins that one wonders whether the sharing of a common name is more misleading than otherwise. In the Introduction a distinction was made between the geographically-local survey, discussed in this book, and the modern sample survey. The same distinction will be used here.

The American social surveys discussed in earlier chapters were carried out apart from, or on the margins of, academic social science as it was constituted from the late nineteenth century onwards. There was some input from academic advisers to Florence Kelley and Paul Kellogg, described in chapters 4 and 9, but in the main the studies were conducted and supported independently of academic auspices, and aimed at a general audience in the wider society. The purposes of the social surveyors were often different from those of the main figures in the developing social science disciplines, so it is not surprising that there was divergence. What *is* surprising, however, is that there was so little borrowing or sharing in terms of the research methods used.

THE SOCIAL SURVEY MOVEMENT

The Social Survey Movement, which developed and flourished in the United States in the first three decades of the twentieth century, owed its existence to the benefactions of Mrs Russell Sage, who relied heavily on her legal counsel, Robert W. De Forest. As well as being lawyer to railroad, banking and insurance companies, De Forest was the leading figure in New York philanthropy, president of both the Charity Organisation Society from 1888 and the National Conference on Charities and Corrections from 1903, and co-author of a study of the tenement house problem.[2] He advised Mrs Russell Sage to adopt a flexible strategy for philanthropic activity since given 'constant change and shift of social conditions, and extension, or it

Social Surveys By State 1854 - 1927

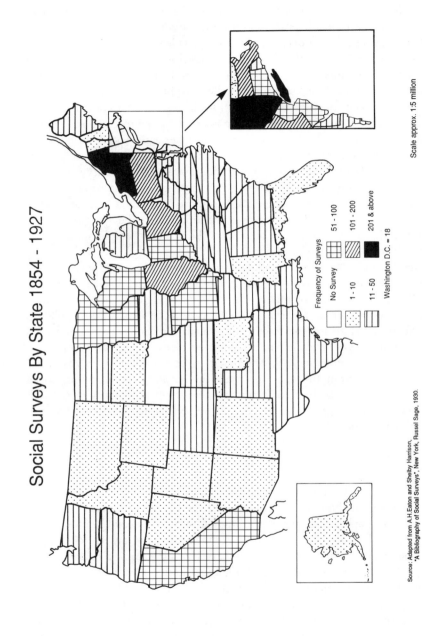

Frequency of Surveys

No Survey	51 - 100
1 - 10	101 - 200
11 - 50	201 & above

Washington D.C. = 18

Scale approx. 1:5 million

Source: Adapted from A.H.Eaton and Shelby Harrison,
"A Bibliography of Social Surveys", New York, Russel Sage, 1930.

Map 8   Social surveys in the United States by state, 1854–1927.

may be contraction, of the sphere of government activity, the future may develop other and greater needs for philanthropic action than any which is now apparent'.[3] The policy of the Foundation, whose trustees included former president of Johns Hopkins University, Daniel Coit Gillman, was 'to take up the larger and more difficult problems' and to pay attention to issues not provided for in existing philanthropic activity.[4]

The Foundation supported the Pittsburgh Survey, discussed by Steven Cohen in chapter 9, after it was initially supported on a small budget by the New York-based Charities Publication Committee. For a period it was the only study of its type apart from a study of the Polish section of the city of Buffalo. Growing interest in the potential of the survey method led to a number of cities seeking advice from the *Survey* magazine and from the Russell Sage Foundation.

The Russell Sage Department of Surveys and Exhibits

In 1912 the Russell Sage Foundation established the Department of Surveys and Exhibits, directed by Shelby M. Harrison, who had worked on the Pittsburg Survey. A graduate of Northwestern University, with graduate work at Harvard and Boston Universities, Harrison had also worked on *The Survey*, directed the Syracuse survey and the fieldwork for the Birmingham, Alabama survey. The purpose of the department was to spread the survey idea and to develop further methods of survey research.[5] The Department's aim also was to present information gathered from such sources to wider audiences through public exhibits.

The purpose was something more than the centralising of inquiries regarding surveys and exhibits. Beyond that was a conviction that the Survey, including the survey and other popular methods of educating the public, was proving a sound and an effective measure for preventing and correcting conditions that are wrong, and for quickening community forces that are showing promise. It was recognised that important changes in our national life and community relationships ... had brought new problems calling for study, and that in dealing with the new needs the usefulness of the survey as an organised method of social discovery, and the exhibit as an agency for popular interpretation, had been demonstrated. The aim always was not to humiliate the city but to inform it.[6]

The Department sponsored the survey of Springfield, Illinois, a town of some 60,000 people. This survey, directed by Harrison, was one of the main studies carried out in this tradition.

The Springfield Survey illustrates the character of surveys conducted in the style of the Social Survey Movement. It relied heavily upon local volunteers to gather the evidence used in the study. It used a diversity of

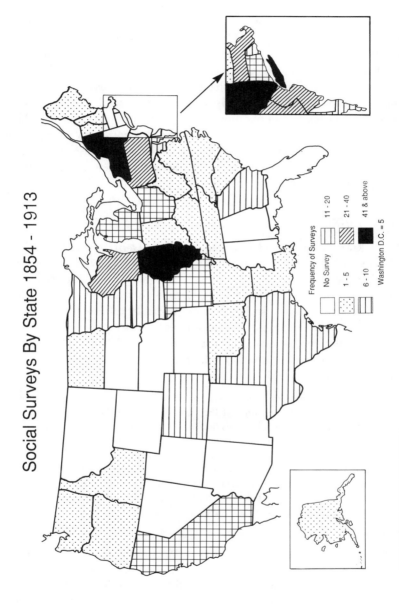

Social Surveys By State 1854 - 1913

Frequency of Surveys

No Survey   11 - 20

1 - 5   21 - 40

6 - 10   41 & above

Washington D.C. = 5

Scale approx. 1:5 million

Source: Adapted from A.H.Eaton and Shelby Harrison,
"A Bibliography of Social Surveys", New York, Russel Sage, 1930.

Map 9   Social surveys in the United States by state, 1854–1913.

methods of gathering data including use of the records of local organisations and institutions, studies of particular agencies in operation, observations of conditions throughout the city, interviews and written inquiries of knowledgeable informants, and some intensive studies in certain sections of the city. It had weighty local sponsorship, and its results were presented in an exhibition in the First Regiment Armory which attracted thousands of visitors. The journalistic element predominated, both in the methods of data collection and in the presentation of the results to a wider public. The Springfield Survey represented a kind of populist version of the social survey, with more emphasis upon the reception of the results by a wide audience than on the penetration of the data collection or analysis.

Shelby Harrison indeed later explicitly acknowledged that the survey movement fostered an amalgam of several different activities.

It is not scientific research alone, nor journalism alone, nor social planning alone, nor any one other type of social or civic endeavour; it is a combination of a number of these. In its best form the survey unites the contributions of the research worker who brings to light new information bearing upon related problems and needs in a definite locality, of the experienced social planner in offering suggestions for improvements based upon new knowledge, and the expert in educational publicity in spreading widely both the information and the suggestions, and in interpreting their significance.[7]

The 1920s and the Survey Graphic

There followed in the 1920s an increasing number of such surveys, some general studies of a community and some specialised investigations of particular topics, more reminiscent of nineteenth-century studies of sanitation and housing. The sponsorship was a mixture of local civic bodies, Schools of Social Welfare, and the Russell Sage Department of Surveys and Exhibits which continued in active existence. Specialist topics investigated included education, recreation, employment, industrial relations and crime. Some surveys had academic sponsorship. In the field of crime, for example, the Cleveland Survey of 1921 was directed by Roscoe Pound and Felix Frankfurter, the Missouri Crime Survey of 1926 by Raymond Moley of Columbia. For the most part, however, such surveys were undertaken by non-academic workers, usually associated with the worlds of social welfare and local philanthropy, with a dash of reform politics.

The Survey, of which Paul Kellogg became the editor, was the main channel of communication among this constituency. From 1922 it was published in two parts, the *Survey Mid-Monthly*, aimed at an audience of professional social workers, and the *Survey Graphic*, an illustrated magazine

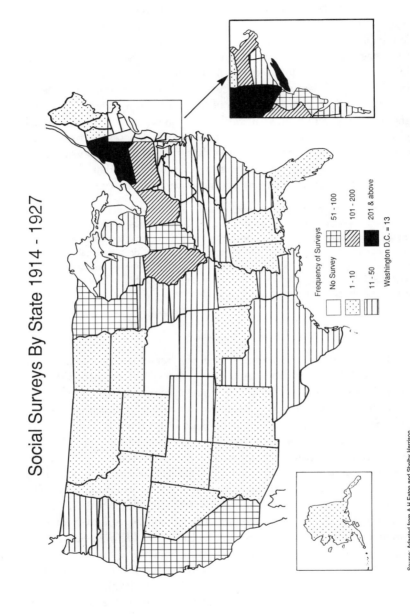

Social Surveys By State 1914 - 1927

Frequency of Surveys

No Survey	51 - 100
1 - 10	101 - 200
11 - 50	201 & above

Washington D.C. = 13

Scale approx. 1:5 million

Source: Adapted from A.H.Eaton and Shelby Harrison,
"A Bibliography of Social Surveys", New York, Russel Sage, 1930.

Map 10   Social surveys in the United States by state, 1914–27.

aiming to popularise the findings of social inquiry to a wide audience.[8] It drew on the work and ideas of social scientists, some of whom were also contributors, but it embodied a particular ideological ethos; 'Robert Marion LaFollette was the *Graphic's* favourite politician – after his death in 1925 there was none until Senator Robert Wagner came along ... The British Fabians and the British labour movement were still its models of what democracy applied might mean for human welfare'.[9] It had, however, a distinctively American character, both in its democratic and populist appeal (reflecting the conception of the social survey as a vehicle for publicity and community consciousness) and it sought to harness expertise to the solution of social problems. The *Survey Graphic* stood for experimentation in all phases of modern life and the application of the latest specialist knowledge to that end. Social and region planning, the engineering of society, featured prominently in its pages, reflecting the ideas of, among others, Patrick Geddes and Lewis Mumford. This, then, was an indication of the type of audience beyond the locality to which the social survey of the 1920s was aimed.

THE SOCIAL SURVEY AND ACADEMIC SOCIAL SCIENCE

The activities of the Social Survey Movement were clearly well-known in the social science community of the time.[10] Several books and articles on the social survey were either written by sociologists or used by them in their courses, there were sociological theses on the social survey, and sessions at the American Sociological Society annual meetings.[11] The discussion here focuses upon sociologists at the University of Chicago, the dominant department in American sociology, particularly at the graduate level, between 1920 and about 1935. The discussion is not intended to suggest that developments elsewhere were unimportant but rather that by looking at the situation in the leading department of the period, which was extremely productive of empirical research, some understanding may be gained of the relationship between the Social Survey Movement and sociology and other social sciences. It may be that this account dwells too strongly upon the academic centre and neglects developments at the periphery – in the West and the South, for example, in state universities and land-grant institutions – as well as in fields such as rural sociology which were marginal to mainstream social science. Chicago was not the only centre, however dominant in the 1920 and 1930s; its influence lay as a centre for graduate training and for establishing some of the main trends in sociological research at this period.

At an earlier period, as Stephen Turner suggests in the previous chapter, Columbia had been as or more dominant than Chicago, and students of Franklin Giddings such as J. M. Williams and N. L. Sims had conducted studies of small towns which might be termed surveys.[12] At this period there were no effective rivals of Chicago dominance in research. Harvard scarcely had any sociologists on its staff, Columbia under an ageing Giddings was in decline, and Chapel Hill, though a strong regional center, had relatively little impact outside the South.[13]

Robert E. Park

At the University of Chicago, W. I. Thomas showed little interest in the social survey as a method of research. He once wrote that 'interviews in the main may be treated as a body of error to be used for purposes of comparison in future observations'.[14] Robert Park, however, whom Thomas persuaded to come to the university from 1913 onwards, was much more interested in the social survey; indeed, he gave courses on the subject. The syllabus of his 1918 course on the social survey read:

An examination of current methods of social investigation, the diagnosis of social problems, and the formulation of community programs; the applications and limitations of the survey method; its relationship to statistical and case studies, the devices employed in the presentation and publication of social facts and survey findings; the role of the expert and the 'survey committee'; the function of publicity as a means of social reform and social control.[15]

Park's interest was not in the survey as a method of research but as the social survey as a social movement, a method of publicity, and a means of shaping public opinion. In his essay on 'The City' in 1915, he suggested that the Russell Sage Foundation surveys, the work of the New York Bureau of Municipal Research, and local social surveys across the country were really higher forms of journalism, dealing with existing conditions critically and seeking through the agency of publicity to bring about radical reforms. He contrasted the American survey with its European counterparts, which were undertaken to inform officials and politicians, not to contribute to public debate.

It is an interesting and singular thing that what we call a 'movement' should connect itself with what is essentially a mere device, a device for investigating and reporting social facts ... it is interesting also that the survey, in the form that it has taken in recent years, is peculiar to America — at least, if not peculiar to America, gained its greatest popularity here and to a lesser extent in England.[16]

Both Park and Ernest Burgess were familiar with the range of surveys carried out and taught their students about them. Park in his lectures distinguished between the more scientific and factual kind of survey, represented by Booth and Rowntree and Elmer's text[17] and the more publicity-oriented survey, represented *par excellence* by the Pittsburgh Survey and Aronovici's text. His lectures in 1917–20 included references to the poverty studies of Booth and Rowntree and to the *Hull-House Maps and Papers*. Writing in 1929, he explicitly linked the urban studies which he, Burgess and their students had undertaken to traditions of local surveys, referring to Booth and Rowntree, surveys associated with the Settlement House movement, the Chicago studies of Edith Abbott and Sophonisba Breckenridge in Social Service Administration, the Pittsburgh and Springfield Surveys, the *Survey of Criminal Justice in Cleveland* of 1922, and *The Negro in Chicago* of the same year.[18] At the same time Park made clear the differences from the type of study he and his collaborators had undertaken.

THE NEGRO IN CHICAGO

The Negro in Chicago was the result of research carried out for the Chicago Commission on Race Relations set up by the Governor of Illinois in the wake of the 1919 race riots in which over fifty people, most of them black, were killed. Robert Park's involvement is instructive in regard to ideas about social investigation among sociologists in the early 1920s. The research work of the Commission was in charge of Graham Romeyn Taylor, the journalist son of Graham Taylor, assisted by black sociology graduate student Charles S. Johnson, a student of Park at the University of Chicago. Johnson conducted the research for the Commission, which bore strong traces of Park's influence.[19] The study used some of the methods later used by Park's students, including the collection of personal documents, direct observation and an intensive content analysis of press coverage of race issues. Official statistics were used, including census returns, and a questionnaire was sent by mail to 860 employers in the city. The research also involved, however, two large-scale surveys of the black population. To find out about housing, 274 families living in all parts of the city were interviewed.

Three negro women, well equipped to deal sympathetically and intelligently with these families, gathered this information. These 274 families lived in 238 blocks, the distribution being such that no type of neighbourhood or division of the Negro population was overlooked. The questionnaire employed contained five pages of questions and required an interview of about two hours. Special effort was made to secure social information without the aid of leading questions.[20]

In the field of labour, the commission carried out personal interviews with black employees in selected industries, including meat packing, iron and steel, laundries, hotels, railroads and the needle trades, to complement interviews with employers and round table conferences. Though few details were given in the report, apparently 865 black employees were interviewed by a black interviewer either at home or at work.

For both surveys, the results were analysed by simple frequency distributions, followed by extended quotation and the use of individual case studies. This study showed an advance on the Social Survey movement type of survey, in that it was focused upon a scientific problem, saw the need to avoid leading questions, and racially matched interviewers. On the other hand, the analysis of data was almost non-existent, reflecting the lack of understanding of the potential of such individualised data for the study of interrelations at the time. (By contrast, the value of aggregate data was well-appreciated.) It was as if there was an intuitive sense of the value of collecting extensive data about individuals in the population being studied, without the necessary knowledge either about sampling or how to handle the data once collected other than compute simple counts of characteristics and then treat respondents on a case-by-case basis.

Ernest Burgess

Ernest Burgess had even closer acquaintance with the social survey than Robert Park. Burgess had gained his PhD at Chicago in 1913, and then taught from 1913 to 1915 at the University of Kansas, While there,

I had come into contact with the social survey movement under Shelby Harrison; I had made the recreation study for the Topeka Survey [carried out by the Russell Sage Department], had cooperated with the Health Department of the university in making a study of Belleville, Kansas, and then made a social survey of Lawrence.[21]

The study of Lawrence was carried out under his head of department, F. W. Blackmar, but Burgess provided the main research input. It followed the conventional pattern for surveys of the period. It was a descriptive account, using data gathered with the cooperation of a committee of local notables, under such headings as land and people, city planning, municipal adminstration, public health and sanitation, housing and charity. The chapters on delinquency and court cases did, however, show an interest in the potentialities of more rigorous measurement, including counts of the number of delinquent children in the city, their distribution by district, and the calculation of rates to show variation.[22]

Shortly after his appointment at the University of Chicago in 1916,

Burgess published an article about the social survey in the *American Journal of Sociology*. His conception of the survey was little different from Park's, placing the main emphasis upon its role as a means of promoting community consciousness. 'Community self-study under expert direction is democracy being at school to the social scientist. The social survey is to the community what the demonstration station is to the farmer.'[23] He did emphasise the value of the survey as a means of research training.

Society is the laboratory of the sociologist. The social survey provides a unique opportunity both for investigation and for social construction, both for the analysis of mental attitudes and for the control of forces in seeming improvement. To the advanced student the social survey affords severe and stimulating training in the technique of investigation and in the art of social action.[24]

The article was in the main a summing up of the Kansas experience rather than a statement of how research was to be conducted at Chicago. Although in the next few years Burgess taught a course of the causes and prevention of poverty, and a surviving document shows that he and Park contemplated carrying out a survey of Hyde Park in the early 1920s,[25] once settled in the department Burgess moved away from the social survey to what he considered more scientific methods of first-hand observation, mapping and the use of aggregate census tract data.

The social survey and the sociological survey

The distinction between the social survey and the research methods Chicago sociologists were using was made clear in Park's Preface to Emory Bogardus' *The New Social Research* in 1926, which gave an account of the methods used in the Race Relations Survey of the Pacific Coast, in which he collaborated with Park. Park concluded that

[t]he social investigators in the past have been very largely social politicians, interested in formulating programs and initiating policies. They are now, however, ambitious to go further, and conduct experiments. They are beginning to check up on the social experiments already in process. Experiment, however, in the scientific sense, seeks to formulate and test hypotheses; and social research, in the strict scientific sense, is confined to investigation based on hypotheses. In the present volume the term research has been used in a somewhat wider sense, to include exploration as well as experiment, In the most limited sense of the word, I should say that a survey is never research, – it is explorations; it seeks to define problems rather than test hypotheses.[26]

The reference to 'social politicians' and interest in problems and policies underlined the extent to which Park saw the social survey as distinct from sociology, which was concerned with the development of a science, which tested hypotheses and sought to frame general explanations of human behaviour.

This distinction was embodied in the research methods text of 1928 written by Vivien Palmer, who was the coordinator of the urban research programme directed by Park and Burgess. Palmer distinguished between the Social Survey Movement and the 'sociological survey', emphasising that the latter was not concerned with reform and amelioration but with 'the scientific discovery of how human societies function'.[27] Though both types of survey focused on particular communities, the sociological survey did so in order to compare them with other communities and to abstract social processes and patterns. The sociologist was interested in normal as well as pathological behaviour. Unlike the reformers, he was not trying to prove particular points and could make an 'unpartisan, unhurried stand that can lead to discoveries of scientific caliber'.[28] The social survey provided a snapshot of existing conditions, while the sociological survey aimed to penetrate beneath the surface to define problems for research and to abstract from the data the processes of social organisation and the processes that had produced those patterns. By comparison, the conventional social survey was a 'stagnant backwater'.[29] The sociologist should not pattern his work on the social survey but develop his own type of research to meet his own particular needs.

The same distinction appears in Pauline Young's text published in 1939. Dr Young was a product of the Chicago Sociology Department whose monograph on *The Pilgrims of Russian Town* had been published by the University of Chicago Press. She distinguished between the Social Survey Movement, which was described in some detail, and social research, the beginnings of which was traced to the work of W. I. Thomas. The social survey was concerned primarily with social problems and social planning and even then did not analyse social problems in great depth. Social research was distinguished by its greater scope, its formulation of hypotheses or propositions about social action, and the attempt to formulate theories or laws to explain social phenomena.[30]

THE INSTITUTE OF SOCIAL AND RELIGIOUS RESEARCH AND *MIDDLETOWN*

The modern social survey had roots earlier in the century in the United States other than the Social Survey Movement. The Country Life Movement in the first decade of the century undertook inquiries into social conditions in rural areas, and had some some influence on the establishment within the Department of Agriculture in 1919 of a department for research into rural life under Charles J. Galpin. Carl C. Taylor, author of a monograph on the social survey, was subsequently director.[31] Another important source of investigation was the Institute of Social and Religious Research (ISSR), set up from the ruins of the Interchurch World Movement in 1921. Concerned with the health of the church in small towns and the countryside, it conducted a number of studies focused around the church, and a massive monograph on *The Town and Country Church in the United States* in 1923.[32]

The importance of the ISSR for the future lay, however, in other studies which it promoted. One which did not have a positive outcome was Robert Park's Race Relations Survey on the Pacific Coast, referred to above. Park clashed with the ISSR in 1924 over their attempts to modify his conclusions, a clear example of the difference in orientation between the more detached scientist and the more committed ameliorist organisation.[33] The ISSR were also the sponsors of the first study of Muncie, Indiana, by Robert and Helen Lynd. 'The result was *Middletown*,[34] the first sociological inquiry to attract wide and enduring public attention ... [which] studied, for the first time, the full round of life of all sectors of the population of an entire urban community.'[35] Robert Lynd was a clergyman who joined the research programme of the Institute to undertake this study of a 'typical' American town. The methods of research used, however, owed more to anthropology than to the social survey, and the eventual study was more important as a model for sociological community research than as securing continuity from the variant of the survey tradition from which it stemmed.[36]

SOCIAL REFORM AND SOCIAL SCIENCE IN THE 1920S

There was apparent by the 1920s an increasingly sharp line between research done with a reformist and ameliorative purpose on the one hand, and research with a scientific purpose on the other. This was a period in the development of the social sciences in the United States at which two tendencies were apparent. One was the thrust toward the much more extensive empirical study of the contemporary world, evident in psychology, economics, political science and sociology alike.[37] In political science, for example, Charles Merriam and his associates turned political science in a much more empirical direction, in the case of Merriam and Harold Gosnell, indeed, carrying out survey studies of non-voting which anticipated modern survey research by some ten years.[38] At the same time,

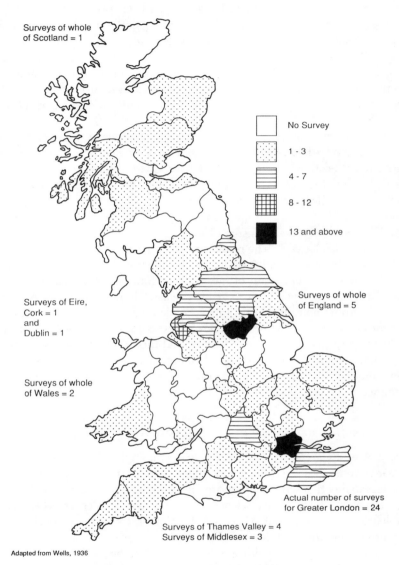

Surveys of whole
of Scotland = 1

No Survey

1 - 3

4 - 7

8 - 12

13 and above

Surveys of Eire,
Cork = 1
and
Dublin = 1

Surveys of whole
of England = 5

Surveys of whole
of Wales = 2

Actual number of surveys
for Greater London = 24

Surveys of Thames Valley = 4
Surveys of Middlesex = 3

Adapted from Wells, 1936

Map 11   Social surveys in Britain by county, 1886–1935.

such social scientists were insistent that their investigations were conducted in a scientific spirit, that is, they were part of a wider scientific enterprise which included the building of theory and the understanding of general processes.

This is clear from Park's preface to *The New Social Research*. The Social Survey Movement was not part of such a scientific movement, and its methods of research were seen as tainted by social involvements and partisanship which ill-befitted the social scientist. This was true in economics, political science and sociology. In economics, Wesley Mitchell in establishing the National Bureau of Economic Research in 1920 was most insistent that it should be free from political partisanship, devising a dual system of control involving an independent board of directors to try to insure impartiality in the results produced. In political science, despite his own earlier involvements in reform politics, Charles Merriam espoused a severely scientific conception of the subject. He made strenuous efforts to separate the study of public administration, for example, from municipal reform movements, though the foundations whom he approached for support, particularly the Laura Spelman Rockefeller Memorial, remained sceptical that the distinction could be quite so sharply drawn.

In sociology, both Robert Park in his programme at Chicago and Robert Lynd in his study of Middletown in different ways distanced themselves from the type of study typical of the Social Survey Movement, though in Lynd's case he was closer to that model at the outset of his fieldwork. In Lynd's case he sought advice from academic social scientists, and it may be that they reinforced his determination to carry out a different kind of study.

This conception of social science reached its apogee in *Recent Social Trends*. Ogburn and Odum aspired to produce a purely objective description of contemporary society in the United States, from which all bias and, indeed, any trace of commitment, were meant to be entirely excluded.[39] In fact, Ogburn and Lynd clashed bitterly over Lynd's chapter on consumer behaviour on precisely this point, Ogburn attempting to insist that all evaluative statements be removed.[40] What is significant here is not the validity of the view that Wesley Mitchell, Merriam, Park, Lynd or Ogburn took of what they were doing, for indeed one can point to inconsistencies and over-optimism in their programmes. The fact that they held such views and acted upon them in seeking to establish their fields as empirical social sciences was what mattered. 'If men define situations as real, they are real in their consequences.' In the process of espousing a scientific conception of social science, the possibility of any continuity between the Social Survey Movement and later developments was undermined.

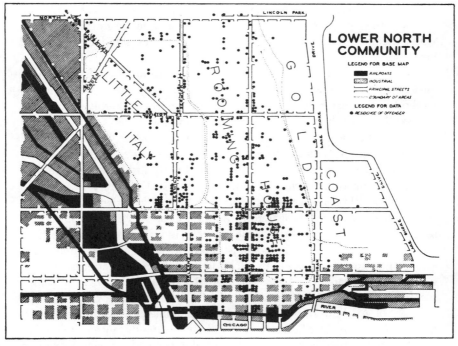

Map 12   Crime in the Lower North Community, Chicago, 1924.

A different type of development, but one with significance for sociological research methods, was the growth of demography in the United States in the inter-war period.[41] In Britain early demographic research had no connection to sociology; in the United States it did, with scholars such as William Ogburn, Samuel Stouffer and Philip Hauser, all connected to the University of Chicago, conducting demographic research. Stouffer in the early 1930s spent time in London with the English statisticians Pearson, Yule and Bowley. Hauser moved later in the 1930s to the US Census Bureau, where he began to recruit significant numbers of sociologists.[42] The close connection between demography and sociology may be traced back to this period. It also had consequences for the modes of analysis used by sociologists. Although these demographers did not conduct surveys, they were developing methods of quantitative analysis with a statistical basis which could be adapted to the sample survey when it was more widely adopted. The research interests of Stouffer exemplify this transition.[43]

THE DECLINE AND DISAPPEARANCE OF THE SOCIAL SURVEY MOVEMENT

The Social Survey Movement, indeed, faded out in the later 1920s. One limitation from which it suffered, which partly accounts for its invisibility in *Recent Social Trends*, was that surveys were local enterprises, confined to a single community. Social scientists were increasingly interested in the regional level, as in Odum's work at Chapel Hill, or the national level, as in the work of the President's Committee. To such concerns the local social survey had little to offer, while notions of national probability samples were still some way off.

A more important change was the growth of alternative sources of support for large-scale social science research, whose conception of investigation was different from that which prevailed in philanthropic circles in New York and in *The Survey* magazine. The entry of the Carnegie Corporation and of the Laura Spelman Rockefeller Memorial into the funding of university social science had a transforming effect, not least because the officials of such foundations were themselves either trained in social science or had themselves been social scientists. James Angell at the Carnegie Corporation had been professor of psychology at the University of Chicago, Beardsley Ruml at the Memorial had a Chicago PhD in psychology and had worked as an applied psychologist at Carnegie University and in the War Department before moving to New York.[44]

These foundations, unlike Russell Sage, were much more oriented to scientific study of society grounded in the basic social sciences. In the case of the Memorial, the attacks on ill-judged Rockefeller Foundation sponsorship of industrial research in 1915 had made the trustees extremely wary of any kind of normative tinge to research supported, and one of Ruml's early measures was to draw up a careful definition of the scope of the Memorial's interests, which specifically excluded support for projects which had reform as one of their aims. The Memorial and on a lesser scale the Carnegie Corporation made possible many of the developments of empirical social science referred to earlier, although to a large extent they reflected trends already taking place in university social science. There was an elective affinity between the two, which were mutually supportive, rather than a change engineered from without by the foundations.

Social investigation had moved from an amateur, episodic, reformist phase in the 1890s to one which was professionalised, scientific in orientation and aspired to be cumulative by the 1930s. This is to overstate the contrast, but there is no doubt that the claims of the social sciences to special expertise in the investigation of society had hardened in the intervening period. If they still found it difficult to get those claims taken seriously in government, they nevertheless embodied a very different conception of social inquiry from that of the early local social surveyors. The stance of social scientists by the end of the period was more detached, more olympian, but at the same time they made implicit claims to greater authority by virtue of their standing as professional experts.[45] They now addressed regional or national issues as much as local ones. Their audience lay with national policy makers and their state counterparts, as well as professional practitioners and other elite groups. Local audiences and publicity for the results of research were of secondary importance; short-run social amelioration was not their primary concern, and they played no part in the education of agents of social intervention, social workers.

To be sure, the advance of 'science' in social science was not simply a matter of the progress of scientific method. Its appeal and authority was not universally recognised, and among historians (and some social scientists) there is much ambivalence about the trends which it represented.[46] This ambivalence is reflected in this collection in the comments by Eileen Yeo in chapter 2 and Seth Koven in chapter 15 about claims of the social sciences to scientific status. The argument of this chapter is that in the inter-war period in the United States, a very significant transition took place in the character of social science and the conceptions held of appropriate methods to use in social investigation.

This transition had the effect of weakening some of the connections which Yeo and Koven suggest existed between the survey method and the wider society in the nineteenth and early twentieth centuries. It is not clear how useful it is to argue, as Yeo does as the basis for her interpretation, that inter-war scientific sociology and later the sample survey were a vehicle for the interests of the middle class, or, as Koven does, that the social survey was a product of and servant to politics and the state. What took place was rather the gradual inter-war emergence of a more autonomous realm of 'expert' activity conducted by social scientists which was marked by disinterestedness and detachment from the political and reform issues of the day. It undoubtedly had its limitations as a conception of social science, but viewed over a longer time scale it represented a significant shift.

Nor is it a matter, as Seth Koven suggests, simply of chosing between surveys as yielding objective facts, and surveys as inherently value-laden. This is a false antithesis. Empirical sociologists as various as Max Weber, William Ogburn, Robert Lynd, Gunnar Myrdal and C. Wright Mills struggled at various points in the first half of the century with these dilemmas of how objective social knowledge could be created. The social sciences have more ambitious agendas than history as a form of scholarly inquiry, with more high-flown aspirations and a greater likelihood of failing to achieve them. But this is not a reason to fall back upon historically particularistic accounts reducible to the political and social agendas which may have shaped the inquiries under discussion. It is a truism that much social knowledge is a creature of the period at which it was produced, but one may legitimately ask general questions about the development of a form of inquiry – in this book the local survey – over a longer period of time. One such set of questions concerns the links between the local survey and the sample survey.

THE RISE OF THE MODERN SAMPLE SURVEY

The emergence of the modern sample survey took place in an intellectual climate and institutional context different from those of the rise of the social survey in the 1890s. The political and social agenda was not the same, and welfare policy was less the preserve in the 1930s of settlement house workers and social work professionals than it had been around 1900. Government activity, partly as a result of their earlier activities, was now more extensive. Though the role of the state over this period is capable of being exaggerated, it was much more of an actor than it had been a generation earlier.[47] Academic social science considerably expanded in scope, conceptualising and investigating social reality in novel ways, and in so doing able to draw on its own sources of external support.

Modern social survey research was also fed from more utilitarian sources. Just as the growth of psychology was encouraged by the demand for its skills in industry and education,[48] so the market for survey research in commercial product testing and particularly in early audience research for the mass media encouraged the development of a style of research which social scientists then took up and used for more serious social inquiry. The paths of social science research and social survey research in the United States have been separate, parallel to each other, from time to time crossing each other and occasionally for short periods merging with each other. They remain distinct activities, as attempts to institutionalise survey research in American universities demonstrate. Jean Converse terms survey research a 'quasi-discipline', but it is perhaps a mistake to see it in these terms at all. The inputs to sample survey research have been more varied, academically from different disciplines including statistics, outside the academic world from commercial product testing, media interests and the demands for political information. Social survey research using probability sampling methods also developed as part of 'big social science' in the postwar period, with increasing support from the federal government, private foundations and other funding sources. That topic, however, is another story and the subject of another book than the present one.

NOTES

1 J. Converse, *Survey Research in the United States: Roots and Emergence 1890–1960* (Berkeley: University of California Press, 1987).

2 R. W. DeForest and L. Veiller (eds.), *The Tenement House Problem* (New York: Macmillan and Co., 1903).

3 J. M. Glenn, L. Brandt and F. E. Andrews, *Russell Sage Foundation 1907–1946* (New York: Russell Sage Foundation, 1947), I, p. 7.

4 Glenn *et al.*, *Russell Sage Foundation*, pp. 4, 18–19.

5 See Shelby M. Harrison, *Community Action through Surveys* (New York: Russell Sage Foundation, 1916). See also S. M. Harrison, *The Social Survey* (New York: Russell Sage Foundation, 1931).

6 Glenn *et al.*, *Russell Sage Foundation*, pp. 177–8, quoting from a document by Shelby M. Harrison.

7 S. M. Harrison, 'Development and Spread of Social Surveys', in A. Eaton and S. M. Harrison, *A Bibliography of Social Surveys* (New York: Russell Sage Foundation, 1930), pp. xxv–xxvi.

8 The publication history of this magazine is complex. It began life in 1898 as *Charities: A Weekly Review of Local and General Philanthropy*, until in 1905 it absorbed *The Commons* to become *Charities and the Commons* until 1909. In that year it was renamed *The Survey* and retained that title until its closure in May 1952. From 1922 to 1948 it was published in two parts, with varying degrees of explicit separation between the two in their titles, the *Survey Mid-monthly*, a journal for professional social workers, and the *Survey Graphic*, an illustrated magazine aimed at a wider audience. The latter was reabsorbed into *The Survey* in 1948. From November 1912 until its closure the editor (of both publications) was Paul U. Kellogg. See *Library of Congress Catalogue* and Clarke A. Chambers, *Paul U. Kellogg and the Survey: Voices for Social Welfare and Social Justice* (Minneapolis: University of Minnesota Press, 1971).

9 Chambers, *Paul U. Kellogg and the Survey*, p. 105.

10 For a discussion of the response of some early American sociologists such as J. L. Gillin, F. W. Blackmar, Franklin Giddings and others to the social survey, see M. Gordon, 'The Social Survey Movement and Sociology in the United States', *Social Problems*, 21 (1973), 284–98.

11 See M. C. Elmer, *The Technique of Social Surveys* (Minneapolis: Minnesota University Printing Company, 1917); C. Aronovici, *The Social Survey* (Philadelphia: Harper, 1916); Carl C. Taylor, *The Social Survey: Its History and Methods*, (Columbia, Missouri: University of Missouri, 1919); E. W. Burgess, 'The Social Survey: A Field for

Constructive Service by Departments of Sociology', *American Journal of Sociology*, 21 (1916), 492–500; C. C. Taylor, 'The Social Survey and the Science of Sociology', *American Journal of Sociology*, 25 (May, 1920), 731–56; H. M. Bartlett, 'The Social Survey and the Charity Organisation Movement', *American Journal of Sociology*, 34, no. 2 (September, 1928); Manuel C. Elmer, 'Social Surveys of Urban Communities', PhD thesis, University of Chicago, 1914; R. W. Stone, 'The Origin of the Survey movement', PhD thesis, University of Chicago, 1919; Robert E. Park (chair), 'Roundtable on the Technique of the Social Survey', with contributions by Shelby M. Harrison and Manuel C. Elmer, *Publications of the American Sociological Association*, 22, [Washington DC meeting 1927] (Chicago: University of Chicago Press, 1928), pp. 223–5.

12 J. L. Williams, *An American Town* (New York, 1906) and N. L. Sims, *A Hoosier Village* (New York: Columbia University Press, 1912).

13 For an elaboration, see Martin Bulmer, *The Chicago School of Sociology: Institutionalisation, Diversity and the Rise of Sociological Research* (Chicago: University of Chicago Press, 1984).

14 W. I. Thomas, 'Race Psychology: Standpoint and Questionnaire with Particular Reference to the Immigrant and the Negro', *American Journal of Sociology*, 17, 6 (May 1912), 771.

15 Circular of the departments of political economy, political science, history, sociology, and anthropology, 1918, *Official Publications of the University of Chicago* (Chicago: University of Chicago Press, 1918).

16 Robert E. Park, 'Notes on the History of the Social Survey, 1917–1920', Robert E. Park Papers, Joseph Regenstein Library, University of Chicago.

17 Elmer, *The Technique of Social Surveys*. Elmer had gained his PhD in sociology from the University of Chicago in 1914 for a dissertation on 'Social Surveys in Urban Communities', but apparently received little encouragement from staff of the sociology department. He received most encouragement from Ernst Freund in the Law School. See Bulmer, *The Chicago School of Sociology*, p. 67. On Freund and his involvements in early social research, see Steven J. Diner, *A City and its Universities: Public Policy in Chicago, 1892–1919* (Chapel Hill: University of North Carolina Press, 1980), pp. 43–4.

18 R. E. Park, 'The City as a Social Laboratory', in T. V. White and L. D. Smith (eds.), *Chicago: An Experiment in Social Science Research* (Chicago: University of Chicago Press, 1929), pp. 1–19.

19 Martin Bulmer, 'Charles S. Johnson, Robert E. Park and the Research Methods of the Chicago Commission on Race Relations, 1919–1922: An Early Experiment in Applied Social Research', *Ethnic and Racial Studies*, 4 (July 1981), 289–306.

20 Chicago Commission on Race Relations, *The Negro in Chicago* (Chicago: University of Chicago Press, 1922), p. 152.

21 E. W. Burgess, 'Research in Urban Society: A Long View', in E. W. Burgess and D. Bogue (eds.), *Contributions to Urban Sociology* (Chicago: University of Chicago Press, 1964), p. 3.

22 F. W. Blackmar and E. W. Burgess, *The Lawrence Social Survey: Report to the Lawrence Social Survey Committee* (Topeka: Kansas State Printing Plant, 1917).

23 E. W. Burgess, 'The Social Survey', pp. 492–500.

24 Burgess, 'The Social Survey', p. 499.

25 Bulmer, *The Chicago School of Sociology*, p. 74.

26 R. E. Park, Preface to Emory S. Bogardus, *The New Social Research* (Los Angeles: J. R. Miller, 1926), pp. 13–14.

27 V. Palmer, *Field Studies in Sociology: A Student's Manual* (Chicago: University of Chicago Press, 1928), p. 48.

28 Palmer, *Field Studies*, p. 49.

29 Palmer, *Field Studies*, pp. 49–51.

30 P. V. Young, *Scientific Social Surveys and Research* (New York: Prentice Hall, 1939), pp. 55–64.

31 C. C. Taylor, 'The Work of the Division of Farm Population and Rural Life', *Rural Sociology*, 4 (1939), 221–8.

32 Converse, *Survey Research in the United States*, pp. 30–1. One product of this work was a guide to the conduct of local surveys by sociologist Edmund de S. Brunner, *Surveying Your Community* (New York: Institute for Social and Religious Research, 1925).

33 For details, see Fred H. Matthews, *Quest for an American Sociology: Robert E. Park and the Chicago School* (Montreal: McGill-Queens University Press, 1977), esp. pp. 112–15.

34 R. S. and H. Lynd, *Middletown; A Study in Contemporary American Culture* (New York: Harcourt, Brace and Co., 1929).

35 E. Shils, 'The Contemplation of Society in America', in *The Calling of Sociology and Other Essays on the Pursuit of Learning* (Chicago: University of Chicago Press, 1980), pp. 104–5.

36 The line between the local survey and the community study is not an altogether clear one, but in the case of *Middletown* is evident enough if one compares it to, for example, *The Pittsburgh Survey*. It differs in coverage and extensiveness, in the range of problems examined, and in the intellectual frame within which the study was conceived.

37 See D. Ross, 'The Development of the Social Sciences', in A. Oleson and J. Voss, (eds.), *The Organization of Knowledge in Modern America* (Baltimore, Md.: Johns Hopkins University Press, 1979), pp. 107–38.

38 Bulmer, *The Chicago School of Sociology*, pp. 164–9.

39 M. Bulmer, 'The Methodology of Early Social Indicator Research: William F. Ogburn and *Recent Social Trends* 1933', *Social Indicators Research*, 13 (1983), 109–30.

40 M. C. Smith, 'Robert S. Lynd and Consumerism in the 1930's', *Journal of the History of Sociology*, 2 (Fall-Winter, 1979–80), 102–4.

41 I owe this observation to Jennifer Platt.

42 See Margo J. Anderson, *The American Census: A Social History* (New Haven, Conn.: Yale University Press, 1988) esp. pp. 192–3.

43 See the range of essays in his collected papers, S. A. Stouffer, *Social Research to Test Ideas* (New York: Free Press, 1962).

44 M. Bulmer and J. Bulmer, 'Philanthropy and Social Science in the 1920's: The Case of Beardsley Ruml and the Laura Spelman Rockefeller Memorial, 1922–1929', *Minerva*, 19 (Autumn, 1981), 347–407.

45 See Thomas Haskell (ed.), *The Authority of Experts* (Bloomington, Indiana: Indiana University Press, 1984).

46 See Robert C. Bannister, *Sociology and Scientism: The American Quest for Objectivity, 1880–1940* (Chapel hill: University of North Carolina Press, 1987).

47 This point is developed in Martin Bulmer, 'Mobilising Social Knowledge for Social Welfare: Intermediary Institutions in the Political Systems of the United States and Great Britain, 1900–1940', unpublished paper.

48 See M. M. Sokal (ed.), *Psychological Testing and American Society 1890–1930* (New Brunswick, NJ: Rutgers University Press, 1987).

CHAPTER TWELVE

The social survey in Germany before 1933[1]

IRMELA GORGES

This chapter focuses on the impact of social change on the development of social research. It claims that the effect of internal academic developments on methods and techniques of social research have to be judged as much less important than the impact of society on the development of the discipline. Changing societal conditions bring forth different groups of social scientists who dominate the development of social research. Radical changes cause abrupt changes within the prevailing research groups who dispose of research questions and research methods.

This essay pursues the impact of society on the early beginnings of empirical social research in Germany between 1871 and 1933. Until the 1870s statistical social surveys were predominantly a concern of government. Aroused by the urgent social issues caused by industrialisation, more and more individuals and groups felt the need for solving social problems that required deeper insights into the social life of workers and new kinds of survey instruments. Ultimately this resulted in the establishment of academic social research. After World War I, due to the change of constitution and the political upheavals during the Weimar Republic, academic sociologists protected their independence from political demands by separating sociology from social policy and political commitment. Sociologists, overemphasising political 'neutrality', also separated sociology from survey research aiming at social issues. As a consequence they failed to develop any precise method of empirical social research to analyse relevant social political and economic conditions of German society. This history of social surveys in Germany is traced in this paper through the work of the Verein für Socialpolitik, the German Society for Sociology and the Research Institute for the Social Sciences at the University of Cologne.

THE ESTABLISHMENT OF THE VEREIN FÜR SOCIALPOLITIK

Non-governmental social surveys started with the commitment of German professors to the 'social issue' before the establishment of the German Kaiser Reich in 1871. Their social concern led to the establishment of the Verein für Socialpolitik (Association for Social Policy) in 1872. To understand the objectives of the Verein's work one has to look back to the events which led to the establishment of the association.

The origins of the Verein für Socialpolitik sprang from the political ambition of German professors of political science and jurisprudence in the nineteenth century. Professors played an important part in the thwarted bourgeois revolution of 1848. About 600 out of 800 members of the revolutionary parliament were academics, 250 of them professors.

When, due to the efforts of Otto Fürst von Bismarck-Schönhausen, the first German Reich was established in 1871, essential political goals of the revolution of 1848 were realised. Bismarck, Minister President of Prussia from 1862 to 1890 and at the same time the first Chancellor of the Reich from 1871 to 1890, was successful in integrating the divergent national political streams and especially in encouraging the educated middle-class members to take part in the building of a new nation. The establishment of the Verein für Socialpolitik in 1872 has to be seen as an attempt to support the government's activities.

The second root of the *Verein* was the academic tradition of the German Historical School of National Economy. This school was an effort to fill the gap between economic theories and economic and social reality. The first phase of industrialisation was marked by a long-lasting economic boom from the mid-1840s until 1873. These commercial activities were accompanied and supported by powerful movements of economic liberalism. Coming from England, 'Manchesterism' prevailed in classical economic theories and the Volkwirtschaftlicher Kongress (Congress for Political Economy, established in 1859) claimed to support and control the economic policy in Germany.

However as early as 1843 Wilhelm Georg Friedrich Roscher (1817–94), professor of political science, pointed out that the theory of liberal economics had to include an analysis of historical economic conditions. Bruno Hildebrand (1812–78) and Karl Knies (1821–98) elaborated Roscher's point of view. They denied the existence of natural laws in economics and insisted that each economic change had to be analysed in detail to detect the singular impetus for the change. Due to this search for historical singularities in economics, Roscher, Hildebrand and Knies were called the founders of the 'Older Historical School'. The most famous representatives of the second, 'younger' generation of the German Historical School were Gustav Schmoller (1838–1917), Lujo von Brentano (1844–1931) and Adolf Wagner (1835–1917). From about 1860 on they implemented the theoretical demands of the generation of Roscher, Hildebrand and Knies and began to investigate historical economic laws. Looking at real economic life, they became aware of declining living conditions of workers and stated that bourgeois society would fall apart if the impoverishment of the proletariat continued. They therefore pleaded for the restriction of economic *laissez-faire* and self-interest principles, and for social policy legislation to benefit workers. Because this point of view seemed to support workers' demands, the advocates of the pure liberal economy called the young professors 'socialists of the chair' (*Kathedersozialisten*).[2]

Their ambition to help build the new German Reich and the political and scientific rivalry with the representatives of the Manchester School led the young professors to agree with the proposal of a journalist, Julius von Eckardt, to establish a counter organisation against the 'Volkswirt-schaftlicher Kongreß'. The new association should be open to everyone who agreed with the idea of social responsibility and the necessity of social legislation. The first president of the Verein für Socialpolitik was Erwin Nasse. However, Gustav Schmoller became the most influential and well-known member of the Verein's first generation because of his ability to integrate diverging political interests as well as practical and scientific standpoints into well-balanced, middle-class positions.

THE EXPERTS FOR THE GOVERNMENT'S SURVEYS

The Verein für Sozialpolitik was created to negotiate the 'social issue'. The participants of the first assembly of the Verein in 1872 decided that each of their debates should be terminated by passing a resolution giving the assembly's view as to what the state would have to do in order to ameliorate the living conditions of the worker. The resolutions were sent to the most important members of Parliament or member of the government. General assemblies were held every two years. Up to 800 members took part in the assemblies before World War II. All expenses of the Verein were paid by membership fees. Up to 33 per cent of the members were professors.

One of the first discussions of the Verein on working conditions in factories made clear to its participants that the members, nearly all coming from middle-class families, did not know much about the living conditions and feelings of working-class people. Moreover, panel members argued that the few surveys carried out by the state so far were inadequate. Usually questionnaires had been sent to factory owners who answered questions about the working and health conditions of workers, the condition of the work-place, and the worker's moral maturity. This information from the entrepreneurs was then used as a starting point to 'improve' the industrial code. The speakers in the Verein, among them one entrepreneur and several trade unionists, maintained that class interest was always intruding into the judgments of the interviewees and that to be fair one needed to question both groups, the workers and the factory owners. Ernst Engel (1821–96), the well-known director of the Prussian statistical bureau, proposed to publish a survey questionnaire in order to provoke a 'statistical counter-movement' against the one-sidedness of the answers. In the end the Verein assembly in 1873 passed a resolution that future state surveys should be organised in the following way: the local government should install a commission, consisting of the local police authority, an equal part of employees and employers and at least one priest, teacher or physician. In the event that an employer refused to participate in the commission's study because it required him to work at the side of a labourer, he might be replaced by an assistant to the factory's director. The commission then should inspect the working conditions and places of work. If necessary they should force their way into the factory and then report their findings to the government.

Five years after the first resolution on the desirable organisation of the government's enquêtes, the Verein published an essay by the secretary of the Chamber of Commerce in Hamburg, G. Embden, (full first name, dates of birth and death unknown) in which he made a distinction between two types of the organisation of surveys. As the term 'enquête' had been adopted from the French term for state survey, Embden made a distinction between a 'completely organised' and an 'incompletely organised' enquête. The incompletely organised enquête, according to Embden, was the survey by administration. This type of enquête was carried out by bureaucratic officials through statistical questionnaires. The questionnaires were sent to the areas under investigation. Decentralised commissions of administrators conducted the investigations, summarised the findings and sent the reports back to the central government officials, who again summarised the local reports. The final reports, which could not be verified in detail, were used as guidelines for administrative acts.

Embden claimed that the completely organised enquête was the survey by Parliament in which a commission of experts, who had been appointed for that very purpose, travelled through the country in order to investigate what the people thought had to be done to solve the problems in question.

The inquiries were recorded in shorthand. The commission summarised the findings. The minutes as well as the reports, which could be verified in every detail, were sent to Parliament.

Embden illustrated the utility of both types of enquêtean organisations with two examples. At one point the government had conducted an incompletely organised enquête in order to improve the situation of the apprentices. The findings of the enquête added more 'facts' to the ones already known without the administration being able to solve the problems. Embden suggested that instead of piling up more and more 'facts' the government should have sent out a commission to discover the ideas interviewees had about solving the problem. By this means one would have found reasonable and adequate solutions for the problems. Embden's second example reported on a completely organised enquête that was conducted in 1866 in Orissa in India. The enquête aimed at preventing the people from suffering a new famine, but the government's commission of experts was not able to extract concrete suggestions out of the numerous reports on the starvation of the people. In the same year a chief of the Statistical Bureau in Bengal had sent out questionnaires to all rural districts in order to list the prices of rice just after the main harvest. He then compared the average income of the people with the assumed increase of the rice prices just before the next harvest and by this means he was able to predict whether the poor would be able to buy the rice at the end of the year.[3]

Embden's definition of the two types of enquêtes as well as the propositions of the General Assembly of the Verein in 1873 were meant to advise the government. During the years between 1872 and 1878 the Verein itself did not conduct surveys because they neither had the authority of governmental commissions, nor saw the necessity to do the government's work. Instead of this, they discussed and published expert opinions on various social subjects, like 'the establishment of joint stock companies (1873), the reform of apprenticeship (1875), punishment for the breach of labour contracts (1874) or the housing problems of the poor (1872)'. The Verein's work was a mixture of an advisory board for the government and a place where the experts accumulated their knowledge of social issues as a quasi enquête commission.

THE DEVELOPMENT OF THE NON-GOVERNMENTAL ENQUÊTE

In 1878 two attempts on the life of Kaiser Wilhelm I upset the public. Because socialists were held responsible for the attempts, Chancellor

Bismarck enacted a law against all socialist or social democratical activities with the one exception that socialists still could be elected as members of Parliament (the Socialist Party was established in 1875). Those who broke the law could be expelled from the country. Conservative and liberal members of Parliament supported Bismarck's efforts. With the additional pressure of slowly deteriorating economic conditions, internal politics moved in a conservative direction. In order to remove the worker from the attraction of the socialist demands, Bismarck prepared the first social security system in Europe. The Health Insurance Act of 1883, the Accident Insurance Act of 1884 and the Disability and Old Age Act of 1889 were meant to integrate industrial workers into the bourgeois state. The activities of the Verein für Socialpolitik did not fall under the law against the socialists. However, in some of its earlier debates the General Assembly of the Verein had supported political demands by the socialists for example, the worker's freedom to organise political coalitions and the right to strike (1872).

In these early years the Verein discussed problems of trade and economy, such as the income taxes (1875) or the German–Austrian trade agreement (1877), but its main concern was with working-class living conditions. In 1878, when it drifted into a more conservative position, the Verein abandoned its identity as the government's advisor and ceased to pass policy-oriented resolutions. In the 1880s the Verein's concern for the industrial worker was more or less replaced by an interest in the living conditions of the rural population, peasants and big landowners. Examples of the General Assembly's issues and the publications of the Verein at that time include rural conditions in Germany (1883), the rural law of succession and the distribution of real estate, (1884) and the migration from east to west Germany (1996). Apparently these subjects were less explosive politically than the industrial labour question.

As a consequence of the retreat from a position advisory to the government, the Verein now intensified its own research activities. In addition to offering expert opinions, the Verein now conducted surveys. In accordance with the government's investigations the surveys were called enquêtes. Using Embden's categories, the Verein conducted incompletely organised enquêtes. The managing committee of the Verein appointed an enquête commission of the Verein's members who outlined a questionnaire consisting of up to 30 open-ended questions. The research commission charged an adequate number of experts to use the questionnaire as a guideline for the collection of facts and the delineation of the report on the results. It was left to the experts to decide how they would collect the required data. The Verein published the reports, appending a short description of the organisation, the participants and the main subject of the enquête commission and the questionnaire.[4]

During the 1870s the Verein's criticism of enquête methods was confined to the governmental reports, but as consequence of their own 'private' inquiries Verein investigators now had to fulfill their own high methodological standards. Their standards for judging governmental enquêtes had been, firstly, fairness to the involved interest groups and, secondly, whether the methods had been adequate for the purpose of the enquête. The critics from outside the Verein as well as from the members themselves agreed on the first criteria. For instance Professor Gottlieb Schnapper-Arndt (1847–1902), member of the Verein and professor for statistics at the Akademie für Handels- und Sozialwissenschaften in Frankfurt-on-Main (Academy for Commercial Science and Social Sciences), criticised an 1887 enquête on the 'rural usury problem'. He found that the enquête commission should have avoided formulating questions that pushed the interviewees in the desired direction. However, the critics disagreed on the second criterion. Schnapper-Arndt wanted the Verein to be able to recommend carefully directed measures against the usury problem on grounds of 'objective' statements. In order to get as precise informations on the rural usury problem as possible, Schnapper-Arndt wanted the questionnaire to go more into details and for complex questions to be broken into different aspects. Schnapper-Arndt's opponent, Hugo Thiel (1839–1918), the leader of the enquête commission and senior administrative officer, admitted that the survey might not have fulfilled all the scientific criteria, but in contrast to Schnapper-Arndt he held that he was not interested in scientific research. Instead he wanted to stir up the public's attention. The presentation of typical cases of rural usury would have been sufficient to prove that social legislation was necessary.

Under the impact of the laws against the socialists and the establishment of the 'private' enquête, the dispute between Schnapper-Arndt and Thiel as to whether the Verein's research should focus on scientific or on political goals was the beginning of a long-lasting dispute between those who supported and those who fought against the 'value-orientated' enquête.

THE VEREIN'S SECOND GENERATION AND THE ACADEMISATION OF ENQUÊTES

During the 1880s public interest in the Verein's activities diminished. Only one third of the former members remained in the *Verein* (between 1872 and

1879 the total number of members was 847; between 1882 and 1888, 252). The professors and administrators now dominated representatives of other professions. Between 1872 and 1879 13 per cent of all members were professors, 17 per cent administrators, 5 per cent journalists, 65 per cent other 'practitioners' like physicians, trade unionists, factory owners. Between 1882 and 1888 30 per cent of all members were professors, 21 per cent administrators, 4 per cent journalists, 54 per cent other 'practitioners'. This change in membership tamed the Verein's engagement with practical social policy.

Thus when the second generation of the Verein began its work between 1888 and 1892, the situation was changed. This generation had studied national economy and political sciences under the politically restrictive conditions of the 1880s. The most famous of them, Max Weber (1864–1920), his brother, Alfred Weber (1868–1956), Werner Sombart (1863–1941) and Ferdinand Tönnies (1855–1936) felt much less attracted to the Kaiserreich (the German Empire) than the generation of Schmoller and the younger Historical School who had founded the Verein für Socialpolitik. The second generation did not intend to support and stabilise the government by discussing problems of social policy. Because many of them had read Marxian writings and tended to be Social Democratic sympathisers, they found the constitution of the Reich and the government to be restrictive, non-democratic and threatening. Their attitude towards the Verein's research therefore stemmed much less from political enthusiasm for the Kaiserreich and much more from the motivation to enhance democratic social movements. However, in order to protect themselves against the conservative government, they pleaded for the separation of science from politics. In their view conducting survey research was an 'academic' activity.

The movement towards making the private enquête more academic appeared in outline in a survey on the working and living conditions of farm-workers, published in three volumes between 1890 and 1892. Although the law against the socialists did not extend beyond 1890, the *Verein* maintained its interest in the 'agrarian issue' as a research subject, while problems of the industrial worker clearly took up less room than in the 1870s. The farm worker enquête was initiated in 1890 by Professor Max Sering (1857–1939), who also presided over the enquête commission. Two questionnaires were developed. One, answered by the rural employer, asked for the general organisation of the worker's life, for the working and income conditions and for 'general requirements' such as insurance, welfare institutions, libraries etc. A second questionnaire was sent to experts who were asked to inform the enquête-commission about the backgrounds and causes for the given economic and social conditions. Questions included: How did the landholder react to the shortage of farm workers? What were the consequences for the remaining workers? Had the situation of the farm worker changed? Had the socialist agitation been successful?

The Verein sent out more than 4,000 questionnaires to landowners; 3,100 were returned. Of the 562 experts, 291 answered the second questionnaire. The original idea that a group of landowners should summarise the answers had to be abandoned. Instead a group of six university assistants was appointed to analyse the data. The most famous among the assistants was Max Weber. He was chosen to present the findings for those questionnaires from areas east of the river Elbe. Prior to Weber's report on the 'eastern Elbian' farm worker, the *Verein's* monographs occasionally included some statistical tables. Weber's analysis for the first time pursued a different strategy. Because he was unable to measure and quantify the complex data to determine why the situation in one part of the country was worse than in the other, Weber decided to describe, or better 'extract' (ideal) typical constellations with respect to the working and living conditions of farm workers in 15 districts.

While the former monographs of the Verein included reports on their own experiences by the researchers, backed up by information from other experts, Max Weber's study was a scientific analysis from which personal or class interests were excluded. Weber also did not discuss the origins of the data but simply tried to structure the material and summarise the findings.[5]

When the General Assembly of the Verein discussed the findings of the enquête in 1893, the socialists were the main critics of the research methods and the sample chosen. Above all they argued against the enquête because the landowners had been questioned instead of the farm-workers. However, Thiel, the leader of the enquête, found that rural workers would be unable to answer questions because their minds were underdeveloped and they would not be able to protect their own interest so that a short interrogation would bring up no valuable information. Max Weber argued that farm-workers would not answer the Verein's questionnaires because they suspected the Verein's members of supporting socialists and in some cases even local priests had been suspected of supporting social-democratic political goals.[6]

Max Weber's statement made clear that there was a shift of objectives between the older and the younger generation of the Verein. The older generation wanted to be informed about the worker's condition in order to be able to give advice about social legislation. The younger generation distinguished 'scientific necessities from political commitment' and kept them separate. Weber's generation agreed on this point. Only 30 years later Werner Sombart explained that the separation of science and policy had been the only way for the young scientists to become independent from the conservative government and the prevailing political values. If they wanted to become professors in Berlin, the centre for economic and social sciences, it was necessary not to be suspected of cooperating with the socialists.

During the second half of the 1890s, the government of Prussia, of which Berlin was the capital, enacted a second 'small' law against the socialists. During these years the Verein conducted an enquête about craftsmen, published in 10 volumes between 1895 and 1897. Other enquêtes were conducted on credit available to peasants (1896–8), on hawkers (1898–9) and on cottage industry (1899). The enquête on craftsmen was attacked by socialists, conservative politicians, and members of the chamber of handicrafts because it seemed to weaken the position of the guilds. There was no discussion on the enquête methods among the Verein's members. It seemed as if the development of even 'scientific' methods of research was paralysed by political reactions.

It was only after the turn of the century, when the more liberal-oriented government of Graf Posadowsky came to power (1899–1907) and Max Weber had recovered from a nervous indisposition, that the younger generation, still feeling the threatening demands from both sides of the political spectrum, began to develop the 'scientific' enquête. In order to study the conditions of sailors in an 'objective' way, Ferdinand Tönnies worked out questionnaires for an enquête on 'the situation of workers in merchant shipping' (1904). He developed a detailed questionnaire that allowed exact comparisons between different respondents and discussed the validity of different sources of information, such as answers from captains, officers or sailors or sailor's unions. Tönnies also advised the ship's crews, who were asked to fill out the Verein's questionnaire, not to write down their comments just after they had had a quarrel with their chiefs or companions but to wait until they had calmed down. Tönnies wished that all information should be as valid as that obtained from juridical hearings involving sailors. However, these hearings did not deal much with the life situations of sailors.

Max Weber carried the academic refinement of enquête-methods forward. In 1908 he outlined the requirements for a 'neutral' and therefore 'academic' method of inquiry. He had been appointed to the Verein's enquête on 'the selection and adaptation of labourers in very large private enterprises', installed in 1907. Lujo Brentano had proposed the research subject because it was said that the public was disturbed by the increasing percentage of workers who were unfit for military service. In several meetings of the Verein's commission, the subject was turned into the more neutral and academic question of workers' life courses. In 1908 Weber presented a paper in which he underlined the academic reasons for the inquiry. Young scientists were chosen to investigate the workers. Weber advised them to perceive even the sentiments of the worker as 'objective' social facts. They should not take part in the worker's lives. The results of the enquête would be useful for the entrepreneur as well as for the unions, and the scientists should refrain from any personal judgement.[7] Weber proposed to develop two questionnaires. The first one outlined the broad purpose of the enquête as a guideline for the investigators, the second one was sent out to be answered by unions.

The enquête on the selection and adaptation of the labourers in large private enterprises is thought to be the first study in the field of industrial sociology in Germany.[8] The findings, those, for instance, of Marie Bernays on the curves of fatigue during working hours, or on 'shop fashions', are still valid. The young generation in the Verein had succeeded in conducting academic enquêtes. Participating in the debate on the results of the enquête in the General Assembly of 1911, Max and Alfred Weber demonstrated their understanding of the separation of science and social politics. As scientists they had found that even the skilled worker was 'worn out' by the age of 40 and that after this age he would disappear from the 'capitalistic working machinery'. As a citizen committed to social policy, Alfred Weber proposed to pension off the forty-year-old worker.

THE METHODOLOGICAL DEBATES

The turn from politically oriented private enquêtes to scientific study during the first decade of the century was accompanied by serious confrontations between the two generations of the Verein, mainly between Gustav Schmoller, the Verein's president, and Max Weber. The confrontations were based on different political positions, which became overt when the political pressure on the *Verein* ceased after the turn of the century. Max and Alfred Weber as well as Werner Sombart and Friedrich Naumann (1860–1919), theologian and liberal politician, ridiculed the older generation's trust in the state. During the discussion on the 'relations of the cartels and the state' in 1905 Max Weber opposed Schmoller's judgement that the state should intervene in the affairs of cartels. The state, Weber said, was much too weak to interfere. Friedrich Naumann added that on the contrary the cartels would control the state and that it would be not only unrealistic but pure nonsense to ask for the state's interference,[9] whereupon Schmoller accused Naumann of supporting a Marxian position. Schmoller announced that he would resign from his position as the Verein's president unless Naumann refrained from such 'oratorical pronouncements'.

According to Max Weber, the political disputes had to be traced back to their methodological origins. Schmoller had called Naumann a 'demagogue' and Weber suspected that Schmoller wanted to suggest that the younger generation would not use scientific methods. Weber picked up this imputation in order to fight for a 'neutral', 'objective' science of sociology against Schmoller's approach to science. Weber argued that Schmoller would combine science and politics in so far as he always tried to support by means of his research those political goals which would strengthen a well-balanced middle-class position. However, to Weber the 'middle line was not an inch more scientific than the extreme left or right wing party'. It would be a severe self-deception if Schmoller thought that the diagonal between several values would result in a scientific position.[10] By contrast, Weber intended to inquire into the 'truth' by stating social 'facts', i.e. actions or situations; even opinions and values held by people would have to be considered as facts. Sociologists would have to 'understand' them by explaining them in terms of their psychological, individual and historical conditions.

Before the turn of the century, the controversy about methodological positions between the older and the younger generation had been profound. At that time Max and Alfred Weber had criticised the 'socialists of the chair' for failing to interpret the huge amount of data they collected within a theory of capitalist society. Thus the Verein's first generation would not succeed in realising its own goal, i.e. rescuing the worker from socialism. However, more violent criticism had come from outside the Verein. Rosa Luxemburg (1870–1919), socialist theorist and politician, found that the economists of the Historical School had buried the general laws of social development under mountains of historical straw and rubbish.[11] In 1895 the Chamber of Handicrafts even published a 'public warning' not to answer the questions of the Verein's 'Enquête on the Handicraft's Ability to Compete with Large Industries' (1895–7) because the Verein's 'twaddle' would hinder and even 'enormously harm' the (conservative) political goals of the chamber.[12]

Just before World War I, when the diverging groups in German society began to unite into working groups preparing for war, when even the social democrats promised 'to do their duty' in case of a defensive war, controversies on the Verein's methods were reduced to the issues of 'neutrality' and 'objectivity'. The first theoretical debate on the term 'productivity' in 1908 and the debate on value judgements in 1914 (*Werturteilsstreit*) proved that the epistemological and the underlying political divergencies could not be solved by discussing the scientific criteria of research methods.

The younger generation's strict adherence to scientific neutrality had an decisive impact on the development of sociologists' attitude towards empirical social research after World War I. The first step towards a neutral science of sociology before the war was the establishment in 1909 of the German Sociological Society (Deutsche Gesellschaft für Soziologie) as a counter-organization to the Verein für Socialpolitik. It was founded by Max and Alfred Weber, Werner Sombart and Ferdinand Tönnies, among others. The association mirrored the structure and general task of the Verein except that it was supposed to conduct exclusively 'neutral, purely scientific' research. In contrast to the Verein für Socialpolitik the terms of admission were constructed in such a way that the Society was protected from political influences from outside. Thus the central committee constituted itself by cooptions and was not elected by members.

THE VEREIN FÜR SOCIALPOLITIK AND THE GERMAN SOCIETY FOR SOCIOLOGY AFTER WORLD WAR I

During World War I the Verein confined its work to the publication of the enquêtes that had been conducted in the prewar period. The first meeting after the war was held in 1919. However, it briefly seemed that the Verein's work had become superfluous because socialists, who took over the government of the new German democracy between 1918 and 1920, enacted most of the important social policy and education laws which fulfilled, and even exceeded, the Verein's demands for social policy in its early years. For instance, the socialists legalised the 8-hour day and franchise for women, and made eligibility and wage agreements between unions and entrepreneurs compulsory.

However, economic and societal conditions changed by the beginning of the 1920s. In 1923 inflation and economic crisis endangered the economic and social status of the middle class, who faced the prospect of becoming working class. Members of the Verein für Socialpolitik, i.e. the representatives of the Historical School of Economics, realised that conducting empirical social research in order to improve and adapt working-class people's life to the middle-class's life style had become an inadequate research issue. Bankers and politicians accused the Verein's members of not being prepared to respond to new situations. The Verein therefore revised its main research subject and turned to research on mainly economic policy problems and conducted only a few surveys on social policy issues. But even empirical economic research had become useless. Even though the academics did not lack any information about the bad economic and social situation, they were incapable of offering solutions to overcome the inflation and the economic crisis. New theoretical concepts were required. The Verein abandoned the methodological position of the Historical School and shifted to discussions on theory-oriented economics. Nearly half the members of the Verein now favoured the marginal utility theory. As only one adherent (Arthur Spiethoff) remained to represent the former Historical School of National Economy, and as nearly all the new experts of economy theory came from directions which competed with the Historical School, one could not identify a 'third generation' within the Verein. The character of the association had changed. This change in research issue, methodological position and membership meant that the Verein slowly drifted out of the centre of sociological and social policy research and out of discussions on sociological methods. After being closed down in 1936 and revived in 1948, the Verein today is devoted exclusively to problems of economic policy.

The German Society for Sociology held two official meetings before World War I, in 1910 and 1912. Ferdinand Tönnies had become the president of the Society. Max Weber, the secretary, planned to conduct two 'enquêtes', one on clubs and societies the other on the daily press. Another member proposed to investigate the leading professions in modern societies. The enquête on journalism had to be interrupted because Max Weber became entangled in a lawsuit from a journalist. Thinking that the litigation would destroy his objectivity towards the subject, he resigned from the enquête commission. Because of the war none of the enquêtes was carried out. After World War I, the Society for Sociology was revived in 1922. This was at a time when the decline of the economy threatened the social security of the middle class and political uproar had become a near daily ritual. The Society guarded itself from being used by political pressure groups or being destroyed by political enemies by restricting the membership to the elite of social scientists and by insisting on strictly value-neutral discussions. Under this shelter it was possible to gather scientists from all political and epistemological positions and to debate the definition, subject and development of the new science of sociology rather than social policy-oriented research.

However, the Society never conducted its own social surveys. Though participants in its assemblies in 1926 and 1928 discussed the methodological implications of social investigation, the discussions mirrored the different epistemological positions of the Society's members and their different attitudes towards empirical research. For those members who emphasised the 'neutral' position, conducting an inquiry seemed to be too closely related to reality and to the riots of the streets. To them, investigating social reality would have meant engaging and taking part in the political activities of one or the other party.

From about 1928 onwards, the beginning of the decline of the Weimar Republic, the younger generation within the Society began to give up this passive attitude and to resume the idea of social research. However, after Max Weber's death in 1920 there was no advocate for social research among the older generation. Even Ferdinand Tönnies and Werner Sombart, who had supported Max Weber's vision of a neutral, objective research before the war, maintained their reserve against a potentially politically-engaged empirical research and did not take an interest in the younger generation's demands, which were presented during the last meeting of the Society in 1930, two years before the National Socialists came into power.[13]

Though all the different groups of sociologists from the Austro-Marxian orientation of Max Adler to the conservative position of Othmar Spann had accepted the postulate of neutrality during the Society's sessions, it was a group of liberal-oriented scientists around Leopold von Wiese (1876–1969), Ferdinand Tönnies and Werner Sombart, that fought for objectivity in a special manner. Leopold von Wiese had the most rigorous attitude towards neutrality. He began to develop a 'pure' sociology, which was to be differentiated from Max Weber's approach. Von Wiese's work can be traced in the investigations of the 'Forschungsinstitut für Sozialwissenschaften an der Universität zu Köln' (Research Institute for the Social Sciences at the University of Cologne).

THE INSTITUT FÜR SOZIALWISSENSCHAFTEN AN DER UNIVERSITÄT ZU KÖLN

The Institut für Sozialwissenschaften was created by Christian Eckert (1874–1952), professor of economic and political sciences at the University of Cologne, and Konrad Adenauer (1876–1967) Mayor of Cologne and, after World War II, the first Chancellor of the Federal Republic of Germany. In the middle of World War I the scientist and the politician decided to establish a research institute for the social sciences that should help build a new democratic society after the war. The institute should be divided into three departments, each working for one of the parties in the chamber of deputies in Cologne. To this purpose the town's government decided in 1919 to establish a Department of Social Policy, which should provide the Social Democratic Party with scientific material and data. The department was headed by Hugo Lindemann (1867–?) a former Social Democratic minister. The second department, the Department of Sociology, was directed by Leopold von Wiese who represented the liberal parties. Allegedly, the government was not able to appoint a director for the third department, representing the conservatives, in 1919. Up to 1928 Max Scheler (1874–1928) was appointed as co-director to represent the conservative Catholic standpoint within the Department of Sociology. The right wing of the conservatives had opposed the Weimar Republic and its democratic constitution during the first half of the 1920s. It was only in 1925 that the right wing of the conservatives, the Deutschnationale Volkspartei (DNVP) (German National Peoples Party), agreed to take part in the government of the Reich after the repayment of war debts was accepted by the former government in 1924 (the DNVP did not want to be responsible for the decision to pay war debts). In 1925 the DNVP was also successful in having their candidate Paul von Beneckendorf und von Hindenburg (1847–1934), imperial field-marshal, elected to the presidency of the Reich, as successor to the late Friedrich Ebert (1871–1925) who was a member of the Social Democratic Party. After the death of Max Scheler in 1928, the conservative parties in the town government of Cologne responded to this increase in power by appointing Theodor Brauer (1880–1942) head of the Institut's third department, the Department of Social Legislation.

The Department for Social Policy started by conducting several surveys at the beginning of the 1920s. However, they had to stop the investigations almost immediately because of the worsening economic situation and because of their shortage of research money. Their surveys, for instance on public assistance for the unemployed, conducted in 1920 and partly published in 1924,[14] were meant to help the Social Democratic Government formulate social legislation between 1918 and 1920. Thereafter, when the Social Democrats opposed the government they confined themselves to cheaper and less elaborate research methods. They did not develop distinctive methods or techniques of social research during the Weimar

Republic due to their exclusion from political and economic power. Thus, they will be excluded from the following presentation of research strategies and methods of the two other departments of the institute in Cologne.

At the beginning of the Weimar Republic, under the influence of riots in the streets between right-wing and left-wing radicals and under the government of socialist councils, von Wiese began to develop a 'pure', 'objective and neutral' sociology. His approach to the science was based on the formal sociology of George Simmel (1858–1918). Von Wiese assumed that societies consisted of only two basic social interrelations, the attraction towards and the dislike of people. His definition of social behaviour was comparable to the definition of economic behaviour of the marginal utility theory of economics insofar as both definitions had recourse to ahistorical basic needs of individuals as the main constituents of behaviour. Up to the middle of the 1920s von Wiese defined a system of interrelations, those which occurred between people, those between the people and abstract entities (for instance the state or the church) and those between these social entities themselves. He admitted that the interrelations occurred because of emotional conditions within individuals. However, his aim was to separate his science from psychology, the task of psychologists being to investigate the internal emotions of individuals, that of the sociologists concerning emotions which were directed towards other people.

The definitions of interrelations were based on unsystematic observations. Everyday observation was the research method of von Wiese's assistants when they investigated 'the mass',[15] 'the Bohemian'[16] or 'fashion'.[17] However, the analysis of interrelations had to go beyond day-to-day observation. After von Wiese had finished his 'table of interrelations' (*Tafel der Beziehungslehre*),[18] he began to teach 'pure' sociology. Each year von Wiese invited his students to practice interrelational analysis in a small project during the Whitsun vacations. The strict neutrality of his scientific approach meant that research subjects were not allowed to have any political relevance; examples used included 'the small village', 'the student's vacation camp' and 'the small island'. The students had to live with the people 'under investigation' for fourteen days. A standardised questionnaire, which was the same every year, guided their inquiries and observations. The questions focused on the interrelations between the people but exceeded 'pure' sociology in so far as additional questions about the 'situation' in which the interrelations took place and a request for a 'holistic' description of the group under research were included. At the end of the fourteen days von Wiese asked the students and the people who had been investigated to discuss the research findings in a local inn. There, the students had to generalise their research results in such a way that not only the people who were investigated but everybody at any time and place of the world would agree on the validity of the findings. That is why the following example of generalized findings of any investigation on working groups in factories could be transferred to every other research object. The students reported: 'There is a typical development of attitudes in homogeneous groups if they are disturbed by an intruder. First there is distrust and doubt, then there is curiosity and finally in many cases the group will be restructured because the intruder will set up new subgroups'.[19]

The presentation of this example should make clear that for von Wiese it was not necessary to conduct social surveys in the sense of questioning a large number of people by means of elaborate questionnaires. Von Wiese claimed that the quality of his data was comparable to that of the natural sciences, and to detect the underlying law it was sufficient if only a few persons were investigated. In von Wiese's view, sociology was a natural science potentially as useful to the solving of social problems as other natural sciences. At the beginning of the 1920s Leopold von Wiese had refrained from going into politics and had accused the social democrats of pursuing social policy instead of scientific work. At the beginning of the National Socialist regime von Wiese offered his help to the new government. He thought he would be able to restructure interrelations within the German society, a society which was, according to the national Socialists, comparable to a natural organism. The Nazis rejected von Wiese's offer because they intended to tolerate only their own organism-oriented sociology.

After World War II Leopold von Wiese's institute was reopened and his approach to sociology was revived. It may be considered one of the sources of the modern sociology of organisations in Germany.

Though von Wiese was well known during the Weimar Republic and though he had much influence in the German Society of Sociology, his pure sociology was not widely accepted. It was considered lifeless. His approach to objectivity went far beyond the neutrality of Max Weber. Nevertheless, empirical social research in the sense of investigating the actual behaviour and attitudes of people was conducted by those sociologists who either took over Max Weber's 'neutral' point of view, or as successors of Gustav Schmoller, were committed to specific political goals. A mixture of both positions was pursued by the Department of Social Legislation, established in 1928 and the third department of the research institute in Cologne.

SURVEY RESEARCH FOR THE CATHOLIC CHRISTIAN UNION

In 1928 Theodor Brauer (1880–1942) was chosen as head of the new Department for Social Legislation. He was one of the leading ideologists of the 'Catholic social reform movement', which dated back to a papal 'rerum novarum' on the relation between the state and the Catholic church in 1891. The social reform movement aimed at realising the church's ideas about a society that was stratified into groups of professions. Each member of society should be ranked and paid according to the efficiency of his or her work for the welfare of the community. The society's activities should have to focus on the development of the industry, as the Catholic church affirmed and supported the capitalist industrial society. From 1908 Brauer was also a secretary in the national and international Christian Catholic Union movement and the research work of the Department of Social Legislation reflected both influences: the alignment with the Catholic point of view of the society and the involvement with the Catholic labour union.

In prefaces to the official publication of the department, the 'Sozialrechtlichte Jahrbücher', Brauer pointed out that the institute would try to trace those tendencies in the everyday life of the Weimar Republic that indicated a societal drift in the direction of the Catholic church's 'industrial society'. The department's research work should strengthen these tendencies, which had not yet become codified, i.e. 'enacted law'. Brauer tried to grasp the hidden tendencies by conducting research on three main fields: (1) The system of professions and its organisation (research was conducted, for instance, on the fate of the old-age worker, the personality of the secretaries of unions, the living condition of the white-collar worker, etc.); (2) 'Industrial pedagogics' (i.e. adult education, vocational guidance, continued education for the unemployed, etc.); (3) The payment system (i.e. on the discussions on the wages policy, critical views on the statistics of wages etc.) (Sozialrechtliche Jahrbücher 1930–1933).[20]

Brauer published thirty-six essays on the three issues mentioned above within the four years from 1930 to 1933. Twenty-one of them were based on empirical social research. They can be divided into the following categories: Christian Union enquêtes, quasi-enquêtes, reports on travels, and statistical analyses. The research with the most elaborate inquiry method was the Christian Union enquête. Because of the political orientation of the Department of Social Legislation, Christian Unions supported these surveys. This is why, unlike most of the pre-war enquêtes of the Verein für Socialpolitik, the members of Christian Unions did not distrust the enquêtes of the Department of Social Legislation. The questions were answered by the persons under investigation themselves, i.e. Christian Union workers, the union secretaries, or the unemployed. The question-naires consisted of carefully conceived questions, which were divided into three main sequences. In the first part the interviewee was asked to give information on his or her social status, in the second part to describe the relevant 'facts' with regard to the problem under research, and in the last part to write down his or her own opinion of the problems and of how the situation might be changed (for instance: 'Do you think it is possible for the aged worker to take over jobs which require more responsibility but which are less exhausting? How could one organise this kind of work?' Or: 'Do you think that the proceedings in the labour court are too slow? If the answer is yes, could you suggest how this might be changed?').

The construction of the questionnaires indicated that Theodor Brauer and his group of researchers intended to collect different types of data, similar to data produced by Embden's different types of enquêts-organisations in 1877. Brauer combined the characteristics of the completely organised enquête, which was conducted for democratic purposes, with those of the incompletely organised, administrative enquête. Both types of organisation were designed for practical ends. In the case of the Department of Social Legislation, it meant that the Catholic ideal of industrialised society could be translated into reality. However, at the same time Brauer pointed out that the enquêtes were conducted for exclusively academic reasons, indicating that he had accepted the demands for 'neutral' empirical research and thus that no practical political purpose should be connected with an investigation. Brauer solved this contradiction by combining the positions of Gustav Schmoller and Max Weber. He tried to collect as much 'objective, non-biased and therefore valid' data as possible with respect to his general research question, namely, which social movements would speed up the realisation of Catholic industrial society? Brauer always tried to include all the different interests groups in his sample so that he would get well-balanced data. However, he was not always successful because the social democratic and liberal unions usually refused to take part in his research. The data were analysed simply by counting the answers or by summarising and interpreting the interviewee's statements.

The research work of Brauer was lavish. Often more than 500 questionnaires were sent out and it took several scientists to analyse the data. While Brauer had conducted more than twenty studies within five years between 1928 and 1933, the other departments of the Research Institute for the Social Sciences in Cologne, as well as the Verein für Socialpolitik, had to reduce their research activities because of the increasingly critical condition of the world economy from 1929 on. This scale of research activity was possible because of the close relation of the department with the party that had become strongest between 1930 and 1933 and it may be that Brauer received additional funding from the Catholic church.

Another reason for Brauer's increasing enthusiasm for research on social legislation was that he mistook the National Socialist movement which finally brought Hitler to power for a conservative social movement that would pacify the nation. It was only after the Nazis had begun to 'coordinate' (gleichschalten) the academic institutions of different epistemological and political orientation during spring 1933, that Theodor Brauer realised that National Socialism was striving for a 'harmonious' society which was centred round solely national, racial and military goals. The Nazis shut down the Department of Social Legislation in December 1933. The institute was not reopened after World War II.

SUMMARY

The History School of Economics promoted the emergence of empirical social research in Germany between 1870 and 1890. The development of enquête research in turn supported the establishment of a survey-oriented 'objective' and 'neutral' sociology from the beginning of the century until World War I. Anti-socialist legislation at the end of the century and political uproar at the beginning of the 1920s led to the withdrawal of sociology from political commitment and from social survey research during the Weimar Republic. The survey became the frequently used research method in social policy during the same period. The formation of the social survey can be traced in several stages of development from about 1870 to 1933.

The first stage was characterised by the political engagement of scientists. At the beginning of the Kaiserreich, the Verein analysed and criticised the state's statistical enquêtes on grounds of expert opinions. Data collection of the government's enquêtes was discussed mainly from the point of view of lacking 'fairness' towards the opinions and perceptions of the social conditions of workers. The Verein's General Assemblies passed resolutions in order to inform the government about the necessary social legislation.

The second stage was characterised by the withdrawal of the Verein's members from being government advisors. Under the impact of the anti-socialist legislation during the 1880's, the Verein ignored the most expolsive research object, the industrial worker, and turned instead to the state's second important social and political problem, the agrarian issue. At the same time the Verein intensified and extended its research activities. Monographs of experts were published under the designation, 'enquêtes'.

The stage from the end of the 1880s to the turn of the century can be characterised as the transition from the politically-engaged to the academic professional survey research. Under the impact of severe attacks from outside, the Verein's second generation began to discuss the 'value orientation of survey research' and to demand the separation of politics and science. However, the criticism from outside prevented arguments between the two generations inside the Verein and new academic research methods were not yet developed.

The fourth stage was characterised by the separation of survey research and politics. After the turn of the century up until World War I under a liberal government, the Verein's second generation succeeded in formulating rules for 'exact', i.e. highly differentiated and value neutral, research methods. These methods led to the first 'academic' investigation in sociology of industries. The German Society of Sociology was established as an academic counter organisation to the Verein für Socialpolitik.

The fifth stage, which took place after World War I up to the beginning of the Nazi regime in 1933, was characterised by the separation of sociology from social policy. Survey research was assigned to social policy. However, the policy-oriented research institutes developed only a few comprehensive methods of survey research. Due to the new constitution, the social policy legislation of the new government and the economic crisis, the Verein für Socialpolitik replaced its research on social issues with economics-orientated policy studies. These studies required theoretical revision of the former Historical School of National Economy and the Verein neglected the development of survey methods for social issues. The Social Democratic-oriented Department of Social Policy of the Institut für Sozialwissenschaften at the University of Cologne had to reduce its survey research after the loss of political power of the Social Democrats and lack of funds because of the economic crisis. Most developed survey researches were conducted by the Catholic Union-oriented Department of Social Legislation of the same Institute after the conservative parties had participated in the governments after 1925 and had come to power after 1930.

Due to the stance of value-neutrality in sociology, members of the German Society for Sociology refrained from all practical empirical research after world War I. According to their view, survey research entangled 'academic' sociologists with the political uproars between right-wing and left-wing parties during the 1920s. The Department of Sociology of the Institut für Sozialwissenschaften at the University of Cologne, which was supposed to represent liberal politics, confined itself to the building of a value-neutral, ahistoric, sociology as a natural science. The institute conducted research on formal social interrelations by means of unsystematic observations.

Between 1933 and 1936 the National Socialists shut down all the research institutes discussed above and a dictatorship of applied survey research for exclusively national Socialistic purposes began.

NOTES

1 This essay draws on Irmela Gorges, *Sozialforschung in Deutschland 1872–1914* (Frankfurt-on-Main: Hain, 1986), and *Sozialforschung in der Weimarer Republik 1918–1933* (Frankfurt-on-Main: Hain, 1986).

2 Gorges, *Sozialforschung in Deutschland*.

3 G. Embden, 'Wie sind Enquêten zu organisieren?', in *Schriften des Vereins für Sozialpolitik* (Munich, Leipzig: Duncker & Humblot, 1877), XIII, pp. 1–15.

4 Gorges, *Sozialforschung in Deutschland*.

5 Martin Riesebrodt (ed.), *Max Weber, die Lage der Landarbeiter im ostelbischen Deutschland 1892*, 2 vols. (Tübingen: J. C. B. Mohr, 1984); Michaël Pollak, 'Enquête sur la situation des ouvrieres agricoles à l'est de l'Elbe: conclusions prospectives', *Actes de la recherche en sciences sociales*, 65 (1986), 69–76.

6 Anthony Oberschall, *Empirical Social Research in Germany 1848–1914* (The Hague: Mouton, 1965), p. 63.

7 Max Weber, 'Die Objektivität sozialwissenschaftlicher und sozialpolitischer Erkenntnis', in *Archiv für Sozialwissenschaft und Sozialpolitik* (Tübingen: J. C. B. Mohr, 1904), XIX, pp. 22–87.

8 Burkhart Lutz and Gert Schmidt, 'Industriesoziologie', in Rene König (ed.), *Handbuch der empirischen Sozialforschung*, vol. 8: *Beruf, Industrie, Sozialer Wandel* (Stuttgart: Ferdinand Enke, 1977), pp. 101–262.

9 *Schriften des Vereins für Socialpolitik*, CXVI, p. 367.

10 Weber, 'Die Objektivität', p. 154.

11 Rosa Luxemburg, 'Hohl Nüsse,' in *Ausgewählte Reden und Schriften* Vol II (Berlin, Dietz Verlag, 1951), p. 68.

12 *Schriften des Vereins für Socialpolitik*, LXV, pt VII and LXVIII, pt V.

13 Gorges, *Sozialforschung in der Weimarer Republik 1918–1913*.

14 Lore Spindler, 'Studien zur Erwerbslosenfürsorge', in *Kölner Sozialpolitische Vierteljahres-schriften* (Berlin: Hans Robert Engelman, 1924), III, p. 29–58.

15 Wilhelm Vleugels, 'Wesen und eigenschaften der Masse', in *Kölner Vierteljahrshefte für Sozialwissenschaften, Reihe A, Soziologische Hefte* (Munich, Leipzig: Duncker and Humblot, 1922), II, pp. 71–80.

16 Paul Honigsheim, 'Die Boheme', in *Kölner Vierteljahrshefte für Soziologie* (Munich, Leipzig: Duncker and Humblot, 1923/4), III, pp. 60–71.

17 S. R. Steinmetz, 'Die Mode', in *Kölner Vierteljahrshefte für Soziologie* (Munich, Leipzig: Duncker and Humblot, 1926/7), VI, pp. 29–53.

18 Leopold von Wiese, 'Skizze des Aufbaus eines Systems der Beziehungslehre', in *Kölner Vierteljahrshefte für Sozialwissenschaften, Reihe A, Soziologische Hefte* (Munich, Leipzig: Duncker and Humblot, 1922), II, pp. 61–9.

19 Leopold von Wiese, 'Aus der Arbeit meines Soziologischen Obserseminars im Wintersemester 1931/32', in *Kölner Vierteljahrshefte für Soziologie* (Munich, Leipzig: Duncker and Humblot, 1932/3), XI, pp. 65–74.

20 Gorges, *Sozialforschung in der Weimarer Republik 1918–1933*.

Anglo-American contacts in the development of research methods before 1945

JENNIFER PLATT

Research methods tend to be treated, at least in textbooks, as an area of cumulative technical knowledge, where the repertoire in existence at any one time is equally available to all users. From a textbook point of view this may make perfectly good sense, but as history or sociology it is questionable. Britain and America may form one English-language community, but their intellectual developments cannot be conflated – although they cannot be treated as entirely independent either. This chapter examines the processes by which research methods, especially survey method, were or were not transmitted across the Atlantic. The focus is on sociology, though without defining it closely. There was, for much of the time covered, little in Britain that was 'sociology' by any standard, and less of that went by the name or took place under academic auspices, so we shall not limit ourselves to what was done by academic sociologists.

Research methods are not merely technical knowledge, in the sense of abstract ideas, but also concrete practices, and the detail of these practices is very often not conveyed in reports of research. In this area, therefore, personal contact is likely to be particularly important to accuracy of transmission.[1] Hence the emphasis, in what follows, on personal contacts, even when no record has been left of what took place during them. Attention will also be paid to the content of publications, but the risky practice of inferring influence from the observation of similarities will be avoided.

To what extent were Britain and America generally in touch intellectually over our period? No serious effort can be made here to answer this question systematically, but a few relevant points can be high-lighted. Novels and well-known marriage patterns are sufficient to suggest that the upper classes mixed socially. Books were published and distributed in both countries. There was active contact between those involved in social reform

340

and social work activities on both sides of the Atlantic, and this was one of the important strands in the development of both the survey and sociology. Particularly active were the contacts between those involved in social settlements, research and reform in Chicago, and the British Fabians and settlement workers; Britain was still looked up to as playing a leading role. Jane Addams of Hull House in Chicago exchanged visits with the warden of London's Toynbee Hall,[2] and with the Webbs,[3] and she also met Octavia Hill and members of the British Labour movement. Her circle had 'enormous interest ... in 1909 in the brilliant minority report issued by the Royal Poor-Law Commission'.[4] Edith Abbott took a Chicago PhD and then spent a year at the London School of Economics (LSE) *c.* 1906 before returning to Hull-House and jobs in sociology at the University of Chicago.[5] Zueblin, an early Chicago sociologist and Hull House resident, was a Fabian, knew the Webbs and had visited Toynbee Hall.[6] (He also visited Geddes' 'laboratory' in Edinburgh). Harvard's Henry Lee Travelling Fellowships provided opportunities for some Americans to visit Britain, and several used their fellowships to visit settlements. The Webbs' *Methods of Social Study* (1932) cites numbers of American works, including what was then a very up-to-date book on interviewing. Booth had business interests in the US, though it is unclear whether these led to contacts with social reformers or researchers (see in chapter 3 above). Seebohm Rowntree visited the USA many times in the interwar period, finding on his visit in 1921 that his work was already well known; on that trip he met members of the Chicago social science faculty and Jane Addams. He had close friendships with American businessmen with whom he exchanged ideas, and sent others to the US and invited Americans to Britain to study industrial conditions.[7] Clarence Northcott, who studied with Giddings at Columbia, went to work for Rowntree's firm in Britain. Cyril Burt in his very influential book *The Young Delinquent* cites many US sources, and in an appendix on psychiatric clinics for juvenile delinquents describes Healy's work in Chicago as 'a model for all such enterprises'.[8] *The Study of Society* (Bartlett *et al.*, 1939), the first British academic near-textbook on social research methods, contains many references to American social-psychological and sociological works, including some exemplifying, or about, surveys.

The importance in the inter-war period of the Rockefeller Foundation to the funding of social science research can hardly be over-estimated, and it was active in Britain as well as the USA – indeed, Fisher shows that it, along with Carnegie and Harkness money, was 'the mainstay of the support that social science received'.[9] Rockefeller fellowships and scholarships supported a two-way traffic across the Atlantic. American Social Science Research Council (SSRC) fellowships also allowed a number of Americans to come to Britain, and Commonwealth Fund fellowships took Britons to the USA. Harold Laski of LSE used his personal contacts to help a number of British social scientists find fellowships in the US.[18] The Tavistock Institute (at that stage a purely psychiatric institution) had innumerable US connections, and received much of its research funding from US sources.[11] Numbers of articles by American authors were published in *The Sociological Review* (then the only British sociological journal), and there was at least the occasional British one in an American journal.[12] From time to time there were also articles in one country about the current state of sociology in the other.[13] During World War II there was US–British cooperation, both general and in relation to wartime social research, even before the USA entered the war; once it had, this intensified, and many Americans were in Britain playing their part in the war effort. Thus there were many contacts and opportunities for interchange.

Against this background, we turn to consider some key developments in method and the ways in which they were or were not transmitted across the Atlantic, treating first the British and then the American contributions. Three items stand out as known British contributions to social research method: the 'survey' of Booth and Rowntree, statistical theory, and Mass Observation.

THE 'SURVEY' OF BOOTH

The work of Booth was very widely known in the USA and, though much of the interest in it came from those with social welfare concerns rather than sociological ones, it was drawn on in graduate training and referred to in textbooks on research methods.[14] How far the interest in Booth's work should be defined in terms of method is doubtful, since the meaning of 'survey' in the early US literature – and 'survey' was certainly the category to which Booth's work was assigned – was not a methodological one; the term was used to refer to a study carried out by any (and usually multiple) methods which collected intensive data about an area for purposes of social betterment. (Converse suggests, however, that there are common elements of continuing significance in the conduct of fieldwork, in the emphasis on wide scope, the examination of particulars on individual cases, and the counting of cases to give an overview.[15])

In both countries the term 'survey' was sometimes used simply as the equivalent of what we would now call 'community study'. Wells refers to both *Middletown* and the classic Chicago area studies as surveys.[16] Insofar as method is concerned, therefore, the interest was not so much in how the data were collected as in what was done with them. A focus here is on Booth's use of plotting what he had found on maps. Mapping of the distribution of social characteristics was very important in the Chicago department of sociology in the 1920s.[17] It seems likely that, despite the claims to originality sometimes made, this came from Booth mediated by Hull House.[18] W. E. B. Du Bois' *Philadelphia Negro* also included maps produced on Booth's model. Converse points out that the very early US surveys inspired by Booth none the less were also somewhat different in character, with much emphasis on citizen participation and community organisation rather than the recommendation of reforms from above; it is not hard to associate this with well-known differences between British and American society. The 'survey movement' in America became sufficiently large and related to local conditions to constitute its own tradition fairly rapidly; Parten suggests that it did not take on the much more efficient procedures of Bowley when these were available from Britain, and that her own study in 1931 may have been one of the first to employ his scientific sampling (on which see below).[19] There is little obvious trace, either, of the developing US 'survey movement' having influence in Britain; the later British works in the tradition refer back to the earlier ones, and acknowledge the help of their authors, rather than showing overt signs of any influence from elsewhere. To the extent that the movement was oriented to social problems, and the perceived problems of the two countries were different, this is not surprising.

STATISTICAL THEORY

The preeminence of the British statisticians — Pearson, Fisher, Yule, Gosset — was widely recognised, and their innovations in research design and analysis taken up. None of these worked specifically in the social sciences, but there Bowley, a less distinguished theorist but of vital importance in the theory and practice of sampling in social research, had his place. What contacts were involved in the diffusion of knowledge of their work? James Field, an economist who taught a statistics course taken by early Chicago sociologists, met Pearson and Bowley in London (one opportunity arising through service in World War I), and drew on what he learnt from them in his courses.[20] Columbia sociology students such as Ogburn and Chapin in the 1910s learned the new statistics from the econometrician Moore, who frequently visited Galton and Pearson in London.[21] Dorothy S. Thomas, wife of W. I. Thomas and herself President of the American Sociological Association in 1954 and an important contributor to quantitative sociology, did graduate work at the London School of Economics (LSE), winning a medal there in 1924. Samuel Stouffer, a vital figure in the history of survey methods, held an SSRC fellowship in 1931–2 to study the statistical treatment of small samples of sociological data with the British statisticians; he reports that he worked with Fisher and attended a seminar by Bowley and lectures by Karl and Egon Pearson[22] and it may have been from Yule that he learned the technique of using the four-fold table which he transmitted to Lazarsfeld and on which Lazarsfeld elaborated so fruitfully.[23] Mildred Parten, later the author of an important textbook on survey methods, also held an SSRC fellowship in the same year to study the methods of the *New London Survey of Life and Labour* at the LSE, and acknowledges the influence then of Bowley.[24] British statisticians also visited the USA. Iowa State University was an important centre of statistics, especially in agricultural applications. Distinguished visitors were regularly invited to spend the summer session at Iowa, and Fisher did this in both 1931 and 1936, also using the opportunity to visit other US centres, including Chicago where he met Wright (of path analysis fame). A member of the Iowa department went to work with him in London in 1933 and 1935–6.[25] On one of his visits he also lectured at the US Department of Agriculture's Mathematics and Statistics section.[26] (Neyman and Yates also visited the USA in the 1930s.[27]) E. S. (son of K.) Pearson also spent a summer session at Iowa.[28] W. G. Cochran, a Cambridge graduate, worked at Fisher's Rothamsted Experimental Station in 1934–9, and then moved to Iowa and spent the rest of his career in the USA, ending up at Harvard; he made important contributions to survey sampling, especially in the early postwar years.[39] These connections with Iowa are particularly significant because it was the home state of Henry Wallace, Roosevelt's Secretary of State for Agriculture and later Vice-President. Wallace had a personal interest and competence in statistics, and was responsible for the introduction of systematic research on farmers' opinions to the Department of Agriculture. The team built up there under Likert took advice from Iowa to introduce one of the first applications of national random sampling, and later became one of the key postwar survey units, the Institute for Social Research at Michigan.[30] Finally, there was one more line of contact. Margaret Hogg, Bowley's research assistant at the LSE until 1925, then went to America and from 1927 worked as a statistician in the Russell Sage Foundation's department of statistics. Russell Sage played a leading role in the early survey, but also did its own empirical work of other kinds. One of Hogg's studies was on the incidence of unemployment, and a main purpose was to demonstrate the practicability of random sampling.[31] (This study used a sample drawn by Parten.[32]) Hogg's job also included the provision of statistical advice both to other departments at Russell Sage and to outside bodies; in 1932, she was seconded to the federal government's Committee on Government Statistics and Information Services, where she worked on topics such as a cost of living index and a survey of consumer expenditure. She also did some teaching in the Fordham School of Sociology and Social Service.[33] Deming, who was in a position to know, says that she was an important influence in the US in the 1930s.[34]

MASS OBSERVATION

Mass Observation (MO) started in 1937 entirely outside academic life and the social sciences; it rapidly acquired many academic contacts in Britain, although it also had its opponents. Its methods started as observational, informal and unstructured, without formal sampling, but by the postwar period it had become a market research agency using relatively conventional survey methods, although traces of the original ideology remained. The earlier period is, thus, the one where it had a distinctive influence to contribute. Several articles on MO appeared in American academic journals. The well-known 1938 article by Lazarsfeld and Fiske introducing the idea of panel studies has a section on MO;[35] this does not fit into their general argument very well, but is included because 'the study [i.e. *First Year's Work*] is attracting so much attention'. (Those employed by MO as full-time observers during 1938–40 included Gertrud Wagner, a friend of Lazarsfeld's from their days in Vienna.) Willcock and Ferraby of MO had articles on it in the *American Journal of Sociology* in 1943 and 1945 respectively.[36] In 1941 Hadley Cantril, one of the leading US pollsters, was corresponding with Tom Harrisson of MO and wrote: 'I have followed your mass observations most closely and think I have the most complete file of your work of anyone around'.[37]

In the early stages of World War II MO worked for the Ministry of Information, and it is possibly as a consequence of this that an American emissary collecting material on how Britain had been dealing with various practical wartime problems visited Harrisson in 1942.[38] The files of the Ministry of Information show that in 1940 there was a discussion of sending MO material to the US because it might be valuable if they entered the war, and anyway there was more interest in it there; one copy should go to the Library of Congress and one to the University of Chicago, where MO already had contacts. (Ministry of Information). Numbers of other Americans also visited MO during the war, including Margaret Mead in connection with her wartime work for the government on food.[39] Ernest

Burgess of Chicago was a leading sociologist, and had a special interest in
the systematic analysis of qualitative data. It is probable that some MO
materials were sent to him; he certainly knew of MO's work, because
minutes of the (US) SSRC show that he thought of using methods
developed by them (SSRC). There was some talk of founding Mass
Observation groups in the USA. The only one I have identified consisted
of Harold Orlans, then a young graduate of City College of New York
employed as a journalist but later a sociologist, and a group of his socialist-
Zionist friends; their attention was drawn to MO in 1942–3 by Zellig
Harris, their political mentor, a professor of linguistics at the University of
Pennsylvania who knew of it because of his interest in socialism and grass-
roots political response.[40] They did a study of reactions to the death of
President Roosevelt using MO methods.[42] There is in the MO archive an
undated, but postwar, publicity handout which says that a new commercial
outfit in America 'with a programme extensively publicised as based on the
principles of MO' has been set up.[42] By this stage, however, many other
sources for relatively intensive interviewing – such as the quite independent
Division of Program Surveys[43] – also existed.

The larger bulk and more cumulative nature of American contributions
makes it harder to isolate particular items, but we shall none the less
attempt to do so.

POLITICAL POLLING

The early history of polls in the work of Gallup, Roper and Crossley is well
known, and the interest in election results ensured that they were widely
reported. The most direct possible transmission of this to Britain occurred,
in that in 1936 Gall up set up a British branch, the British Institution of
Public Opinion (BIPO). Henry Durant, a graduate of the LSE, was put in
charge of this. Durant maintained American connections; he visited the US
for briefing on Gallup methods and was on the editorial board of the early
Public Opinion Quarterly.

MARKET RESEARCH

Many of the same agencies that did political polls also did more general
market research. Important early practical developments in sampling,
question wording and the organisation and training of field forces were
made there, although the people most important to the development of
academic research, Likert and Lazarsfeld, moved at an early stage into

governmental and academic work. The 1930s saw the major growth. There was market research using questionnaire methods in Britain in the early 1930s, but it appears to have been fairly primitive. P. Redmayne and H. Weeks in *Market Research* (1931), for a long time the only British textbook on the subject, suggest that no questionnaire should have more than eight questions, that these should not be asked in any fixed order, and the answers should be recorded later from memory; the appendix on the theory of statistics gets as far as recommending deviations as measures of dispersion. (But some US research was not necessarily more sophisticated at this stage.) Some US references appear in its twelve-book bibliography, but none on surveys or general research method. Mark Abrams entered market research with the London Press Exchange (LPE) in 1933, and he and the LPE from then on were involved in many significant pieces of work outside the commercial field – which he attributes to the lack of competition at the time; in effect they acted as a general survey agency. Abrams had just returned from two years at the Brookings Institution; the people he met there were mostly political scientists and statisticians, but they included Daniel Starch, who had invented a method of surveying newspaper readership which on his return Abrams used for the *Manchester Guardian*. He met Lazarsfeld in London when the latter passed through on first leaving Vienna; as a result of this, Gertrud Wagner worked with him at the LPE in the mid-thirties. He was involved in much wartime research, including the content analysis of German media output. Americans were sent over to see what his team was doing on this, and in 1942 he was sent to the Political Warfare Division in Washington to explain his methods; one of the first people he met there was Likert, then head of DPS, which was making important innovations in open-ended interviewing, coding and sampling.[44] He gave talks to Likert and his colleagues on Britain's food rationing. He spent a lot of his spare time with Lazarsfeld (as well as with Geoffrey Gorer, then working in Washington, and with Margaret Mead and Harold Lasswell). On another visit, in 1943, he met Gabriel Almond and Daniel Lerner, and turned down an invitation to come back after the war to create an institute for survey research at Stanford.[45] Marie Jahoda, Lazarsfeld's collaborator in Vienna, came to England from Austria and did some work in market research before joining the early WarTime Social Survey (WTSS). Frederick Brown, of the LSE, was a statistician by training, but worked in the Department of Business Administration and took a special interest in methods of market research, writing about it in quite a sophisticated way (with references to Lazarsfeld's work) in the later 30s.[46] He later became responsible for the initial methods and organisation of the early WTSS.[47] The National Institute for Industrial Psychology did some market research, and also undertook attitude surveys, usually in individual companies, and Winifred Raphael directed many of these.[48] She had held a Rockefeller fellowship to study sociology in the USA and Canada in 1928–9; that was an early stage in US developments, but suggests a possible channel of some US influence.[39]

Once again, thus, there were Anglo-American contacts, though how consequential they were specifically for market research is not clear. Mark Abrams felt that US market research tended to concentrate on the measurement of attention to advertisements and on opinions, while British market research was more concerned with who buys what, and in that field was more advanced because of the long tradition of fact-finding surveys.[50] It has also been suggested that most people then in market research in Britain had been trained in economics and statistics; the Americans probably came more often from psychology.[51] It is harder to write about practice in market research than in most other areas because most of it is not published. Lazarsfeld, however, often managed to get from it academically publishable material, and our next heading relates to an area he developed.

PANEL STUDIES

The panel study, as repeated measurements on the same group to assess change over time, grew from the older practice of having a group of consumers recruited to comment on new products.[52] Lazarsfeld applied it, famously, to election campaigns.[53] This idea was very directly transplanted to Britain. When Edward Shils was at the LSE after the war he was, by Benney's account, shocked at the absence of sophisticated empirical research in British sociology and persuaded people at the LSE to undertake an election study modelled on *The People's Choice*.[54] Mark Abrams adapted the design to British conditions, Henry Durant's BIPO did the fieldwork, and Benney (an ex-burglar who had been introduced to systematic fieldwork by Abrams) directed it. The result was *How People Vote* (1956). The second author for the work, A. P. Gray, was an Australian who had done graduate work at Columbia and been employed on the *Voting* study.[55] The third, R. H. Pear, then at the LSE, had studied political science at Chicago in 1939–41. All this was, however, after the war, and so too late really to fall within our period.

Modern survey method generally

There were some other points of contact in addition to those already mentioned, most of them in connection with the war effort in World War II. David Glass held a Rockefeller fellowship to study sociology in the USA in 1940–1,[56] and played an important role in British demographic and survey research; his wife Ruth Glass was a Senior Research Officer at Lazarsfeld's Bureau of Applied Social Research in 1940–2. It is possible that the advanced methods of the US Census may have influenced the British Census, though I have no data on that. It has been suggested that the two countries' censuses did influence each other, and it seems likely that the inevitable census problems of dealing with large numbers made methods of machine tabulation an important area for imitation.[57] However, it has also been pointed out that the British Census over our period had a narrowly economistic perspective which limited its range, while the US Census was broader and both used and was used by sociologists to a much greater extent.[58] There seems to have been some exchange of information among wartime research units, though this may not have been extensive. Lord (then Dr) Taylor, who was at the Ministry of Information, says he knew of the work of Likert's DPS, whose function was closely analogous to that of the later WTSS that he was in charge of, although he did not think highly of it.[59] F. Brown of the earlier WTSS went to the USA in 1940, and wrote a report on what he had been doing with them which he said aroused much interest there, presumably in the Polls and/or Surveys Divisions of The Bureau of Intelligence to whose superior it was addressed.[60] It is perhaps not very surprising that I have found no trace of direct contact with the work done in the US Army under Stouffer, later published as *The American Soldier*;[61] it is hard to imagine the British Army encouraging surveys of its soldiers' attitudes. (In an interview in 1987, however Jack Davies reports that a proposal for a system of selection for officers which would draw on Moreno's sociometric technique came quite near to acceptance. He attributes this and some other openings to the anxiety caused by the very poor British war situation in 1941–2.) What was done in the British armed forces appears to have been psychological, psychiatric, or in the new field of what became known as operational research.[62] Psychological work on selection in the Army drew heavily on American work, some of it from World War I; J. R. Rees describes a volume of the US Army's medical history of that war as his bible when he became Consulting Psychiatrist to the Army at Home.[63] Rees was a key figure at the Tavistock Institute, some of whose leading members, as a result of their wartime work on issues of leadership and morale, after the war set up the Institute of Human Relations, which made major contributions to industrial sociology. This was closely linked to the Center for Group Dynamics at Michigan, a part of Likert's postwar continuation of his wartime survey group the Division of Program Surveys; in this way there came later to be a connection with US surveys.[64] These Tavistock interests converged with those of the people coming from operational research, supported by money and enthusiasm from the programme for postwar reconstruction, to produce a major flowering of interest in industrial sociology. Elton Mayo, who regularly spent his winters at Harvard and his summers in England, was also a significant figure in the genesis of this movement.[65] The US British commonality was, thus, substantive rather than methodological, and so, it seems, was the important exchange of ideas.

Radio research is worth a special mention, although surveys were not its only method, because it was so important in Lazarsfeld's early career. Rudolf Arnheim, a refugee from Berlin, worked briefly for the British Broadcasting Corporation (BBC) before getting a Rockefeller fellowship which he held at Lazarsfeld's Office of Radio Research in 1941; it is not clear if he returned to the BBC, but from 1943 his career was in the US.[66] Ernst Kris, another refugee, worked with Abrams on propaganda analysis at the BBC before going on to do closely related work in the US, using material provided by the BBC's monitoring service.[67] The BBC started research on its own listeners in 1936; this was directed by Robert Silvey, formerly of the LPE's statistical department (where Abrams had joined him). He know Lazarsfeld's work, and visited his project in the US at least once.[68] How far his work was actually influenced by what was done in the US was not clear, although Durant at Gallup did some fieldwork for the BBC; certainly as late as 1944 it is clear that it retained some characteristically British features.[69] Lazarsfeld's early work on radio refers to British listener research only once briefly,[70] and this seems to be about the analysis of listeners' letters. Thus the real potential influence may not have had a great effect on practice. Clearly the ethos of the BBC may have had something to do with this; there was strong initial resistance to finding out listeners' preferences, on the ground that what they wanted should not determine what was given to them![71] The issues raised in American commercial radio were bound to differ.

Finally, what is in some ways a different intellectual stream may be mentioned, that of more 'qualitative' research. There was considerable contact between British and American anthropologists, but this probably did not have the impact on sociology which has sometimes been assumed,[72] The early work of the Chicago school appears to have been widely known, though often understood in a very British way. One little-known direct contact is by way of Sibyl Clement Brown, a psychiatric social worker at the LSE. She held a Rockefeller fellowship for sociology in the US in 1924–7, and studied juvenile delinquency. This led her to meet C. Shaw and W. I. Thomas, as well as working closely with some of the social workers who provided the cases used in much of the early Chicago sociological work; she did case studies and a delinquent's life history while there.[73] Later F. Brown, her colleague at the LSE, brought her in to advise on interviewing method in the early, 'qualitative' days of WTSS, and most of its first interviewers were psychiatric social workers who had been her students. However, this phase of WTSS broke up[74] and its personnel dispersed, so it had little later influence; many historical accounts date the start of WTSS from Louis Moss's arrival on the scene as Director and his reconstitution of the organisation after the old staff left. It is interesting to note that Marie Jahoda, as one of the key staff members in the early phase, brought to it analytical skills developed working with Lazarsfeld and others in Vienna, so that in that sense there is a connection with what became American survey method. E. Wight Bakke from Yale held a fellowship in England in 1931–2 and did the work which led to *The Unemployed Man* (1933). This used methods along the spectrum from semi-structured interview to participant observation. Curiously, however, this seems to have drawn little on qualitative methods developing in America at the time; the participant observation was actually suggested by John Hilton, well known for his direction of the Ministry of Labour's highly statistical sample enquiries into unemployment, apparently as a spontaneous original idea.[75] The book was admired and quoted widely, but again does not seem to have led to anything.

Reading about British social research in the period 1920–40, one can hardly fail to note what a small world it was. The same names crop up again and again in different contexts and permutations. To that extent, some of the separations between spheres suggested by the distinctions made above between subheadings are of little practical importance. To a considerable extent there was one world of social research, and it cut across the boundaries between academic and non-academic. To a considerable extent, too, this world centred on the London School of Economics and the metropolitan institutions and networks with which this intersected, although there were also nuclei at Oxford, Cambridge and Liverpool. Of crucial importance, however, is the fact that the highest levels of technical skill and interest in methodological issues were located outside academia.

Perhaps it could be said that the academic world was too small to allow for the differentiation necessary to support methods specialists, and there is something to that, but presumably a greater interest in what they could offer would have led to room being made for them. However, the close metropolitan connections among academic, policy and commercial worlds may have helped to make the development of the more distinctively academic and analytical type of survey seem unnecessary to those most likely to be interested in it.

CONCLUSION

Major British contributions did have some influence in the USA. The work of the statisticians was widely taken up, elaborated, built upon and incorporated into practice. The surveys of Booth and Rowntree were also known, imitated and developed. It is less clear that MO had any real impact, though much interest was shown in it. A likely reason for this is that, insofar as what it had to offer was research methods rather than a socio-political movement, these were on the one hand overtaken by and subsumed under the emerging new conception of 'participant observation'[76] and sophisticated postwar survey techniques for the use of open-ended questions, while on the other hand what was distinctive about them was in any case eroded with time.

It is harder to point to US influences on Britain, even though there were so many more of them available, except – significantly – in commercial rather than academic work. To account for this, we may point to some well-known characteristics of the British academic sociology of the period. First, there was very little of it, and those who went by the name of sociologists had little interest in empirical research. Those who did the empirical work that might be regarded as more or less sociological could be practically anything but a professional sociologist: businessman (Seebohm Rowntree), demographer/geographer (David Glass), civil servant (John Hilton), journalist (Charles Madge), statistician (Frederick Brown), anthropologist (Kenneth Little), economist (P. Sargant Florence), social worker (Marie Paneth) or just plain amateur (Pearl Jephcott). Numbers of those most directly involved in empirical work were of foreign origin and training: E. Wight Bakke, Ruth Glass, Marie Jahoda, Ernst Kris, Oscar Oeser, Hans Singer (*Men Without Work*), Gertrud Wagner. Indeed, social research generally was not institutionalised within the universities; even after the war, when large-scale studies were undertaken the fieldwork was likely to be carried out by market research firms. Such a high proportion of what was done was financed by the Rockefeller Foundation that it seems likely that it would not have taken place at all without that external impetus.[77] (In

America part of the New Deal's response to the Depression was to set up the Works Progress Administration, whose job-creation activities funded a large amount of empirical research; there was no equivalent response to unemployment in Britain.) The sociology degree course at LSE did not teach research methods, although students could take courses on the practical uses of social statistics taught by Bowley and Brown; even after the war Banks reports that the course with 'methods' in the title, taught by Ginsberg, referred only to the 'comparative method' of Hobhouse.[78] It is striking that the 1939 *The Study of Society* is explicitly aimed at amateurs as well as students ('it is recognised that invaluable services can be rendered by persons who have had little opportunity to obtain technical instruction ... attempts have been made to indicate how the amateur investigator can best assist in the development of social studies'[79]). The small number of students would hardly have created a sufficient market for a purely professional textbook at the time. If textbooks are not being written, that discourages systematic reflection on the morals to be drawn from practice and the ways in which they can be generalised beyond immediate practical needs, and hence makes the development of an articulated tradition harder. In these circumstances, it is not surprising that there was little sign of a cumulative tradition handed on from sociological generation to generation. The lack of graduate training − or funding for it − was also important in this. It is probably only with the first postwar cohort described by Halsey that the serious possibility of passing on an intellectual tradition to students who would stay in the discipline existed.[80]

It was possible before then to make some sort of career in social research, but for those not in the civil service or the commercial world it would be an insecure one pieced together from fragments. Discussions of method took place within market research or at the Government Social Survey. One of the most striking features for anyone with American experience is the dominance of statisticians in discussions of survey method, and the importance of the Royal Statistical Society and its publications as a methodological forum. Consequently those who wrote on survey method in Britain normally had as their paradigm primarily the survey of an atheoretical or demographic character, of a kind commonly done for the government, and secondarily that of market research.[81] Abrams suggests that one reason for lack of mutual influence was that in the interwar period US surveys were more sociologically oriented, testing hypotheses, while British ones were almost entirely policy-oriented.[82]

As Kent points out, the lack of continuity meant that much of the research that was done effectively started almost from scratch − with luck, reinventing the wheel. The only area where there was some real continuity, with minor technical improvements, was that of the 'survey' as known to Booth and Rowntree,[83] This persisted within academic life, as it did not in the USA. In the University of Chicago's department of sociology one can trace how the early interests of key members in the old-style survey gradually evolved from the 1910s as fresh theoretical questions were raised, new empirical topics approached, and a distinctive professional identity established; Stephen Turner shows, earlier in this book, how another sort of development took place at Columbia. In a sense the old survey kept out the new in Britain.

It is suggested, therefore, that there were in Britain many of the contacts and opportunities which could have diffused American methodological ideas, but none the less they were not effectively implanted. Rockefeller money was used for old-style surveys, or for the kind done by economists at the National Institute for Economic and Social Research and the Oxford Institute of Statistics. Several refugees or other foreigners with valuable experience went on to America (Jahoda, Kris) or elsewhere (Wagner, Gray, Oeser). Some of the most intensive contacts were maintained by people outside the opportunities of academic life. For the effective transmission of ideas their public availability and personal contacts with their originators may be necessary, but are not sufficient, conditions. There must be something for them to articulate with if they are to have a real effect; merely to be known in principle does not ensure application in practice. In the case of Britain, this set of sufficient conditions was not complete. In the case of the USA it was, and what Britain had to offer was taken, but it tended to vanish from sight with so much else going on and with cumulative work building on it. Paradoxically, therefore, the smaller country with less active social science appears to have influenced the larger and more active one more than it was influenced by it, because in the USA there was a substantial empirical social science to influence.[84]

NOTES

1 Cf. H. M. Collins, *Changing Order* (Beverly Hills: Sage, 1985).

2 J. Addams, *20 Years at Hull-House* (New York: Macmillan, 1919), pp. 74–207.

3 M. I. Cole (ed.), *Beatrice Webb's Diaries 1912–17* (London: Longmans, Green, 1952), p. 40.

4 J. Addams, *The Second 20 Years at Hull-House* (New York: Macmillan, 1930), p. 13.

5 M. J. Deegan, *Jane Addams and the Men of the Chicago School, 1892–1918* (New Brunswick: Transaction Books, 1988), p. 44.

6 Deegan, *Jane Addams*, pp. 90–2.

7 A. Briggs, *Social Thought and Social Action: A Study of the Work of Seebohm Rowntree* (London: Longmans, Green, 1961), ch. 6.

8 Cyril Burt, *The Young Delinquent* (London: University of London Press, 1925).

9 D. Fisher, 'American Philanthropy and the Social Sciences in Britain, 1919–39: The Reproduction of a Conservative Ideology', *Sociological Review*, 28 (1980), 285.

10 M. Abrams, personal communication.

11 H. V. Dicks, *50 Years of the Tavistock Clinic* (London: Routledge and Kegan Paul, 1970), passim.

12 H. Mess, 'The Social Survey of Tyneside', *American Journal of Sociology*, 33 (1928), 424–30.

13 For instance, C. Zueblin, 'The World's First Sociological Laboratory', *American Journal of Sociology*, 4 (1899), 577–92, and V. Palmer, 'Impressions of Sociology in Great Britain', *American Journal of Sociology*, 32 (1927), 756–61.

14 M. Bulmer, *The Chicago School of Sociology* (Chicago: Chicago University Press, 1984), pp. 64, 80.

15 J. M. Converse, *Survey Research in the US: Roots and Emergence 1890–1960* (Berkeley: University of Chicago Press, 1987), p. 21.

16 A. F. Wells, 'Social Surveys and Sociology', *Sociological Review*, 28 (1936), 285–6.

17 Bulmer, *Chicago School*, pp. 154–6.

18 Deegan, *Jane Addams*, pp. 46, 64. There is, however, also a hint that it may have had supplementary origins elsewhere in Chicago. Mrs Ethel Dummer, though never a professional, was active in Chicago sociological circles and made significant intellectual contributions to others' work. In her autobiography she describes how her husband, who had a hobby of maps and an interest in the geographical distribution of ethnic groups, when she told him about her interest in places like saloons made a map with pins of different colours to stand for saloons, settlements and churches. Unfortunately there is no date for this episode, but other evidence makes the mid-1900s seem likely. See E. S. Dummer, *Why I Think So* (Chicago: Clarke-McElroy, 1937), p. 38. However, it would have been very surprising if Mr and Mrs Dummer had not known of Hull-House's mapping activities, though Mrs Dummer took up her active social concerns relatively late in life. There is also the possibility that the tradition of agricultural mapping may have contributed via rural sociology.

19 M. Parten, *Surveys, Polls, and Samples* (New York: Harper, 1950), pp. 9, 12.

20 Bulmer, *Chicago School*, p. 163.

21 P. Halfpenny, *Positivism and Sociology* (London: Allen and Unwin, 1982), p. 40.

22 S. Stouffer, 'Karl Pearson – An Appreciation ...', *Journal of the American Statistical Association*, 53 (1958), 23.

23 J. Platt, 'Qualitative Research for the State', *Quarterly Journal of Social Affairs*, 2 (1986), 104.

24 Parten, *Surveys*, p. xii.

25 J. F. Box, *R. A. Fisher. The Life of a Scientist* (New York: Wiley, 1978), pp. 314–18.

26 P. M. Hauser Papers, University of Chicago Archives, box 8, Folder 11.

27 F. F. Stephan, 'History of the Uses of Modern Sampling Procedures', *Journal of the American Statistical Association*, 43 (1948), 31.

28 Box, *R. A. Fisher*, p. 313.

29 P. Rao and Sedransk, *W. G. Cochran's Impact on Statistics* (New York: Wiley, 1984).

30 It is possible that the agricultural connection was particularly important, It is easily forgotten how important farming still was to the American economy and politics between the wars. The Agricultural Experiment Stations at land-grant universities housed agricultural scientists and sociologists in close proximity, and provided both jobs and research funding for a rural sociology which was of considerable professional importance. Thus Fisher's essentially accidental agricultural connections probably helped rather than hindering here.

31 M. H. Hogg, *The Incidence of Work Shortage* (New York: Russell Sage, 1932), p. 13.

32 Parten, *Surveys*, p. 12.

33 J. M. Glenn *et al.*, *The Russell Sage Foundation 1907–46* (New York: Russell Sage, 1947), pp. 398, 606–9.

34 W. E. Deming, 'Sample Surveys: The Field', in W. H. Kruskal and J. M. Tanur (eds.), *International Encyclopaedia of Statistics* (New York: Free Press, 1978), pp. 567–84.

35 P. F. Lazarsfeld and M. Fiske, 'The Panel as a New Tool for Measuring Opinion', *Public Opinion Quarterly*, 2 (1938), 596–612.

36 H. D. Willcock, 'Mass Observation', *AJS*, 48 (1943), 455–56; J. G. Ferraby, 'Planning a Mass Observation Investigation', *AJS*, 51 (1945), 1–6.

37 Letter, 27 March 1941, USA folder, International contacts, MO Archive, University of Sussex.

38 Folder 1B, box 247, MO Archive.

39 D. Chapman, Interview (1979) by Nick Stanley, MO Archive.

40 Z. Harris, personal communication (1988).

41 H. Orlans, 'An Anthropologist without a Tribe: A Memoir', *The American Scholar*, 50 (1981), 465–78; personal communication (1987).

42 'Statement on policy', folder, fieldwork etc. Box, MO Archive.

43 Platt, 'Qualitative Research'.

44 M. Abrams, 'Founding Fathers: Mark Abrams', *Market Research Society Newsletter* 149 (1978), 8–9; interview (1985).

45 M. Abrams, personal communication (1987).

46 F. Brown, 'Some Problems in Market Research', in A. Plant (ed.), *Some Modern Business Problems* (London: Longmans, Green, 1937).

47 Platt, 'Qualitative Research'.

48 J. Davies, Interview (1987).

49 *Directory of Fellowships and Scholarships 1917–70* (New York: Rockefeller Foundation, 1972).

50 Abrams, 'Founding Fathers', p. 9.

51 J. W. Downham *et al.*, Intro. in E. S. Edwards (ed.), *Readings in Market Research* (London: BMRB, 1956), p. xxviiii.

52 Converse, *Survey Research*, p. 143.

53 P. F. Lazarsfeld *et al.*, *The People's Choice* (New York: Duell, Sloan and Pearce, 1944).

54 M. Benney, *Almost a Gentleman* (London: Peter Davies, 1966).

55 M. Benney, A. P. Gray and R. H. Pear, *How People Vote* (London: Routledge and Kegan Paul, 1956).

56 *Directory.*

57 M. Conk, 'Labor Statistics in the American and English Census...', *Journal of Social History*, 16 (1983), 83–102.

58 Cf. P. M. Hauser, 'Social Accounting', in P. F. Lazarsfeld *et al.*, *The Uses of Sociology* (New York: Basic Books, 1967).

59 S. (Lord) Taylor, Interview (1986).

60 Platt, 'Qualitative Research'; Clement Brown, Interviews (1986).

61 S. A. Stouffer *et al.*, *The American Soldier* (Princeton, NJ: Princeton University Press, 1949).

62 R. Stansfield, 'Operational Research and Sociology...', *Science and Public Policy*, 8 (1981), 252–80; T. T. Paterson, *Morale in War and Work* (London: Parrish, 1955).

63 J. R. Rees, *Reflections* (New York: US Committee of the World Federation for Mental Health, 1966), p. 40.

64 H. V. Dicks, *Fifty Years of the Tavistock Clinic* (London: Routledge and Kegan Paul, 1970), pp. 5–8.

65 J. H. Smith, 'Elton Mayo and the English Dream', *Sociological Review*, 35 (1987), 602–21.

66 D. Fleming and B. Bailyn (eds.), *The Intellectual Migration* (Cambridge, Mass: Harvard University Press, 1969).

67 E. Kris and H. Speier, *German Radio Propaganda* (New York: Oxford University Press, 1944), p. v.

68 R. Silvey, *Who's Listening?* (London: Allen and Unwin, 1974), pp. 85–6.

69 R. Silvey, 'Methods of Listener Research Employed by the BBC', *JRSS*, 107 (1944), 190–211.

70 P. F. Lazarsfeld, *Radio and the Printed Page* (New York: Duell, Sloan and Pearce, 1940), p. 113.

71 A. Briggs, *The Golden Age of Wireless* (London: Oxford University Press, 1965), pp. 257–62.

72 J. Platt, 'The Development of the Participant Observation Method...', *Journal for the History of the Behavioral Sciences*, 19 (1983), 392–3.

73 S. C. Brown, Interview (1986).

74 Platt, 'Qualitative Research'.

75 E. W. Bakke, *The Unemployed Man* (London: Nisbet, 1933), p. xiv.

76 Platt, 'Participant Observation Method'.

77 D. Fisher 'American Philanthropy and the Social Sciences in Britain, 1919–39: The Reproduction of a Conservative Ideology', *Sociological Review*, 28 (1980), 277–315.

78 J. A. Banks, personel communication (1988).

79 F. C. Bartlett *et al.* (eds.), *The Study of Society* (London: Routledge and Kegan Paul, 1939), p. viii.

80 A. H. Halsey, 'Provincials and Professionals...', in M. Bulmer (ed.), *Essays on the History of British Sociological Research* (Cambridge: Cambridge University Press, 1985).

81 Cf. A. McKennell , 'The Links between Policy, Survey Research and Academic Social Science: America and Britain Compared, in M. Bulmer (ed.), *Social Science Research and Government* (Cambridge: Cambridge University Press, 1987), p. 255. Vivien Palmer of Chicago pointed out in 1927 ('Impressions of Sociology in Great Britain', *American Journal of Sociology*, 32, 758–9) that in British sociology '... the main trend has been

toward bringing the sociological point of view into economic studies rather than toward developing sociological studies of contemporaneous British life ... there is still a strong and rather prevalent aversion to "prying into the individual's innermost recesses" to obtain those personal documents which are proving so important in advancing sociological knowledge in this country ...' Sixteen years later Rowntree reviewed the first two volumes of Lloyd Warner's Yankee City studies with a stiff and distant lack of comprehension: 'The purpose of the inquiry is quite different from that of the ordinary investigations into social and economic conditions which have been made in many cities ... Has it added new and valuable knowledge about the influences which determine the character and quality of the social life of a community? Will it guide social reformers? Quite frankly the answer to both questions is that it will do so only very slightly ...' (*Sociological Review*, 35 (1943), 50–1).

82 Abrams, personel communication.

83 Perhaps associated with this is the prevalence in Britain of the curious practice, possibly stemming from Booth (cf. Marsh 1985), of collecting secondhand data, by getting volunteers seen as well-informed to report on the activities of others. (See C. Marsh, 'Informants, Respondents and Citizens', in M. Bulmer (ed.), *Essays in the History of British Sociological Research* (Cambridge: Cambridge University Press, 1985.) BBC Audience Research used it (Silvey, 'Methods of Listener Research', pp. 209–11), so did the Ministry of Information in World War II, and there was a strong element of it in Mass Observation. Insofar as there is a US equivalent, it is the heavy use made in the 'case-study method' of social workers' case records. The British tradition, however, did not have room for the 'own story' which often appeared alongside or as part of this; social distance was maintained.

84 It is of interest to note that, despite the societal and social-scientific differences referred to, there were some apparently independent inventions of similar ideas: both the early WTSS and DPS turned to psychiatric techniques for methods of open-ended survey interviewing, and the 'thermometer' which Converse suggests was reinvented several times in the USA also appeared as a 'barometer' in BBC listener research (Silvey, *Who's Listening'*, p. 79).

CHAPTER FOURTEEN

The social survey in historical perspective: a governmental perspective

ROGER DAVIDSON

The papers gathered in this volume well illustrate the difficulties of any attempt at a comparative analysis of the history of social investigation. The emergence of the social survey in countries of very different cultures reveals important parallels and contrasts that invite interpretation. However, to gain traction on these issues is problematic. Although the sociology of knowledge presents suggestive theories for explaining the diffusion of information and the contrasting development of investigative techniques,[1] the historian is faced with a range of social and intellectual linkages which is far from easy to document. What *is* clear is that these case studies reveal a set of cultural and institutional factors which provide the key variables shaping the knowledge base of industrialised society. Among these could be cited contemporary perceptions of social and economic crisis, the role of information in dominant ideologies, societal attitudes to investigation and quantification, and the institutional framework within which social knowledge is produced and deployed.

The last raises important issues of the relationships of the State to the social survey. In focusing on the internal history and politics of specific surveys, such as those of Booth and Rowntree or of Hull House or Du Bois, there is a danger of losing leverage on their broader implications for the growth of 'the knowledge state'. In particular, the relationship of government to the social survey may reveal important aspects of its origins and use.

Within the British context, one would have expected the late-nineteenth- and early-twentieth-century surveys to have been closely integrated with government investigation. The debt of government inquiry to private research (both institutional and individual) has been documented. Official investigations, such as those into working-class patterns of expenditure and destitution, often used the research of organisations such as relief agencies,

359

trade unions, chambers of commerce, churches and statistical societies as well as the data collected by individuals such as Booth and Rowntree in their surveys. Moreover, this was far from being a one-way process. There existed a symbiotic relationship between the social investigators inside and outside Whitehall. They frequently shared the same social and cultural background, emerging from the University Settlement and Extension Movements or from involvement in the Charity Organisation Society and other relief agencies. They shared the same social scientific milieu at the Royal Statistical Society, the Economic Society and the British Association for the Advancement of Science. They also shared similar social concerns (at the breakdown of industrial relations, at the socio-economic crisis of the urban economy, and at the competitive failure of the British economy) that motivated their quest for information. Moreover, although it operated unevenly, a pattern of incorporation within State investigation can be discerned. Significantly, many of the leading participants of Booth's *Survey of the Life and Labour of the People of London*, such as Llewellyn Smith, Ernest Aves, Clara Collet and David Schloss were subsequently appointed to senior investigative posts within Whitehall. It is also notable that the same group of social statisticians corresponded with social surveyors in America, such as Edith Abbott of Hull House.[2]

Yet, for all this, there is little evidence that Whitehall paid any significant regard to either the form or the findings of the social survey movement before 1930. (In this respect, Kevin Bales' claims for the policy implications of the Booth Survey appear somewhat inflated.) The bulk of inquiries into the labour market or social conditions were aggregative rather than intensive community studies and were based upon schedules sent to selected groups such as large employers or poor law guardians with supplementary information from local newspapers and fee-paid correspondents. A trawl of the published and unpublished material relating to official social investigation in late-nineteenth- and early-twentieth-century Britain reveals few examples of the social survey being explicitly discussed and all reveal both the logistical and ideological constraints operating upon government inquiry.

In 1895, the first Labour Commissioner, Llewellyn Smith, responded vigorously in a Cabinet paper to pressure upon the Board of Trade to use social survey methods as a means of establishing the extent of unemployment.

classification of the people according to poverty is determined by the nett impression left on the mind of Mr Booth and his secretaries by cross-examination of School-Board visitors...It may be doubted whether a work like this, however possible to a private individual, could be justifiably carried out by a government department...[I]t is doubtful if the State could undertake with propriety to assess the value of the impressions left on the minds of a number of persons by certain facts and make a statistical record of these impressions. Government statistics as a rule must be records or facts or statements derived first-hand and resting on a perfectly definite and tangible basis, such as the statements of the persons enumerated.[3]

Pressure in 1903 for survey methods to be employed to establish the extent of poverty nationwide and the ability of the working classes to sustain price increases consequent upon tariff reform encountered similar resistance from within Whitehall.[4] Although the subsequent cost of living inquiries drew upon budget data obtained in the Booth and Rowntree surveys, their methodology was not adopted and developed.[5] This evasion of social survey techniques was also a feature of interwar government in Britain. The major surveys continued to be undertaken by private enterprise and it is significant that Hubert Llewellyn Smith returned to survey methods as coordinator of the New London Survey only after his retirement from the Civil Service.

A range of explanations may be advanced for this lack of diffusion. First, rightly or wrongly, the social survey was viewed in some official circles, and especially within the Treasury and the Registrar General's Office as a collectivist device. The Treasury viewed all social inquiries that were not specific to the routine needs of the administrative machine as a conspiracy for extravagance. Booth's work in particular was identified with London progressivism and the interest of a small clique of social scientific populists within the Royal Statistical Society. Until 1909, the Registrar General's Office was similarly cautious in its approach and resistant to pressure from social scientists for greater use of the census to monitor broader social trends than vital statistics had traditionally targetted. This proved to be a major constraint on any attempt to link government investigation with social survey methods for it was only by the systematic use of the census that government statisticians could have used sampling as a means of extrapolating national trends in welfare from local investigations.[6]

The association of the social survey with collectivism also engendered resistance from powerful figures within the statistical establishment of government who, like Robert Giffen, head of the Statistical Department of the Board of Trade or William Ogle, Superintendant of Statistics at the General Register Office still subscribed to a tradition of liberal utilitarian individualism. According to this view-point, official investigations were essentially a means of facilitating self-help and the voluntary and local resolution of social problems and conflict. By revealing the fundamental community of interest between industrial management and workforce and eliminating irrational conflict, and by focusing voluntary effort more effectively upon the crisis points of urban deprivation, collectivist measures would be rendered unnecessary and efficient and economical government secured.[7] Amidst the wealth of literature on the rise of New Liberalism and other collectivist ideologies such as the National Efficiency Movement, there has been a tendency to ignore the tenacity with which this investigative philosophy survived within late-Victorian and Edwardian Whitehall.

Secondly, in many respects extensive local investigation on the scale of social surveys was viewed as part of the responsibility of civil society and private enterprise. The failure of the State to take up the mantle of Booth and Rowntree was consistent with the continuing strength of voluntarist forces within late-Victorian and Edwardian society; forces which are very effectively captured in Jane Lewis' study of Helen Bosanquet's approach to social investigation. In some respects, local surveys with their connections with the Settlement movement and relief organisations were viewed as part of a philanthropic tradition.

Thirdly, it is clear that in Britain the social survey was closely associated in both the public and official mind with the measurement of urban destitution and hence the definition of a poverty line. The concepts of primary and secondary poverty were regarded as highly contentious and as fulfilling a normative and prescriptive role at odds with the legitimate functions of State intelligence. Any official poverty line would mean official endorsement of desirable income and consumption patterns and this in turn would serve to politicise the conduct and the methodology of investigation undertaken by the State.[8]

Fourthly, the lack of diffusion of social survey methodology to government inquiries in Britain in the late-nineteenth- and early-twentieth centuries may relate to the lack of consensus within the social science profession as to the validity and value of new statistical and other investigative methodologies, especially those involving sampling and the mathematical theory of statistics. It can be argued that, during this period, British empirical social research lacked the unified professional identity, institutional setting and theoretical consensus necessary for the sustained diffusion of ideas and techniques. Ease of entry meant that the investigation of urban poverty and other social problems by individuals such as Booth and Rowntree and by organisations such as the Royal Statistical Society remained dominated by generalists. The discipline of statistical investigation remained eclectic and fragmented and its links with the machinery of government ad hoc and often informal, thus reducing the status of new techniques and methods of enquiry, such as the Social Survey.[9]

Fifthly, the type of statistical expertise that would have been necessary had the British state taken up the mantle of Booth and Rowntree and used sampling techniques as a means of monitoring nationwide patterns of destitution threatened the status and operational philosophy of career statisticians within Whitehall. Technical zeal such as that exhibited by A. L. Bowley and G. Udny Yule when seeking as consultants to shape the celebrated cost of living enquiries of the Board of Trade after 1903 was viewed as in conflict with overriding administrative priorities: those of rationalising procedures, minimising the vulnerability of the department to public and parliamentary criticism, and of sustaining, as far as possible, belief in the infallibility of government statistics.

Finally, it could be argued that community studies along the lines of the Booth Survey lacked relevance to the aggregative issues of efficiency and stability being addressed by British governments. Moreover, within policy-making circles, these were issues that were primarily conceived within a set of economic rather than social priorities and parameters. It is noteworthy that in spite of the fact that social issues intrude upon high politics to an unprecedented degree after 1880, and despite the *distributive* orientation of reformist ideologies, the bulk of social and labour statistics remain an adjunct of economic and fiscal surveys focusing on the *productive* efficiency of the workforce and the economy. Indeed, in this respect, the recent research of Jungwoon Choi of the University of Chicago is highly suggestive. He argues on the basis of evidence drawn from France, Britain and the United States that, faced with the stresses of a maturing economy, the State typically develops patterns of social statistics – preeminently labour statistics – designed to institutionalise class struggle and to reduce it to the game of rational class politics played in the arena of public policy. In structuring government information, the prime objective was to provide categories of analysis consistent with the social relations of industry, hence the stress on labour as opposed to working class statistics. Within this context, the social survey with its open-ended structure and sociological intent would have been inappropriate.

It is difficult to obtain a clear picture of the relationship of the State to the social survey in Germany. While there is extensive literature on the development of empirical social research in Germany,[10] it tends to lack focus on the precise interaction between private and public investigative enterprise. Although Gorges' provides in her paper an illuminating analysis of the social politics surrounding the German survey movement, she conveys relatively little on the interface between non-governmental and official investigation. However, one feature *can* be clearly discerned in the literature. In comparison with Britain, the social survey was very much more a part of the machinery of State investigation. In part, this reflected, as Bulmer and Bales stress, the strong Statist tradition of social research in nineteenth- century Germany. Whereas in England and France the pioneers of social surveys were physicians, clergymen, philanthropists, and other well-to-do reformers who carried out their work outside the universities and the government, in Germany the conduct of social surveys was highly institutionalised.[11]

In its early years, the Verein für Sozialpolitik sustained this close association between social survey research and the State. Within the Verein, the survey was explicitly conceived as:

an undertaking, authorised by law, to ascertain economic and social facts and their causal relationships, the ultimate purpose of which is the preparation of legislative or administrative acts ... [12]

Moreover, this policy-orientated advisory role, dedicated to the creation of a consensus around a programme of moderate social reforms, clearly shaped the scope and methodology of the social survey in late-nineteenth-century Germany.

Subsequently, the picture becomes more complex. In some respects, the ideological forces shaping German surveys at the turn of the century, such as investigations into the nature of work and the social psychology of the proletariat, had statist implications analogous to those of the National Efficiency Movement in Britain. The Verein's empirical research continued to focus on public issues both before and after the First World War as did, according to Gorges, the work of the Institut fur Sozialwissenschaften.

Yet, it would appear that after the 1870s, with the conservative shift of German politics towards Bismarkian collectivism, the influence of survey work upon government was significantly eroded. The concern of the Verein to disengage its surveys from political debate and the resistance of State authorities to a research discipline and methodology that had been so closely identified with 'leftist political sympathies' produced a partial retreat of the social survey from the domain of social politics to that of academic sociology. Toennies' abortive pleas for State-sponsored sociological observatories in the 1920s reflected the hiatus that had been created by the division of labour between the social book-keeping of administrative statistics within government and the more analytical sociography of the surveyors.[13]

Locating the relationship between the social survey and the State in the USA is equally problematic. Many of the papers in this volume examine the social and intellectual networks surrounding major social surveys but tend to focus on their linkages with academic and philanthropic institutions rather than with government agencies. None the less, if one views the social survey less as a specialist methodology and more as a civic practice, the importance of the State (whether Federal or local) to its development in the USA becomes readily apparent.

It is clear that, as with the Verein in Germany, American social surveyors were heavily action- and policy-orientated. Turner's study of survey developments at Columbia reveals the Cameralistic ideals of Mayo Smith and Willcox according to which private and public investigative enterprise would be mutually inter-dependent. Cohen refers to similarly close connections between private research and government in the 'famous Wisconsin idea'. Perhaps the most explicit example of investigative symbiosis is provided in Sklar's study of the Hull House Maps and Papers with their links with the slum investigations of Carroll Wright and the US Department of Labor which echo the earlier interplay within the Massachusetts Bureau of Labour Statistics between official investigations and the scope and methodology of non-governmental survey work.[14]

One might speculate that the greater diffusion of survey methodology within American government as compared with the British experience owed something to the structure of government and the more 'open' pattern of career development of statisticians and investigators. While the career migrations between private research and government employment of investigators such as Francis Walker, Carroll Wright, and Florence Kelley can be compared with those in Britain of, for example, Llewellyn Smith and Clara Collet, it remains true that American government was markedly more receptive to outside influences. While Whitehall, especially after the Northcote-Trevelyan Reforms, became introspective and exclusive with an 'almost monastic quality of shared commitments and collective separateness', Washington displayed a 'lateral openness' and a powerful tendency to radiate outwards into external communities.[15]

The greater receptivity of American government to the social survey also reflected the more democratic and pluralist philosophy of information inherent in the new Liberal positivism of late-nineteenth century America. The typical public investigations of the Progressive era were hybrid enterprises with privately funded surveys and government inquiries playing complementary roles in the process of civic education.[16] The research 'community' embraced the bureaus, the municipalities and research foundations in a pattern of social enquiry and social learning that was markedly more decentralised and participatory than its British counterpart.[17] For example, the work of the Bureaus of Labour and of Education lacked that 'territorial imperative' which seems to have constrained the investigative work of so many Whitehall departments.[18] Nor was there the same concern to dominate the production and deployment of social data in the interests of crisis management. The operation of the American census reflected this more open philosophy of information brokerage. As many of the papers convey, the census was conceived broadly as a massive periodical survey of social and economic conditions and as a resource for the social scientific community. Such an operational philosophy was symptomatic of a political and intellectual culture that enabled the social survey to operate freely between the State and civil society.

NOTES

1 See for example, H. C. Selvin, 'Durkheim, Booth and Yule: The Non-Diffusion of an Intellectual Innovation', *European Journal of Sociology* (Archives Europeenes de Sociologie), 16 (1976), 39–51.

2 See, for example, Clara Collet papers, correspondence from Edith Abbott, Hull House, Chicago.

3 PRO CAB 37/38, memorandum on 'The Unemployed' by H. Llewellyn Smith, 23 Jan., 1895, pp. 6–7.

4 PRO LAB 2/1555, memoranda on the measurement of national levels of poverty, July, 1903.

5 See R. Davidson, 'The Measurement of Urban Poverty: A Missing Dimension', *Economic History Review*, 45, 2 (1988), 299–301.

6 R. Davidson, *Whitehall and the Labour Problem in Late-Victorian and Edwardian Britain: A Study in Official Statistics and Social Control* (London: Croom Helm, 1985), chs. 7–8.

7 See, for example, Hicks Beach Papers (County Record Office, Gloucester), PC/PP/60, memorandum on 'Board of Trade Labour Statistics and the Labour Commission' by R. Giffen, 30 April, 1892.

8 I. Levitt, 'The Use of Official Statistics', *Quantitative Sociology Newsletter*, 22 (1979), 72.

9 See especially, S. Cole, 'Continuity and Institutionalisation in Science: A Case Study in Failure', in A. Oberschall (ed.), *The Establishment of Empirical Sociology: Studies in Continuity, Discontinuity and Institutionalisation* (New York: Harper and Row, 1972), pp. 73–129.

10 See, for example, A. Oberschall, *Empirical Social Research in Germany 1848–1914* (The Hague: Mouton, 1965).

11 Oberschall, *Empirical Social Research*, pp. 3–4.

12 Oberschall, *Empirical Social Research*, p. 16.

13 Oberschall, *Empirical Social Research*, pp. 77, 138–41; J. J. Sheehan, *German Liberalism in the Nineteenth Century* (Chicago: University of Chicago Press, 1978), pp. 181–218; D. MacRAe, *Weber* (Glasgow; William Collins, 1974), p. 25.

14 In addition, there was strong continuity between the survey work of the Country Life Movement and the subsequent inquiries of the Department of Agriculture into rural

life. See Jean M. Converse, *Survey Research in the United States: Roots and Emergence 1890–1960* (Berkeley: University of California Press, 1987), pp. 27–8.

15 H. Heclo, 'Washington and Whitehall Revisited: An Essay in Constitutional Lore', unpublished paper presented to British/American Festival, North Carolina (1984).

16 See Mary Furner, *Advocacy and Objectivity: A Crisis in the Professionalisation of American Social Science, 1865–1905* (Lexington: University of Kentucky Press, 1975).

17 Converse, *Survey Research*, p. 23, characterises the American social survey as 'a more sprawling affair of community participation' in which civic volunteer groups, church organisations, local and state government agencies, social scientists and their students, all participated.

18 It was not, however, entirely absent. See Converse, *Social Research*, p. 27.

CHAPTER FIFTEEN

The dangers of castle building – surveying the social survey

SETH KOVEN

A history of the social survey movement is a utopian adventure in 'castle building'. To borrow Jerome Bruner's evocative phrase, it is one of those 'possible castles' we imaginatively construct which seeks to combine the methodological premises and claims of the sciences and the humanities.[1] Bruner poses the question: if in walking in the Danish countryside, we stumble upon a castle, and later learn that it is Hamlet's castle, can we ever view it in the same way? Do the ghosts of Hamlet and Shakespeare irrevocably change its meaning for us? The history of the social survey is also a kind of Hamlet's castle. Once we know when and why it emerged, for what motives and with what consequences, is our conception of it fundamentally altered? Like all utopian endeavors, the history of the social survey has proved invigorating and problematic in both its conception and execution. And, like the social survey, these essays reflect a wide range of competing, though not necessarily contradictory, conceptions of social knowledge and reality.

On the one hand, the social survey was an instrument of positivist social science. For many social scientists, surveys defined measurable and verifiable social realities, just as sociology, as a discipline, was objective and politically neutral. Such a view resonates in the contributions of Bulmer and Bales to this volume.

On the other hand, the social survey can be viewed as inherently value-laden, a product of and servant to politics and the state. Historically, the survey played a pivotal role in shaping social policy, social reform and social work in Europe and the United States. Each of the social surveys discussed in this volume bears the imprint of the political and social agendas that led to their execution. Charles Tilly even claims that the survey emerged not as a tool of scientific research but as a mechanism used by the elite to explain and contain social disorder.[2] While these two views of the survey and social science need not be viewed as mutually exclusive, they historically existed in an uneasy and at times even divisive tension.

Gorges' study of the debates within the Verein für Sozialpolitik between Gustav Schmoller and Max Weber (chapter 12) suggests that the articulation of these two conceptions coincided historically with the emergence of the social survey and the discipline of sociology itself in the late-nineteenth century. In Germany, where universities and hence academic sociology were essentially a branch of the civil service (where professors were *Beamte*),[3] Schmoller believed that sociology and the social survey should respond to the political agendas and exigencies of the state. Max Weber, by contrast, proclaimed that sociology was scientifically objective and politically neutral. Gorges subverts the Weberian stance of ethical and political neutrality by demonstrating that the position of neutrality was itself politically determined. Neutrality can and did cloak political impotence; in this light, Weber's plea for neutrality is recast as a political strategy shaped by his political marginality and opposition to both the conservative politics of the Wilhelmine Reich and the radical politics of the socialists.[4]

If we reject the Weberian aspiration for value-freedom and acknowledge the political instrumentality of surveys, their importance no longer rests on the claim to represent social truths or realities. Instead, we can use them as windows into the perceptions and attitudes of the surveyors and those whom they surveyed. Historians have begun to read surveys with an eye to exposing the assumptions about race, class and gender embedded in them.[5] The notion that surveys were and are neutral documents recording fact seems increasingly untenable in the wake of feminist and post-structuralist analyses.

Bulmer and Bales, in chapter 1, confidently define the characteristics of the survey and offer a precise periodisation of the movement, beginning in 1889 with the first volume of Booth's *Life and Labour of London*. And yet as Eileen Yeo insists in chapter 2, Mayhew's investigations in the 1840s and 50s were collectively an embryonic survey satisfying Bulmer and Bales's defining criteria.

If it has proved difficult to agree on the point of origin of the survey movement, the question of its trajectory into the twentieth century is equally problematic. By what criteria, for example, can community studies like Howarth and Wilson's[6] for West Ham in 1917 be included but Wilmott and Young's[7] for Bethnal Green in the 1950s be excluded? Should the criteria of what constitutes a social survey shift according to the technologies of information gathering and analysis available at any given time? If so, we must acknowledge that the definition of the social survey is contingent and historically constructed.

The rise of the social survey marked an important development in the collection and analysis of large quantities of data about social structures. At the outset, surveys emerged as a means to know the unknown slums of the great cities of industrial capitalism. The survey was a distinct kind and form of knowledge that was produced in response to a crisis in class relations in the late nineteenth century. Class conflict had been figured for several decades as rooted in and perhaps even caused by the mutual ignorance, the lack of knowledge, of rich and poor for one another.[8] Middle-class philanthropists imagined that the survey would enable them to know, to contain, to control, and to speak about the poor in a new way. One innovation of the social survey was that unlike previous government statistical reports, surveyors solicited their data directly from the populations being surveyed: workers, inhabitants of a community, city or region, etc.[9] While survey workers, settlement house residents and charitable visitors extolled the virtues of personal contact and exchange between rich and poor, the survey was emphatically not dialogic: its language of graphs, tables and statistics defined an elite readership and excluded those whom it surveyed.[10]

The Pittsburgh Survey was a notable exception. Its results were disseminated among the inhabitants of the areas included in the survey.[11] The Pittsburgh survey can be viewed as a tentative initiative to make the survey the basis for dialogue across class lines between the surveyors and the community. At the very least, it defined the community not only as objects but as consumers of the survey. Could or did such a vision of the function of the survey threaten to empower working-class communities by demystifying it as a form of knowledge? Would this have undermined the efficacy of the survey as a tool of policy makers within and outside the state? While Cohen does not explicitly take up these questions in chapter 9, he argues that the Pittsburgh Survey was 'a sociological road not taken' and its vision of 'social liberalism' denounced by the Chicago School as jeopardizing the scientific purity of sociology.

Alain Desrosières in chapter 8 analyses the ways in which the social survey, and in particular, representative sampling techniques, sought to reconcile the 'parts with the whole'. This tension was mirrored in the competing ideological and political demands of liberal individualism and collectivism in the 1890s. The leaders of the social survey movement in England and America were committed to the value of the individual as object and agent of social reform and change. But they also were forced to confront the overwhelming scale of poverty of the modern city; that torchbearer of COS parsimony, Charles Loch, likened the insatiable appetite of the poor for relief to a sea anemone swallowing 'flies and chopped beef' and perpetually thrusting its 'many fingered fringe' out for more.[12] The twin spectres of aggregation and segregation haunted social reformers who desperately sought to construct a comprehensive vision that could accommodate the needs of the individual and of the social whole.

The survey was peculiarly well suited to providing reformers which such a vision. While ambitiously mapping the whole community, it also remained extraordinarily attentive to the details of each street and household within the city. Booth's maps and graphs were accompanied by charts in which the location, size, occupations and other more highly personal comments were included about individual households. In this way, the survey constructed narratives, albeit fragmentary, of tens of thousands of otherwise inarticulate individual men, women and children. It vividly reminded its readers that the city was made up of individuals within households, and not impersonal averages or wholes. The authority of the survey rested not only upon its claim to scientific objectivity and comprehensiveness but upon its specificity and particularity. The social survey offered reformers a way to reconcile parts with wholes and suggested a middle ground that helped them mediate between the political logic and attraction of individualism and collectivism.

In an age increasingly preoccupied with imperialism, the bipolar tropes of civilisation and barbarism, exploration and conquest, were as frequently invoked to describe the work of explorers of the 'Nether' worlds of the slums of industrial capitalism as for those actual voyagers to the far corners of empire. Not surprisingly, social surveys were implicated in this discourse. Could it have been mere coincidence that Booth's maps encoded the racist assumptions of Victorian imperialism: the blackest parts of the maps designated the dens of thieves and street arabs; the pinkest, the villas of the rich?

The social survey map should be viewed as part of a larger project undertaken by late-nineteenth century reformers, many of whom were involved in or closely allied with the Social Survey movement, to reshape the physical and mental landscape of the urban working class. Booth's maps appeared to confirm the connection between disorderly social groups and class relations and the chaotic and irrational spaces in which poverty lurked.[13]

The actual physical shape and use of urban space was hotly contested in East London in the years immediately following the publication of the first volumes of Booth's *Life and Labour*. Booth's poverty maps and volumes became the Baedecker's of social reformers committed to a tidier, more sanitary and rational city. As early as 1890, the LCC began to plan the first of its massive efforts in urban renewal, knocking down the infamous Old Nichol, displacing thousands of East Londoners, and erecting in its place the Boundary Street Estate as model housing for the respectable working class.[14]

In *A Child of the Jago* (1896), the working-class novelist, Arthur Morrison, brilliantly exposed the conflation of these two distinct projects: one ostensibly scientific, the mapping of survey results; and the other political and reformist, clearing and rebuilding the slums. The first piece of visual text the reader confronts is a map of the Nichol (called the Jago in the novel), a self-conscious echo of Booth's maps. The illusion of knowing the Jago by virtue of possessing its map is immediately shattered by the written text which plunges the reader into a darkness and confusion out of which he slowly emerges into the partial light of the distinctive social and cultural norms of the Jago. The destruction of the Old Jago and the construction of the New (the Boundary Street Estate) occurs at the mid-point of the novel. This event ominously adumbrates the intrusion of alien forces into the Jago seeking to destroy all who refuse to conform to the order the redrawn map imposes upon them. Ultimately, the protagonist's outlaw father is a victim of the reconfigured space: his familiar escape routes destroyed by the work of urban planners, he is entrapped by the police and surrenders to bourgeois institutions of authority and justice. Morrison's novel depicts the social and political uses of mapping poverty even as it satirises the claim of the map's creators to know the world contained within its boundaries.

The arduous task of collecting, mapping and analysing survey data required a group of people trained in social work and sociological research methods and techniques. Sklar contends, in chapter 4, that the social survey in the United States, and in particular, the maps produced by Hull House were woman's work.[15] According to Sklar, the *Hull-House Maps and Papers* were the fruit of an activist, female political culture that flourished alongside and within settlements in the United States.

Sklar and Lewis (chapters 4 and 5) both draw attention to women's voluntary associations as important sites of both social work and sociological analysis. Victorian women in England and America, propelled by an evangelical culture that enjoined them to use their special moral gifts to purify their homes and uplift the poor, played a crucial role in the development of social science, sociology and social work. If a woman's proper sphere was the home, an idea many Victorian women engaged in social work accepted, it was but a small step to extend her housekeeping duties from the private world of the home to the surrounding community. Women in England and America used voluntary associations like settlement houses to enter into the public sphere of social work; and this in turn led many to enter into the male-dominated arena of politics and social policy formulation.[16]

In England, the feminisation of social work was achieved at a considerable cost: the virtual exclusion of social work and hence most women from the academic discipline of sociology. The attitudes that encouraged this differentiation are explored by Lewis in her comparison of the Fabian socialist, Beatrice Webb and the Charity Organisation Society leader, Helen Bosanquet. Bosanquet, typically dismissed as a last gasp of anachronistic and condescending COS policies, emerges as more intellectually coherent than Webb whose empirical researches did not neatly conform to her political programme. Bosanquet, and women trained at the COS and settlement houses, were often remarkably attentive to and interested in the language and distinctive cultural norms of the working class: they accepted cultural difference across class lines without embracing a cultural relativism that would have challenged their authority in the social worker–client relationship.

Webb, Lewis asserts, believed that 'in entering the world of social investigation, she also made the decision to leave the women's world of practical social work'. But we need not accept Webb's own gender-specific vision of social work and sociology. In fact, Webb's assessment is a gross distortion of the historical evolution of professional social work and sociology in Great Britain, both of which had roots in 'woman's' work in settlement houses in London and Liverpool and the COS.

The Women's University Settlement in Southwark,[17] under the leadership of Margaret Sewell and Edith Argles, began setting up a training course for the profession of social work as early as 1889.[18] Helen Bosanquet's husband, Bernard Bosanquet delivered the inaugural lectures.[19] Shortly thereafter, the settlement declared its intention to serve as 'a school, a training college for workers'.[20] In 1896 the settlement joined forces with the COS and the National Union of Women Workers, to form a Joint Lectures Committee. This in turn became the first School of Sociology, under the aegis of E. J. Urwick, a former resident of the first two settlement houses, Oxford House and Toynbee Hall.

The curriculum of the School of Sociology significantly joined practical training in social work with serious study of the foundation texts of social science and political economy in Great Britain: readings included Hobbes, Smith, Bentham, T. H. Green, Jevons and Marx. The first School of Sociology in Britain was emphatically created to serve the needs of female students. One of the premises of the school was the essential integrity of theory and practice, of sociological research and analysis and social work.[21]

The sharp division along the lines of sex between sociology as men's labour, and social work as women's labor, gained momentum after the School of Sociology moved to the London School of Economics. The amalgamation of the School with the LSE on the eve of World War I suggests that the professionalisation of social work was a goal shared by both the leaders of the COS, including the Bosanquets, and the leaders of the LSE, most prominently the Webbs. However, at the LSE, women students at the School, overwhelmingly single and committed to their independent lives, were condescendingly and inappropriately known as 'Urwick's harem'.[22] Male-dominated academic sociology anxiously distanced itself from its first institutional incarnation in the female dominated Schools of Sociology. Academic sociologists in England erected powerful professional and disciplinary borders between sociology and social work – borders that were buttressed by gendered notions of male and female labour and which continue to be carefully policed.[23]

In surveying the Social Survey Movement, the reader of these essays has been asked to consider the impact of differing state structures, political agendas and national cultures, race, class and gender relations on the meaning and nature of the social survey. The social survey is not a castle; and its categories, codes, graphs, tables and maps, like the stones of Hamlet's castle, remain unchanged – but we cannot see them in quite the same way.

NOTES

I would like to thank my colleague, Peter Knapp, for his suggestions and criticisms.

1 Jerome Bruner, 'Possible Castles', in *Actual minds, Possible Worlds*, (Cambridge, MA.: Harvard University Press, 1986), ch. 3.

2 Tilly contents that 'much the same spirit that brought burghers and bureaucrats to worry about rising disorder induced social reformers and officials to undertake surveys of living condition.' Charles Tilly, *Big Structures, Large Processes, Huge Comparisons*, (New York: Russell Sage Foundation, 1984), p. 13.

3 See Fritz K. Ringer, *The Decline of the German Mandarins, The German Academic Community, 1890–1933* (Cambridge, MA.: Harvard University Press, 1969), especially chapter 3. Also see Jane Caplan, *Government Without Administration, State and Civil Service in Wimar and Nazi Germany* (Oxford: Clarendon Press, 1989), ch. 1.

4 The issue of interpreting Weber's politics is cogently examined from a variety of points of view in Otto Stammer (ed.), *Max Weber and Sociology Today*, trans. Kathleen Morris (Oxford: Basil Blackwell, 1971).

5 For example, Susan Pedersen argues that 'scientific sociology used questionable statistics to redefine male maintenance as the normal family situation, and thus the only reasonable basis for welfare policy.' 'The Failure of Feminism in the making of the British Welfare State', *Radical History Review*, 43 (Winter, 1989), 87. Pedersen examines the gender bias of Rowntree's survey of 13,000 women workers conducted for his study *The Responsibility of Women Workers for Dependents* which obscured women's economic contribution to supporting dependents.

6 Edward G. Howarth and Mona Wilson, compilers, *West Ham: A Study in Social and Industrial Problems* (London: J. M. Dent, 1907).

7 Michael Young and Peter Willmott, *Family and Kinship in East London* (London: Routledge and Kegan Paul, 1957).

8 Many mid-Victorian novels including Gaskell's industrial novels, *North and South* and *Mary Barton*, Disraeli's *Sybil*, Eliot's *Felix Holt* develop this theme of the dire consequences of mutual ignorance of rich and poor. It was also a recurring theme in pamphlet literature such as Kay-Shuttleworth's famous *The Moral and Physical Condition of the Working Class in Manchester*, written in the wake of the 1832 cholera epidemic.

9 As Bales shows in chapter 3, Booth and his survey team relied on the accounts of school visitors for the poverty volumes.

10 Booth asked the transient young male settlers at Oxford House Settlement and Roynbee Hall to review his poverty maps, not the actual residents of Bethnal Green and Whitechapel.

11 See Clarke Chambers *Paul U. Kellogg and the Survey* (Minneapolis, Minnesota: Minnesota Press, 1971), pp. 33–40.

12 Charles Loch, Diary, 13 Sept., 1888, Goldsmith Library, Ms. 801, Senate House, University of London.

13 Among other things, of course, Booth's maps showed that poverty was not confined to the East End and that there were pockets of poverty scattered throughout London.

14 For an account of the role of LCC architects in this experiment in slum clearance, see Susan Beattie, *A Revolution in London Housing, LCC Housing Architects and Their Work, 1893–1914*, (London: 1984.) See also Anthony Wohl, *The Eternal Slum* (London: Edward Arnold, 1977) and R. V. Steffel, 'The Boundary Street Estate – An Example of Urban Redevelopment by the London County Council 1880–1914.' *Town Planning Review*, 47 (1976), 161–72. On Arthur Morrison, see Peter Keating, *The Working Classes in Victorian Fiction* (London: Routledge and Kegan Paul, 1971) and his Introduction to the reprint of *A Child of the Jago*, (London: Boydell Press, 1982).

15 Some of Booth's most able assistants and authors were women, including Clara Collet, Jesse Argyle and Beatrice Potter.

16 See Seth Koven and Sonya Michel, 'Gender and the Origins of the Welfare State', *Radical History Review*, 43 (Winter, 1989).

17 See Martha Vicinus, *Independent Women* (London: Virago, 1985), 6, for treatment of women's settlement house movement as locations in which single woman created

communities for themselves. See Seth Koven, 'Culture and Poverty: the London Settlement House Movement, 1870 to 1914', PhD, thesis, Harvard University, 1987, for a detailed account of women's settlements in London and in particular for the history of the School of Sociology. On the School of Sociology, also see Noel Parry, Michael Rustin and Carole Satyamurti (eds.), *Social Work, Welfare and the State* (London: Edward Arnold, 1979) ch. 2 and 4; and Marjorie Smith, *Professional Education for Social Work in Britain* (London: Allen and Unwin, 1953).

18 The Victoria Women's Settlement in Liverpool established the program which became the second School of Sociology in England.

19 His topics included 'Civic Education', 'The Difficulty of Doing Good by Merely Giving Away Money', 'The Duty of Understanding and Enforcing the Sanitary Conditions of Life', and 'Socialism Criticized'.

20 Mrs Maitland, Report of General Meeting, Women's University Settlement, *Annual Report*, 1891, p. 7.

21 In 1964, Richard Titmuss affirmed the vision of linking social work with sociology and social research and condemned the exaltation of 'pure research' as superior to applied work. See Richard Titmuss, 'The Relationship Between Schools of Social Work, Social Research and Social Policy', in *Commitment to Welfare* (London: Allen and Unwin, 1968), pp. 37–47.

22 Mary Danvers Stocks, *My Commonplace Book* (London: Peter Davies 1970), p. 82.

23 Dr Mark Abrams, one of the most distinguished social surveyors of the century, in commenting on Jennifer Platt's contribution to this volume at the Conference, explained that in the 1930s and 40s the Anglo-American survey community was sustained by an old-boy network, centred around Harold Laski, to which women had limited access.

Index

Abbott, Edith, 28, 36, 112, 301, 341, 360
Abrams, Mark, 3–4, 347
Addams, Jane, 28, 36, 112, 133–5, 341
Adenauer, Konrad, 330
Adler, Max, 330
American Economic Assoiation, 273
American sectionalism, 273
American Social Science Association, 271–2
American Sociological Society, 299
American Soldier, The, 349
American Statistical Association, 273, 275
Americanisation, 280–1
Angell, James, 309
Association for the Promotion of Profit-Sharing, 273
Aves, Ernest, 360

Babbage, Charles, 7
Barnett, Canon Samuel, 24–5, 154 *see also* Toynbee Hall
Beard, Charles, 279
Bernays, Mary, 326
Blackmar, F. W., 302
Blane, Gilbert, 7
Booth, Charles, 2, 4, 19–23, 31–2, 49, 56, 66–110, 122–3, 154, 174, 181, 189, 291, 369–70
  classification, 189
  comparison with US social scientists, 122–9
  criticisms of, 91–2
  data collection of, 77–82
  data used by, 93–8
  impact of work, 67–70, 93, 98–9

personal philosophy of, 66–7
poverty, causes of 196–7
poverty, definition of, 189, 196–7
and old age pensions, 230
research methods of, 69–77, 190–1, 341–2
and School Board Visitors, 83–9
Booth, Mary, 73
Bortkiewicz, L., 236
Bosanquet, Bernard, 158, 165
Bosanquet, Helen Dendy, 22, 56, 57–8, 91, 148–66, 202, 362, 365–6
  beliefs about social work, 158–62
  methods of research, 161–2
  and the Royal Commission on Poor Laws, 162–6
  and social investigation, 161–2
Bowley, Arthur, 22, 40, 205–13, 228, 230–1, 343, 363
  comparison with Rowntree, 205–13, 217
  poverty, definition of, 207–9
  random sampling, 205–6
Branford, Victor, 16
Brauer, Theodor, 331, 334–6
Breckinridge, Sophonisba, 301
Brentano, Lujo, 317–18
British Association for the Advancement of Science, 360
British Institute of Public Opinion (BIPO), 41
Brown, Sibyl Clement, 351
Bureau of Indian Ethnology, 273
Bureaux of 'Labor Statistics', 269–72
Burgess, John, 274, 301